Modern Full-Stack React Projects

Build, maintain, and deploy modern web apps using
MongoDB, Express, React, and Node.js

Daniel Bugl

Modern Full-Stack React Projects

Group Product Manager: Rohit Rajkumar

Publishing Product Manager: Kushal Dave

Book Project Manager: Aishwarya Mohan

Senior Editor: Rakhi Patel

Technical Editor: K Bimala Singha

Copy Editor: Safis Editing

Indexer: Pratik Shirodkar

Production Designer: Prashant Ghare

DevRel Marketing Coordinators: Anamika Singh and Nivedita Pandey

First published: June 2024

Production reference: 1090524

Published by Packt Publishing Ltd.

Grosvenor House

11 St Paul's Square

Birmingham

B3 1RB, UK

ISBN 978-1-83763-795-9

www.packtpub.com

Contributors

About the author

Daniel Bugl is a full-stack developer, product designer, and entrepreneur focusing on web technologies. He has a Bachelor of Science degree in business informatics and information systems and a Master of Science degree in data science from the Vienna University of Technology (TU Wien). He is a contributor to many open source projects and a member of the React community. He also founded and runs his own hardware/software start-up, TouchLay, which helps other companies present their products and services. At his company, he constantly works with web technologies, particularly making use of React and Next.js. In the past couple of years, he has, together with Georg Schelkshorn and Matthias Zronek, worked as a technical advisor and full-stack developer for large enterprises and the public sector, among other things working on citizen services for the Austrian government.

I want to thank the people involved in the production of this book; my co-founder, Georg Schelkshorn; my business partner, Matthias Zronek; my family and friends; and my girlfriend, Junxian Wang.

About the reviewers

Matthias Zronek is a senior software engineer and technical advisor with more than 20 years of professional experience. He loves coding and is passionate about every new programming language he learns. His current focus is on the development of full-stack web frameworks to enable frontend teams to create scalable and sustainable web applications using React and TypeScript. In his free time, he writes highly optimized applications for PC benchmarking in C++ or tries to reverse-engineer interesting binaries. If he is not in front of a (disassembled) computer, he spends time with his loving wife, their newborn son, and their fascinatingly weird cat.

Georg Schelkshorn is a full-stack React enthusiast with excitement for DevOps and crafting user-friendly interfaces. Alongside Daniel Bugl, he co-manages TouchLay, a company specializing in interactive hardware and software solutions as well as advising enterprises on successfully implementing modern web projects. Through many challenging projects, he has gained deep knowledge of what makes a full-stack React project work at scale. Georg loves diving into new areas of learning and hopes you'll enjoy exploring this book's learning journey.

Kirill Ezhemenskii is a visionary CTO who leads a healthcare company with cutting-edge software solutions. He is a master of functional programming and a guru of modern web and mobile development. He leverages the power of React, Next.js, GraphQL, and TypeScript to create stunning and performant applications that run on any platform. He is also a generous mentor who shares his expertise and passion for React Native with aspiring developers.

Foreword

I met Daniel for the first time 14 years ago. He is a close friend of my wife's family, so he was often invited to family gatherings. Back then, Daniel was already a bright young mind with a curiosity for everything. One day, he excitedly asked me to visit his "lab" – simply a room in the family's basement back then – to show me his latest project. Together with my wife's cousin, he had built a touch table out of a wooden box. It was an early prototype, but already fully functional. Daniel was only 13 years old at that time. The years passed and I saw him diving into web development, creating a successful business and adopting React as early as 2015.

Today, Daniel is the same age as I was back then and I am honored to review his third book. I have also been very fortunate to work closely with Daniel for the past five years on corporate React projects. This book reflects his well-structured approach to the challenges of enterprise web applications. He carefully extracts the essence of complex concepts and presents them so clearly, that even the most difficult chapters in this book will feel manageable. The provided source code prevents you from getting sidetracked by unnecessary details.

Daniel starts your journey by handing you the basic tools you need to create a modern full-stack React project from scratch. Every step is guided and thoroughly explained. Later on, as chapters get more and more challenging, the focus will shift away from the basics, giving your newly learned skills the chance to fill the gaps. That's why it is important to work through the basics as well, so you can focus on the advanced topic at hand.

Five years ago, I was where you, the reader, are right now. I was eager to learn full-stack React but didn't know where to start. I had the chance to learn from Daniel directly. With this book, you finally have that chance as well.

Matthias Zronek
Senior Software Engineer and Technical Advisor

Table of Contents

Part 2: Building and Deploying Our First Full-Stack Application with a REST API

3

Implementing a Backend Using Express, Mongoose ODM, and Jest   51

4

Integrating a Frontend Using React and TanStack Query   91

5

Deploying the Application with Docker and CI/CD   119

Part 3: Practicing Development of Full-Stack Web Applications

6

Adding Authentication with JWT   149

7

Improving the Load Time Using Server-Side Rendering   183

8

Making Sure Customers Find You with Search Engine
Optimization   213

14

Creating a Frontend to Consume and Send Events   341

15

Adding Persistence to Socket.IO Using MongoDB   359

Part 5: Advancing to Enterprise-Ready Full-Stack Applications

16

17

18

19

Deploying a Next.js App   445

20

Diving Deeper into Full-Stack Development   455

Preface

Hi there – I am Daniel, an entrepreneur, technical advisor, and full-stack developer with a focus on technologies in the React ecosystem.

In my time as a technical advisor and developer for enterprises and the public sector, I have noticed that more and more companies look to reduce the gap between frontend and backend developers. Their business requirements often result in the need for a so-called "backend for frontend," where data is fetched from different backend systems and prepared in a way that can be easily displayed in the frontend.

As an entrepreneur, I also have experience with starting new projects with smaller teams, where it is essential that every developer on your team can do everything, not just the frontend or the backend. In such cases, it often makes sense to develop the backend and frontend in the same language, which is often JavaScript (or TypeScript), because there is a big ecosystem and a large number of developers available.

In both cases, becoming a full-stack developer is getting increasingly more important. I have been coaching developers to learn more about full-stack development for a long time and have noticed that there are common issues and misunderstandings that most developers encounter when learning full-stack development. In this book, I want to summarize all my learnings and teachings about full-stack development, giving you pointers on where and how to learn more about the ever-growing ecosystem of full-stack development in JavaScript.

Nowadays, many companies use a stack consisting of MongoDB, Express, React, and Node.js, called the MERN stack. In this book, I will teach you how to build modern full-stack React applications by using these technologies. I will teach these technologies from the ground up, using as few libraries as possible, so that you can learn the essential concepts. This will allow you to adapt to new technologies for years to come, even when the specific tools used in this book become outdated. Additionally, I will teach about the deployment of apps and DevOps, as I found that this sector is often neglected and there are not enough developers who know about it. In the last part of the book, I will introduce Next.js as a full-stack framework and give an outlook on new developments in this sector, such as React Server Components and Server Actions.

I hope you enjoy reading this book. If you have any questions or feedback, feel free to reach out to me!

Who this book is for

This book is for developers who already have experience with React and want to learn how to create, integrate, and deploy various backend systems to become a full-stack developer. You should already have a good understanding of JavaScript and React, but do not need to have any prior knowledge of the development, creation, integration, and deployment of backend systems. If you face one of the following challenges, this book will be perfect for you:

- You know how to make a frontend with React but have no idea how to properly integrate it with a backend

- You want to create a full-stack project from scratch but do not know how to

- You want to learn more about the deployment of apps and DevOps

- You want to learn more about modern React development, such as React Server Components, Server Actions, and Next.js

This book will provide you with real-world projects and includes all the steps needed to become a full-stack developer, including but not limited to backend development, frontend development, testing (unit tests and end-to-end tests), and deployment.

What this book covers

Chapter 1, *Preparing for Full-stack Development*, gives a brief overview of the contents of the book and teaches you how to set up a project that will be used as a basis for the development of your full-stack projects.

Chapter 2, *Getting to Know Node.js and MongoDB*, provides information on how to write and run scripts with Node.js. Then, it explains how to use Docker to set up a database service. It also introduces MongoDB, a document database, and how to access the MongoDB database via Node.js.

Chapter 3, *Implementing a Backend Using Express*, puts into practice what you learned in *Chapter 2* by creating a backend service. Express is used to provide a REST API, Mongoose ODM to interface with MongoDB, and Jest to write unit tests for the backend code.

Chapter 4, *Integrating a Frontend Using React and TanStack Query*, provides instructions on how to create a frontend that interfaces with the previously created backend service. It uses Vite to set up a React project, in which we create a basic user interface. Then, it teaches you how to use TanStack Query, a data-fetching library, to handle backend state and integrate the backend API with the frontend.

Chapter 5, *Deploying the Application with Docker and CI/CD*, deep-dives into DevOps by teaching you about Docker and how to package an app with it. Then, it provides instructions on how to deploy an app to a cloud provider and how to configure CI/CD to automate the deployment.

Chapter 6, Adding Authentication with JWT, teaches you about JSON Web Tokens, a way to add authentication to web applications. It also provides instructions on how to set up multiple routes using React Router.

Chapter 7, Improving the Load Time Using Server-Side Rendering, covers benchmarking an application and teaches you about Web Vitals. Then, it gives instructions on how to implement a way to render React components on a server from scratch and how to pre-fetch data on the server.

Chapter 8, Making Sure Customers Find You with Search Engine Optimization, focuses on how to optimize an app to be found by search engines, such as Google or Bing. Additionally, it provides information on how to create meta tags for easier integration with various social media sites.

Chapter 9, Implementing End-to-End Tests Using Playwright, introduces Playwright as a tool for writing end-to-end tests, which automatically performs actions in an app to find out whether your code still runs as designed after making changes. It also covers how to run Playwright in CI using GitHub Actions.

Chapter 10, Aggregating and Visualizing Statistics Using MongoDB and Victory, provides instructions on how to collect events in an app. Then, it teaches you how to aggregate data with MongoDB to generate summary statistics, such as the number of views or session duration. Finally, it covers creating graphs to visualize those aggregated statistics using the Victory library.

Chapter 11, Building a Backend with a GraphQL API, introduces GraphQL as an alternative to REST APIs, and you will learn when it is useful to use and how to implement it in a backend.

Chapter 12, Interfacing with GraphQL on the Frontend Using Apollo Client, teaches you how to use Apollo Client on the frontend to interface with the previously implemented GraphQL backend.

Chapter 13, Building an Event-Based Backend Using Express and Socket.IO, introduces an event-based architecture, which is useful for apps that deal with real-time data, such as collaborative applications (Google Docs or an online whiteboard) or financial applications (Kraken crypto exchange). It teaches you about WebSockets and how to use Socket.IO to implement an event-based backend.

Chapter 14, Creating a Frontend to Consume and Send Events, implements a frontend for the previously created event-based backend and interfaces with it using Socket.IO.

Chapter 15, Adding Persistence to Socket.IO Using MongoDB, teaches you how to properly integrate a database into an event-based app to persist (and later replay) events.

Chapter 16, Getting Started with Next.js, introduces Next.js as an enterprise-ready full-stack web application framework for React. It highlights the differences between using a framework and a simple bundler such as Vite. It also teaches you about the Next.js App Router, a new paradigm for defining routes and pages.

Chapter 17, Introducing React Server Components, teaches you about a new concept in React, Server Components, allowing you to directly integrate React apps with a database without needing a REST or GraphQL API. Additionally, it teaches you about Server Actions, which allow you to call functions on the server via the frontend.

Chapter 18, Advanced Next.js Concepts and Optimizations, dives deeper into the Next.js framework, providing information on how caching works in Next.js and how it can be used to optimize applications. It also teaches you about defining API routes in Next.js and how to add metadata for search engine optimization. Lastly, it teaches you how to optimally load images and fonts in Next.js.

Chapter 19, Deploying a Next.js App, teaches you two ways to deploy a Next.js app. The easiest way is using the Vercel platform, with which we can quickly get our app up and running. However, it also teaches you how to create a custom deployment setup using Docker.

Chapter 20, Diving Deeper into Full-stack Development, briefly covers various advanced topics that have not been covered in this book yet. It starts with an overview of other full-stack frameworks and then summarizes concepts such as maintaining large-scale projects, optimizing the bundle size, an overview of UI libraries, and advanced state management solutions.

To get the most out of this book

Software/hardware covered in the book	Operating system requirements
Node.js v20.10.0	Windows, macOS, or Linux
Git v2.43.0	
Visual Studio Code v1.84.2	
Docker v24.0.6	
Docker Desktop v4.25.2	
MongoDB Shell v2.1.0	

If you are using the digital version of this book, we advise you to type the code yourself or access the code from the book's GitHub repository (a link is available in the next section). Doing so will help you avoid any potential errors related to the copying and pasting of code.

Download the example code files

You can download the example code files for this book from GitHub at `https://github.com/PacktPublishing/Modern-Full-Stack-React-Projects`. If there's an update to the code, it will be updated in the GitHub repository.

We also have other code bundles from our rich catalog of books and videos available at `https://github.com/PacktPublishing/`. Check them out!

Code in Action

The *Code in Action* videos for this book can be viewed at `https://packt.link/VINfo`.

Conventions used

There are a number of text conventions used throughout this book.

`Code in text`: Indicates code words in text, database table names, folder names, filenames, file extensions, pathnames, dummy URLs, user input, and Twitter handles. Here is an example: "First, you need to create a `robots.txt` file to allow search engines whether they are allowed to crawl parts of your website, and which parts they are allowed to crawl."

A block of code is set as follows:

```
export const getPostById = async (postId) => {
  const res = await fetch(`${import.meta.env.VITE_BACKEND_URL}/
posts/${postId}`)
  return await res.json()
}
```

When we wish to draw your attention to a particular part of a code block, the relevant lines or items are set in bold:

```
{fullPost ? (
  <h3>{title}</h3>
) : (
  <Link to={`/posts/${_id}`}>
    <h3>{title}</h3>
  </Link>
)}
```

Any command-line input or output is written as follows:

```
$ npm install node-emoji
```

Bold: Indicates a new term, an important word, or words that you see on screen. For instance, words in menus or dialog boxes appear in **bold**. Here is an example: "Connect to the database, then expand the **Playgrounds** section (if it is not expanded already) and click on the **Create New Playground** button."

> **Tips or important notes**
> Appear like this.

Get in touch

Feedback from our readers is always welcome.

General feedback: If you have questions about any aspect of this book, email us at `customercare@packtpub.com` and mention the book title in the subject of your message.

Errata: Although we have taken every care to ensure the accuracy of our content, mistakes do happen. If you have found a mistake in this book, we would be grateful if you would report this to us. Please visit `www.packtpub.com/support/errata` and fill in the form.

Piracy: If you come across any illegal copies of our works in any form on the internet, we would be grateful if you would provide us with the location address or website name. Please contact us at `copyright@packt.com` with a link to the material.

If you are interested in becoming an author: If there is a topic that you have expertise in and you are interested in either writing or contributing to a book, please visit `authors.packtpub.com`.

Share Your Thoughts

Once you've read *Modern Full-Stack React Projects*, we'd love to hear your thoughts! Scan the QR code below to go straight to the Amazon review page for this book and share your feedback.

`https://packt.link/r/1837637954`

Your review is important to us and the tech community and will help us make sure we're delivering excellent quality content.

Download a free PDF copy of this book

Thanks for purchasing this book!

Do you like to read on the go but are unable to carry your print books everywhere?

Is your eBook purchase not compatible with the device of your choice?

Don't worry, now with every Packt book you get a DRM-free PDF version of that book at no cost.

Read anywhere, any place, on any device. Search, copy, and paste code from your favorite technical books directly into your application.

The perks don't stop there, you can get exclusive access to discounts, newsletters, and great free content in your inbox daily

Follow these simple steps to get the benefits:

1. Scan the QR code or visit the link below

https://packt.link/free-ebook/978-1-83763-795-9

2. Submit your proof of purchase
3. That's it! We'll send your free PDF and other benefits to your email directly

Part 1:
Getting Started with
Full-Stack Development

In this part, you will learn how to set up a project and tools for **full-stack development**. You will also get to know and make the first steps with **Node.js**, **Docker**, and **MongoDB**. After this part, you will have a basic project setup that can be used for further projects developed throughout this book.

This part includes the following chapters:

- *Chapter 1, Preparing For Full-Stack Development*
- *Chapter 2, Getting to Know Node.js and MongoDB*

1

Preparing for Full-Stack Development

In this chapter, I am first going to give a brief overview of the contents of the book and explain why the skills taught in this book are important in a modern development environment. Then, we will jump into action and set up a project that will be used as a basis for the development of our full-stack projects. At the end of this chapter, you will have an **integrated development environment (IDE)** and project set up and ready for full-stack development and will understand which tools can be used for setting up such projects.

In this chapter, we are going to cover the following main topics:

- Motivation to become a full-stack developer

- What is new in the third edition?

- Getting the most out of this book

- Setting up the development environment

Technical requirements

This chapter will guide you through setting up all the necessary technologies needed for developing full-stack web applications throughout this book. Before we start, please install the following, if you do not already have them installed:

- Node.js v20.10.0

- Git v2.43.0

- Visual Studio Code v1.84.2

Those versions are the ones used in the book. While installing a newer version should not be an issue, please note that certain steps might work differently on a newer version. If you are having an issue with the code and steps provided in this book, please try using the mentioned versions.

You can find the code for this chapter on GitHub: `https://github.com/PacktPublishing/Modern-Full-Stack-React-Projects/tree/main/ch1`.

The CiA video for this chapter can be found at: `https://youtu.be/dyf3nECvKAE`.

> **Important**
>
> If you cloned the full repository for the book, Husky may not find the `.git` directory when running `npm install`. In that case, just run `git init` in the root of the corresponding chapter folder.

Motivation to become a full-stack developer

Understanding full-stack development is becoming increasingly important, as companies seek to increase the cooperation – and reduce the gap – between the frontend and the backend. The frontend is becoming more deeply integrated with the backend, using technologies such as server-side rendering. Throughout this book, we are going to learn about the development, integration, testing, and deployment of full-stack projects.

What is new in this release of Full-Stack React Projects?

Unlike previous releases of Full-Stack React Projects, this new release focuses more on the integration of the frontend with the backend than the previous two editions, and thus intentionally does not focus so much on creating a **user interface** (**UI**) or using UI libraries, such as **Material UI** (**MUI**), on the frontend. This edition gives the essential knowledge for integrating and deploying full-stack web applications. The deployment of apps was missing completely from previous editions, and testing was only briefly introduced. This edition focuses more on these essential parts of full-stack development such that, after reading this book, you will be able to develop, integrate, test, and deploy a full-stack web application.

Getting the most out of this book

To keep the book short and to the point, we are going to use specific technologies and tools. The concepts, however, apply to other technologies as well. We will attempt to briefly introduce alternatives so that if something is not a good fit for your project, you can pick and choose different tools. I recommend first trying out the technologies introduced in this book to be able to follow the instructions, but do not hesitate to try out the alternatives on your own later.

It is highly recommended that you write the code on your own. Do not simply run the code examples that are provided. It is important to write the code yourself in order to learn and understand it properly. However, if you run into any issues, you can always refer to the code examples.

With that said, let's start with setting up our development environment in the next section.

Setting up the development environment

In this book, we are going to use **Visual Studio Code** (**VS Code**) as our code editor. Feel free to use whichever editor you prefer, but keep in mind that the extensions used and settings configured may be slightly different in the editor of your choice.

Let's now install VS Code and useful extensions, and then continue setting up all the tools needed for our development environment.

Installing VS Code and extensions

Before we can get started developing and setting up the other tools, we need to set up our code editor by following these steps:

1. Download VS Code for your operating system from the official website (at the time of writing, the URL is `https://code.visualstudio.com/`). We are going to use version *1.84.2* in this book.

2. After downloading and installing the application, open it, and you should see the following window:

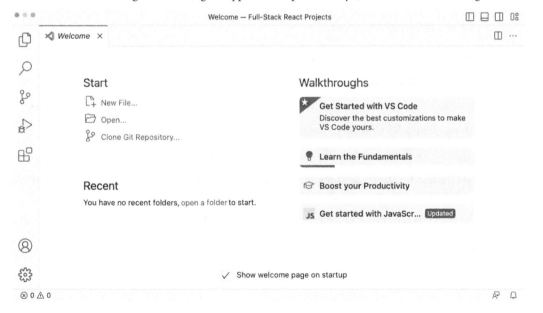

Figure 1.1 – A fresh installation of VS Code (on macOS)

3. To make things easier later, we are going to install some extensions, so click on the **Extensions** icon, which is the fifth icon from the top on the left in the screenshot. A sidebar should open, where you will see **Search Extensions in Marketplace** at the top. Enter an extension name here and click on **Install** to install it. Let's start by installing the **Docker** extension:

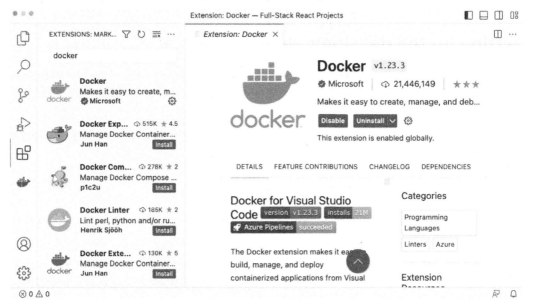

Figure 1.2 – Installing the Docker extension in VS Code

4. Install the following extensions:

    -   Docker (by Microsoft)
    -   ESLint (by Microsoft)
    -   Prettier – Code formatter (by Prettier)
    -   MongoDB for VS Code (by MongoDB)

    Support for JavaScript and Node.js already comes built-in with VS Code.

5. Create a folder for the projects made in this book (for example, you can call it `Full-Stack-React-Projects`). Inside this folder, create a new folder called `ch1`.

6. Go to the **Files** tab (first icon from top) and click the **Open Folder** button to open the empty `ch1` folder.

7. If you get a dialog asking **Do you trust the authors of the files in this folder?**, check **Trust the authors of all files in the parent folder 'Full-Stack-React-Projects'** and then click on the **Yes, I trust the authors** button.

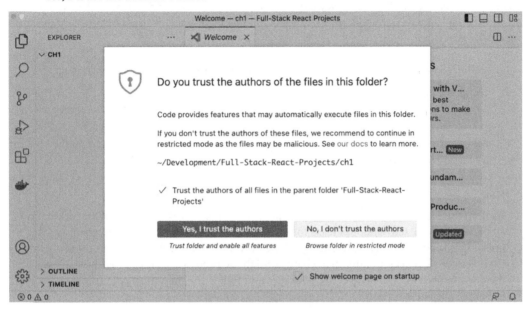

Figure 1.3 – Allowing VS Code to execute files in our project folder

> **Tip**
> You can safely ignore this warning in your own projects, as you can be sure that those do not contain malicious code. When opening folders from untrusted sources, you can press **No, I don't trust the authors**, and still browse the code. However, when doing so, some features of VS Code will be disabled.

We have now successfully set up VS Code and are ready to start setting up our project! If you have cloned the folder from the GitHub code examples provided, a notification telling you that a Git repository was found will also pop up. You can simply close this one, as we only want to open the ch1 folder.

Now that VS Code is ready, let's continue by setting up a new project with Vite.

Setting up a project with Vite

For this book, we are going to use **Vite** to set up our project, as it is the most popular and liked according to *The State of JS 2022* survey (`https://2022.stateofjs.com/`). Vite also makes it easy to set up a modern frontend project, while still making it possible to extend the configuration later if needed. Follow these steps to set up your project with Vite:

1. In the VS Code menu bar, go to **Terminal | New Terminal** to open a new Terminal.

2. Inside the Terminal, run the following command:

    ```
    $ npm create vite@5.0.0 .
    ```

    Make sure there is a period at the end of the command to create the project in the current folder instead of creating a new folder.

> **Note**
>
> To keep the instructions in this book working even when new versions are released, we pin all packages to a fixed version. Please follow the instructions with the given versions. After finishing this book, when starting new projects on your own, you should always try using the latest versions but keep in mind that changes might be needed to get them working. Consult the documentation of the respective packages and follow the migration path from the book version to the latest version.

3. When asked if `create-vite` should be installed, simply type `y` and press the *Return/Enter* key to proceed.

4. When asked about the framework, use the arrow keys to select **React** and press *Return*. If you are being asked for a project name, press *Ctrl + C* to cancel, then run the command again, making sure there is a period at the end to select the current folder.

5. When asked about the variant, select **JavaScript**.

6. Now, our project is set up and we can run `npm install` to install the dependencies.

7. Afterward, run `npm run dev` to start the dev server, as shown in the following screenshot:

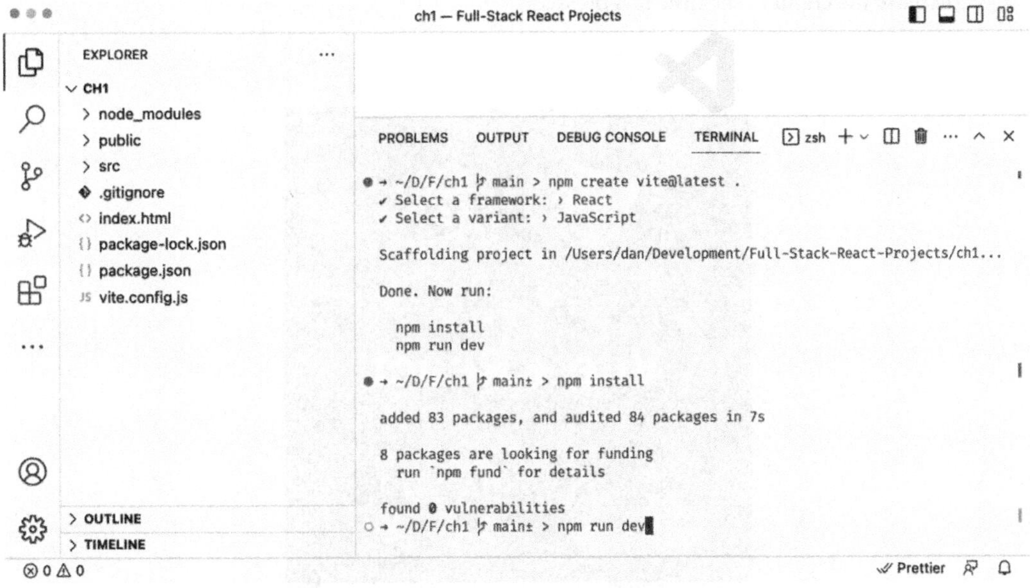

Figure 1.4 – The Terminal after setting up a project with Vite and before starting the dev server

---

Note

For simplicity in setting up, we just used npm directly. If you prefer `yarn` or pnpm, you can instead run `yarn create vite` or pnpm `create vite`, respectively.

---

8. In the Terminal, you will see a URL telling you where your app is running. You can either hold *Ctrl* (*Cmd* on macOS) and click on the link to open it in your browser, or manually enter the URL in a browser.

9. To test whether your app is interactive, click the button with the text **count is 0**, and it should increase the count every time it is pressed.

Figure 1.5 – Our first React app running with Vite

Alternatives to Vite

Alternatives to Vite are bundlers, such as webpack, Rollup, and Parcel. These are highly configurable but often do not offer a great experience for dev servers. They first must bundle all our code together before serving it to the browser. Instead, Vite natively supports the **ECMAScript module (ESM)** standard. Furthermore, Vite requires very little configuration to get started. A downside of Vite is that it can be hard to configure certain more complex scenarios with it. An upcoming bundler that is promising is Turbopack; however, it is still very new at the time of writing. For full-stack development with server-side rendering, we will later get to know Next.js, which is a React framework that also provides a dev server out of the box.

Now that our boilerplate project is up and running, let's spend some time setting up tools that will enforce best practices and a consistent code style.

Setting up ESLint and Prettier to enforce best practices and code style

Now that our React app is set up, we are going to set up **ESLint** to enforce coding best practices with JavaScript and React. We are also going to set up **Prettier** to enforce a code style and automatically format our code.

Installing the necessary dependencies

First, we are going to install all the necessary dependencies:

1. In the Terminal, click on the **Split Terminal** icon at the top right of the **Terminal** pane to create a new **Terminal** pane. This will keep our app running while we run other commands.

2. Click on this newly opened pane to focus it. Then, enter the following command to install ESLint, Prettier, and the relevant plugins:

    ```
    $ npm install --save-dev prettier@3.1.0 \
      eslint@8.54.0 \
      eslint-plugin-react@7.33.2 \
      eslint-config-prettier@9.0.0 \
      eslint-plugin-jsx-a11y@6.8.0
    ```

    The packages installed are the following:

    - `prettier`: Formats our code automatically according to a defined code style

    - `eslint`: Analyzes our code and enforces best practices

    - `eslint-config-react`: Enables rules in ESLint relevant to React projects

    - `eslint-config-prettier`: Disables rules relating to code style in ESLint so that Prettier can handle them instead

    - `eslint-plugin-jsx-a11y`: Allows ESLint to check for accessibility (`a11y`) issues in our JSX code

> **Note**
>
> The `--save-dev` flag in npm saves those dependencies as `dev` dependencies, which means that they will only be installed for development. They will not be installed and included in a deployed app. This is important in order to keep the size of our containers as small as possible later.

After the dependencies are installed, we need to configure Prettier and ESLint. We will start with configuring Prettier.

Configuring Prettier

Prettier will format the code for us and replace the default code formatter for JavaScript in VS Code. It will allow us to spend more time writing code, automatically formatting it for us properly when we save the file. Follow these steps to configure Prettier:

1. Right-click below the files list in the left sidebar of VS Code (if it is not opened, click the **Files** icon) and press **New file...** to create a new file. Call it `.prettierrc.json` (do not forget the period at the beginning of the file name!).

2. The newly created file should open automatically, so we can start writing the following configuration into it. We first create a new object and set the `trailingComma` option to `all` to make sure objects and arrays that span over multiple lines always have a comma at the end, even for the last element. This reduces the number of touched lines when committing a change via Git:

    ```
    {
        "trailingComma": "all",
    ```

3. Then, we set the `tabWidth` option to 2 spaces:

    ```
        "tabWidth": 2,
    ```

4. Set the `printWidth` to 80 characters per line to avoid long lines in our code:

    ```
        "printWidth": 80,
    ```

5. Set the `semi` option to `false` to avoid semicolons where not necessary:

    ```
        "semi": false,
    ```

6. Finally, we enforce the use of single quotes instead of double quotes:

    ```
        "jsxSingleQuote": true,
        "singleQuote": true
    }
    ```

> **Note**
>
> These settings for Prettier are just an example of a coding style convention. Of course, you are free to adjust these to your own preferences. There are many more options, all of which can be found in the Prettier docs (`https://prettier.io/docs/en/options.html`).

Configuring the Prettier extension

Now that we have a configuration file for Prettier, we need to make sure the VS Code extension is properly configured to format the code for us:

1. Open the VS Code settings by going to **File | Preferences... | Settings** on Windows/Linux, or **Code | Settings... | Settings** on macOS.

2. In the newly opened settings editor, click on the **Workspace** tab. This ensures that we save all our settings in a `.vscode/settings.json` file in our project folder. When other developers open our project, they will automatically be using those settings as well.

3. Search for `editor format on save` and check the checkbox to enable formatting code on save.

4. Search for `editor default formatter` and select **Prettier - Code formatter** from the list.

5. To verify that Prettier works, open the `.prettierrc.json` file, add some extra spaces to the beginning of a line, and save the file. You should notice that Prettier reformatted the code to adhere to the defined code style. It will reduce the number of spaces for indentation to two.

Now that Prettier is set up properly, we do not need to worry about formatting our code manually anymore. Feel free to just type in code as you go and save the file to get it formatted for you!

Creating a Prettier ignore file

To improve performance and avoid running Prettier on files that should not be automatically formatted, we can ignore certain files and folders by creating a Prettier ignore file. Follow these steps:

1. Create a new file called `.prettierignore` in the root of our project, similar to how we created the `.prettierrc.json` file.

2. Add the following contents to it to ignore the transpiled source code:

   ```
   dist/
   ```

   The `node_modules/` folder is automatically ignored by Prettier.

Now that we have successfully set up Prettier, we are going to configure ESLint to enforce coding best practices.

Configuring ESLint

While Prettier focuses on the style and formatting of our code, ESLint focuses on the actual code, avoiding common mistakes or unnecessary code. Let's configure it now:

1. Delete the automatically created `.eslintrc.cjs` file.

2. Create a new `.eslintrc.json` file and start writing the following configuration into it. First, we set `root` to `true` to make sure ESLint does not look at parent folders for more configuration:

    ```
    {
      "root": true,
    ```

3. Define an `env` object, in which we set the browser environment to `true` so that ESLint understands browser-specific globals such as `document` and `window`:

    ```
    "env": {
      "browser": true
    },
    ```

4. Define a `parserOptions` object, where we specify that we are using the latest ECMAScript version and ESM:

    ```
    "parserOptions": {
      "ecmaVersion": "latest",
      "sourceType": "module"
    },
    ```

5. Define an `extends` array to extend from recommended configurations. Specifically, we extend from ESLint's recommended rules and the recommended rules for the plugins we installed:

    ```
    "extends": [
      "eslint:recommended",
      "plugin:react/recommended",
      "plugin:react/jsx-runtime",
      "plugin:jsx-a11y/recommended",
    ```

6. As the last element of the array, we use `prettier` to disable all code style-related rules in ESLint and let Prettier handle it:

    ```
    "prettier"
    ],
    ```

7. Now, we define settings for the plugins. First, we tell the `react` plugin to detect our installed React version automatically:

    ```
    "settings": {
      "react": {
    ```

```
            "version": "detect"
        }
    },
```

8. Finally, outside of the `settings` section, we define an `overrides` array, in which we specify that ESLint should only lint `.js` and `.jsx` files:

```
    "overrides": [
        {
            "files": ["*.js", "*.jsx"]
        }
    ]
}
```

9. Create a new `.eslintignore` file, with the following contents:

```
dist/
vite.config.js
```

The `node_modules/` folder is automatically ignored by ESLint.

10. Save the files and run `npx eslint src` in the Terminal to run the linter. You will see that there are some errors already due to our configured rules not matching the source provided by the default project in Vite:

```
⊗ → ~/D/F/ch1 ⨍ main± > npx eslint src

/Users/dan/Development/Full-Stack-React-Projects/ch1/src/App.jsx
  12:9  error  Using target="_blank" without rel="noreferrer" (which implies rel="noopener") is a security risk in
older browsers: see https://mathiasbynens.github.io/rel-noopener/#recommendations  react/jsx-no-target-blank
  15:9  error  Using target="_blank" without rel="noreferrer" (which implies rel="noopener") is a security risk in
older browsers: see https://mathiasbynens.github.io/rel-noopener/#recommendations  react/jsx-no-target-blank

✗ 2 problems (2 errors, 0 warnings)
  2 errors and 0 warnings potentially fixable with the `--fix` option.
```

Figure 1.6 – When running ESLint for the first time, we get some errors about rule violations

11. Fortunately, all these issues are automatically fixable by ESLint. Run `npx eslint src --fix` to fix the issues automatically. Now, when you run `npx eslint src` again, you will not get any output. This means that there were no linter errors!

Tip

The `npx` command allows us to execute commands provided by npm packages, in a similar context as running them in `package.json` scripts would do. It can also run remote packages without installing them permanently. If the package is not installed yet, it will ask you whether it should do this.

Adding a new script to run our linter

In the previous section, we have been calling the linter by running `npx eslint src` manually. We are now going to add a `lint` script to `package.json`:

1. In the Terminal, run the following command to define a `lint` script in the `package.json` file:

    ```
    $ npm pkg set scripts.lint="eslint src"
    ```

2. Now, run `npm run lint` in the Terminal. This should execute `eslint src` successfully, just like `npx eslint src` did:

    ```
    ● → ~/D/F/ch1  main± > npm run lint

    > ch1@0.0.0 lint
    > eslint src

    ○ → ~/D/F/ch1  main± > █
    ```

    Figure 1.7 – The linter running successfully, with no errors

After setting up ESLint and Prettier, we still need to make sure that they run before we commit code. Let's set up Husky to make sure we commit proper code now.

Setting up Husky to make sure we commit proper code

After setting up Prettier and ESLint, we will now get our code automatically formatted on save by Prettier and see errors from ESLint in VS Code when we make mistakes or ignore best practices. However, we might miss some of these errors and accidentally commit code that is invalid. To avoid this, we can set up **Husky** and **lint-staged**, which run before we commit our code to Git and ensure that Prettier and ESLint are executed successfully on the source code before it is committed.

> **Important**
>
> If you cloned the full repository for the book, Husky may not find the `.git` directory when running `npm install`. In that case, just run `git init` in the root of the corresponding chapter folder.

Let's set Husky and lint-staged up by following these steps:

1. Run the following command to install Husky and lint-staged as `dev` dependencies:

    ```
    $ npm install --save-dev husky@8.0.3 \
        lint-staged@15.1.0
    ```

2. Open the package.json file and add the following lint-staged configuration to it in a new object after devDependencies, then save the file. This will run Prettier and ESlint on all committed .js and .jsx files and attempt to automatically fix code style and linter errors, if possible:

```
"lint-staged": {
  "**/*.{js,jsx}": [
    "npx prettier --write",
    "npx eslint --fix"
  ]
}
```

3. Initialize a Git repository in the ch1 folder and make an initial commit with just the package.json file, as lint-staged does not get executed on the initial commit:

```
$ git init
$ git add package.json
$ git commit -m "chore: initial commit"
```

4. Add the husky install script to a prepare script in package.json, so that Husky gets installed automatically when the project is cloned and npm install is executed:

```
$ npm pkg set scripts.prepare="husky install"
```

5. Since we do not need to run npm install again right now, we need to manually run the prepare script this time:

```
$ npm run prepare
```

6. Add a pre-commit hook for lint-staged, so that ESLint and Prettier run every time we do git commit:

```
$ npx husky add .husky/pre-commit "npx lint-staged"
```

7. Now, add all files to Git and attempt to make a commit:

```
$ git add .
$ git commit -m "chore: basic project setup"
```

If everything worked successfully, you should see husky running lint-staged, which, in turn, runs prettier and eslint, after you run git commit. If you are getting a configuration error, ensure that all files are saved properly and then run git commit again.

```
● → ~/D/F/ch1 ⅙ main± > git commit -m "chore: basic project setup"
  ✓ Preparing lint-staged...
  ✓ Running tasks for staged files...
  ✓ Applying modifications from tasks...
  ✓ Cleaning up temporary files...
[main f226bcd] chore: basic project setup
```

Figure 1.8 – Husky and lint-staged successfully enforcing code style and best practices before we commit

Setting up commitlint to enforce a standard for our commit messages

In addition to linting our code, we can also lint our commit messages. You may have noticed that we were prefixing our commit messages with a type already (the chore type). Types make it easier to follow what was changed in a commit. To enforce the use of types, we can set up **commitlint**. Follow these steps to set it up:

1. Install commitlint and a conventional config for commitlint:

    ```
    $ npm install --save-dev @commitlint/cli@18.4.3 \
        @commitlint/config-conventional@18.4.3
    ```

2. Create a new .commitlintrc.json file in the root of our project and add the following contents:

    ```
    {
        "extends": ["@commitlint/config-conventional"]
    }
    ```

3. Add a commit-msg hook to Husky:

    ```
    $ npx husky add .husky/commit-msg \
        'npx commitlint --edit ${1}'
    ```

4. Now, if we try adding our changed files and committing without a type or a wrong type, we will get an error from commitlint and will not be able to make such a commit. If we add the correct type, it will succeed:

    ```
    $ git add .
    $ git commit -m "no type"
    $ git commit -m "wrong: type"
    $ git commit -m "chore: configure commitlint"
    ```

The following figure shows Husky in action. If we write an incorrect commit message, it will reject it and not let us commit the code. Only if we enter a properly formatted commit message will the commit go through:

```
⊗ → ~/D/F/ch1 ⸝ main± > git commit -m "no type"
→ No staged files match any configured task.
✘   input: no type
✘   subject may not be empty [subject-empty]
✘   type may not be empty [type-empty]

✘   found 2 problems, 0 warnings
ⓘ   Get help: https://github.com/conventional-changelog/commitlint/#what-is-commitlint

husky - commit-msg hook exited with code 1 (error)
⊗ → ~/D/F/ch1 ⸝ main± > git commit -m "wrong: type"
→ No staged files match any configured task.
✘   input: wrong: type
✘   type must be one of [build, chore, ci, docs, feat, fix, perf, refactor, revert, style, test] [type-enum]

✘   found 1 problems, 0 warnings
ⓘ   Get help: https://github.com/conventional-changelog/commitlint/#what-is-commitlint

husky - commit-msg hook exited with code 1 (error)
● → ~/D/F/ch1 ⸝ main± > git commit -m "chore: configure commitlint"
→ No staged files match any configured task.
[main e5e8cd0] chore: configure commitlint
 4 files changed, 2019 insertions(+), 57 deletions(-)
 create mode 100644 .commitlintrc.json
 create mode 100755 .husky/commit-msg
```

Figure 1.9 – commitlint working successfully and preventing
commits without a type and with wrong types

Commit messages in the commitlint conventional config (https://www.conventionalcommits.org/) are structured in a way where a type must be listed first, then an optional scope follows, and then the description follows, such as type(scope): description. Possible types are as follows:

- fix: For bug fixes

- feat: For new features

- refactor: For restructuring the code without adding features or fixing bugs

- build: For changes in the build system or dependencies

- ci: For changes in the CI/CD configuration

- docs: For changes in the documentation only

- perf: For performance optimizations

- style: For fixing code formatting

- test: For adding or adjusting tests

The scope is optional and best used in a monorepo to specify that changes were made to a certain app or library within it.

Summary

Now that we have successfully set up our project and started enforcing standards, we can continue working on our project without worrying about a consistent code style, consistent commit messages, or making small mistakes. ESLint, Prettier, Husky, and commitlint have got us covered.

In the next chapter, *Chapter 2, Getting to Know Node.js and MongoDB*, we are going to learn how to write and run small Node.js scripts and how MongoDB, a database system, works.

2

Getting to Know Node.js and MongoDB

In the previous chapter, we set up our IDE and a basic project for frontend development. In this chapter, we will first learn how to write and run scripts with Node.js. Then, we will move on to introducing Docker as a way to set up a database service. Once we have set up Docker and a container for our database, we are going to access it to learn more about MongoDB, the document database that we will use going forward. Finally, we will connect everything we have learned in this chapter by accessing MongoDB via Node.js scripts.

By the end of this chapter, you will have an understanding of the most important tools and concepts in backend development with JavaScript. This chapter gives us a good foundation to create a backend service for our first full-stack application in the upcoming chapters.

In this chapter, we are going to cover the following main topics:

- Writing and running scripts with Node.js

- Introducing Docker, a platform for containers

- Introducing MongoDB, a document database

- Accessing the MongoDB database via Node.js

Technical requirements

Before we start, please install the following (in addition to all technical requirements from *Chapter 1, Preparing for Full-stack Development*), if you do not already have them installed:

- Docker v24.0.6

- Docker Desktop v4.25.2

- MongoDB Shell v2.1.0

The versions listed are the ones used in the book. While installing a newer version should not be an issue, please note that certain steps might work differently on a newer version. If you are having an issue with the code and steps provided in this book, please try using the mentioned versions.

You can find the code for this chapter on GitHub: `https://github.com/PacktPublishing/Modern-Full-Stack-React-Projects/tree/main/ch2`.

The CiA video for this chapter can be found at: `https://youtu.be/q_LHsdJEaPo`.

> **Important**
> If you cloned the full repository for the book, Husky may not find the `.git` directory when running `npm install`. In that case, just run `git init` in the root of the corresponding chapter folder.

Writing and running scripts with Node.js

For us to become full-stack developers, it is important to get familiar with backend technologies. As we are already familiar with JavaScript from writing frontend applications, we can use Node.js to develop backend services using JavaScript. In this section, we are going to create our first simple Node.js script to get familiar with the differences between backend scripts and frontend code.

Similarities and differences between JavaScript in the browser and in Node.js

Node.js is built on V8, the JavaScript engine used by Chromium-based browsers (Google Chrome, Brave, Opera, Vivaldi, and Microsoft Edge). As such, JavaScript code will run the same way in the browser and Node.js. However, there are some differences, specifically in the environment. The environment is built on top of the engine and allows us to render something on a website in the browser (using the `document` and `window` objects). In Node.js, there are certain modules provided to interface with the operating system, for tasks such as creating files and handling network requests. These modules allow us to create a backend service using Node.js.

Let's have a look at the Node.js architecture versus JavaScript in the browser:

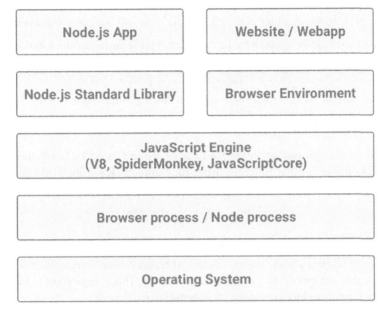

Figure 2.1 – The Node.js architecture versus JavaScript in the browser

As we can see from the visualization, both Node.js and browser JavaScript run on a JavaScript engine, which is always V8 in Node.js, and can be V8 for Chromium-based browsers, SpiderMonkey for Firefox, or JavaScriptCore for Safari.

Now that we know that we can run JavaScript code in Node.js, let's try it out!

Creating our first Node.js script

Before we can start writing backend services, we need to get familiar with the Node.js environment. So, let's start by writing a simple "hello world" example:

1. Copy the ch1 folder from the previous chapter to a new ch2 folder, as follows:

    ```
    $ cp -R ch1 ch2
    ```

> **Note**
>
> On macOS, it is important to run the command with a capitalized -R flag, not -r. The -r flag deals differently with symlinks and causes the node_modules/ folder to break. The -r flag only exists for historic reasons and should not be used on macOS. Always prefer using the -R flag instead.

2. Open the new ch2 folder in VS Code.

3. Create a new `backend` folder in the `ch2` folder. This will contain our backend code.

4. In the `backend` folder, create a `helloworld.js` file and enter the following code:

```
console.log('hello node.js world!')
```

5. Open a Terminal in the `ch2` folder and run the following command to execute the Node.js script:

```
$ node backend/helloworld.js
```

You will see that the console output shows `hello node.js world!`. When writing Node.js code, we can make use of familiar functions from the frontend JavaScript world and run the same JavaScript code on the backend!

> **Note**
>
> While most frontend JavaScript code will run just fine in Node.js, not all code from the frontend will automatically work in a Node.js environment. There are certain objects, such as `document` and `window`, that are specific to a browser environment. This is important to keep in mind, especially when we introduce server-side rendering later.

Now that we have a basic understanding of how Node.js works, let's get started handling files with Node.js.

Handling files in Node.js

Unlike in the browser environment, Node.js provides functions to handle files on our computer via the `node:fs` (filesystem) module. For example, we could make use of this functionality to read and write various files or even use files as a simple database.

Follow these steps to create your first Node.js script that handles files:

1. Create a new `backend/files.js` file.

2. Import the `writeFileSync` and `readFileSync` functions from the `node:fs` internal Node.js module. This module does not need to be installed via npm, as it is provided by the Node.js runtime.

```
import { writeFileSync, readFileSync } from 'node:fs'
```

3. Create a simple array containing users, with a name and email address:

```
const users = [{ name: 'Adam Ondra', email: 'adam.ondra@climb.
ing' }]
```

4. Before we can save this array to a file, we first need to convert it to a string by using `JSON.stringify`:

```
const usersJson = JSON.stringify(users)
```

5. Now we can save our JSON string to a file by using the `writeFileSync` function. This function takes two arguments – first the filename, then the string to be written to the file:

    ```
    writeFileSync('backend/users.json', usersJson)
    ```

6. After writing to the file, we can attempt reading it again using `readFileSync` and parsing the JSON string using `JSON.parse`:

    ```
    const readUsersJson = readFileSync('backend/users.json')
    const readUsers = JSON.parse(readUsersJson)
    ```

7. Finally, we log the parsed array:

    ```
    console.log(readUsers)
    ```

8. Now we can run our script. You will see that the array gets logged and a `users.json` file was created in our `backend/` folder:

    ```
    $ node backend/files.js
    ```

You may have noticed that we have been using `writeFileSync`, and not `writeFile`. The default behavior in Node.js is to run everything asynchronously, which means that if we used `writeFile`, the file may not have been created yet at the time when we called `readFile`, as asynchronous code is not executed in order.

This behavior might be annoying when writing simple scripts like we did, but is very useful when dealing with, for example, network requests, where we do not want to block other users from accessing our service while dealing with another request.

After learning about handling files with Node.js, let's learn more about how asynchronous code is executed in the browser and Node.js.

Concurrency with JavaScript in the browser and Node.js

An essential and special trait of JavaScript is that most API functions are asynchronous by default. This means that code does not simply run in the sequence in which it is defined. Specifically, JavaScript is event-driven. In the browser, this means that JavaScript code will run because of user interactions. For example, when a button is clicked, we define an `onClick` handler to execute some code.

On the server side, input/output operations, such as reading and writing files, and network requests, are handled asynchronously. This means that we can handle multiple network requests at once, without having to deal with threads or multiprocessing ourselves. Specifically, in Node.js, `libuv` is responsible for assigning threads for I/O operations while giving us, as a programmer, access to a single runtime thread to write our code in. However, this does not mean that each connection to our backend will create a new thread. Threads are created on the fly when advantageous. As a developer, we do not have to deal with multi-threading and can focus on developing with asynchronous code and callbacks.

If code is synchronous, it is executed directly by putting it on the **call stack**. If code is asynchronous, the operation is started, and the instance of that operation is stored in a queue, together with a callback function. The Node.js runtime will first execute all code left in the stack. Then, the **event loop** will come in and check whether there are any completed tasks in the queue. If that is the case, the callback function is executed by putting it on the stack. A callback function can then again either execute synchronous or asynchronous code. When we add an event listener – for example, an `onClick` listener in the browser – when the user clicks the related element, the callback will also be put in the task queue, which means it will be executed when nothing else is left on the stack. Similarly, in Node. js, we can add listeners for network events, and execute a callback when a request comes in.

In contrast to multi-threaded servers, a Node.js server accepts all requests in a single thread, which contains the event loop. Multi-threaded servers have the disadvantage that threads can block I/O completely and slow down the server. Node.js, however, delegates operations in a fine-grained way on the fly to threads. This results in less blocking of I/O operations by default. The downside with Node.js is that we have less control over how the multi-threading happens and thus need to be careful to avoid using synchronous functions whenever possible. Otherwise, we will block the main Node.js thread and slow down our server. For simplicity, we still use synchronous functions in this chapter. Going forward, in the next chapters, we will avoid using those and rely solely on asynchronous functions (when possible) to get the best performance.

The following diagram visualizes the difference between multi-threaded servers and a Node.js server:

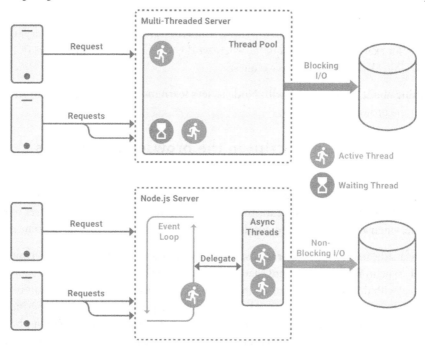

Figure 2.2 – The difference between multi-threaded servers and a Node.js server

We can see this asynchrony in action by using `setTimeout`, a function that you may be familiar with from frontend code. It waits a specified number of milliseconds and then executes the code specified in the callback function. For example, if we run the following code (with a Node.js script or in the browser, the result is the same for both):

```
console.log('first')
setTimeout(() => {
  console.log('second')
}, 1000)
console.log('third')
```

We can see that they get printed in the following order:

```
first
third
second
```

This makes sense, because we are delaying the "second" `console.log` by a second. However, the same output will happen if we execute the following code:

```
console.log('first')
setTimeout(() => {
  console.log('second')
}, 0)
console.log('third')
```

Now that we are waiting zero milliseconds before executing the code, you would think that "second" gets printed after "first." However, that is not the case. Instead, we get the same output as before:

```
first
third
second
```

The reason is that when we use `setTimeout`, the JavaScript engine calls either a web API (on the browser) or a native API (on Node.js). This API runs in native code in the engine, tracks the timeout internally, and puts the callback into the task queue, because the timer completes right away. While this is happening, the JavaScript engine continues processing the other code by pushing it onto the stack and executing it. When the stack is empty (there is no more code to execute), the event loop advances. It sees that there is something in the task queue, so it executes that code, resulting in "second" being printed last.

> **Tip**
> You can use the Loupe tool to visualize the inner workings of the Call Stack, web APIs, Event Loop, and Callback/Task Queue: `http://latentflip.com/loupe/`

Now that we have learned how asynchronous code is handled in the browser and Node.js, let's create our first web server with Node.js!

Creating our first web server

Now that we have learned the basics of how Node.js works, we can use the node:http library to create a simple web server. For our first simple server, we are just going to return a **200 OK** response and some plain text on any request. Let's get started with the steps:

1. Create a new backend/simpleweb.js file, open it, and import the createServer function from the node:http module:

    ```
    import { createServer } from 'node:http'
    ```

2. The createServer function is asynchronous, so it requires us to pass a callback function to it. This function will be executed when a request comes in from the server. It has two arguments, a request object (req) and a response object (res). Use the createServer function to define a new server:

    ```
    const server = createServer((req, res) => {
    ```

3. For now, we will ignore the request object and only return a static response. First, we set the status code to 200:

    ```
    res.statusCode = 200
    ```

4. Then, we set the Content-Type header to text/plain, such that the browser knows what kind of response data it is dealing with:

    ```
    res.setHeader('Content-Type', 'text/plain')
    ```

5. Lastly, we end the request by returning a Hello HTTP world! string in the response:

    ```
    res.end('Hello HTTP world!')
    })
    ```

6. After defining the server, we need to make sure to listen on a certain host and port. These will define where the server will be available. For now, we use localhost on port 3000 to make sure our server is available via http://localhost:3000/:

    ```
    const host = 'localhost'
    const port = 3000
    ```

7. The `server.listen` function is also asynchronous and requires us to pass a callback function, which will execute as soon as the server is up and running. We can simply log something here for now:

```
server.listen(port, host, () => {
  console.log(`Server listening on http://${host}:${port}`)
})
```

8. Run the Node.js script as follows:

```
$ node backend/simpleweb.js
```

9. You will notice that we get our **Server listening on http://localhost:3000** log message, so we know the server was started successfully. This time, the Terminal does not return control to us; the script keeps running. We can now open `http://localhost:3000` in a browser:

Hello HTTP world!

Figure 2.3 – A plaintext response from our first web server!

Now that we have set up a simple web server, we can extend it to serve a JSON file instead of simply returning plaintext.

Extending the web server to serve our JSON file

We can now try combining our knowledge of the `node:fs` module with the HTTP server to create a server that serves the previously created `users.json` file. Let's get started with the steps:

1. Copy the `backend/simpleweb.js` file to a new `backend/webfiles.js` file.

2. At the beginning of the file, add an import of `readFileSync`:

```
import { readFileSync } from 'node:fs'
```

3. Change the `Content-Type` header to `application/json`:

```
res.setHeader('Content-Type', 'application/json')
```

4. Replace the string in `res.end()` with the JSON string from our file. In this case, we do not need to parse the JSON, as `res.end()` expects a string anyway:

```
res.end(readFileSync('backend/users.json'))
```

5. If it is still running, stop the previous server script via *Ctrl + C*. We need to do this because we cannot listen on the same port twice.

6. Run the server and refresh the page to see the JSON from the file being printed. Try changing the `users.json` file and see how it is read again on the next request (when refreshing the website):

```
$ node backend/webfiles.js
```

While useful as an exercise, files are not a proper database to be used in production. As such, we are later going to introduce MongoDB as a database. We are going to run the MongoDB server in Docker, so let's first briefly have a look at Docker.

Introducing Docker, a platform for containers

Docker is a platform that allows us to package, manage, and run applications in loosely isolated environments, called **containers**. Containers are lightweight, are isolated from each other, and include all dependencies needed to run an application. As such, we can use containers to easily set up various services and apps without having to deal with managing dependencies or conflicts between them.

> **Note**
>
> There are also other tools, such as Podman (which even has a compatibility layer for the Docker CLI commands), and Rancher Desktop, which also supports Docker CLI commands.

We can use Docker locally to set up and run services in an isolated environment. Doing so avoids polluting our host environment and ensures that there is a consistent state to build upon. This consistency is especially important when working in larger development teams, as it ensures that everyone is working with the same state.

Additionally, Docker makes it easy to deploy containers to various cloud services and run them in a **continuous integration/continuous delivery (CI/CD)** workflow.

In this section, we will first get an overview of the Docker platform. Then, we will learn how to create a container and how to access Docker from VS Code. At the end, we will understand how Docker works and how it can be used to manage services.

The Docker platform

The Docker platform essentially consists of three parts:

- **Docker Client**: Can run commands by sending them to the **Docker daemon**, which is either running on the local machine or a remote environment.

- **Docker Host**: Contains the Docker daemon, images, and containers.

- **Docker Registry**: Hosts and stores docker images, extensions, and plugins. By default, the public registry **Docker Hub** will be used to search for images.

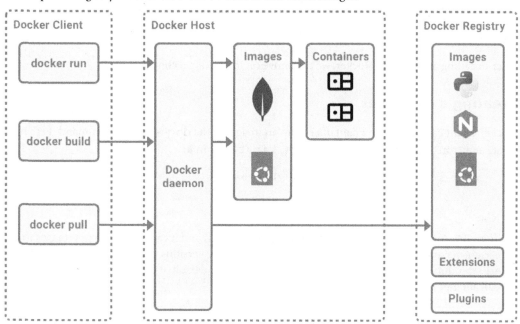

Figure 2.4 – Overview of the Docker platform

Docker images can be thought of as read-only templates and are used to create containers. Images can be based on other images. For example, the mongo image, which contains a MongoDB server, is based on the ubuntu image.

Docker containers are instances of images. They run an operating system with a configured service (such as a MongoDB server on Ubuntu). Additionally, they can be configured, for example, to forward some ports from within the container to the host, or to mount a storage volume in the container that stores data on the host machine. By default, a container is isolated from the host machine, so if we want to access ports or storage from it on the host, we need to tell Docker to allow this.

Installing Docker

The easiest way to set up the Docker platform for local development is using Docker Desktop. It can be downloaded from the official Docker website (`https://www.docker.com/products/docker-desktop/`). Follow the instructions to install it and start the Docker engine. After installation, you should have a `docker` command available in your Terminal. Run the following command to verify that it is working properly:

```
$ docker -v
```

This command should output the Docker version, like in the following example:

```
Docker version 24.0.6, build ed223bc
```

After installing and starting Docker, we can move on to creating a container.

Creating a container

Docker Client can instantiate a container from an image via the `docker run` command. Let's now create an `ubuntu` container and run a shell (`/bin/bash`) in it:

```
$ docker run -i -t ubuntu:24.04 /bin/bash
```

> **Note**
>
> The `:24.04` string after the image name is called the **tag**, and it can be used to pin images to certain versions. In this book, we use tags to pull specific versions of images so that the steps are reproducible even when new versions are released. By default, if no tag is specified, Docker will attempt to use the `latest` tag.

A new shell will open. We can verify that this shell is running in the container by executing the following command to see which operating system is running:

```
$ uname -a
```

If you get a version number that ends with `-linuxkit`, you have successfully run a command in the container, because LinuxKit is a toolkit to create small Linux VMs!

You can now type the following command to exit the shell and the container:

```
$ exit
```

The following figure shows the result of running these commands:

```
● → ~/D/F/ch2 ⑂ main± > docker run -i -t ubuntu /bin/bash
  Unable to find image 'ubuntu:latest' locally
  latest: Pulling from library/ubuntu
  d0a4bfa485d1: Pull complete
  Digest: sha256:2adf22367284330af9f832ffefb717c78239f6251d9d0f58de50b86229ed1427
  Status: Downloaded newer image for ubuntu:latest
  root@d05b654cc753:/# uname -a
  Linux d05b654cc753 5.15.49-linuxkit #1 SMP PREEMPT Tue Sep 13 07:51:32 UTC 2022
   aarch64 aarch64 aarch64 GNU/Linux
  root@d05b654cc753:/# exit
  exit
○ → ~/D/F/ch2 ⑂ main± > █
```

Figure 2.5 – Running our first Docker container

The docker run command does the following:

- If you have never run a container based on the ubuntu image before, Docker will start by pulling the image from the Docker registry (this is equivalent to executing docker pull ubuntu).

- After the image is downloaded, Docker creates a new container (the equivalent to executing docker container create).

- Then, Docker configures a read-write filesystem for the container and creates a default network interface.

- Finally, Docker starts the container and executes the specified command. In our case, we specified the /bin/bash command. Because we passed the -i (keeps STDIN open) and -t (allocates a pseudo-tty) options, Docker attaches the container's shell to our currently running Terminal, allowing us to use the container as if we were directly accessing a Terminal on our host machine.

As we can see, Docker is very useful for creating self-contained environments for our apps and services to run in. Later in this book, we are going to learn how to package our own apps in Docker containers. For now, we are only going to use Docker to run services without having to install them on our host system.

Accessing Docker via VS Code

We can also access Docker via the VS Code extension we installed in *Chapter 1, Preparing for Full-stack Development*. To do so, click the Docker icon in the left sidebar of VS Code. The Docker sidebar will open, showing you a list of containers, images, registries, networks, volumes, contexts, and relevant resources:

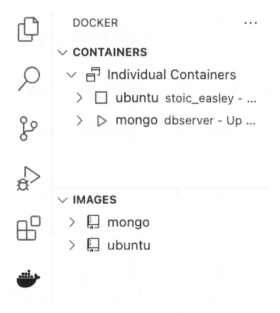

Figure 2.6 – The Docker sidebar in VS Code

Here, you can see which containers are stopped and which ones are running. You can right-click on a container to start, stop, restart, or remove it. You can also view its logs to debug what is going on inside the container. Additionally, you can attach a shell to the container to get access to its operating system.

Now that we know the essentials of Docker, we can create a container for our MongoDB database server.

Introducing MongoDB, a document database

MongoDB, at the time of writing, is the most popular NoSQL database. Unlike **Structured Query Language (SQL)** databases (such as MySQL or PostgreSQL), NoSQL means that the database specifically does not use SQL to query the database. Instead, NoSQL databases have various other ways to query the database and often have a vastly different structure of how data is stored and queried.

The following main types of NoSQL databases exist:

- Key-value stores (for example, Valkey/Redis)
- Column-oriented databases (for example, Amazon Redshift)
- Graph-based databases (for example, Neo4j)
- Document-based databases (for example, MongoDB)

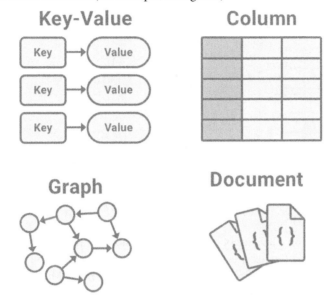

Figure 2.7 – Overview of NoSQL databases

MongoDB is a document-based database, which means that each entry in the database is stored as a document. In MongoDB, these documents are basically JSON objects (internally, they are stored as BSON – a binary JSON format to save space and improve performance, among other advantages). Instead, SQL databases store data as rows in tables. As such, MongoDB provides a lot more flexibility. Fields can be freely added or left out in documents. The downside of such a structure is that we do not have a consistent schema for documents. However, this can be solved by using libraries, such as Mongoose, which we will learn about in *Chapter 3, Implementing a Backend Using Express, Mongoose ODM, and Jest.*

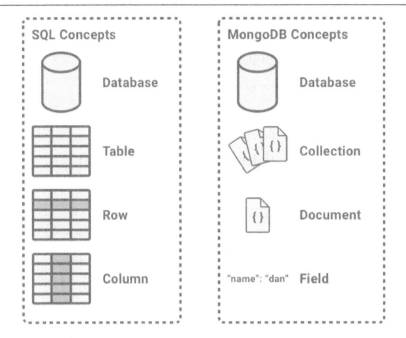

Figure 2.8 – Comparison between MongoDB and SQL databases

MongoDB is also based on a JavaScript engine. Since version 3.2, it has been using SpiderMonkey (the JavaScript engine that Firefox uses) instead of V8. Nevertheless, this still means we can execute JavaScript code in MongoDB. For example, we can use JavaScript in the **MongoDB Shell** to help with administrative tasks. Again, we must be careful with this, though, as the MongoDB environment is vastly different from a browser or Node.js environment.

In this section, we will first learn how to set up a MongoDB server using Docker. Then, we will learn more about MongoDB and how to access it directly using the MongoDB Shell for the administration of our database and the data. We are also going to learn how to use VS Code to access MongoDB. At the end of this section, you will have an understanding of how CRUD operations work in MongoDB.

> **Note**
> CRUD is an acronym for create, read, update, and delete, which are the common operations that backend services usually provide.

Setting up a MongoDB server

Before we can start using MongoDB, we need to set up a server. Since we already have Docker installed, we can make things easier for ourselves by running MongoDB in a Docker container. Doing so also allows us to have separate, clean MongoDB instances for our apps by creating separate containers. Let's get started with the steps:

1. Make sure Docker Desktop is running and Docker is started. You can verify this by running the following command, which lists all running containers:

    ```
    $ docker ps
    ```

    If Docker is not started properly, you will get a **Cannot connect to the Docker daemon** error. In that case, make sure Docker Desktop is running and the Docker Engine is not paused.

    If Docker is started properly, you will see the following output:

    ```
    CONTAINER
    ID   IMAGE    COMMAND   CREATED   STATUS   PORTS    NAMES
    ```

    If you already have some containers running, it will be followed by a list of started containers.

2. Run the following Docker command to create a new container with a MongoDB server:

    ```
    $ docker run -d --name dbserver -p 27017:27017 --restart unless-
    stopped mongo:6.0.4
    ```

    The docker run command creates and runs a new container. The arguments are as follows:

    - -d: Runs the container in the background (daemon mode).

    - --name: Specifies a name for the container. In our case, we named it dbserver.

    - -p: Maps a port from the container to the host. In our case, we map the default MongoDB server port 27017 in the container to the same port on our host. This allows us to access the MongoDB server running within our container from outside of it. If you already have a MongoDB server running on that port, feel free to change the first number to some other port, but make sure to also adjust the port number from 27017 to your specified port in the following guides.

    - --restart unless-stopped: Makes sure to automatically start (and restart) the container unless we manually stop it. This ensures that every time we start Docker, our MongoDB server will already be running.

    - mongo: This is the image name. The mongo image contains a MongoDB server.

3. Install the MongoDB Shell on your host system (not within the container) by following the instructions on the MongoDB website (https://www.mongodb.com/docs/mongodb-shell/install/).

4. On your host system, run the following command to connect to the MongoDB server using the MongoDB Shell (`mongosh`). After the hostname and port, we specify a database name. We are going to call our database `ch2`:

```
$ mongosh mongodb://localhost:27017/ch2
```

You will see some output from the database server, and at the end, we get a shell running on our selected database, as can be seen by the `ch2 >` prompt. Here, we can enter commands to be executed on our database. Interestingly, MongoDB, like Node.js, also exposes a JavaScript engine, but with yet another different environment. So, we can run JavaScript code, such as the following:

```
ch2> console.log("test")
```

The following figure shows JavaScript code being executed in the MongoDB Shell:

```
○ → ~/D/F/ch2 ⨉ main± > mongosh mongodb://localhost:27017/ch2
Current Mongosh Log ID: 6564926d8342fc83e3545366
Connecting to:      mongodb://localhost:27017/ch2?directConnection=true&serverSelectionTimeoutMS=2000&appName=mongosh+2.1.0
(node:51213) [DEP0040] DeprecationWarning: The `punycode` module is deprecated. Please use a userland alternative instead.
(Use `node --trace-deprecation ...` to show where the warning was created)
Using MongoDB:      6.0.4
Using Mongosh:      2.1.0

For mongosh info see: https://docs.mongodb.com/mongodb-shell/

------
   The server generated these startup warnings when booting
   2023-11-27T12:58:10.497+00:00: Using the XFS filesystem is strongly recommended with the WiredTiger storage engine. See http://
/dochub.mongodb.org/core/prodnotes-filesystem
   2023-11-27T12:58:11.204+00:00: Access control is not enabled for the database. Read and write access to data and configuration
is unrestricted
   2023-11-27T12:58:11.204+00:00: /sys/kernel/mm/transparent_hugepage/enabled is 'always'. We suggest setting it to 'never'
   2023-11-27T12:58:11.204+00:00: vm.max_map_count is too low
------

ch2> console.log("test")
test

ch2> ▌
```

Figure 2.9 – Connecting to our MongoDB database server running in a Docker container

Now that we have a shell connected to our MongoDB database server, we can start practicing running commands directly on the database.

Running commands directly on the database

Before we get started creating a backend service that interfaces with MongoDB, let's spend some time getting familiar with MongoDB itself via the MongoDB Shell. The MongoDB Shell is very important for debugging and doing maintenance tasks on the database, so it is a good idea to get to know it well.

Creating a collection and inserting and listing documents

Collections in MongoDB are the equivalent of tables in relational databases. They store documents, which are like JSON objects. To make it easier to understand, a collection can be seen as a very large JSON array containing JSON objects. Unlike simple arrays, collections support the creation of indices, which speed up the lookup of certain fields in documents. In MongoDB, a collection is automatically created when we attempt to insert a document into it or create an index for it.

Let's use the MongoDB Shell to insert a document into our database in the `users` collection:

1. To insert a new user document into the `users` collection, run the following command in the MongoDB Shell:

    ```
    > db.users.insertOne({ username: 'dan', fullName: 'Daniel Bugl',
    age: 26 })
    ```

    Commands that access the database are prefixed with `db`, then the collection name follows, and finally comes the operation, all separated by periods.

    > **Note**
    >
    > While `insertOne()` allows us to insert a single document into the collection, there is also an `insertMany()` method, where we can pass an array of documents to add to the collection.

2. We can now list all documents from the `users` collection by running the following command:

    ```
    > db.users.find()
    ```

    Doing so will return an array with our previously inserted document:

    ```
    [
      {
        _id: ObjectId("6405f062b0d06adeaeefc3bc"),
        username: 'dan',
        fullName: 'Daniel Bugl',
        age: 26
      }
    ]
    ```

As we can see, MongoDB automatically created a unique ID (`ObjectId`) for our document. This ID consists of 12 bytes in hexadecimal format (so each byte is displayed as two characters). The bytes are defined as follows:

- The first 4 bytes are a timestamp, representing the creation of the ID measured in seconds since the Unix epoch

- The next 5 bytes are a random value unique to the machine and currently running database process

- The last 3 bytes are a randomly initialized incrementing counter

> **Note**
>
> The way `ObjectId` identifiers are generated in MongoDB ensures that IDs are unique, avoiding ID collisions even when two ids are generated at the same time from different instances, without requiring a form of communication between the instances, which would slow down the creation of documents when scaling the database.

Querying and sorting documents

Now that we have inserted some documents, we can query them by accessing different fields from the object. We can also sort the list of documents returned from MongoDB. Follow these steps:

1. Before we get started querying, let's insert two more documents into our `users` collection:

```
> db.users.insertMany([
  { username: 'jane', fullName: 'Jane Doe', age: 32 },
  { username: 'john', fullName: 'John Doe', age: 30 }
])
```

2. Now we can start querying for a certain username by using `findOne` and passing an object with the `username` field. When using `findOne`, MongoDB will return the first matching object:

```
> db.users.findOne({ username: 'jane' })
```

3. We can also query for full names, or any other field in the documents from the collection. When using `find`, MongoDB will return an array of all matches:

```
> db.users.find({ fullName: 'Daniel Bugl' })
```

4. An important thing to watch out for is that when querying an `ObjectId`, we need to wrap the ID string with an `ObjectId()` constructor, as follows:

```
> db.users.findOne({ _id: ObjectId('6405f062b0d06adeaeefc3bc')
})
```

Make sure to change the string passed to the `ObjectId()` constructor to a valid `ObjectId` returned from the previous commands.

5. MongoDB also provides certain query operators, prefixed by $. For example, we can find everyone above the age of 30 in our collection by using the `$gt` operator, as follows:

```
> db.users.find({ age: { $gt: 30 } })
```

You will notice that `John Doe` does not get returned, because his age is exactly 30. If we want to match ages greater than or equal to 30, we need to use the `$gte` operator.

6. If we want to sort our results, we can use the `.sort()` method after `.find()`. For example, we can return all items from the `users` collection, sorted by age ascending (`1` for ascending, `-1` for descending):

```
> db.users.find().sort({ age: 1 })
```

Updating documents

To update a document in MongoDB, we combine the arguments from the query and insert operations into a single operation. We can use the same criteria to filter documents as we did for `find()`. To update a single field from the document, we use the `$set` operator:

1. We can update the `age` field for the user with the username `dan` as follows:

```
> db.users.updateOne({ username: 'dan' }, { $set: { age: 27 } })
```

> **Note**
>
> Just like `findOne`, `updateOne` only updates the first matching document. If we want to update all documents that match, we can use `updateMany`.

MongoDB will return an object with information about how many documents matched (`matchedCount`), how many were modified (`modifiedCount`), and how many were upserted (`upsertedCount`).

2. The `updateOne` method accepts a third argument, which is an `options` object. One useful option here is the `upsert` option, which, if set to `true`, will insert a document if it does not exist yet, and update it if it does exist already. Let's first try to update a non-existent user with `upsert: false`:

```
> db.users.updateOne({ username: 'new' }, { $set: { fullName:
'New User' } })
```

3. Now we set `upsert` to `true`, which inserts the user:

```
> db.users.updateOne({ username: 'new' }, { $set: { fullName:
'New User' } }, { upsert: true })
```

> **Note**
>
> If you want to remove a field from a document, use the `$unset` operator. If you want to replace the whole document with a new document, you can use the `replaceOne` method and pass a new document as the second argument to it.

Deleting documents

To delete documents from the database, MongoDB provides the `deleteOne` and `deleteMany` methods, which have a similar API to the `updateOne` and `updateMany` methods. The first argument is, again, used to match documents.

Let's say the user with the username new wants to delete their account. To do so, we need to remove them from the `users` collection. We can do so as follows:

```
> db.users.deleteOne({ username: 'new' })
```

That's all there is to it! As you can see, it is very simple to do CRUD operations in MongoDB if you already know how to work with JSON objects and JavaScript, making it the perfect database for a Node.js backend.

Now that we have learned how to access MongoDB using the MongoDB Shell, let's learn about accessing it from within VS Code.

Accessing the database via VS Code

Up until now, we have been using the Terminal to access the database. If you remember, in *Chapter 1*, *Preparing for Full-stack Development*, we installed a MongoDB extension for VS Code. We can now use this extension to access our database in a more visual way:

1. Click on the MongoDB icon on the left sidebar (it should be a leaf icon) and click on the **Add Connection** button:

Figure 2.10 – The MongoDB sidebar in VS Code

2. A new **MongoDB** tab will open up. In this tab, click on **Connect** in the **Connect with Connection String** box:

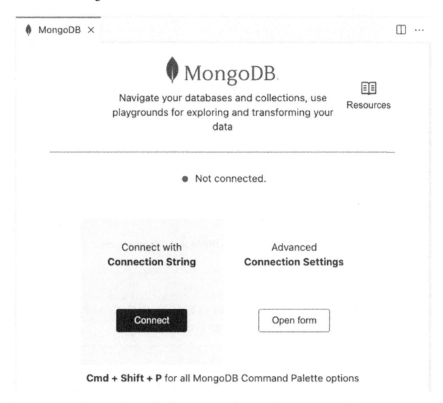

Figure 2.11 – Adding a new MongoDB connection in VS Code

3. A popup should open at the top. In this popup, enter the following connection string to connect to your local database:

```
mongodb://localhost:27017/
```

4.   Press *Return/Enter* to confirm. A new connection will be listed in the MongoDB sidebar. You can browse the tree to view databases, collections, and documents. For example, click the first document to view it:

Figure 2.12 – Viewing a document in the MongoDB extension in VS Code

> **Tip**
> You can also directly edit a document by editing a field in VS Code and saving the file. The updated document will automatically be saved to the database.

The MongoDB extension is very useful for debugging our database, as it lets us visually spot problems and quickly make edits to documents. Additionally, we can right-click on **Documents** and **Search for documents…** to open a new window where we can run MongoDB queries, just like we did in the Terminal. The queries can be executed on the database by clicking on the **Play** button in the top right. You may need to confirm a dialog with **Yes**, and then the results will show in a new pane, as can be seen in the following screenshot:

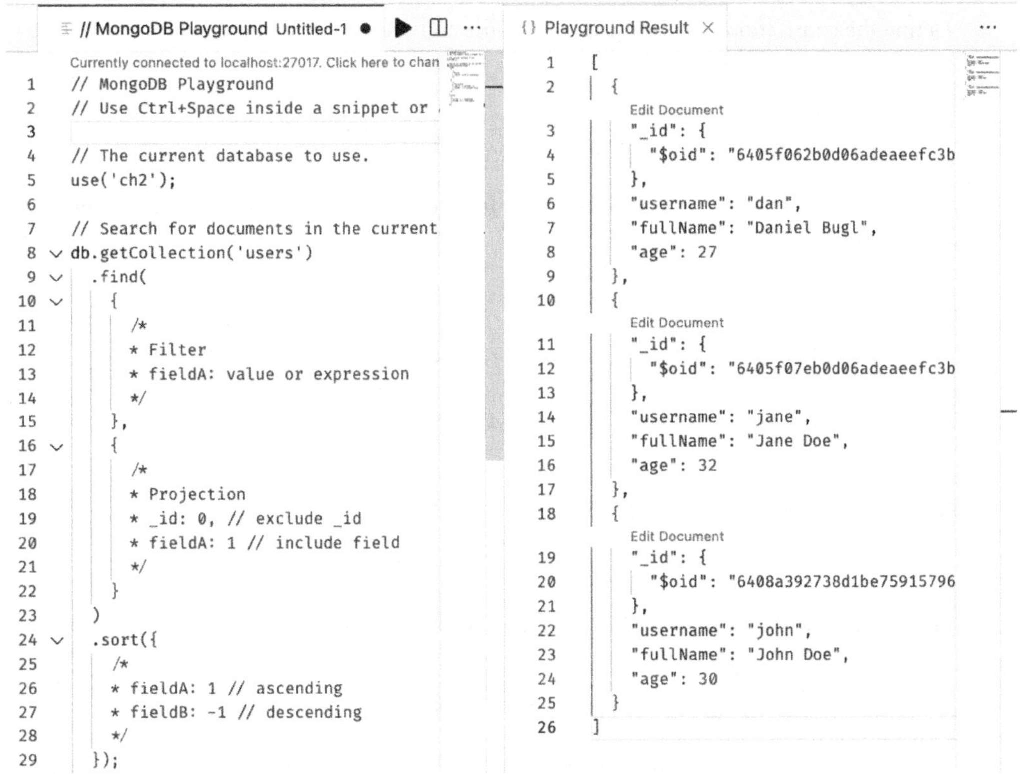

Figure 2.13 – Querying MongoDB in VS Code

Now that we have learned the basics of using and debugging MongoDB databases, we can start integrating our database in a Node.js backend service, instead of simply storing and reading information from files.

Accessing the MongoDB database via Node.js

We are now going to create a new web server that, instead of returning users from a JSON file, returns the list of users from our previously created `users` collection:

1. In the `ch2` folder, open a Terminal. Install the `mongodb` package, which contains the official MongoDB driver for Node.js:

    ```
    $ npm install mongodb@6.3.0
    ```

2. Create a new `backend/mongodbweb.js` file and open it. Import the following:

    ```
    import { createServer } from 'node:http'
    import { MongoClient } from 'mongodb'
    ```

3. Define the connection URL and database name and then create a new MongoDB client:

```
const url = 'mongodb://localhost:27017/'
const dbName = 'ch2'
const client = new MongoClient(url)
```

4. Connect to the database and log a message after we are connected successfully, or when there is an error with the connection:

```
try {
  await client.connect()
  console.log('Successfully connected to database!')
} catch (err) {
  console.error('Error connecting to database:', err)
}
```

5. Next, create an HTTP server, like we did before:

```
const server = createServer(async (req, res) => {
```

6. Then, select the database from the client, and the `users` collection from the database:

```
const db = client.db(dbName)
const users = db.collection('users')
```

7. Now, execute the `find()` method on the `users` collection. In the MongoDB Node.js driver, we also need to call the `toArray()` method to resolve the iterator to an array:

```
const usersList = await users.find().toArray()
```

8. Finally, set the status code and response header, and return the users list:

```
res.statusCode = 200
res.setHeader('Content-Type', 'application/json')
res.end(JSON.stringify(usersList))
})
```

9. Now that we have defined our server, copy over the code from before to listen to `localhost` on port `3000`:

```
const host = 'localhost'
const port = 3000
server.listen(port, host, () => {
  console.log(`Server listening on http://${host}:${port}`)
})
```

10. Run the server by executing the script:

```
$ node backend/mongodbweb.js
```

11. Open `http://localhost:3000` in your browser and you should see the list of users from our database being returned:

```
[{"_id":"6405f062b0d06adeaeefc3bc","username":"dan","fullName":"Daniel Bugl","age":27},
{"_id":"6405f07eb0d06adeaeefc3bd","username":"jane","fullName":"Jane Doe","age":32},
{"_id":"6408a392738d1be75915796e","username":"john","fullName":"John Doe","age":30}]
```

Figure 2.14 – Our first Node.js service retrieving data from a MongoDB database!

As we have seen, we can use similar methods that we have used in the MongoDB Shell in Node.js as well. However, the APIs of the `node:http` module and the `mongodb` package are very low-level, requiring a lot of code to create an HTTP API and talk to the database.

In the next chapter, we are going to learn about libraries that abstract these processes to allow for easier creation of HTTP APIs and handling of the database. These libraries are Express and Mongoose. Express is a web framework that allows us to easily define API routes and handle requests. Mongoose allows us to create schemas for documents in our database to more easily create, read, update, and delete objects.

Summary

In this chapter, we learned how to use Node.js to develop scripts that can run on a server. We also learned how to create containers with Docker, and how MongoDB works and can be interfaced with. At the end of this chapter, we even successfully created our first simple backend service using Node.js and MongoDB!

In the next chapter, *Chapter 3, Implementing a Backend Using Express, Mongoose ODM, and Jest*, we are going to learn how to put together what we learned in this chapter to extend our simple backend service to a production-ready backend for a blog application.

Part 2:
Building and Deploying Our First Full-Stack Application with a REST API

In this part, we are going to be building and deploying our first full-stack application with a **REST API**. We will start by implementing a backend service using **Express** and **Mongoose ODM**. Then, we will create unit tests for it using **Jest**. After that, we will create a frontend with **React** and integrate it with our backend service using **TanStack Query**. Finally, we will deploy the application using **Docker** and learn how to set up a CI/CD pipeline.

This part includes the following chapters:

- *Chapter 3, Implementing a Backend Using Express, Mongoose ODM, and Jest*
- *Chapter 4, Integrating a Frontend Using React and TanStack Query*
- *Chapter 5, Deploying the Application with Docker and CI/CD*

3

Implementing a Backend Using Express, Mongoose ODM, and Jest

After learning the basics of Node.js and MongoDB, we will now put them into practice by building our first backend service using Express to provide a REST API, Mongoose **object data modeling** (**ODM**) to interface with MongoDB, and Jest to test our code. We will first learn how to structure a backend project using an architectural pattern. Then, we will create database schemas using Mongoose. Next, we will make service functions to interface with the database schemas and write tests for them using Jest. Then, we will learn what REST is and when it is useful. Finally, we provide a REST API and serve it using Express. At the end of this chapter, we will have a working backend service to be consumed by a frontend developed in the next chapter.

In this chapter, we are going to cover the following main topics:

- Designing a backend service
- Creating database schemas using Mongoose
- Developing and testing service functions
- Providing a REST API using Express

Technical requirements

Before we start, please install all requirements from *Chapter 1, Preparing for Full-stack Development*, and *Chapter 2, Getting to Know Node.js and MongoDB*.

The versions listed in those chapters are the ones used in the book. While installing a newer version should not be an issue, please note that certain steps might work differently on a newer version. If you are having an issue with the code and steps provided in this book, please try using the versions mentioned in *Chapters 1* and *2*.

You can find the code for this chapter on GitHub at `https://github.com/PacktPublishing/ Modern-Full-Stack-React-Projects/tree/main/ch3`.

If you cloned the full repository for the book, Husky may not find the `.git` directory when running `npm install`. In that case, just run `git init` in the root of the corresponding chapter folder.

The CiA video for the chapter can be found at: `https://youtu.be/fFHVVn03rc`.

Designing a backend service

To design our backend service, we are going to use a variation of an existing architectural pattern called **model–view–controller** (**MVC**) pattern. The MVC pattern consists of the following parts:

- **Model**: Handles data and basic data logic

- **Controller**: Controls how data is processed and displayed

- **View**: Displays the current state

In traditional full-stack applications, the backend would render and display the frontend completely, and an interaction would usually require a full-page refresh. The MVC architecture was designed mainly for such applications. However, in modern applications, the frontend is usually interactive and rendered in the backend only through server-side rendering. In modern applications, we thus often distinguish between the actual backend service(s) and the backend for frontend (which handles static site generation and server-side rendering):

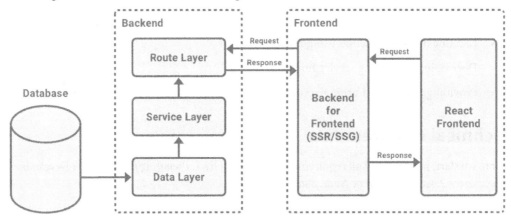

Figure 3.1 – A modern full-stack architecture, with a single backend service and a frontend with server-side rendering (SSR) and static-site generation (SSG)

For modern applications, the idea is that the backend service only deals with processing and serving requests and data and does not render the user interface anymore. Instead, we have a separate application that handles the frontend and server-side rendering of user interfaces specifically. To adapt to this change, we adjust the MVC architectural pattern to a data-service-route pattern for the backend service as follows:

- **Route layer**: Defines routes that consumers can access and handles user input by processing the request parameters and body and then calling service functions

- **Service layer**: Provides service functions, such as **create–read–update–delete** (**CRUD**) functions, which access the database through the data layer

- **Data layer**: Only deals with accessing the database and does basic validation to ensure that the database is consistent

This separation of concerns works best for services that only expose routes and do not deal with rendering user interfaces. Each layer in this pattern only deals with one step in processing the request.

After learning about the design of backend services, let's get started creating a folder structure reflecting what we have learned.

Creating the folder structure for our backend service

We are now going to create a folder structure for our backend service based on this pattern. Follow these steps:

1. First, copy the ch2 folder to a new ch3 folder to create a new folder for our backend service, as follows:

   ```
   $ cp -R ch2 ch3
   ```

2. Open the new ch3 folder in VS Code.

3. Edit the .eslintrc.json file and replace the browser env with the node and es6 env, as follows:

   ```
   "env": {
     "node": true,
     "es6": true
   },
   ```

4. Also, *remove* the react and jsx-ally plugins from the .eslintrc.json file. We can also remove the React-related settings and overrides now by removing the highlighted lines:

   ```
   "extends": [
     "eslint:recommended",
     "plugin:react/recommended",
   ```

```
      "plugin:react/jsx-runtime",
      "plugin:jsx-a11y/recommended",
      "prettier"
    ],
    "settings": {
      "react": {
        "version": "detect"
      }
    },
    "overrides": [
      {
        "files": ["*.js", "*.jsx"]
      }
    ]
```

5. *Delete* the index.html and vite.config.js files.

6. We can now also *remove* the vite.config.js file from the .eslintignore file:

    ```
    dist/
    vite.config.js
    ```

7. *Delete* the public, backend, and src folders.

8. Open the ch3 folder in VS Code, open a Terminal and run the following commands to remove vite and react:

    ```
    $ npm uninstall --save react react-dom
    $ npm uninstall --save-dev vite @types/react \
      @types/react-dom @vitejs/plugin-react \
      eslint-plugin-jsx-a11y eslint-plugin-react
    ```

9. Edit the package.json file and *remove* the dev, build, and preview scripts from it:

    ```
    "scripts": {
      "dev": "vite",
      "build": "vite build",
      "lint": "eslint src",
      "preview": "vite preview",
      "prepare": "husky install"
    },
    ```

10. Now, create a new src/ folder, and within it, create src/db/ (for the data layer), src/services/ (for the services layer), and src/routes/ (for the routes layer) folders.

Our first application is going to be a blog application. For such an application, we are going to need the API to be able to do the following:

- Get a list of posts

- Get a single post

- Create a new post

- Update an existing post

- Delete an existing post

To provide these functions, we first need to create a database schema to define what a blog post object should look like in our database. Then, we need service functions to handle CRUD functionality for blog posts. Finally, we are going to define our REST API to query, create, update, and delete blog posts.

Creating database schemas using Mongoose

Before we can get started defining the database schemas, we first need to set up Mongoose itself. Mongoose is a library that simplifies MongoDB object modeling by reducing the boilerplate code needed to interface with MongoDB. It also includes common business logic such as setting `createdAt` and `updatedAt` timestamps automatically and validation and type casting to keep the database state consistent.

Follow these steps to set up the `mongoose` library:

1. First, install the `mongoose` library:

    ```
    $ npm install mongoose@8.0.2
    ```

2. Create a new `src/db/init.js` file and import `mongoose` there:

    ```
    import mongoose from 'mongoose'
    ```

3. Define and export a function that will initialize the database connection:

    ```
    export function initDatabase() {
    ```

4. First, we define `DATABASE_URL` to point to our local MongoDB instance running via Docker and specify `blog` as the database name:

    ```
    const DATABASE_URL = 'mongodb://localhost:27017/blog'
    ```

    The connection string is similar to what we used in the previous chapter when directly accessing the database via Node.js.

5. Then, add a listener to the open event on the Mongoose connection so that we can show a log message once we are connected to the database:

```
mongoose.connection.on('open', () => {
  console.info('successfully connected to database:',
DATABASE_URL)
})
```

6. Now, use the mongoose.connect() function to connect to our MongoDB database and return the connection object:

```
const connection = mongoose.connect(DATABASE_URL)
return connection
}
```

7. Create a new src/example.js file and import and run the initDatabase function there:

```
import { initDatabase } from './db/init.js'
initDatabase()
```

8. Run the src/example.js file using Node.js to see Mongoose successfully connecting to our database:

```
$ node src/example.js
```

As always, you can stop the server by pressing *Ctrl* + *C* in the Terminal.

We can see our log message being printed to the Terminal, so we know that Mongoose was able to successfully connect to our database! If there is an error, for example, because Docker (or the container) is not running, it will hang for a while and then throw an error about the connection being refused (ECONNREFUSED). In that case, make sure the Docker MongoDB container is running properly and can be connected to.

Defining a model for blog posts

After initializing the database, the first thing we should do is define the data structure for blog posts. Blog posts in our system should have a title, an author, contents, and some tags associated with the post. Follow these steps to define the data structure for blog posts:

1. Create a new src/db/models/ folder.

2. Inside that folder, create a new src/db/models/post.js file, import the mongoose and the Schema classes:

```
import mongoose, { Schema } from 'mongoose'
```

3. Define a new schema for posts:

```
const postSchema = new Schema({
```

4. Now specify all properties of a blog post and the corresponding types. We have a required `title`, an `author`, and `contents`, which are all strings:

```
title: { type: String, required: true },
author: String,
contents: String,
```

5. Lastly, we have `tags`, which are a string array:

```
tags: [String],
})
```

6. Now that we have defined the schema, we can create a Mongoose model from it by using the `mongoose.model()` function:

```
export const Post = mongoose.model('post', postSchema)
```

> **Note**
>
> The first argument to `mongoose.model()` specifies the name of the collection. In our case, the collection will be called `posts` because we specified `post` as the name. In Mongoose models, we need to specify the name of the document in singular form.

Now that we have defined the data structure and model for blog posts, we can start using it to create and query posts.

Using the blog post model

After creating our model, let's try using it! For now, we are simply going to access it in the `src/example.js` file because we have not defined any service functions or routes yet:

1. Import the `Post` model in the `src/example.js` file:

```
import { initDatabase } from './db/init.js'
import { Post } from './db/models/post.js'
```

2. The `initDatabase()` function we defined earlier is an `async` function, so we need to `await` it; otherwise, we would be attempting to access the database before we are connected to it:

```
await initDatabase()
```

3. Create a new blog post by calling `new Post()`, defining some example data:

    ```
    const post = new Post({
        title: 'Hello Mongoose!',
        author: 'Daniel Bugl',
        contents: 'This post is stored in a MongoDB database using
    Mongoose.',
        tags: ['mongoose', 'mongodb'],
    })
    ```

4. Call `.save()` on the blog post to save it to the database:

    ```
    await post.save()
    ```

5. Now we can use the `.find()` function to list all posts, and log the result:

    ```
    const posts = await Post.find()
    console.log(posts)
    ```

6. Run the example script to see our post being inserted and listed:

    ```
    $ node src/example.js
    ```

    You will get the following result after running the preceding script:

    ```
    ○ → ~/D/F/ch3 ⑂ main± > node src/test.js
      successfully connected to database: mongodb://localhost:27017/ch3
      [
        {
          _id: new ObjectId("64281a742bd96957bf8bde51"),
          title: 'Hello Mongoose!',
          author: 'Daniel Bugl',
          contents: 'This post is stored in a MongoDB database using Mongoose.',
          tags: [ 'mongoose', 'mongodb' ],
          __v: 0
        }
      ]
    ```

Figure 3.2 – Our first document inserted via Mongoose!

As you can see, using Mongoose is very similar to using MongoDB directly. However, it offers us some wrappers around models for convenience, making it easier to deal with documents.

Defining creation and last update dates in the blog post

You may have noticed that we have not added any dates to our blog post. So, we do not know when a blog post is created or when it was last updated. Mongoose makes implementing such functionality simple, let's try it out now:

1. Edit the `src/db/models/post.js` file and add a second argument to the `new Schema()` constructor. The second argument specifies options for the schema. Here, we set the `timestamps: true` setting:

    ```
    const postSchema = new Schema(
      {
        title: String,
        author: String,
        contents: String,
        tags: [String],
      },
      { timestamps: true },
    )
    ```

2. Now all we need to do is create a new blog post by running the example script, and we will see that the last post inserted now has `createdAt` and `updatedAt` timestamps:

    ```
    $ node src/example.js
    ```

3. To see if the `updatedAt` timestamp works, let's try updating the created blog post by using the `findByIdAndUpdate` method. Save the result of `await post.save()` in a `createdPost` constant, then add the following code close to the end of the `src/example.js` file, before the `Post.find()` call:

    ```
    const createdPost = await post.save()

    await Post.findByIdAndUpdate(createdPost._id, {
      $set: { title: 'Hello again, Mongoose!' },
    })
    ```

4. Run the server again to see the blog posts being updated:

    ```
    $ node src/example.js
    ```

You will get three posts, and the last one of them now looks as follows:

```
{
  _id: new ObjectId("64281e304e7d65f85ce07e1f"),
  title: 'Hello again, Mongoose!',
  author: 'Daniel Bugl',
  contents: 'This post is stored in a MongoDB database using Mongoose.',
  tags: [ 'mongoose', 'mongodb' ],
  createdAt: 2023-04-01T12:06:08.303Z,
  updatedAt: 2023-04-01T12:06:08.312Z,
  __v: 0
}
```

Figure 3.3 – Our updated document with the automatically updated timestamps

As we can see, using Mongoose makes dealing with MongoDB documents much more convenient! Now that we have defined our database model, let's start developing (and writing tests for) service functions!

Developing and testing service functions

Up until now, we have always been testing code by putting it in the `src/example.js` file. Now, we are going to write some service functions and learn how to write actual tests for them by using Jest.

Setting up the test environment

First, we are going to set up our test environment by following these steps:

1. Install `jest` and `mongodb-memory-server` as dev dependencies:

    ```
    $ npm install --save-dev jest@29.7.0 \
      mongodb-memory-server@9.1.1
    ```

    Jest is a test runner used to define and execute unit tests. The `mongodb-memory-server` library allows us to spin up a fresh instance of a MongoDB database, storing data only in memory, so that we can run our tests on a fresh database instance.

2. Create a `src/test/` folder to put the setup for our tests in.

3. In this folder, create a `src/test/globalSetup.js` file, where we will import `MongoMemoryServer` from the previously installed library:

    ```
    import { MongoMemoryServer } from 'mongodb-memory-server'
    ```

4. Now define a `globalSetup` function, which creates a memory server for MongoDB:

    ```
    export default async function globalSetup() {
      const instance = await MongoMemoryServer.create({
    ```

5. When creating the `MongoMemoryServer`, set the binary version to `6.0.4`, which is the same version that we installed for our Docker container:

```
binary: {
  version: '6.0.4',
},
})
```

6. We will store the MongoDB instance as a global variable to be able to access it later in the `globalTeardown` function:

```
global.__MONGOINSTANCE = instance
```

7. We will also store the URL to connect to our test instance in the `DATABASE_URL` environment variable:

```
process.env.DATABASE_URL = instance.getUri()
}
```

8. Edit `src/db/init.js` and adjust the `DATABASE_URL` to come from the environment variable so that our tests will be using the correct database:

```
export function initDatabase() {
  const DATABASE_URL = process.env.DATABASE_URL
```

9. Additionally, create a `src/test/globalTeardown.js` file to stop the MongoDB instance when our tests are finished and add the following code inside it:

```
export default async function globalTeardown() {
  await global.__MONGOINSTANCE.stop()
}
```

10. Now, create a `src/test/setupFileAfterEnv.js` file. Here, we will define a `beforeAll` function to initialize our database connection in Mongoose before all tests run and an `afterAll` function to disconnect from the database after all tests finish running:

```
import mongoose from 'mongoose'
import { beforeAll, afterAll } from '@jest/globals'

import { initDatabase } from '../db/init.js'

beforeAll(async () => {
  await initDatabase()
})

afterAll(async () => {
```

```
    await mongoose.disconnect()
  })
```

11. Then, create a new `jest.config.json` file in the root of our project where we will define the config for our tests. In the `jest.config.json` file, we first set the test environment to `node`:

```
{
  "testEnvironment": "node",
```

12. Next, tell Jest to use the `globalSetup`, `globalTeardown`, and `setupFileAfterEnv` files we created earlier:

```
  "globalSetup": "<rootDir>/src/test/globalSetup.js",
  "globalTeardown": "<rootDir>/src/test/globalTeardown.js",
  "setupFilesAfterEnv": ["<rootDir>/src/test/setupFileAfterEnv.
js"]
}
```

> **Note**
>
> In this case, `<rootDir>` is a special string that automatically gets resolved to the root directory by Jest. You do not need to manually fill in a root directory here.

13. Finally, edit the `package.json` file and add a `test` script, which will run Jest:

```
  "scripts": {
    "test": "NODE_OPTIONS=--experimental-vm-modules jest",
    "lint": "eslint src",
    "prepare": "husky install"
  },
```

> **Note**
>
> At the time of writing, the JavaScript ecosystem is still in the process of moving to the **ECMAScript module (ESM)** standard. In this book, we already use this new standard. However, Jest does not support it yet by default, so we need to pass the `--experimental-vm-modules` option when running Jest.

14. If we attempt running this script now, we will see that there are no tests found, but we can still see that Jest is set up and working properly:

```
$ npm test
```

```
⊛ → ~/D/F/ch3 ⑂ main± > npm run test

> ch3@0.0.0 test
> NODE_OPTIONS=--experimental-vm-modules jest

No tests found, exiting with code 1
Run with `--passWithNoTests` to exit with code 0
In /Users/dan/Development/Full-Stack-React-Projects/ch3
  14 files checked.
  testMatch: **/__tests__/**/*.[jt]s?(x), **/?(*.)+(spec|test).[tj]s?(x) - 0 matches
  testPathIgnorePatterns: /node_modules/ - 14 matches
  testRegex:  - 0 matches
Pattern:  - 0 matches
```

Figure 3.4 – Jest is set up successfully, but we have not defined any tests yet

Now that our test environment is set up, we can start writing our service functions and unit tests. It is always a good idea to write unit tests right after writing service functions, as it means we will be able to debug them right away while still having their intended behavior fresh in our minds.

Writing our first service function: createPost

For our first service function, we are going to make a function to create a new post. We can then write tests for it by verifying that the create function creates a new post with the specified properties. Follow these steps:

1. Create a new `src/services/posts.js` file.

2. In the `src/services/posts.js` file, first import the `Post` model:

    ```
    import { Post } from '../db/models/post.js'
    ```

3. Define a new `createPost` function, which takes an object with `title`, `author`, `contents`, and `tags` as arguments and creates and returns a new post:

    ```
    export async function createPost({ title, author, contents, tags
    }) {
      const post = new Post({ title, author, contents, tags })
      return await post.save()
    }
    ```

    We specifically listed all properties that we want the user to be able to provide here instead of simply passing the whole object to the `new Post()` constructor. While we need to type more code this way, it allows us to have control over which properties a user should be able to set. For example, if we later add permissions to the database models, we may be accidentally allowing users to set those permissions here, if we forget to exclude those properties. For those security reasons, it is always good practice to have a list of allowed properties instead of simply passing down the whole object.

After writing our first service function, let's continue by writing test cases for it.

Defining test cases for the createPost service function

To test if the `createPost` function works as expected, we are going to define unit test cases for it using Jest:

1. Create a new `src/__tests__/` folder, which will contain all test definitions.

> **Note**
>
> Alternatively, test files can also be co-located with the related files that they are testing. However, in this book, we use the `__tests__` directory to make it easier to distinguish tests from other files.

2. Create a new `src/__tests__/posts.test.js` file for our tests related to posts. In this file, start by importing `mongoose` and the `describe`, `expect`, and `test` functions from `@jest/globals`:

    ```
    import mongoose from 'mongoose'
    import { describe, expect, test } from '@jest/globals'
    ```

3. Also import the `createPost` function from our services and the `Post` model:

    ```
    import { createPost } from '../services/posts.js'
    import { Post } from '../db/models/post.js'
    ```

4. Then, use the `describe()` function to define a new test. This function describes a group of tests. We can call our group `creating posts`:

    ```
    describe('creating posts', () => {
    ```

5. Inside the group, we will define a test by using the `test()` function. We can pass an `async` function here to be able to use async/await syntax. We call the first test `creating posts with all parameters should succeed`:

    ```
    test('with all parameters should succeed', async () => {
    ```

6. Inside this test, we will use the `createPost` function to create a new post with some parameters:

    ```
    const post = {
        title: 'Hello Mongoose!',
        author: 'Daniel Bugl',
        contents: 'This post is stored in a MongoDB database using
    Mongoose.',
        tags: ['mongoose', 'mongodb'],
    ```

```
  }
  const createdPost = await createPost(post)
```

7. Then, verify that it returns a post with an ID by using the expect() function from Jest and the toBeInstanceOf matcher to verify that it is an ObjectId:

```
expect(createdPost._id).toBeInstanceOf(mongoose.Types.
ObjectId)
```

8. Now use Mongoose directly to find the post with the given ID:

```
const foundPost = await Post.findById(createdPost._id)
```

9. We expect() the foundPost to equal an object containing at least the properties of the original post object we defined. Additionally, we expect the created post to have createdAt and updatedAt timestamps:

```
expect(foundPost).toEqual(expect.objectContaining(post))
expect(foundPost.createdAt).toBeInstanceOf(Date)
expect(foundPost.updatedAt).toBeInstanceOf(Date)
})
```

10. Additionally, define a second test, called creating posts without title should fail. As we defined the title to be required, it should not be possible to create a post without one:

```
test('without title should fail', async () => {
  const post = {
    author: 'Daniel Bugl',
    contents: 'Post with no title',
    tags: ['empty'],
  }
```

11. Use a try/catch construct to catch the error and expect() the error to be a Mongoose ValidationError, which tells us that the title is required:

```
  try {
    await createPost(post)
  } catch (err) {
    expect(err).toBeInstanceOf(mongoose.Error.ValidationError)
    expect(err.message).toContain('`title` is required')
  }
})
```

12. Finally, make a test called `creating posts with minimal parameters should succeed` and only enter the `title`:

```
test('with minimal parameters should succeed', async () => {
  const post = {
    title: 'Only a title',
  }
  const createdPost = await createPost(post)
  expect(createdPost._id).toBeInstanceOf(mongoose.Types.
ObjectId)
  })
})
```

13. Now that we have defined our tests, run the script we defined earlier:

```
$ npm test
```

As we can see, using unit tests we can do isolated tests on our service functions without having to define and manually access routes or write some manual test setups. These tests also have the added advantage that when we change code later, we can ensure that the previously defined behavior did not change by re-running the tests.

Defining a function to list posts

After defining a function to create posts, we are now going to define an internal `listPosts` function, which allows us to query posts and define a sort order. Then, we are going to use this function to define `listAllPosts`, `listPostsByAuthor`, and `listPostsByTag` functions:

1. Edit the `src/services/posts.js` file and define a new function at the end of the file.

   The function accepts a `query` and an `options` argument (with `sortBy` and `sortOrder` properties). With `sortBy`, we can define which field we want to sort by, and the `sortOrder` argument allows us to specify whether posts should be sorted in ascending or descending order. By default, we list all posts (empty object as query) and show the newest posts first (sorted by `createdAt`, in descending order):

   ```
   async function listPosts(
     query = {},
     { sortBy = 'createdAt', sortOrder = 'descending' } = {},
   ) {
   ```

2. We can use the `.find()` method from our Mongoose model to list all posts, passing an argument to sort them:

   ```
   return await Post.find(query).sort({ [sortBy]: sortOrder })
   }
   ```

3. Now we can define a function to list all posts, which simply passes an empty object as query:

```
export async function listAllPosts(options) {
  return await listPosts({}, options)
}
```

4. Similarly, we can create a function to list all posts by a certain author by passing `author` to the query object:

```
export async function listPostsByAuthor(author, options) {
  return await listPosts({ author }, options)
}
```

5. Lastly, define a function to list posts by tag:

```
export async function listPostsByTag(tags, options) {
  return await listPosts({ tags }, options)
}
```

In MongoDB, we can simply match strings in an array by matching the string as if it was a single value, so all we need to do is add a query for `tags: 'nodejs'`. MongoDB will then return all documents that have a `'nodejs'` string in their `tags` array.

> **Note**
>
> The `{ [variable]: … }` operator resolves the string stored in the `variable` to a key name for the created object. So, if our variable contains `'createdAt'`, the resulting object will be `{ createdAt: … }`.

After defining the list post function, let's also write test cases for it.

Defining test cases for list posts

Defining test cases for list posts is similar to create posts. However, we now need to create an initial state where we already have some posts in the database to be able to test the list functions. We can do this by using the `beforeEach()` function, which executes some code before each test case is executed. We can use the `beforeEach()` function for a whole test file or only run it for each test inside a `describe()` group. In our case, we are going to define it for the whole file, as the sample posts will come in handy when we test the delete post function later:

1. Edit the `src/__tests__/posts.js` file, adjust the `import` statement to import the `beforeEach` function from `@jest/globals` and import the various functions to list posts from our services:

```
import { describe, expect, test, beforeEach } from '@jest/
globals'
```

```
import { createPost,
        listAllPosts,
        listPostsByAuthor,
        listPostsByTag,
} from '../services/posts.js'
```

2. At the end of the file, define an array of sample posts:

```
const samplePosts = [
  { title: 'Learning Redux', author: 'Daniel Bugl', tags:
['redux'] },
  { title: 'Learn React Hooks', author: 'Daniel Bugl', tags:
['react'] },
  {
    title: 'Full-Stack React Projects',
    author: 'Daniel Bugl',
    tags: ['react', 'nodejs'],
  },
  { title: 'Guide to TypeScript' },
]
```

3. Now, define an empty array, which will be populated with the created posts. Then, define a
    beforeEach function, which first clears all posts from the database and clears the array of
    created sample posts and then creates the sample posts in the database again for each of the
    posts defined in the array earlier. This ensures that we have a consistent state of the database
    before each test case runs and that we have an array to compare against when testing the list
    post functions:

```
let createdSamplePosts = []

beforeEach(async () => {
  await Post.deleteMany({})
  createdSamplePosts = []
  for (const post of samplePosts) {
    const createdPost = new Post(post)
    createdSamplePosts.push(await createdPost.save())
  }
})
```

To ensure that our unit tests are modular and independent from each other, we insert posts into
the database directly by using Mongoose functions (instead of the createPost function).

4. Now that we have some sample posts ready, let's write our first test case, which should simply list all posts. We will define a new test group for `listing posts` and a test to verify that all sample posts are listed by the `listAllPosts()` function:

```
describe('listing posts', () => {
  test('should return all posts', async () => {
    const posts = await listAllPosts()
    expect(posts.length).toEqual(createdSamplePosts.length)
  })
```

5. Next, make a test that verifies that the default sort order shows newest posts first. We sort the `createdSamplePosts` array manually by `createdAt` (descending) and then compare the sorted dates to those returned from the `listAllPosts()` function:

```
test('should return posts sorted by creation date descending
by default', async () => {
  const posts = await listAllPosts()
  const sortedSamplePosts = createdSamplePosts.sort(
    (a, b) => b.createdAt - a.createdAt,
  )
  expect(posts.map((post) => post.createdAt)).toEqual(
    sortedSamplePosts.map((post) => post.createdAt),
  )
})
```

> **Note**
>
> The `.map()` function applies a function to each element of an array and returns the result. In our case, we select the `createdAt` property from all elements of the array. We cannot directly compare the arrays with each other because Mongoose returns documents with a lot of additional information in hidden metadata, which Jest will attempt to compare.

6. Additionally, define a test case where the `sortBy` value is changed to `updatedAt`, and the `sortOrder` value is changed to `ascending` (showing oldest updated posts first):

```
test('should take into account provided sorting options',
async () => {
  const posts = await listAllPosts({
    sortBy: 'updatedAt',
    sortOrder: 'ascending',
  })
  const sortedSamplePosts = createdSamplePosts.sort(
    (a, b) => a.updatedAt - b.updatedAt,
  )
  expect(posts.map((post) => post.updatedAt)).toEqual(
```

```
                sortedSamplePosts.map((post) => post.updatedAt),
          )
      })
```

7. Then, add a test to ensure that listing posts by author works:

```
test('should be able to filter posts by author', async () => {
    const posts = await listPostsByAuthor('Daniel Bugl')
    expect(posts.length).toBe(3)
})
```

> **Note**
>
> We are controlling the test environment by creating a specific set of sample posts before each test case runs. We can make use of this controlled environment to simplify our tests. As we already know that there are only three posts with that author, we can simply check if the function returned exactly three posts. Doing so keeps our tests simple, and they are still safe because we control the environment completely.

8. Finally, add a test to verify that listing posts by tag works:

```
test('should be able to filter posts by tag', async () => {
    const posts = await listPostsByTag('nodejs')
    expect(posts.length).toBe(1)
})
})
```

9. Run the tests again and watch them all pass:

```
$ npm test

PASS  src/__tests__/posts.test.js
  creating posts
    √ with all parameters should succeed (16 ms)
    √ without title should fail (5 ms)
    √ with minimal parameters should succeed (6 ms)
  listing posts
    √ should return all posts (4 ms)
    √ should return posts sorted by creation date descending by default (4 ms)
    √ should take into account provided sorting options (4 ms)
    √ should be able to filter posts by author (3 ms)
    √ should be able to filter posts by tag (4 ms)

Test Suites: 1 passed, 1 total
Tests:       8 passed, 8 total
Snapshots:   0 total
Time:        0.349 s, estimated 1 s
Ran all test suites.
```

Figure 3.5 – All our tests passing successfully!

As we can see, for some tests, we need to prepare an initial state. In our case, we only had to create some posts, but this initial state may become more sophisticated. For example, on a more advanced blogging platform, it may be necessary to create a user account first, then create a blog on the platform, and then create blog posts for that blog. In that case, we could create test utility functions, such as `createTestUser`, `createTestBlog`, `createTestPost` and import them in our tests. We can then use these functions in `beforeEach()` across multiple test files instead of manually doing it every single time. Depending on your application structure, different test utility functions may be needed, so feel free to define them as you see fit.

After defining the test cases for the list posts function, let's continue by defining the get single post, update post, and delete post functions.

Defining the get single post, update and delete post functions

The get single post, update and delete post functions can be defined very similarly to the list posts function. Let's do that quickly now:

1. Edit the `src/services/posts.js` file and define a `getPostById` function as follows:

```
export async function getPostById(postId) {
    return await Post.findById(postId)
}
```

It may seem a bit trivial to define a service function that just calls `Post.findById`, but it is good practice to define it anyway. Later, we may want to add some additional restrictions, such as access control. Having the service function allows us to change it only in one place and we do not have to worry about forgetting to add it somewhere. Another benefit is that if we, for example, want to change the database provider later, the developer only needs to worry about getting the service functions working again, and they can be verified with the test cases.

2. In the same file, define the `updatePost` function. It will take an ID of an existing post, and an object of parameters to be updated. We are going to use the `findOneAndUpdate` function from Mongoose, together with the `$set` operator, to change the specified parameters. As a third argument, we provide an options object with `new: true` so that the function returns the modified object instead of the original:

```
export async function updatePost(postId, { title, author,
contents, tags }) {
    return await Post.findOneAndUpdate(
        { _id: postId },
        { $set: { title, author, contents, tags } },
        { new: true },
    )
}
```

3. In the same file, also define a `deletePost` function, which simply takes the ID of an existing post and deletes it from the database:

```
export async function deletePost(postId) {
  return await Post.deleteOne({ _id: postId })
}
```

> **Tip**
>
> Depending on your application, you may want to set a `deletedOn` timestamp instead of deleting it right away. Then, set up a function that gets all documents that have been deleted for more than 30 days and delete them. Of course, this means that we need to always filter out already deleted posts in the `listPosts` function and that we need to write test cases for this behavior!

4. Edit the `src/__tests__/posts.js` file and import the `getPostById` function:

```
  getPostById,
} from '../services/posts.js'
```

5. Add tests for getting a post by ID and failing to get a post because the ID did not exist in the database:

```
describe('getting a post', () => {
  test('should return the full post', async () => {
    const post = await getPostById(createdSamplePosts[0]._id)
    expect(post.toObject()).toEqual(createdSamplePosts[0].
toObject())
  })

  test('should fail if the id does not exist', async () => {
    const post = await getPostById('000000000000000000000000')
    expect(post).toEqual(null)
  })
})
```

In the first test, we use `.toObject()` to convert the Mongoose object with all its internal properties and metadata to a **plain old JavaScript object** (**POJO**) so that we can compare it to the sample post object by comparing all properties.

6. Next, import the `updatePost` function:

```
  updatePost,
} from '../services/posts.js'
```

7. Then, add tests for updating a post successfully. We add one test to verify that the specified property was changed and another test to verify that it does not interfere with other properties:

```
describe('updating posts', () => {
  test('should update the specified property', async () => {
    await updatePost(createdSamplePosts[0]._id, {
      author: 'Test Author',
    })
    const updatedPost = await Post.
findById(createdSamplePosts[0]._id)
    expect(updatedPost.author).toEqual('Test Author')
  })

  test('should not update other properties', async () => {
    await updatePost(createdSamplePosts[0]._id, {
      author: 'Test Author',
    })
    const updatedPost = await Post.
findById(createdSamplePosts[0]._id)
    expect(updatedPost.title).toEqual('Learning Redux')
  })
```

8. Additionally, add a test to ensure the `updatedAt` timestamp was updated. To do so, first convert the `Date` objects to numbers by using `.getTime()`, and then we can compare them by using the `expect(...).toBeGreaterThan(...)` matcher:

```
  test('should update the updatedAt timestamp', async () => {
    await updatePost(createdSamplePosts[0]._id, {
      author: 'Test Author',
    })
    const updatedPost = await Post.
findById(createdSamplePosts[0]._id)
    expect(updatedPost.updatedAt.getTime()).toBeGreaterThan(
        createdSamplePosts[0].updatedAt.getTime(),
    )
  })
```

9. Also add a failing test to see if the `updatePost` function returns `null` when no post with a matching ID was found:

```
  test('should fail if the id does not exist', async () => {
    const post = await updatePost('000000000000000000000000', {
      author: 'Test Author',
    })
```

```
        expect(post).toEqual(null)
      })
  })
```

10. Lastly, import the `deletePost` function:

    ```
      deletePost,
    } from '../services/posts.js'
    ```

11. Then, add tests for successful and unsuccessful deletes by checking if the post was deleted and verifying the returned `deletedCount`:

    ```
    describe('deleting posts', () => {
      test('should remove the post from the database', async () => {
        const result = await deletePost(createdSamplePosts[0]._id)
        expect(result.deletedCount).toEqual(1)
        const deletedPost = await Post.
    findById(createdSamplePosts[0]._id)
        expect(deletedPost).toEqual(null)
      })

      test('should fail if the id does not exist', async () => {
        const result = await deletePost('000000000000000000000000')
        expect(result.deletedCount).toEqual(0)
      })
    })
    ```

12. Finally, run all tests again; they should all pass:

    ```
    $ npm test
    ```

Writing tests for service functions may be tedious, but it will save us a lot of time in the long run. Adding additional functionality later, such as access control, may change the basic behavior of the service functions. By having the unit tests, we can ensure that we do not break existing behavior when adding new functionality.

Using the Jest VS Code extension

Up until now, we have run our tests by using Jest via the Terminal. There is also a Jest extension for VS Code, which we can use to make running tests more visual. The extension is especially helpful for larger projects where we have many tests in multiple files. Additionally, the extension can automatically watch and re-run tests if we change the definitions. We can install the extension as follows:

1. Go to the **Extensions** tab in the VS Code sidebar.

2. Enter `Orta.vscode-jest` in the search box to find the Jest extension.

3. Install the extension by pressing the **Install** button.

4. Now go to the newly added test icon on the sidebar (it should be a chemistry flask icon):

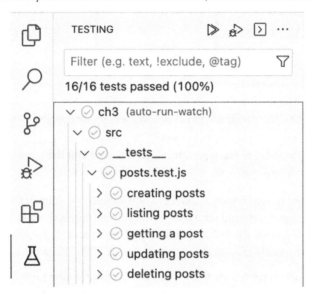

Figure 3.6 – The Testing tab in VS Code provided by the Jest extension

The Jest extension provides us an overview of all tests that we have defined. We can hover over them and press on the **Play** icon to re-run a specific test. By default, the Jest extension enables **auto-run-watch** (as can be seen in *Figure 3.6*). If **auto-run-watch** is enabled, the extension will re-run tests automatically when test definition files are saved. That's pretty handy!

Now that we have defined and tested our service functions, we can start using them when defining routes, which we are going to do next!

Providing a REST API using Express

Having our data and service layers set up, we have a good framework for being able to write our backend. However, we still need an interface that lets users access our backend. This interface will be a **representational state transfer** (**REST**) API. A REST API provides a way to access our server via HTTP requests, which we can make use of when we develop our frontend.

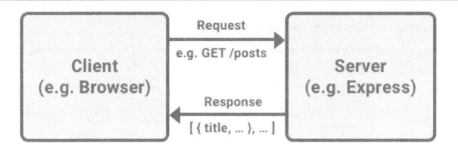

Figure 3.7 – The interaction between client and server using HTTP requests

As we can see, clients can send requests to our backend server, and the server will respond to them. There are five commonly used methods in a REST-based architecture:

- **GET**: This is used to read resources. Generally, it should not influence the database state and, given the same input, it should return the same output (unless the database state was changed through other requests). This behavior is called **idempotence**. In response to a successful GET request, a server usually returns the resource(s) with a 200 OK status code.

- **POST**: This is used to create new resources, from the information provided in the request body. In response to a successful POST request, a server usually either returns the newly created object with a 201 Created status code or returns an empty response (with 201 Created status code) with a URL in the **Location** header that points to the newly created resource.

- **PUT**: This is used to update an existing resource with a given ID, replacing the resource completely with the new data provided in the request body. In some cases, it can also be used to create a new resource with a client-specified ID. In response to a successful PUT request, a server either returns the updated resource with a 200 OK status code, 204 No Content if it does not return the updated resource, or 201 Created if it created a new resource.

- **PATCH**: This is used to modify an existing resource with a given ID, only updating the fields specified in the request body instead of replacing the whole resource. In response to a successful PATCH request, a server either returns the updated resource with 200 OK or 204 No Content if it does not return the updated resource.

- **DELETE**: This is used to delete a resource with a given ID. In response to a successful DELETE request, a server either returns the deleted resource with 200 OK or 204 No Content if it does not return the deleted resource.

HTTP REST API routes are usually defined in a folder-like structure. It is always a good idea to prefix all routes with /api/v1/ (v1 being the version of the API definition, starting with 1). If we want to change the API definition later, we can then easily run /api/v1/ and /api/v2/ in parallel for a while until everything is migrated.

Defining our API routes

Now that we have learned how HTTP REST APIs work, let's start by defining routes for our backend, covering all functionality we have already implemented in the service functions:

- `GET /api/v1/posts`: Get a list of all posts
- `GET /api/v1/posts?sortBy=updatedAt&sortOrder=ascending`: Get a list of all posts sorted by `updatedAt` (ascending)

> **Note**
>
> Everything after the `?` symbol is called a query string and follows the format `key1=value1&key2=value2&...`. The query string can be used to provide additional optional parameters to a route.

- `GET /api/v1/posts?author=daniel`: Get a list of posts by author "daniel"
- `GET /api/v1/posts?tag=react`: Get a list of posts with the tag `react`
- `GET /api/v1/posts/:id`: Get a single post by ID
- `POST /api/v1/posts`: Create a new post
- `PATCH /api/v1/posts/:id`: Update an existing post by ID
- `DELETE /api/v1/posts/:id`: Delete an existing post by ID

As we can see, by putting together our already developed service functions and what we have learned about REST APIs, we can easily define routes for our backend. Now that we have defined our routes, let's set up Express and our backend server to be able to expose those routes.

> **Note**
>
> This is just one example of how a REST API can be designed. It is intended as an example to get you started with full-stack development. Later, on your own time, feel free to check out other resources, such as `https://standards.rest`, to deepen your knowledge of REST API designs.

Setting up Express

Express is a web application framework for Node.js. It provides utility functions to easily define routes for REST APIs and serve HTTP servers. Express is also very extensible, and there are many plugins for it in the JavaScript ecosystem.

> **Note**
>
> While Express is the most well-known framework at the time of writing, there are also newer ones, such as Koa (https://koajs.com) or Fastify (https://fastify.dev). Koa is designed by the team behind Express but aims to be smaller, more expressive, and more robust. Fastify focuses on efficiency and low overhead. Feel free to check these out on your own time to see if they fit your requirements better.

Before we can set up the routes, let's take some time to set up our Express application and backend server by following these steps:

1.   First, install the express dependency:

     ```
     $ npm install express@4.18.2
     ```

2.   Create a new src/app.js file. This file will contain everything needed to set up our Express app. In this file, first import express:

     ```
     import express from 'express'
     ```

3.   Then create a new Express app, as follows:

     ```
     const app = express()
     ```

4.   Now we can define routes on the Express app. For example, to define a GET route, we can write the following code:

     ```
     app.get('/', (req, res) => {
        res.send('Hello from Express!')
     })
     ```

5.   We export the app to be able to use it in other files:

     ```
     export { app }
     ```

6.   Next, we need to create a server and specify a port, similar to what we did before when creating an HTTP server. To do so, we create a new src/index.js file. In this file, we import the Express app:

     ```
     import { app } from './app.js'
     ```

7.   Then, we define a port, make the Express app listen to it, and log a message telling us where the server is running:

     ```
     const PORT = 3000
     app.listen(PORT)
     console.info(`express server running on http://
     localhost:${PORT}`)
     ```

8. Edit `package.json` and add a `start` script to run our server:

    ```
    "scripts": {
      "start": "node src/index.js",
    ```

9. Run the backend server by executing the following command:

    ```
    $ npm start
    ```

10. Now, navigate to `http://localhost:3000/` in your browser and you will see **Hello from Express!** Being printed, just like before with the plain http server:

Figure 3.8 – Accessing our first Express app from the browser!

That's all there is to setting up a simple Express app! We can now keep defining routes by using `app.get()` for GET routes, `app.post()` for POST routes, etc. However, before we start developing our routes, let's take some time to improve our development environment. First, we should make `PORT` and `DATABASE_URL` configurable so that we can change them without having to change the code. To do so, we are going to use environment variables.

Using dotenv for setting environment variables

A good way to load environment variables is using `dotenv`, which loads environment variables from `.env` files into our `process.env`. This makes it easy to define environment variables for local development while keeping it possible to set them differently in, for example, a testing environment. Follow these steps to set up `dotenv`:

1. Install the `dotenv` dependency:

    ```
    $ npm install dotenv@16.3.1
    ```

2. Edit `src/index.js`, import `dotenv` there, and call `dotenv.config()` to initialize the environment variables. We should do this before we call any other code in our app:

    ```
    import dotenv from 'dotenv'
    dotenv.config()
    ```

3. Now we can start replacing our static variables with environment variables. Edit `src/index.js` and replace the static port `3000` with `process.env.PORT`:

```
const PORT = process.env.PORT
```

4. We have already migrated the `initDatabase` function to use `process.env.DATABASE_URL` earlier when we set up Jest. Now, we can edit `src/index.js` and import `initDatabase` there:

```
import { initDatabase } from './db/init.js'
```

5. Adjust the existing code to first call `initDatabase`, and only when the database initialized, start the Express app. We can now also handle errors while connecting to the database by adding a try/catch block:

```
try {
  await initDatabase()
  const PORT = process.env.PORT
  app.listen(PORT)
  console.info(`express server running on http://
localhost:${PORT}`)
} catch (err) {
  console.error('error connecting to database:', err)
}
```

6. Finally, create a `.env` file in the root of the project and define the two environment variables there:

```
PORT=3000
DATABASE_URL=mongodb://localhost:27017/blog
```

7. We should exclude the `.env` file from the Git repository, as it is only used for local development. Edit `.gitignore` and add `.env` to it in a new line:

```
.env
```

    At the moment, we have no sensible information in our environment variables, but it is still a good practice to do this already now. Later, we may have some credentials in the environment variables, which we do not want to accidentally push to a Git repository.

8. To make it easier for someone to get started with our project, we can create a copy of our `.env` file and duplicate it to `.env.template`, making sure that it does not contain any sensitive credentials, of course! Sensitive credentials could instead be stored in, for example, a shared password manager.

9. If it is still running from before, stop the server (by pressing *Ctrl* + *C* in the Terminal) and start it again as follows:

```
$ npm start
```

You will get the following result:

```
○ → ~/D/F/ch3 ⌥ main± > npm start

> ch3@0.0.0 start
> node src/index.js

successfully connected to database: mongodb://localhost:27017/ch3
express server running on http://localhost:3000
```

Figure 3.9 – Initializing the database connection and the Express server with environment variables

As we can see, dotenv makes it easy to maintain environment variables for development while still allowing us the possibility to change them in a continuous integration, testing, or production environment.

You may have noticed that we need to manually restart the server after making some changes. This is a stark contrast to the hot reloading we got out of the box from Vite, where any changes we make are applied to the frontend in the browser instantly. Let's now spend some time to improve the development experience by making the server auto-restart on changes.

Using nodemon for easier development

To make our server auto-restart on changes, we can use the nodemon tool. The nodemon tool allows us to run our server, similarly to the node CLI command. However, it offers the possibility to auto-restart the server on changes to the source files.

1. Install the nodemon tool as a dev dependency:

```
$ npm install –save-dev nodemon@3.0.2
```

2. Create a new nodemon.json file in the root of your project and add the following contents to it:

```
{
    "watch": ["./src", ".env", "package-lock.json"]
}
```

This makes sure that all code in the src/ folder is watched for changes, and it will refresh if any files inside it are changed. Additionally, we specified the .env file in case environment variables are changed and the package-lock.json file in case packages are added or upgraded.

3. Now, edit package.json and define a new "dev" script that runs nodemon:

    ```
    "scripts": {
      "dev": "nodemon src/index.js",
    ```

4. Stop the server (if it is currently running) and start it again by running the following command:

    ```
    $ npm run dev
    ```

5. As we can see, our server is now running through nodemon! We can try it out by changing the port in the .env file:

    ```
    PORT=3001
    DATABASE_URL=mongodb://localhost:27017/blog
    ```

6. Edit .env.template as well to change the port to 3001:

    ```
    PORT=3001
    ```

7. Keep the server running.

```
[nodemon] 2.0.22
[nodemon] to restart at any time, enter `rs`
[nodemon] watching path(s): src/**/* .env package.json
[nodemon] watching extensions: js,mjs,json
[nodemon] starting `node src/index.js`
successfully connected to database: mongodb://localhost:27017/ch3
express server running on http://localhost:3000
[nodemon] restarting due to changes...
[nodemon] starting `node src/index.js`
successfully connected to database: mongodb://localhost:27017/ch3
express server running on http://localhost:3001
```

Figure 3.10 – Nodemon automatically restarting the server after we changed the port

After making the change, nodemon automatically restarted the server for us with the new port. We now have something like hot reloading, but for backend development—awesome! Now that we have improved the developer experience on the backend, let's start writing our API routes with Express. Keep the server running (via nodemon) to see it restart and update live while coding!

Creating our API routes with Express

We can now start creating our previously defined API routes with express. We start by defining the GET routes:

1. Create a new `src/routes/posts.js` file and import the service functions there:

    ```
    import {
      listAllPosts,
      listPostsByAuthor,
      listPostsByTag,
      getPostById,
    } from '../services/posts.js'
    ```

2. Now create and export a new function called `postsRoutes`, which takes the Express app as an argument:

    ```
    export function postsRoutes(app) {
    ```

3. In this function, define the routes. Start with the GET `/api/v1/posts` route:

    ```
    app.get('/api/v1/posts', async (req, res) => {
    ```

4. In this route, we need to make use of query params (`req.query` in Express) to map them to the arguments of our functions. We want to be able to add query params for `sortBy`, `sortOrder`, `author`, and `tag`:

    ```
    const { sortBy, sortOrder, author, tag } = req.query
    const options = { sortBy, sortOrder }
    ```

5. Before we call our service functions, which might throw an error if we pass invalid data to the database functions, we should add a try-catch block to handle potential errors properly:

    ```
    try {
    ```

6. We now need to check if the `author` or `tag` was provided. If both were provided, we return a `400 Bad Request` status code and a JSON object with an error message by calling `res.json()`:

    ```
    if (author && tag) {
      return res
        .status(400)
        .json({ error: 'query by either author or tag, not
    both' })
    ```

7. Otherwise, we call the respective service function and return a JSON response in Express by calling `res.json()`. In case an error happened, we catch it, log it, and return a 500 status code:

```
        } else if (author) {
          return res.json(await listPostsByAuthor(author,
options))
        } else if (tag) {
          return res.json(await listPostsByTag(tag, options))
        } else {
          return res.json(await listAllPosts(options))
        }
      } catch (err) {
        console.error('error listing posts', err)
        return res.status(500).end()
      }
    })
```

8. Next, we define an API route to get a single post. We use the `:id` param placeholder to be able to access it as a dynamic parameter in the function:

```
    app.get('/api/v1/posts/:id', async (req, res) => {
```

9. Now, we can access `req.params.id` to get the `:id` part of our route and pass it to our service function:

```
      const { id } = req.params
      try {
        const post = await getPostById(id)
```

10. If the result of the function is `null`, we return a 404 response because the post was not found. Otherwise, we return the post as a JSON response:

```
        if (post === null) return res.status(404).end()
        return res.json(post)
      } catch (err) {
        console.error('error getting post', err)
        return res.status(500).end()
      }
    })
  }
```

By default, Express will return the JSON response with status 200 OK.

11. After defining our GET routes, we still need to mount them in our app. Edit `src/app.js` and import the `postsRoutes` function there:

```
import { postsRoutes } from './routes/posts.js'
```

12. Then, call the `postsRoutes(app)` function after initializing our Express app:

```
const app = express()
postsRoutes(app)
```

13. Go to `http://localhost:3001/api/v1/posts` to see the route in action!

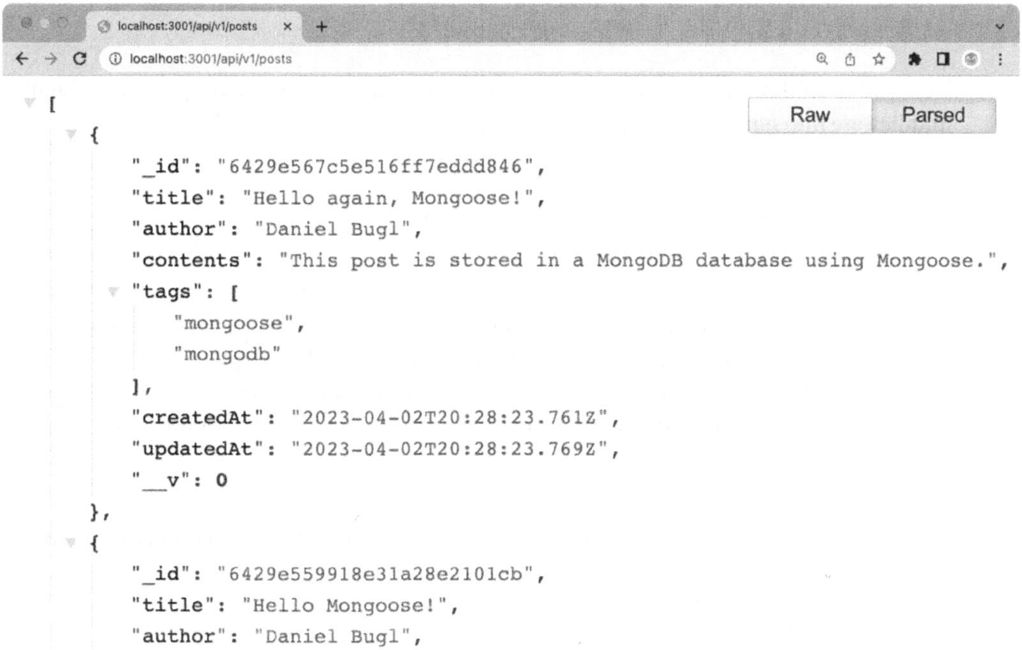

Figure 3.11 – Our first real API route in action!

Tip

You can install a **JSON Formatter** extension in your browser to format the JSON response nicely, like in *Figure 3.11*.

After defining the GET routes, we need to define the POST routes. However, these accept a body, which will be formatted as JSON objects. As such, we need a way to parse this JSON body in Express.

Defining routes with a JSON request body

To define routes with a JSON request body in Express, we need to use the `body-parser` module. This module detects if a client sent a JSON request (by looking at the `Content-Type` header) and then automatically parses it for us so that we can access the object in `req.body`.

1. Install the `body-parser` dependency:

    ```
    $ npm install body-parser@1.20.2
    ```

2. Edit `src/app.js` and import the `body-parser` there:

    ```
    import bodyParser from 'body-parser'
    ```

3. Now add the following code after our app is initialized to load the `body-parser` plugin as middleware into our Express app:

    ```
    const app = express()
    app.use(bodyParser.json())
    ```

> **Note**
>
> Middleware in Express allows us to do something before and after each request. In this case, `body-parser` is reading the JSON body for us, parsing it as JSON and giving us a JavaScript object that we can easily access from our route definitions. It should be noted that only routes defined after the middleware have access to it, so the order of defining middleware and routes is important!

4. After loading the `body-parser`, we edit `src/routes/posts.js` and import the service functions needed to make the rest of our routes:

    ```
      createPost,
      updatePost,
      deletePost,
    } from '../services/posts.js'
    ```

5. Now, we define the `POST /api/v1/posts` route by using `app.post` and `req.body`, inside of the `postsRoutes` function:

    ```
    app.post('/api/v1/posts', async (req, res) => {
      try {
        const post = await createPost(req.body)
        return res.json(post)
      } catch (err) {
        console.error('error creating post', err)
        return res.status(500).end()
    ```

```
      }
  })
```

6. Similarly, we can define the update route, where we need to make use of the `id` param and the request body:

```
app.patch('/api/v1/posts/:id', async (req, res) => {
  try {
    const post = await updatePost(req.params.id, req.body)
    return res.json(post)
  } catch (err) {
    console.error('error updating post', err)
    return res.status(500).end()
  }
})
```

7. Finally, we define the delete route, which does not require the `body-parser`; we just need to get the `id` param here. We return 404 if the post was not found, and 204 No Content if the post was deleted successfully:

```
app.delete('/api/v1/posts/:id', async (req, res) => {
  try {
    const { deletedCount } = await deletePost(req.params.id)
    if (deletedCount === 0) return res.sendStatus(404)
    return res.status(204).end()
  } catch (err) {
    console.error('error deleting post', err)
    return res.status(500).end()
  }
})
```

As we can see, Express makes defining and handling routes, requests, and responses much easier. It already detects and sets headers for us, and thus it can read and send JSON responses properly. It also allows us to change the HTTP status code easily.

Now that we finished defining the routes with a JSON request body, let's allow access to our routes from other URLs using **cross-origin resource sharing (CORS)**.

Allowing access from other URLs using CORS

Browsers have a safety feature to only allow us to access APIs on the same URL as the page we are currently on. To allow access to our backend from other URLs than the backend URL itself (for example, when we run the frontend on a different port in the next chapter), we need to allow CORS requests. Let's set that up now by using the cors library with Express:

1. Install the cors dependency:

    ```
    $ npm install cors@2.8.5
    ```

2. Edit src/app.js and import cors there:

    ```
    import cors from 'cors'
    ```

3. Now add the following code after our app is initialized to load the cors plugin as middleware into our Express app:

    ```
    const app = express()
    app.use(cors())
    app.use(bodyParser.json())
    ```

Now that CORS requests are allowed, we can start trying out the routes in a browser!

Trying out the routes

After defining our routes, we can try them out by using the fetch() function in the browser:

1. In your browser, go to http://localhost:3001/, open the console by right-clicking on a page and clicking **Inspect**, then go to the **Console** tab.

2. In the console, enter the following code to make a GET request to get all posts:

    ```
    fetch('http://localhost:3001/api/v1/posts')
      .then(res => res.json())
      .then(console.log)
    ```

3. Now we can modify this code to make a POST request by specifying the Content-Type header to tell the server that we will be sending JSON and then sending a body with JSON.stringify (as the body has to be a string):

    ```
    fetch('http://localhost:3001/api/v1/posts', {
        headers: { 'Content-Type': 'application/json' },
        method: 'POST',
        body: JSON.stringify({ title: 'Test Post' })
    })
      .then(res => res.json())
      .then(console.log)
    ```

4. Similarly, we can also send a PATCH request, as follows:

```
fetch('http://localhost:3001/api/v1/
posts/642a8b15950196ee8b3437b2', {
    headers: { 'Content-Type': 'application/json' },
    method: 'PATCH',
    body: JSON.stringify({ title: 'Test Post Changed' })
})
    .then(res => res.json())
    .then(console.log)
```

Make sure to replace the MongoDB IDs in the URL with the one returned from the POST request made before!

5. Finally, we can send a DELETE request:

```
fetch('http://localhost:3001/api/v1/
posts/642a8b15950196ee8b3437b2', {
    method: 'DELETE',
})
    .then(res => res.status)
    .then(console.log)
```

6. When doing a GET request, we can see that our post has now been deleted again:

```
fetch('http://localhost:3001/api/v1/
posts/642a8b15950196ee8b3437b2')
    .then(res => res.status)
    .then(console.log)
```

This request should now return a 404.

> **Tip**
>
> Instead of the browser console, you can also use command line tools such as curl or apps such as Postman to make the requests. Feel free to use different tools to try out the requests if you are already familiar with them.

We have now successfully defined all routes needed to handle a simple blog post API!

Summary

The first version of our backend service is now complete, allowing us to create, read, update, and delete blog posts via a REST API (using Express), which then get stored in a MongoDB database (using Mongoose). Additionally, we have created service functions with unit tests, defined using the Jest test suite. All in all, we managed to create a solid foundation for our backend in this chapter.

In the next chapter, *Chapter 4, Integrating a Frontend Using React and TanStack Query*, we are going to integrate our backend into a React frontend using TanStack Query, a library to handle asynchronous state and thus data fetched from our server. This means that, after the next chapter, we will have developed our first full-stack application!

Integrating a Frontend Using React and TanStack Query

After designing, implementing, and testing our backend service, it's now time to create a frontend to interface with the backend. First, we will start by setting up a full-stack React project based on the Vite boilerplate and the backend service created in the previous chapters. Then, we are going to create a basic user interface for our blog application. Finally, we will use TanStack Query, a data fetching library to handle backend state, to integrate the backend API into the frontend. By the end of this chapter, we will have successfully developed our first full-stack application!

In this chapter, we are going to cover the following main topics:

- Principles of React
- Setting up a full-stack React project
- Creating the user interface for our application
- Integrating the backend service using TanStack Query

Technical requirements

Before we start, please install all requirements from *Chapter 1, Preparing for Full-stack Development*, and *Chapter 2, Getting to Know Node.js and MongoDB*.

The versions listed in those chapters are the ones used in the book. While installing a newer version should not be an issue, please note that certain steps might work differently on a newer version. If you are having an issue with the code and steps provided in this book, please try using the versions mentioned in *Chapter 1* and *2*.

You can find the code for this chapter on GitHub: `https://github.com/PacktPublishing/Modern-Full-Stack-React-Projects/tree/main/ch4`

If you cloned the full repository for the book, Husky may not find the `.git` directory when running `npm install`. In that case, just run `git init` in the root of the corresponding chapter folder.

The CiA video for this chapter can be found at: `https://youtu.be/WXqJu2Ut7Hs`

Principles of React

Before we start learning how to set up a full-stack React project, let's revisit the three fundamental principles of React. These principles allow us to easily write scalable web applications:

- **Declarative**: Instead of telling React how to do things, we tell it what we want it to do. As a result, we can easily design our applications and React will efficiently update and render just the right components when the data changes. For example, the following code, which duplicates strings in an array is imperative, which is the opposite of declarative:

```
const input = ['a', 'b', 'c']
let result = []
for (let i = 0; i < input.length; i++) {
  result.push(input[i] + input[i])
}
console.log(result) // prints: [ 'aa', 'bb', 'cc' ]
```

  As we can see, in imperative code, we need to tell JavaScript exactly what to do, step by step. However, with declarative code, we can simply tell the computer what we want, as follows:

```
const input = ['a', 'b', 'c']
const result = input.map(str => str + str)
console.log(result) // prints: ['aa', 'bb', 'cc']
```

  In this declarative code, we tell the computer that we want to map each element of the `input` array from `str` to `str + str`. As you can see, declarative code is much more concise.

- **Component-based**: React encapsulates components that manage their own state and views and then allows us to compose them in order to create complex user interfaces.

- **Learn once, write anywhere**: React does not make assumptions about your technology stack and tries to ensure that you can develop apps without rewriting existing code as much as possible.

React's three fundamental principles make it easy to write code, encapsulate components, and share code across multiple platforms. Instead of reinventing the wheel, React tries to make use of existing JavaScript features as much as possible. As a result, we will learn software design patterns that will be applicable in many more cases than just designing user interfaces.

Now that we have learned the fundamental principles of React, let's get started setting up a full-stack React project!

Setting up a full-stack React project

Before we can start developing our frontend application, we first need to merge our previously created frontend boilerplate based on Vite with the backend service created in *Chapter 3, Implementing a Backend Using Express, Mongoose ODM, and Jest*. Let's merge them now by following these steps:

1. Copy the ch1 folder to a new ch4 folder, as follows:

    ```
    $ cp -R ch1 ch4
    ```

2. Copy the ch3 folder to a new ch4/backend folder, as follows:

    ```
    $ cp -R ch3 ch4/backend
    ```

3. *Delete* the .git folder in the copied ch4/backend folder, as follows:

    ```
    $ rm -rf ch4/backend/.git
    ```

4. Open the new ch4 folder in VS Code.

5. *Remove* the Husky prepare script (the line is highlighted in the code snippet) from the backend/package.json file, as we already have Husky set up in the root directory:

    ```
    "scripts": {
      "dev": "nodemon src/index.js",
      "start": "node src/index.js",
      "test": "NODE_OPTIONS=--experimental-vm-modules jest",
      "lint": "eslint src",
      "prepare": "husky install"
    },
    ```

6. Also *remove* the following lint-staged config from the backend/package.json file:

    ```
    "lint-staged": {
      "**/*.{js,jsx}": [
        "npx prettier --write",
        "npx eslint --fix"
      ]
    }
    ```

7. Then, *remove* the backend/.husky, backend/.vscode, and backend/.git folders.

8. To make sure all dependencies are installed properly, run the following command in the root of the ch4 folder:

    ```
    $ npm install
    ```

9. Also go to the `backend/` directory and install all dependencies there:

    ```
    $ cd backend/
    $ npm install
    ```

10. We can now also remove the `husky`, `lint-staged`, and `@commitlint` packages from the backend project, as we already have it set up in the main project folder:

    ```
    $ npm uninstall husky lint-staged \
      @commitlint/cli @commitlint/config-conventional
    ```

Tip

It is always a good idea to regularly check which packages you still need and which you can get rid of, to keep your project clean. In this case, we copied code from another project, but do not need the Husky / lint-staged / commitlint setup, as we already have it set up in the root of our project.

---

11. Now go back to the root of the `ch4` folder and run the following command to start the frontend server:

    ```
    $ cd ../
    $ npm run dev
    ```

12. Open the frontend in your browser by going to the URL shown by Vite: `http://localhost:5173/`

13. Open `src/App.jsx`, change the title as follows, and save the file:

    ```
    <h1>Vite + React + Node.js</h1>
    ```

14. You will see that the change is reflected instantly in the browser!

After successfully setting up our full-stack project by combining our projects from previous chapters, let's now get started designing and creating the user interface for our blog application.

Creating the user interface for our application

When designing the structure of a frontend, we should also consider the folder structure, so that our app can grow easily in the future. Similar to how we did for the backend, we will also put all our source code into a `src/` folder. We can then group the files in separate folders for the different features. Another popular way to structure frontend projects is to group code by routes. Of course, it is also possible to mix them, for example, in Next.js projects we can group our components by features and then create another folder and file structure for the routes, where the components are used. For full-stack projects, it additionally makes sense to first separate our code by creating separate folders for the API integration and UI components.

Now, let's define the folder structure for our project:

1. Create a new `src/api/` folder.

2. Create a new `src/components/` folder.

> **Tip**
>
> It is a good idea to start with a simple structure at first, and only nest more deeply when you actually need it. Do not spend too much time thinking about the file structure when starting a project, because usually, you do not know upfront how files should be grouped, and it may change later anyway.

After defining the high-level folder structure for our projects, let's now take some time to consider the component structure.

Component structure

Based on what we defined in the backend, our blog application is going to have the following features:

- Viewing a single post

- Creating a new post

- Listing posts

- Filtering posts

- Sorting posts

The idea of components in React is to have each component deal with a single task or UI element. We should try to make components as fine-grained as possible, in order to be able to reuse code. If we find ourselves copying and pasting code from one component to another, it might be a good idea to create a new component and reuse it in multiple other components.

Usually, when developing a frontend, we start with a UI mock-up. For our blog application, a mock-up could look as follows:

Title: [   ]

Author: [   ]

[   ]

[Create]

author: [   ]
Sort By: [createdAt ∨] / Sort Order: [descending ∨]

Full-Stack React Projects

Let's become full-stack developers!

*Written by **Daniel Bugl***

Hello React!

Figure 4.1 – An initial mock-up of our blog application

> **Note**
>
> In this book, we will not cover UI or CSS frameworks. As such, the components are designed and developed without styling. Instead, the book focuses on the full-stack aspect of the integration of backends with frontends. Feel free to use a UI framework (such as MUI), or a CSS framework (such as Tailwind) to style the blog application on your own.

When splitting up the UI into components, we use the **single-responsibility principle**, which states that every module should have responsibility over a single encapsulated part of the functionality.

In our mock-up, we can draw boxes around each component and subcomponent, and give them names. Keep in mind that each component should have exactly one responsibility. We start with the fundamental components that make up the app:

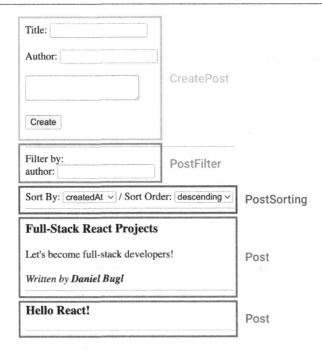

Figure 4.2 – Defining the fundamental components in our mock-up

We defined a CreatePost component, with a form to create a new post, a PostFilter component to filter the list of posts, a PostSorting component to sort posts, and a Post component to display a single post.

Now that we have defined our fundamental components, we are going to look at which components logically belong together, thereby forming a group: we can group the Post components together in PostList, then make an App component to group everything together and define the structure of our app.

Now that we are done with structuring our React components, we can move on to implementing the static React components.

Implementing static React components

Before integrating with the backend, we are going to model the basic features of our application as static React components. Dealing with the static view structure of our application first makes sense, as we can play around and re-structure the application UI if needed, before adding integration to the components, which would make it harder and more tedious to move them around. It is also easier to deal only with the UI first, which helps us to get started quickly with projects and features. Then, we can move on to implementing integrations and handling state.

Let's get started implementing the static components now.

The Post component

We have already thought about which elements a post has during the creation of the mock-up and the design of the backend. A post should have a `title`, `contents`, and an `author`.

Let's implement the `Post` component now:

1. First, create a new `src/components/Post.jsx` file.

2. In that file, import `PropTypes`:

    ```
    import PropTypes from 'prop-types'
    ```

3. Define a function component, accepting `title`, `contents`, and `author` props:

    ```
    export function Post({ title, contents, author }) {
    ```

4. Next, render all props in a way that resembles the mock-up:

    ```
    return (
      <article>
        <h3>{title}</h3>
        <div>{contents}</div>
        {author && (
          <em>
            <br />
            Written by <strong>{author}</strong>
          </em>
        )}
      </article>
    )
    }
    ```

> **Tip**
>
> Please note that you should always prefer spacing via CSS, rather than using the `<br />` HTML tag. However, we are focusing on the UI structure and integration with the backend in this book, so we simply use HTML whenever possible.

5. Now, define `propTypes`, making sure only `title` is required:

    ```
    Post.propTypes = {
      title: PropTypes.string.isRequired,
      contents: PropTypes.string,
      author: PropTypes.string,
    }
    ```

> **Info**
>
> `PropTypes` are used to validate the props passed to React components and to ensure that we are passing the correct props when using JavaScript. When using a type-safe language, such as TypeScript, we can instead do this by directly typing the props passed to the component.

6. Let's test out our component by *replacing* the `src/App.jsx` file with the following contents:

    ```jsx
    import { Post } from './components/Post.jsx'

    export function App() {
      return (
        <Post
          title='Full-Stack React Projects'
          contents="Let's become full-stack developers!"
          author='Daniel Bugl'
        />
      )
    }
    ```

7. Edit `src/main.jsx` and update the import of the App component, because we are now not using `export default` anymore:

    ```jsx
    import { App } from './App.jsx'
    ```

> **Info**
>
> I personally tend to prefer not using default exports, as they make it harder to re-group and re-export components and functions from other files. Also, they allow us to change the names of the components, which could be confusing. For example, if we change the name of a component, the name when importing it is not changed automatically.

8. Also, *remove* the following line from `src/main.jsx`:

    ```jsx
    import './index.css'
    ```

9. Finally, we can *delete* the `index.css` and `App.css` files, as they are not needed anymore.

Now that our static `Post` component has been implemented, we can move on to the `CreatePost` component.

The CreatePost component

We'll now implement a form to allow for the creation of new posts. Here, we provide fields for `author` and `title` and a `<textarea>` element for the contents of the blog post.

Let's implement the CreatePost component now:

1. Create a new src/components/CreatePost.jsx file.

2. Define the following component, which contains a form to enter the title, author, and contents of a blog post:

```
export function CreatePost() {
  return (
    <form onSubmit={ (e) => e.preventDefault() }>
      <div>
        <label htmlFor='create-title'>Title: </label>
        <input type='text' name='create-title' id='create-title'
/>
      </div>
      <br />
      <div>
        <label htmlFor='create-author'>Author: </label>
        <input type='text' name='create-author' id='create-
author' />
      </div>
      <br />
      <textarea />
      <br />
      <br />
      <input type='submit' value='Create' />
    </form>
  )
}
```

In the preceding code block, we defined an onSubmit handler and called e.preventDefault() on the event object to avoid a page refresh when the form is submitted.

3. Let's test the component out by *replacing* the src/App.jsx file with the following contents:

```
import { CreatePost } from './components/CreatePost.jsx'

export function App() {
  return <CreatePost />
}
```

As you can see, the CreatePost component renders fine. We can now move on to the PostFilter and PostSorting components.

> **Tip**
>
> If you want to test out multiple components at once and keep the tests around for later, or build a style guide for your own component library, you should look into Storybook (`https://storybook.js.org`), which is a useful tool to build, test, and document UI components in isolation.

The PostFilter and PostSorting components

Similar to the `CreatePost` component, we will be creating two components that provide input fields to filter and sort posts. Let's start with `PostFilter`:

1. Create a new `src/components/PostFilter.jsx` file.

2. In this file, we import `PropTypes`:

   ```
   import PropTypes from 'prop-types'
   ```

3. Now, we define the `PostFilter` component and make use of the `field` prop:

   ```
   export function PostFilter({ field }) {
     return (
       <div>
         <label htmlFor={`filter-${field}`}>{field}: </label>
         <input
           type='text'
           name={`filter-${field}`}
           id={`filter-${field}`}
         />
       </div>
     )
   }

   PostFilter.propTypes = {
     field: PropTypes.string.isRequired,
   }
   ```

   Next, we are going to define the `PostSorting` component.

4. Create a new `src/components/PostSorting.jsx` file.

5. In this file, we create a `select` input to select which field to sort by. We also create another `select` input to select the sort order:

   ```
   import PropTypes from 'prop-types'

   export function PostSorting({ fields = [] }) {
     return (
   ```

```
      <div>
        <label htmlFor='sortBy'>Sort By: </label>
        <select name='sortBy' id='sortBy'>
          {fields.map((field) => (
            <option key={field} value={field}>
              {field}
            </option>
          ))}
        </select>
        {' / '}
        <label htmlFor='sortOrder'>Sort Order: </label>
        <select name='sortOrder' id='sortOrder'>
          <option value={'ascending'}>ascending</option>
          <option value={'descending'}>descending</option>
        </select>
      </div>
    )
}

PostSorting.propTypes = {
    fields: PropTypes.arrayOf(PropTypes.string).isRequired,
}
```

Now we have successfully defined UI components to filter and sort posts. In the next step, we are going to create a `PostList` component to combine the filter and sorting with a list of posts.

The PostList component

After implementing the other post-related components, we can now implement the most important part of our blog app, that is, the feed of blog posts. For now, the feed is simply going to show a list of blog posts.

Let's start implementing the `PostList` component now:

1. Create a new `src/components/PostList.jsx` file.

2. First, we import `Fragment`, `PropTypes`, and the `Post` component:

    ```
    import { Fragment } from 'react'
    import PropTypes from 'prop-types'
    import { Post } from './Post.jsx'
    ```

3. Then, we define the `PostList` function component, accepting a `posts` array as a prop. If `posts` is not defined, we set it to an empty array, by default:

    ```
    export function PostList({ posts = [] }) {
    ```

4. Next, we render all posts by using the `.map` function and the spread syntax:

```
return (
  <div>
    {posts.map((post) => (
      <Post {...post} key={post._id} />
    ))}
  </div>
)
}
```

We return the `<Post>` component for each post, and pass all the keys from the `post` object to the component as props. We do this by using the spread syntax, which has the same effect as listing all the keys from the object manually as props, like so:

```
<Post
  title={post.title}
  author={post.author}
  contents={post.contents}
/>
```

> **Note**
>
> If we are rendering a list of elements, we have to give each element a unique `key` prop. React uses this `key` prop to efficiently compute the difference between two lists when the data has changed.

We used the `map` function, which applies a function to all the elements of an array. This is similar to using a `for` loop and storing all the results, but it is more concise, declarative, and easier to read! Alternatively, we could do the following instead of using the `map` function:

```
let renderedPosts = []
let index = 0
for (let post of posts) {
  renderedPosts.push(<Post {...post} key={post._id} />)
  index++
}

return (
  <div>
    {renderedPosts}
  </div>
)
```

However, using this style is *not* recommended with React.

5. We also still need to define the prop types. Here, we can make use of the prop types from the `Post` component, by wrapping it inside the `PropTypes.shape()` function, which defines an object prop type:

```
PostList.propTypes = {
  posts: PropTypes.arrayOf(PropTypes.shape(Post.propTypes)).
isRequired,
}
```

6. In the mock-up, we have a horizontal line after each blog post. We can implement this without an additional `<div>` container element, by using `Fragment`, as follows:

```
{posts.map((post) => (
  <Fragment key={post._id}>
    <Post {...post} />
    <hr />
  </Fragment>
))}
```

> **Note**
>
> The `key` prop always has to be added to the uppermost parent element that is rendered within the map function. In this case, we had to move the `key` prop from the `Post` component to `Fragment`.

7. Again, we test our component by editing the `src/App.jsx` file:

```
import { PostList } from './components/PostList.jsx'

const posts = [
  {
    title: 'Full-Stack React Projects',
    contents: "Let's become full-stack developers!",
    author: 'Daniel Bugl',
  },
  { title: 'Hello React!' },
]

export function App() {
  return <PostList posts={posts} />
}
```

Now we can see that our app lists all the posts that we defined in the `posts` array.

As you can see, listing multiple posts via the `PostList` component works fine. We can now move on to putting the app together.

Putting the app together

After implementing all the components, we now have to put everything together in the App component. Then, we will have successfully reproduced the mock-up!

Let's start modifying the App component and putting our blog app together:

1. Open `src/App.jsx` and add imports for the `CreatePost`, `PostFilter`, and `PostSorting` components:

```
import { PostList } from './components/PostList.jsx'
import { CreatePost } from './components/CreatePost.jsx'
import { PostFilter } from './components/PostFilter.jsx'
import { PostSorting } from './components/PostSorting.jsx'
```

2. Adjust the App component to contain all the components:

```
export function App() {
  return (
    <div style={{ padding: 8 }}>
      <CreatePost />
      <br />
      <hr />
      Filter by:
      <PostFilter field='author' />
      <br />
      <PostSorting fields={['createdAt', 'updatedAt']} />
      <hr />
      <PostList posts={posts} />
    </div>
  )
}
```

3. After saving the file, the browser should automatically refresh, and we can now see the full UI:

Figure 4.3 – Full implementation of our static blog app, according to the mock-up

As we can see, all of the static components that we defined earlier are rendered together in one App component. Our app now looks just like a mock-up. Next, we can move on to integrating our components with the backend service.

Integrating the backend service using TanStack Query

After finishing creating all the UI components, we can now move on to integrating them with the backend we created in the previous chapter. For the integration, we are going to use TanStack Query (previously called React Query), which is a data fetching library that can also help us with caching, synchronizing, and updating data from a backend.

TanStack Query specifically focuses on managing the state of fetched data (server state). While other state management libraries can also deal with server state, they specialize in managing client state instead. Server state has some stark differences from client state, such as the following:

- Being persisted remotely in a location the client does not control directly
- Requiring asynchronous APIs to fetch and update state

- Having to deal with shared ownership, which means that other people can change the state without your knowledge

- State becoming stale ("out of date") at some point when changed by the server or other people

These challenges with server state result in issues such as having to cache, deduplicate multiple requests, update "out of date" state in the background, and so on.

TanStack Query provides solutions to these issues out of the box and thus makes dealing with server state simple. You can always combine it with other state management libraries that focus on client state as well. For use cases where the client state essentially just reflects the server state though, TanStack Query on its own can be good enough as a state management solution!

> **Note**
> The reason why React Query got renamed to TanStack Query is that the library now also supports other frameworks, such as Solid, Vue, and Svelte!

Now that you know why and how TanStack Query can help us integrate our frontend with the backend, let's get started using it!

Setting up TanStack Query for React

To set up TanStack Query, we first have to install the dependency and set up a query client. The query client is provided to React through a context and will store information about active requests, cached results, when to periodically re-fetch data, and everything needed for TanStack Query to function.

Let's get started setting it up now:

1. Open a new Terminal (do not quit Vite!) and install the `@tanstack/react-query` dependency by running the following command in the root of our project:

   ```
   $ npm install @tanstack/react-query@5.12.2
   ```

   We are now going to move our current `App` component to a new `Blog` component, as we are going to use the `App` component for setting up libraries and contexts instead.

2. Rename the `src/App.jsx` file to `src/Blog.jsx`.

   Do not update imports yet. If VS Code asks you to update imports, click **No**.

3. Now, in `src/Blog.jsx`, change the function name from `App` to `Blog`:

   ```
   export function Blog() {
   ```

4. Create a new `src/App.jsx` file. In this file, import `QueryClient` and `QueryClientProvider` from TanStack React Query:

    ```
    import { QueryClient, QueryClientProvider } from '@tanstack/
    react-query'
    ```

5. Also, import the `Blog` component:

    ```
    import { Blog } from './Blog.jsx'
    ```

6. Now, create a new query client:

    ```
    const queryClient = new QueryClient()
    ```

7. Define the `App` component and render the `Blog` component wrapped inside `QueryClientProvider`:

    ```
    export function App() {
      return (
        <QueryClientProvider client={queryClient}>
          <Blog />
        </QueryClientProvider>
      )
    }
    ```

That's all there is to setting up TanStack Query! We can now make use of it inside our `Blog` component (and its children).

Fetching blog posts

The first thing we should do is fetch the list of blog posts from our backend. Let's implement that now:

1. First of all, in the second Terminal window opened (not where Vite is running), run the backend server (do not quit Vite!), as follows:

    ```
    $ cd backend/
    $ npm start
    ```

    If you get an error, make sure Docker and MongoDB are running properly!

> **Tip**
>
> If you want to develop the backend and frontend at the same time, you can start the backend using `npm run dev` to make sure it hot reloads when you change the code.

2. Create a `.env` file in the root of the project, and enter the following contents into it:

```
VITE_BACKEND_URL="http://localhost:3001/api/v1"
```

Vite supports `dotenv` out of the box. All environment variables that should be available to be accessed within the frontend need to be prefixed with `VITE_`. Here, we set an environment variable to point to our backend server.

3. Create a new `src/api/posts.js` file. In this file, we are going to define a function to fetch posts, which accepts the query params for the `/posts` endpoint as an argument. These query params are used to filter by author and tag and define sorting using `sortBy` and `sortOrder`:

```
export const getPosts = async (queryParams) => {
```

4. Remember that we can use the `fetch` function to make a request to a server. We need to pass the environment variable to it and add the `/posts` endpoint. After the path, we add query params, which are prefixed with the `?` symbol:

```
const res = await fetch(
    `${import.meta.env.VITE_BACKEND_URL}/posts?` +
```

5. Now we need to use the `URLSearchParams` class to turn an object into query params. That class will automatically escape the input for us and turn it into valid query params:

```
new URLSearchParams(queryParams),
```

6. Like we did before in the browser, we need to parse the response as JSON:

```
)
    return await res.json()
}
```

7. Edit `src/Blog.jsx` and *remove* the sample `posts` array:

```
const posts = [
    {
        title: 'Full-Stack React Projects',
        contents: "Let's become full-stack developers!",
        author: 'Daniel Bugl',
    },
    { title: 'Hello React!' },
]
```

8. Also, import the `useQuery` function from `@tanstack/react-query` and the `getPosts` function from our `api` folder in the `src/Blog.jsx` file:

```
import { useQuery } from '@tanstack/react-query'
import { PostList } from './components/PostList.jsx'
```

```
import { CreatePost } from './components/CreatePost.jsx'
import { PostFilter } from './components/PostFilter.jsx'
import { PostSorting } from './components/PostSorting.jsx'
import { getPosts } from './api/posts.js'
```

9. Inside the `Blog` component, define a `useQuery` hook:

```
export function Blog() {
    const postsQuery = useQuery({
        queryKey: ['posts'],
        queryFn: () => getPosts(),
    })
```

The `queryKey` is very important in TanStack Query, as it is used to uniquely identify a request, among other things, for caching purposes. Always make sure to use unique query keys. Otherwise, you might see requests not triggering properly.

For the `queryFn` option, we just call the `getPosts` function, without query params for now.

10. After the `useQuery` hook, we get the posts from our query and fall back to an empty array if the posts are not loaded yet:

```
const posts = postsQuery.data ?? []
```

11. Check your browser, and you will see that the posts are now loaded from our backend!

Now that we have successfully fetched blog posts, let's get the filters and sorting working!

Implementing filters and sorting

To implement filters and sorting, we need to handle some local state and pass it as query params to `postsQuery`. Let's do that now:

1. We start by editing the `src/Blog.jsx` file and importing the `useState` hook from React:

```
import { useState } from 'react'
```

2. Then we add state hooks for the `author` filter and the sorting options inside the `Blog` component, before the `useQuery` hook:

```
const [author, setAuthor] = useState('')
const [sortBy, setSortBy] = useState('createdAt')
const [sortOrder, setSortOrder] = useState('descending')
```

3. Then, we adjust `queryKey` to contain the query params (so that whenever a query param changes, TanStack Query will re-fetch unless the request is already cached). We also adjust `queryFn` to call `getPosts` with the relevant query params:

```
const postsQuery = useQuery({
    queryKey: ['posts', { author, sortBy, sortOrder }],
    queryFn: () => getPosts({ author, sortBy, sortOrder }),
})
```

4. Now pass the values and relevant `onChange` handlers to the filter and sorting components:

```
<PostFilter
  field='author'
  value={author}
  onChange={(value) => setAuthor(value)}
/>
<br />
<PostSorting
  fields={['createdAt', 'updatedAt']}
  value={sortBy}
  onChange={(value) => setSortBy(value)}
  orderValue={sortOrder}
  onOrderChange={(orderValue) => setSortOrder(orderValue)}
/>
```

> **Note**
>
> For simplicity's sake, we are only using state hooks for now. A state management solution or context could make dealing with filters and sorting much easier, especially for larger applications. For our small blog application, it is fine to use state hooks though, as we are focusing mostly on the integration of the backend and frontend.

5. Now, edit `src/components/PostFilter.jsx` and add the `value` and `onChange` props:

```
export function PostFilter({ field, value, onChange }) {
  return (
    <div>
      <label htmlFor={`filter-${field}`}>{field}: </label>
      <input
        type='text'
        name={`filter-${field}`}
        id={`filter-${field}`}
        value={value}
```

```
        onChange={(e) => onChange(e.target.value)}
      />
    </div>
  )
}

PostFilter.propTypes = {
  field: PropTypes.string.isRequired,
  value: PropTypes.string.isRequired,
  onChange: PropTypes.func.isRequired,
}
```

6. We also do the same for `src/components/PostSorting.jsx`:

```
export function PostSorting({
  fields = [],
  value,
  onChange,
  orderValue,
  onOrderChange,
}) {
  return (
    <div>
      <label htmlFor='sortBy'>Sort By: </label>
      <select
        name='sortBy'
        id='sortBy'
        value={value}
        onChange={(e) => onChange(e.target.value)}
      >
        {fields.map((field) => (
          <option key={field} value={field}>
            {field}
          </option>
        ))}
      </select>
      {' / '}
      <label htmlFor='sortOrder'>Sort Order: </label>
      <select
        name='sortOrder'
        id='sortOrder'
        value={orderValue}
```

```
        onChange={(e) => onOrderChange(e.target.value)}
      >
        <option value={'ascending'}>ascending</option>
        <option value={'descending'}>descending</option>
      </select>
    </div>
  )
}

PostSorting.propTypes = {
  fields: PropTypes.arrayOf(PropTypes.string).isRequired,
  value: PropTypes.string.isRequired,
  onChange: PropTypes.func.isRequired,
  orderValue: PropTypes.string.isRequired,
  onOrderChange: PropTypes.func.isRequired,
}
```

7. In your browser, enter `Daniel Bugl` as the author. You should see TanStack Query re-fetch the posts from the backend as you type, and once a match is found, the backend will return all posts by that author!

8. After testing it out, make sure to clear the filter again, so that newly created posts are not filtered by the author anymore later on.

> **Tip**
>
> If you do not want to make that many requests to the backend, make sure to use a debouncing state hook, such as `useDebounce`, and then pass only the debounced value to the query param. If you are interested in gaining further knowledge about the `useDebounce` hook and other useful hooks, I recommend checking out my book titled *Learn React Hooks*.

The application should now look as follows, with the posts being filtered by the author entered in the field, and sorted by the selected field, in the selected order:

Figure 4.4 – Our first full-stack application – a frontend fetching posts from a backend!

Now that sorting and filtering are working properly, let's learn about mutations, which allow us to make requests to the server that change the state of the backend (for example, inserting or updating entries in the database).

Creating new posts

We are now going to implement a feature to create posts. To do this, we need to use the useMutation hook from TanStack Query. While queries are meant to be idempotent (meaning that calling them multiple times should not affect the result), mutations are used to create/update/delete data or perform operations on the server. Let's get started using mutations to create new posts now:

1. Edit src/api/posts.js and define a new createPost function, which accepts a post object as an argument:

    ```
    export const createPost = async (post) => {
    ```

2. We also make a request to the /posts endpoint, like we did for getPosts:

    ```
    const res = await fetch(`${import.meta.env.VITE_BACKEND_URL}/
    posts`, {
    ```

3. However, now we also set method to a POST request, pass a header to tell the backend that we will be sending a JSON body, and then send our post object as a JSON string:

    ```
    method: 'POST',
    headers: { 'Content-Type': 'application/json' },
    body: JSON.stringify(post),
    ```

4. Like with getPosts, we also need to parse the response as JSON:

    ```
    })
    return await res.json()
    }
    ```

    After defining the createPost API function, let's use it in the CreatePost component by creating a new mutation hook there.

5. Edit src/components/CreatePost.jsx and import the useMutation hook from @tanstack/react-query, the useState hook from React, and our createPost API function:

    ```
    import { useMutation } from '@tanstack/react-query'
    import { useState } from 'react'
    import { createPost } from '../api/posts.js'
    ```

6. Inside the CreatePost component, define state hooks for title, author, and contents:

    ```
    const [title, setTitle] = useState('')
    const [author, setAuthor] = useState('')
    const [contents, setContents] = useState('')
    ```

7. Now, define a mutation hook. Here, we are going to call our createPost function:

    ```
    const createPostMutation = useMutation({
      mutationFn: () => createPost({ title, author, contents }),
    })
    ```

8. Next, we are going to define a handleSubmit function, which will prevent the default submit action (which refreshes the page), and instead call .mutate() to execute the mutation:

    ```
    const handleSubmit = (e) => {
      e.preventDefault()
      createPostMutation.mutate()
    }
    ```

9. We add the `onSubmit` handler to our form:

```
<form onSubmit={handleSubmit}>
```

10. We also add the `value` and `onChange` props to our fields, as we did before for the sorting and filters:

```
<div>
  <label htmlFor='create-title'>Title: </label>
  <input
    type='text'
    name='create-title'
    id='create-title'
    value={title}
    onChange={(e) => setTitle(e.target.value)}
  />
</div>
<br />
<div>
  <label htmlFor='create-author'>Author: </label>
  <input
    type='text'
    name='create-author'
    id='create-author'
    value={author}
    onChange={(e) => setAuthor(e.target.value)}
  />
</div>
<br />
<textarea
  value={contents}
  onChange={(e) => setContents(e.target.value)}
/>
```

11. For the submit button, we make sure it says `Creating...` instead of `Create` while we are waiting for the mutation to finish, and we also disable the button if no title was set (as it is required), or if the mutation is currently pending:

```
<br />
<br />
<input
  type='submit'
  value={createPostMutation.isPending ? 'Creating...' :
'Create'}
  disabled={!title || createPostMutation.isPending}
/>
```

12. Lastly, we add a message below the submit button, which will be shown if the mutation is successful:

```
{createPostMutation.isSuccess ? (
    <>
        <br />
        Post created successfully!
    </>
) : null}
</form>
```

> **Note**
>
> In addition to isPending and isSuccess, mutations also return isIdle (when the mutation is idle or in a fresh/reset state) and isError states. The same states can also be accessed from queries, for example, to show a loading animation while posts are fetching.

13. Now we can try adding a new post, and it seems to work fine, but the post list is not updating automatically, only after a refresh!

The issue is that the query key did not change, so TanStack Query does not refresh the list of posts. However, we also want to refresh the list when a new post is created. Let's fix that now.

Invalidating queries

To ensure that the post list is refreshed after creating a new post, we need to invalidate the query. We can make use of the query client to do this. Let's do it now:

1. Edit src/components/CreatePost.jsx and import the useQueryClient hook:

```
import { useMutation, useQueryClient } from '@tanstack/react-
query'
```

2. Use the query client to invalidate all queries starting with the 'posts' query key. This will work with any query params to the getPosts request, as it matches all queries starting with 'posts' in the array:

```
const queryClient = useQueryClient()
const createPostMutation = useMutation({
  mutationFn: () => createPost({ title, author, contents }),
  onSuccess: () => queryClient.invalidateQueries(['posts']),
})
```

Try creating a new post, and you will see that it works now, even with active filters and sorting! As we can see, TanStack Query is great for handling server state with ease.

Summary

In this chapter, we learned how to create a React frontend and integrate it with our backend using TanStack Query. We have covered the main functionality of our backend: listing posts with sorting, creating posts, and filtering by author. Dealing with tags and deleting and editing posts are similar to the already explained functionalities and are left as an exercise for you.

In the next chapter, *Chapter 5, Deploying the Application with Docker and CI/CD*, we are going to deploy our application with Docker and set up CI/CD pipelines to automate the deployment of our application.

5

Deploying the Application with Docker and CI/CD

Now that we have successfully developed our first full-stack application with a backend service and a frontend, we are going to package our app into Docker images and learn how to deploy them using **continuous integration** (**CI**) and **continuous delivery** (**CD**) principles. We have already learned how to start Docker containers in *Chapter 2, Getting to Know Node.js and MongoDB*. In this chapter, we will learn how to create our own Docker images to instantiate containers from. Then, we are going to manually deploy our application to a cloud provider. Finally, we are going to configure CI/CD to automate the deployment of our application. At the end of this chapter, we will have successfully deployed our first full-stack **MongoDB Express React Node.js** (**MERN**) application, and set it up for future automated deployments!

In this chapter, we are going to cover the following main topics:

- Creating Docker images
- Deploying our full-stack application to the cloud
- Configuring CI to automate testing
- Configuring CD to automate the deployment

Technical requirements

Before we start, please install all requirements from *Chapter 1, Preparing For Full-Stack Development*, and *Chapter 2, Getting to Know Node.js and MongoDB*.

The versions listed in those chapters are the ones used in the book. While installing a newer version should not be an issue, please note that certain steps might work differently on a newer version. If you are having an issue with the code and steps provided in this book, please try using the versions mentioned in *Chapter 1* and *Chapter 2*.

You can find the code for this chapter on GitHub: `https://github.com/PacktPublishing/Modern-Full-Stack-React-Projects/tree/main/ch5`.

The CiA video for this chapter can be found at: `https://youtu.be/aQplfCQGWew`

Creating Docker images

In *Chapter 2, Getting to Know Node.js and MongoDB*, we learned that in the Docker platform, we use Docker images to create containers, which can then run services. We have already learned how to use the existing `mongo` image to create a container for our database service. In this section, we are going to learn how to create our own image to instantiate a container from. To do so, we first need to create a **Dockerfile**, which contains all the instructions needed to build the Docker image. First, we will create a Docker image for our backend service and run a container from it. Then, we will do the same for our frontend. Finally, we will create a **Docker Compose file** to start our database and backend services together with our frontend.

Creating the backend Dockerfile

A Dockerfile tells Docker step by step how to build the image. Each line in the file is an instruction telling Docker what to do. The format of a Dockerfile is as follows:

```
# comment
INSTRUCTION arguments
```

Every Dockerfile must begin with a FROM instruction, which specifies which image the newly created image should be based on. You can extend your image from existing images, such as `ubuntu` or `node`.

Let's get started by creating the Dockerfile for our backend service:

1. Copy the `ch4` folder to a new `ch5` folder, as follows:

    ```
    $ cp -R ch4 ch5
    ```

2. Create a new `backend/Dockerfile` file inside the `ch5` folder.

3. In this file, we first define a base image for our image, which will be version 20 of the node image:

    ```
    FROM node:20
    ```

    This image is provided by Docker Hub, similar to the `ubuntu` and `mongo` images we created containers from before.

> **Note**
>
> Be careful to only use official images and images created by trusted authors. The node image, for example, is officially maintained by the Node.js team.

4. Then, we set the working directory, which is where all files of our service will be placed inside the image:

    ```
    WORKDIR /app
    ```

    The WORKDIR instruction is similar to using cd in the terminal. It changes the working directory so that we do not have to prefix all the following commands with the full path. Docker creates the folder for us if it does not exist yet.

5. Next, we copy the package.json and package-lock.json files from our project to the working directory:

    ```
    COPY package.json package-lock.json ./
    ```

    The COPY instruction copies files from your local file system into the Docker image (relative to the local working directory). Multiple files can be specified, and the last argument to the instruction is the destination (in this case, the current working directory of the image).

    The package-lock.json file is needed to ensure that the Docker image contains the same versions of the npm packages as our local build.

6. Now, we run npm install to install all dependencies in the image:

    ```
    RUN npm install
    ```

    The RUN instruction executes a command in the working directory of the image.

7. Then, we copy the rest of our application from the local file system to the Docker image:

    ```
    COPY . .
    ```

    > **Note**
    >
    > Are you wondering why we initially just copied package.json and package-lock.json? Docker images are built layer by layer. Each instruction forms a layer of the image. If something changes, only the layers following the change are rebuilt. So, in our case, if any of the code changes, only this last COPY instruction is re-executed when rebuilding the Docker image. Only if dependencies change are the other COPY instruction and npm install re-executed. Using this order of instruction reduces the time required to rebuild the image immensely.

8. Finally, we run our application:

    ```
    CMD ["npm", "start"]
    ```

    The CMD instruction is not executed while building the image. Instead, it stores information in the metadata of the image, telling Docker which command to run when a container is instantiated from the image. In our case, the container is going to run npm start when using our image.

> **Note**
>
> You may have noticed that we passed a JSON array to the CMD instruction instead of simply writing CMD npm start. The JSON array version is called **exec form** and, if the first argument is an executable, will run the command directly without invoking a shell. The form without the JSON array is called **shell form** and will execute the command with a shell, prefixing it with /bin/sh -c. Running a command without a shell has the advantage of allowing the application to properly receive signals, such as a SIGTERM or SIGKILL signal when the application is terminated. Alternatively, the ENTRYPOINT instruction can be used to specify which executable should be used to run a certain command (it defaults to /bin/sh -c). In some cases, you may even want to run the script directly using CMD ["node", "src/index.js"], so that the script can properly receive *all* signals. However, this would require us to implement the SIGINT signal in our backend server to allow closing the container via *Ctrl + C*, so, to keep things simple, we just use npm start instead.

After creating our Dockerfile, we should also create a .dockerignore file to make sure unnecessary files are not copied into our image.

Creating a .dockerignore file

The COPY command, where we copy all files, would also copy the node_modules folder and other files, such as the .env file, which we do not want to go into our image. To prevent certain files from being copied into our Docker image, we need to create a .dockerignore file. Let's do that now:

1.   Create a new backend/.dockerignore file.

2.   Open it and enter the following contents to ignore the node_modules folder and all .env files:

    ```
    node_modules
    .env*
    ```

Now that we have defined a .dockerignore file, the COPY instructions will ignore these folders and files. Let's build the Docker image now.

Building the Docker image

After successfully creating the backend Dockerfile and a .dockerignore file to prevent certain files and folders from being added to our Docker image, we can now get started building our Docker image:

1.   Open a Terminal.

2.   Run the following command to build the Docker image:

    ```
    $ docker image build -t blog-backend backend/
    ```

We specified blog-backend as the name of our image and backend/ as the working directory.

After running the command, Docker will start by reading the Dockerfile and .dockerignore file. Then, it will download the node image and run our instructions one by one. Finally, it will export all layers and metadata into our Docker image.

The following screenshot shows the output of creating a Docker image:

```
● → ~/D/F/ch5 ⟩ main± > docker image build -t blog-backend backend/
 [+] Building 120.8s (11/11) FINISHED
 => [internal] load build definition from Dockerfile
 => => transferring dockerfile: 159B
 => [internal] load .dockerignore
 => => transferring context: 59B
 => [internal] load metadata for docker.io/library/node:latest
 => [auth] library/node:pull token for registry-1.docker.io
 => [1/5] FROM docker.io/library/node:latest@sha256:db2672e3c200b85e0b813cdb294fac16764711d7a66b41315e6261f2231f2331
 => => resolve docker.io/library/node:latest@sha256:db2672e3c200b85e0b813cdb294fac16764711d7a66b41315e6261f2231f2331
 => => sha256:05962e2d2a19f217fca55ed6b61aae16070c7c220c690aee1b60564e03bfb377 7.54kB / 7.54kB
 => => sha256:df2021ddb7d686bdbb125598b2a6163d63035f080356b3014595f354ea0b40d6 49.61MB / 49.61MB
 => => sha256:8d647f1dd7e741209a8a75083ccc889e39cb3e94c17f45441eae96e1a679d971 23.58MB / 23.58MB
 => => sha256:db2672e3c200b85e0b813cdb294fac16764711d7a66b41315e6261f2231f2331 1.21kB / 1.21kB
 => => sha256:63d8ba1a9663e2daa5fa8f49bce6b048cc5e31565f9786b1eca7d8be3f911ec5 2.00kB / 2.00kB
 => => sha256:5cdd9a70365f741a6b9f7a4e32cdb7d4aa29ac73da0b78ca0a83e937f285fdd5 63.99MB / 63.99MB
 => => sha256:95089c600b361807380090316c250b0b8eaf4fa2175b11ac8f49bb7581c61125 202.45MB / 202.45MB
 => => sha256:00e0658e345c7433de5051c897a98b802ae91e6375952104fa0fbf7d969ab581 3.37kB / 3.37kB
 => => sha256:95f3e8ec3833596867c7796e2860de73800b5599a63bec578722cd6ebe857b3f 49.00MB / 49.00MB
 => => extracting sha256:df2021ddb7d686bdbb125598b2a6163d63035f080356b3014595f354ea0b40d6
 => => sha256:335e1806199ff1916aeecfe3a5571fcd0012f56e3abfdbbfdbf0df6e8a859eef 2.23MB / 2.23MB
 => => sha256:764c4860e9c44928a589ad3af023dddd3bcff4b1bddff7c8377393e57fd47db9 452B / 452B
 => => extracting sha256:8d647f1dd7e741209a8a75083ccc889e39cb3e94c17f45441eae96e1a679d971
 => => extracting sha256:5cdd9a70365f741a6b9f7a4e32cdb7d4aa29ac73da0b78ca0a83e937f285fdd5
 => => extracting sha256:95089c600b361807380090316c250b0b8eaf4fa2175b11ac8f49bb7581c61125
 => => extracting sha256:00e0658e345c7433de5051c897a98b802ae91e6375952104fa0fbf7d969ab581
 => => extracting sha256:95f3e8ec3833596867c7796e2860de73800b5599a63bec578722cd6ebe857b3f
 => => extracting sha256:335e1806199ff1916aeecfe3a5571fcd0012f56e3abfdbbfdbf0df6e8a859eef
 => => extracting sha256:764c4860e9c44928a589ad3af023dddd3bcff4b1bddff7c8377393e57fd47db9
 => [internal] load build context
 => => transferring context: 297.81kB
 => [2/5] WORKDIR /app
 => [3/5] COPY package.json package-lock.json ./
 => [4/5] RUN npm install
 => [5/5] COPY . .
 => exporting to image
 => => exporting layers
 => => writing image sha256:df44d3116a1f3adf1445f2aed7fd220e45083da7388ce6ffa8699a7e80babaf0
 => => naming to docker.io/library/blog-backend
```

Figure 5.1 – The output when creating a Docker image

Now that we have successfully created our own image, let's create and run a container based on it!

Creating and running a container from our image

We have already created Docker containers based on the ubuntu and mongo images in *Chapter 2, Getting to Know Node.js and MongoDB*. Now, we are going to create and run a container from our own image. Let's get started doing that now:

1. Run the following command to list all available images:

    ```
    $ docker images
    ```

    This command should return the blog-backend image that we just created, and the mongo and ubuntu images that we previously used.

2. Make sure the dbserver container with our database is already running.

3. Then, start a new container, as follows:

```
$ docker run -it -e PORT=3001 -e DATABASE_URL=mongodb://host.
docker.internal:27017/blog -p 3001:3001 blog-backend
```

Let's break down the arguments to the docker run command:

- -it runs the container in interactive mode (-t to allocate a pseudo Terminal and -i to keep the input stream open).

- -e PORT=3001 sets the PORT environment variable inside the container to 3001.

- -e DATABASE_URL=mongodb://host.docker.internal:27017/blog sets the DATABASE_URL environment variable. Here, we replaced localhost with host.docker.internal, as the MongoDB service runs in a different container on the Docker host (our machine).

- -p 3001:3001 forwards port 3001 from inside the container to port 3001 on the host (our machine).

- blog-backend is the name of our image.

4. The blog-backend container is now running, which looks very similar to running the backend directly on our host in the Terminal. Go to http://localhost:3001/api/v1/posts to verify that it is running properly like before and returning all posts.

5. Keep the container running for now.

We have successfully packaged our backend as a Docker image and started a container from it! Now, let's do the same for our frontend.

Creating the frontend Dockerfile

After creating a Docker image for the backend service, we are now going to repeat the same process to create an image for the frontend. We will do so by first creating a Dockerfile, then the .dockerignore file, building the image, and then running a container. Now, we will start with creating the frontend Dockerfile.

In the Dockerfile for our frontend, we are going to use two images:

- A build image to build our project using **Vite** (which will be discarded, with only the build output kept)

- A final image, which will serve our static site using nginx

Let's make the Dockerfile now:

1. Create a new Dockerfile in the root of our project.

2. In this newly created file, first, use the `node` image again, but this time we tag it `AS build`. Doing so enables multi-stage builds in Docker, which means that we can use another base image later for our `final` image:

    ```
    FROM node:20 AS build
    ```

3. During build time, we also set the `VITE_BACKEND_URL` environment variable. In Docker, we can use the `ARG` instruction to define environment variables that are only relevant when the image is being built:

    ```
    ARG VITE_BACKEND_URL=http://localhost:3001/api/v1
    ```

> **Note**
>
> While the `ARG` instruction defines an environment variable that can be changed at build time using the `--build-arg` flag, the `ENV` instruction sets the environment variable to a fixed value, which will persist when a container is run from the resulting image. So, if we want to customize environment variables during build time, we should use the `ARG` instruction. However, if we want to customize environment variables during runtime, `ENV` is better suited.

4. We set the working directory to `/build` for the `build` stage, and then repeat the same instructions that we defined for the backend to install all necessary dependencies and copy over the necessary files:

    ```
    WORKDIR /build
    COPY package.json .
    COPY package-lock.json .
    RUN npm install
    COPY . .
    ```

5. Additionally, we execute `npm run build` to create a static build of our Vite app:

    ```
    RUN npm run build
    ```

6. Now, our `build` stage is completed. We use the `FROM` instruction again to create the `final` stage. This time, we base it off the `nginx` image, which runs an nginx web server:

    ```
    FROM nginx AS final
    ```

7. We set the working directory for this stage to `/var/www/html`, which is the folder that nginx serves static files from:

    ```
    WORKDIR /usr/share/nginx/html
    ```

8. Lastly, we copy everything from the /build/dist folder (which is where Vite puts the built static files) from the build stage into the final stage:

    ```
    COPY --from=build /build/dist .
    ```

    A CMD instruction is not needed in this case, as the nginx image already contains one to run the web server properly.

We successfully created a multi-stage Dockerfile for our frontend! Now, let's move on to creating the .dockerignore file.

Creating the .dockerignore file for the frontend

We also need to create a .dockerignore file for the frontend. Here, we also exclude, in addition to the node_modules/ folder and .env files, the backend/ folder containing our backend service and the .vscode, .git, and .husky folders. Let's create the .dockerignore file now:

1. Create a new .dockerignore file in the root of our project.

2. Inside this newly created file, enter the following contents:

    ```
    node_modules
    .env*
    backend
    .vscode
    .git
    .husky
    .commitlintrc.json
    ```

Now that we have ignored the files not necessary for the Docker image, let's build it!

Building the frontend Docker image

Just like before, we execute the docker build command to build the image, giving it the name blog-frontend and specifying the root directory as the path:

```
$ docker build -t blog-frontend .
```

Docker will now use the node image to build our frontend in the build stage. Then, it will switch to the final stage, use the nginx image, and copy over the built static files from the build stage.

Now, let's create and run the frontend container.

Creating and running the frontend container

Similarly to what we did for the backend container, we can also create and run a container from the blog-frontend image by executing the following command:

```
$ docker run -it -p 3000:80 blog-frontend
```

The nginx image runs the web server on port 80, so, if we want to use the port 3000 on our host, we need to forward from port 80 to 3000 by passing -p 3000:80.

After running this command and navigating to http://localhost:3000 in your browser, you should see the frontend being served properly and showing blog posts from the backend.

Now that we have created images and containers for the backend and frontend, we are going to learn about a way to manage multiple images more easily.

Managing multiple images using Docker Compose

Docker Compose is a tool that allows us to define and run multi-container applications with Docker. Instead of manually building and running the backend, frontend, and database containers, we can use Compose to build and run them all together. To get started using Compose, we need to create a compose.yaml file in the root of our project, as follows:

1. Create a new compose.yaml file in the root of our project.

2. Open the newly created file and start by defining the version of the Docker Compose file specification:

    ```
    version: '3.9'
    ```

3. Now, define a services object, in which we are going to define all the services that we want to use:

    ```
    services:
    ```

4. First, we have blog-database, which uses the mongo image and forwards port 27017:

    ```
    blog-database:
      image: mongo
      ports:
        - '27017:27017'
    ```

> **Note**
>
> In YAML files, the indentation of lines is very important to distinguish where properties are nested, so please be careful to put in the correct amount of spaces before each line.

5. Next, we have `blog-backend`, which uses the Dockerfile defined in the `backend/` folder, defines the environment variables for `PORT` and `DATABASE_URL`, forwards the port to the host, and depends on `blog-database`:

```
blog-backend:
  build: backend/
  environment:
    - PORT=3001
    - DATABASE_URL=mongodb://host.docker.internal:27017/blog
  ports:
    - '3001:3001'
  depends_on:
    - blog-database
```

6. Lastly, we have `blog-frontend`, which uses the Dockerfile defined in the root, defines the `VITE_BACKEND_URL` build argument, forwards the port to the host, and depends on `blog-backend`:

```
blog-frontend:
  build:
    context: .
    args:
      VITE_BACKEND_URL: http://localhost:3001/api/v1
  ports:
    - '3000:80'
  depends_on:
    - blog-backend
```

7. After defining the services, save the file.

8. Then, stop the backend and frontend containers running in the terminal by using the *Ctrl + C* key combination.

9. Also, stop the already running `dbserver` container, as follows:

```
$ docker stop dbserver
```

10. Finally, run the following command in the Terminal to start all services using Docker Compose:

```
$ docker compose up
```

Docker Compose will now create containers for the database, backend, and frontend and start all of them. You will start seeing logs being printed from the different services. If you go to `http://localhost:3000`, you can see that the frontend is running. Create a new post to verify that the connection to the backend and database works as well.

The following screenshot shows the output of docker compose up creating and starting all containers:

```
○ → ~/d/F/ch5 ⑂ main± > docker compose up
  [+] Running 3/0
   ✓ Container ch5-blog-database-1  Created
   ✓ Container ch5-blog-backend-1   Created
   ✓ Container ch5-blog-frontend-1  Created
  Attaching to ch5-blog-backend-1, ch5-blog-database-1, ch5-blog-frontend-1
```

Figure 5.2 – Creating and running multiple containers with Docker Compose

The output in the screenshot is then followed by log messages from the various services, including the MongoDB database service and our backend and frontend services.

Just like always, you can press *Ctrl + C* to stop all Docker Compose containers.

Now that we have set up Docker Compose, it's very easy to start all services at once and manage them all in one place. If you look at your Docker containers, you may notice that there are lots of stale containers still left over from previously building the blog-backend and blog-frontend containers. Let's now learn how to clean up those.

Cleaning up unused containers

After experimenting with Docker for a while, there will be lots of images and containers that are not in use anymore. Docker generally does not remove objects unless you explicitly ask it to, causing it to use a lot of disk space. If you want to remove objects, you can either remove them one by one or use one of the prune commands provided by Docker:

- docker container prune: This removes all stopped containers

- docker image prune: This removes all dangling images (images not tagged and not referenced by any container)

- docker image prune -a: This removes all images not used by any containers

- docker volume prune: This removes all volumes not used by any containers

- docker network prune: This cleans up networks not used by any containers

- docker system prune: This prunes everything except volumes

- docker system prune --volumes: This prunes everything

So, if you want to, for example, remove all unused containers, you should first make sure that all of the containers that you still want to use are running. Then, execute docker container prune in the terminal.

Now that we have learned how to use Docker locally to package our services as images and run them in containers, let's move on to deploying our full-stack application to the cloud.

Deploying our full-stack application to the cloud

After creating Docker images and containers locally, it's time to learn how to deploy them to the cloud so that everyone can access our services. In this book, we are going to use **Google Cloud** as an example, but the general process also applies to other providers such as **Amazon Web Services** (**AWS**) and **Microsoft Azure**. For the MongoDB database, we are going to use **MongoDB Atlas** but feel free to use any provider that can host a MongoDB database for you.

Creating a MongoDB Atlas database

To host our database, we are going to use the official cloud solution provided by the MongoDB team called MongoDB Atlas. Let's get started with registering and setting up a database now:

1. Go to `https://www.mongodb.com/atlas` and press **Try Free** to create a new account, or sign in with your existing account.

> **Note**
>
> The following instructions may vary slightly due to updates in the MongoDB Atlas UI. If the options are not available exactly as listed, try to follow the instructions on the website instead to create a database and a user to access it. This applies to all cloud services that we are going to set up throughout this chapter.

2. Select **Database** from the sidebar, then press **Create** to create a new database deployment. If you made a new account, you should be asked to create a new database deployment automatically.

3. Select **Shared / M0 Sandbox** (free instance) on Google Cloud and your preferred region.

4. Give your cluster a name of your choice.

5. Press **Create** to create your M0 sandbox cluster. It will take some time for the database to be accessible (typically around a minute). However, you can continue setting up the user while waiting for the cluster to be set up.

6. Go to the **Database** section in the sidebar and click on the **Connect** button next to your newly created cluster.

7. In the popup, select **Allow Access from Anywhere** and then press **Add IP Address**.

8. Set a username and password for your database user and press **Create database user**.

9. Press **Choose a connection method** and select **Drivers**.

10. A connection string will be shown; copy it and save it for later, inserting your previously set password instead of the `<password>` string. The connection string should have the following format:

```
mongodb+srv://<username>:<password>@<cluster-name>.<cluster-id>.
mongodb.net/?retryWrites=true&w=majority
```

11. Verify that the connection string works by opening a terminal and connecting to it using mongo shell:

```
$ mongosh "<connection-string>"
```

The following screenshot shows how the **Database Deployments** tab looks in MongoDB Atlas:

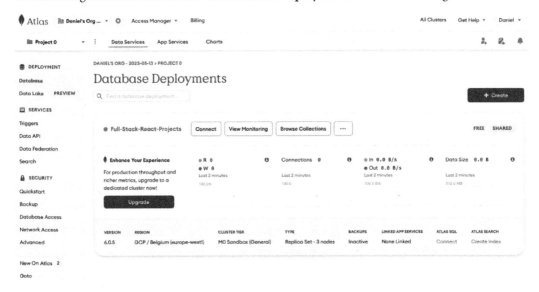

Figure 5.3 – A fresh M0 Sandbox database cluster deployed on MongoDB Atlas

Now that we have successfully created our MongoDB database in the cloud, we can move on to setting up Google Cloud to deploy our backend and frontend.

Creating an account on Google Cloud

Let's get started with Google Cloud by creating an account now. When creating an account, you need to enter billing information, but you will get $300 in free credits to trial using Google Cloud for free:

1. Go to https://cloud.google.com in your browser.

2. Press **Get started for free** if you do not have an account yet or press **Sign in** if you already have an account.

3. Log in with your Google account and follow the instructions until you have access to the Google Cloud console.

You should now see a screen similar to the following figure:

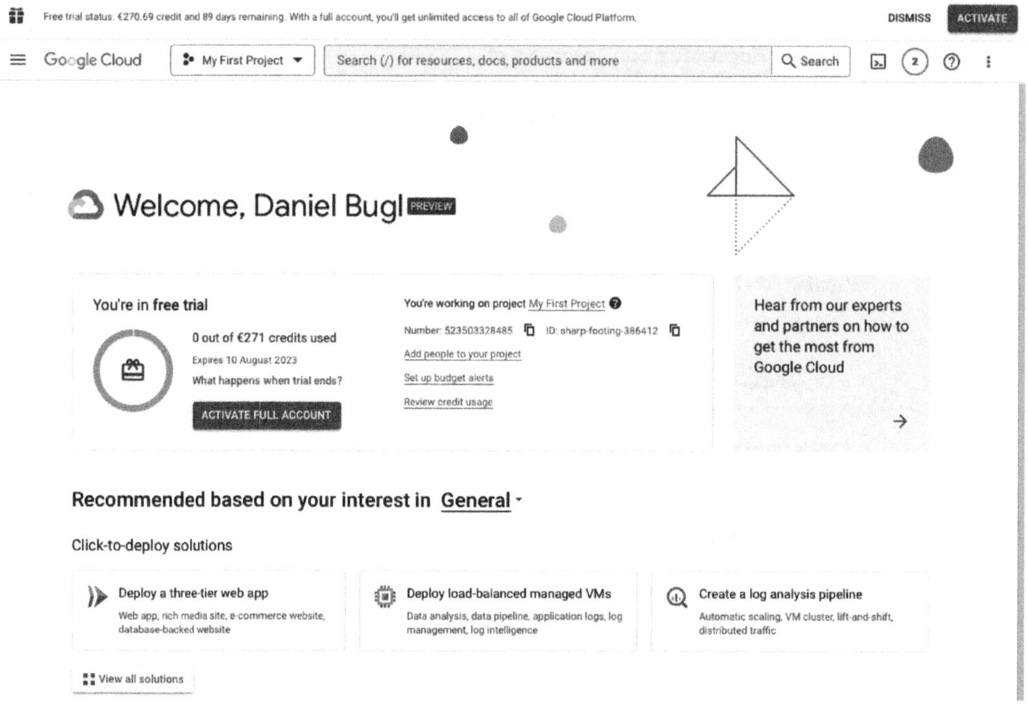

Figure 5.4 – The Google Cloud console after registering

Now that you have an account set up and ready, let's start deploying our services.

Deploying our Docker images to a Docker registry

Before we can deploy a service on a cloud provider, we first need to deploy our Docker image to a **Docker registry** so that the cloud provider can access it from there and create a container from it. Follow these steps to deploy our Docker images to Docker Hub, the official Docker registry:

1. Go to `https://hub.docker.com` and log in or register an account there.

2. Press the **Create repository** button to create a new repository. The repository will contain our image.

3. Enter `blog-frontend` as the repository name and leave the description empty and visibility `public`. Then press the **Create** button.

4. Repeat *Steps 2* and *3*, but this time, enter `blog-backend` as the repository name.

5. Open a new terminal and enter the following command to log in to your Docker Hub account:

```
$ docker login
```

Enter your username and password from Docker Hub and press the *Return* key or *Enter*.

6. Rebuild your image for Linux (to be able to deploy it to Google Cloud later), tag your image with your repository name (replace [USERNAME] with your Docker Hub username), and push it to the repository:

```
$ docker build --platform linux/amd64 -t blog-frontend .
$ docker tag blog-frontend [USERNAME]/blog-frontend
$ docker push [USERNAME]/blog-frontend
```

7. Navigate to backend/ in the terminal and repeat *Step 6* for the blog-backend image:

```
$ cd backend/
$ docker build --platform linux/amd64 -t blog-backend .
$ docker tag blog-backend [USERNAME]/blog-backend
$ docker push [USERNAME]/blog-backend
```

Now that both repositories are set up and the images are pushed to them, they should show up in Docker Hub with the following information: **Contains: Image | Last pushed: a few seconds ago**:

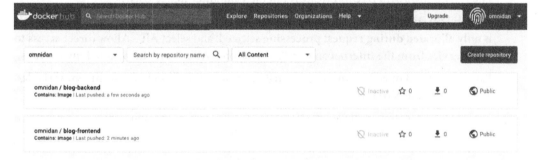

Figure 5.5 – Docker Hub giving an overview of our repositories

Now that our Docker images are published on a public Docker registry (Docker Hub), we can continue setting up Google Cloud to deploy our services.

> **Note**
>
> The repositories created on Docker Hub in this book are *public*. You can also choose to create up to one private repository on Docker Hub for free. Otherwise, you either need to have a Docker Hub subscription, use a different registry, or host your own registry. For example, **Google Artifact Registry** could be used to deploy private Docker images on **Cloud Run**.

Deploying the backend Docker image to Cloud Run

After successfully publishing our Docker images on the Docker Hub registry, it's time to deploy them using Google Cloud Run. Cloud Run is a managed compute platform. It allows us to run containers directly on the Google Cloud infrastructure, making app deployment simple and fast. The alternatives to Cloud Run would be Kubernetes-based infrastructure, such as AWS ECS Fargate or DigitalOcean.

Follow these steps to deploy the backend to Google Cloud Run:

1. Go to `https://console.cloud.google.com/`.

2. In the search bar at the top, enter `Cloud Run` and select the **Cloud Run – Serverless for containerized applications** product.

3. Press the **Create Service** button to create a new service.

> **Note**
>
> You may need to first create a project before you can create a service. In that case, just follow the instructions on the website to create a new project with a name of your choice. Afterward, press the **Create Service** button to create a new service.

4. Enter `[USERNAME]/blog-backend` in the **Container image URL** box.

5. Enter `blog-backend` in the **Service name** box, select a region of your choice, leave **CPU is only allocated during request processing** selected, and select **All – Allow direct access to your service from the Internet** and **Authentication – Allow unauthenticated invocations**.

6. Expand the **Container, Networking, Security** section, scroll down to **Environment variables**, and click on **Add Variable**.

7. Name the new environment variable `DATABASE_URL` and, as the value, enter the connection string from MongoDB Atlas, which you saved earlier.

> **Note**
>
> For simplicity, we are using a regular environment variable here. To make variables that contain credentials more secure, it should instead be added as a secret, which requires enabling the **Secrets API**, adding the secret to the secret manager, and then referencing the secret and choosing it to be exposed as an environment variable.

8. Leave the rest of the options as the default options and press **Create**.

9. You will get redirected to the newly created service, where the container is currently being deployed. Wait until it finishes deploying, which can take up to a couple of minutes.

10. When the service finishes deploying, you should see a checkmark and a URL. Click the URL to open the backend and you will see our **Hello World from Express!** message, which means that our backend was successfully deployed in the cloud!

A deployed service looks as follows in Google Cloud Run:

Figure 5.6 – A successfully deployed service on Google Cloud Run

Deploying the frontend Docker image to Cloud Run

For the frontend, we first need to rebuild the container to change the VITE_BACKEND_URL environment variable, which is statically built into our project. Let's do that first:

1. Open a terminal and run the following command to rebuild the frontend with the environment variable set:

```
$ docker build --platform linux/amd64 --build-arg "VITE_BACKEND_
URL=[URL]/api/v1" -t blog-frontend .
```

Make sure to replace [URL] with the URL to the backend service deployed on Google Cloud Run.

2. Tag it with your Docker Hub username and deploy the new version of the image to Docker Hub:

```
$ docker tag blog-frontend [USERNAME]/blog-frontend
$ docker push [USERNAME]/blog-frontend
```

Now, we can repeat similar steps as we did to deploy the backend to deploy our frontend as well:

1. Create a new Cloud Run service, enter [USERNAME]/blog-frontend in the **Container image URL** box and blog-frontend in the **Service name** box.

2. Pick a region of your choice and enable **Allow unauthenticated invocations**.

3. Expand **Container, Networking, Security** and change the container port from 8080 to 80.

4. Press **Create** to create the service and wait for it to be deployed.

5. Open the URL in your browser and you should see the deployed frontend. Adding and listing blog posts also works now by sending a request to the deployed backend, which then stores the posts in our MongoDB Atlas cluster.

We have successfully manually deployed our first full-stack React and Node.js application with a MongoDB database in the cloud! In the next sections, we are going to focus on automating testing and deployment using CI/CD.

Configuring CI to automate testing

Continuous Integration (**CI**) covers the automation of integrating code changes to find bugs quicker and keep the code base easily maintainable. Usually, this is facilitated by having scripts run automatically when a developer makes a pull/merge request before the code is merged into the main branch. This practice allows us to detect problems with our code early by, for example, running the linter and tests before the code can be merged. As a result, CI gives us more confidence in our code and allows us to make and deploy changes faster and more frequently.

The following figure shows a simple overview of a possible CI/CD pipeline:

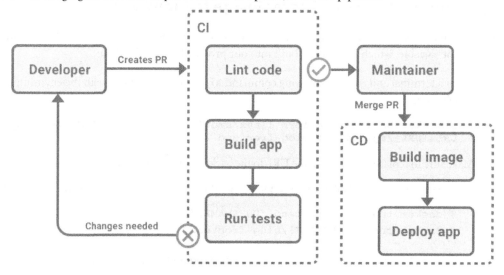

Figure 5.7 – Simple overview of a CI/CD pipeline

> **Note**
>
> In this book, we are going to use **GitHub Actions** for CI/CD. While the syntax and configuration files might look and work differently on other systems, such as GitLab CI/CD or CircleCI, the general principles are similar.

In GitHub Actions, **workflows** can be triggered when **events** occur in the repository, such as pushing to a branch, opening a new pull request, or creating a new issue. Workflows can contain one or multiple **jobs**, which can either run in parallel or sequentially. Each job runs inside its own **runner**, which takes instructions from the CI definition and executes them within a specified container. Inside jobs, **actions** can be performed, which are either existing actions provided on GitHub, or we can write our own actions.

Adding CI for the frontend

Let's get started creating a workflow that will build the frontend when a pull request is created, or a push is made to the main branch:

1. Create a new .github/ folder in the root of our project. Inside it, create a workflows/ folder.

2. Inside the .github/workflows/ folder, create a new file called frontend-ci.yaml.

3. Open the .github/workflows/frontend-ci.yaml file and start by giving the workflow a name:

    ```
    name: Blog Frontend CI
    ```

4. Then, listen to events by using the on keyword. We are going to execute the jobs when a new pull request or push is made to the main branch:

    ```
    on:
      push:
        branches:
          - main
      pull_request:
        branches:
          - main
    ```

5. Now, we define a job that will run the linter and build the frontend:

    ```
    jobs:
      lint-and-build:
    ```

6. We run the job on an ubuntu-latest container:

    ```
    runs-on: ubuntu-latest
    ```

7. We can make use of the matrix strategy to run our tests multiple times with different variables. In our case, we want to run it on multiple Node.js versions:

    ```
    strategy:
      matrix:
        node-version: [16.x, 18.x, 20.x]
    ```

8. Now, we define the steps inside our job. Make sure the `steps` are defined on the same indentation level as `strategy`:

    ```
    steps:
    ```

9. First, we use the `actions/checkout` action, which checks out our repository:

    ```
    - uses: actions/checkout@v3
    ```

10. Then, we use the `actions/setup-node` action, which sets up Node.js inside our container. Here, we make use of the `node-version` variable we defined earlier:

    ```
    - name: Use Node.js ${{ matrix.node-version }}
      uses: actions/setup-node@v3
      with:
        node-version: ${{ matrix.node-version }}
        cache: 'npm'
    ```

    The `cache` option specifies a package manager to be used for caching dependencies.

11. Finally, we install dependencies, run the linter, and build our frontend:

    ```
    - name: Install dependencies
      run: npm install
    - name: Run linter on frontend
      run: npm run lint
    - name: Build frontend
      run: npm run build
    ```

Adding CI for the backend

Now that we have added CI for the frontend, let's also add CI for the backend by building and testing it when a pull request is created or a push is made to the `main` branch:

1. Inside the `.github/workflows/` folder, create a new file called `backend-ci.yaml`.

2. Open the `.github/workflows/backend-ci.yaml` file, start by giving it a name, and listen to the same events as we did for the frontend CI:

    ```
    name: Blog Backend CI
    on:
      push:
        branches:
          - main
      pull_request:
        branches:
          - main
    ```

3. Now, we define a job that will build and test the backend. We set the default working directory to the `backend/` folder to run all actions inside that folder:

```
jobs:
  lint-and-test:
    runs-on: ubuntu-latest
    strategy:
      matrix:
        node-version: [16.x, 18.x, 20.x]
    defaults:
      run:
        working-directory: ./backend
```

4. Then, we use the same actions as for the frontend to check out the repository and set up Node.js:

```
    steps:
      - uses: actions/checkout@v3
      - name: Use Node.js ${{ matrix.node-version }}
        uses: actions/setup-node@v3
        with:
          node-version: ${{ matrix.node-version }}
          cache: 'npm'
      - name: Install dependencies
        run: npm install
```

5. Finally, we run the linter on our backend and run the tests:

```
      - name: Run linter on backend
        run: npm run lint
      - name: Run backend tests
        run: npm test
```

6. Save the workflow files and commit and push them to a GitHub repository by creating a new repository on GitHub and following their instructions to push an existing repository to GitHub.

7. Go to the repository on GitHub and select the **Actions** tab. You should see your workflows running here.

The following screenshot shows our CI workflows successfully running on GitHub:

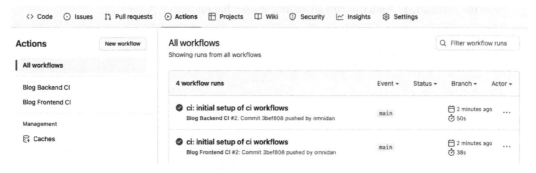

Figure 5.8 – Backend and frontend CI workflows successfully running in GitHub Actions

If we make a new pull request to the `main` branch, we can also see that our CI workflows are running properly on the new code. For example, if we added a way to tag posts from the frontend and accidentally made tags required in the backend without considering our previous rule of only the title being required, we will see that the corresponding tests failed:

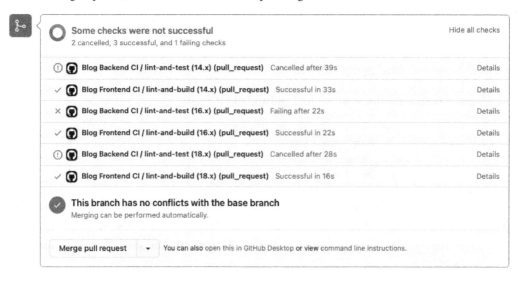

Figure 5.9 – Backend CI workflow failing in a pull request

We can also see that GitHub Actions automatically cancels the jobs running for other Node.js versions after one of them already failed, to avoid wasting time.

Now that we have successfully set up our CI workflows, let's continue by setting up CD to automate the deployment of our full-stack application.

Configuring CD to automate the deployment

After the pull/merge request is merged, **continuous delivery (CD)** comes into play. CD automates the release process by automatically deploying the services and applications for us. Usually, this involves a multi-stage process, where code is first automatically deployed to a staging environment and can then be manually deployed to other environments, up until production. If deployment to production is also an automated process, it is called **continuous deployment** instead of continuous delivery.

First, we need to get the credentials to authenticate with Docker Hub and Google Cloud. Then, we can set up the workflow for deploying our blog.

Getting Docker Hub credentials

Let's start by getting the credentials to access Docker Hub:

1. Go to `https://hub.docker.com/`.
2. Click on your profile and go to your account settings.
3. Click on the **Security** tab and press the **New Access Token** button.
4. As a description, write `GitHub Actions` and press the **Generate** button. Give **Read, Write, Delete** permissions.
5. Copy the access token and store it in a safe place.
6. Go to your GitHub repository and then go to **Settings | Secrets and variables | Actions**.
7. Press the **New repository secret** button to add a new secret. As a name, write `DOCKERHUB_USERNAME`, and as a secret value, use your username on Docker Hub.
8. Add another secret with the name `DOCKERHUB_TOKEN` and paste your previously created access token as the secret value.

Getting Google Cloud credentials

Now, we are going to create a service account to access Google Cloud Run:

1. Go to `https://console.cloud.google.com/`.
2. In the search box on the top, enter **Service accounts** and go to the **IAM and admin – Service accounts** page.
3. Press the **Create Service Account** button.
4. In the **Service account name** box, enter `GitHub Actions`. The ID should automatically be generated as `github-actions`. Press **Create and Continue**.
5. Grant the service access to the **Cloud Run Admin** role and press **Continue**.
6. Press **Done** to finish creating the service account.

7. On the overview list, copy the email of your newly created service account and save it for later use.

8. Go to the default compute service account by clicking on its email address. Go to the **Permissions** tab and press **Grant Access**.

9. Paste the email of your newly created service account into the **New principals** field and assign the **Cloud Run Service Agent** role. Press **Save** to confirm.

10. On the overview list, press the three dots icon to open actions on your `github-actions` service account and select **Manage keys**.

11. On the new page, press **Add Key** | **Create New Key**, and press **Create** in the popup. A JSON file should be downloaded.

12. Go to your GitHub repository, and go to **Settings** | **Secrets and variables** | **Actions**. Press the **New repository secret** button to add a new secret.

13. Add a new secret on your GitHub repository called `GOOGLECLOUD_SERVICE_ACCOUNT` and paste the previously copied email of your newly created service account as a secret value.

14. Add a new secret on your GitHub repository called `GOOGLECLOUD_CREDENTIALS` and as the secret, paste in the contents of the downloaded JSON file.

15. Add a new secret on your GitHub repository called `GOOGLECLOUD_REGION` and set the secret value to the region you selected when creating the Cloud Run services.

> **Note**
>
> For better security, Google recommends using **workload identity federation** instead of exporting service account key JSON credentials. However, setting up workload identity federation is a bit more complicated. More information on how to set it up can be found here: `https://github.com/google-github-actions/auth#setup`.

Defining the deployment workflow

Now that the credentials are available as secret values to our CI/CD workflows, we can get started defining the deployment workflow:

1. Inside the `.github/workflows/` folder, create a new file called `cd.yaml`.

2. Open the `.github/workflows/cd.yaml` file and start by giving it a name:

    ```
    name: Deploy Blog Application
    ```

3. For CD, we only execute the workflow when pushing to the `main` branch:

    ```
    on:
      push:
        branches:
          - main
    ```

4. We start defining a `deploy` job, in which we set `environment` to `production` and point the URL to the deployed frontend URL:

```
jobs:
  deploy:
    runs-on: ubuntu-latest
    environment:
      name: production
      url: ${{ steps.deploy-frontend.outputs.url }}
```

We will define a step with the `deploy-frontend` ID later, which stores a variable in `steps.deploy-frontend.outputs.url`.

5. For the steps, as we did before, we first need to check out our repository:

```
steps:
  - uses: actions/checkout@v3
```

6. Then, we log in to Docker Hub using the credentials we set earlier in our secrets:

```
- name: Login to Docker Hub
  uses: docker/login-action@v2
  with:
    username: ${{ secrets.DOCKERHUB_USERNAME }}
    password: ${{ secrets.DOCKERHUB_TOKEN }}
```

7. Next, we log in to Google Cloud using the credentials we set earlier:

```
- uses: google-github-actions/auth@v1
  with:
    service_account: ${{ secrets.GOOGLECLOUD_SERVICE_
ACCOUNT }}
    credentials_json: ${{ secrets.GOOGLECLOUD_CREDENTIALS
}}
```

8. Now, we build and push the backend Docker image using `docker/build-push-action`, which builds and pushes an image to a Docker registry:

```
- name: Build and push backend image
  uses: docker/build-push-action@v4
  with:
    context: ./backend
    file: ./backend/Dockerfile
    push: true
    tags: ${{ secrets.DOCKERHUB_USERNAME }}/blog-
backend:latest
```

9. After pushing the Docker image for the backend, we can now deploy it on Cloud Run, using the `google-github-actions/deploy-cloudrun` action:

```
- id: deploy-backend
  name: Deploy backend
  uses: google-github-actions/deploy-cloudrun@v1
  with:
    service: blog-backend
    image: ${{ secrets.DOCKERHUB_USERNAME }}/blog-
backend:latest
    region: ${{ secrets.GOOGLECLOUD_REGION }}
```

We gave this step the `deploy-backend` ID, as we need to use it to reference the backend URL to build the frontend image in the next step.

10. After building and deploying the backend, we build the frontend in a similar way, making sure to pass `VITE_BACKEND_URL` as `build-args`:

```
- name: Build and push frontend image
  uses: docker/build-push-action@v4
  with:
    context: .
    file: ./Dockerfile
    push: true
    tags: ${{ secrets.DOCKERHUB_USERNAME }}/blog-
frontend:latest
    build-args: VITE_BACKEND_URL=${{ steps.deploy-backend.
outputs.url }}/api/v1
```

11. Finally, we can deploy the frontend, giving this step the `deploy-frontend` ID, such that our environment URL can be set properly:

```
- id: deploy-frontend
  name: Deploy frontend
  uses: google-github-actions/deploy-cloudrun@v1
  with:
    service: blog-frontend
    image: ${{ secrets.DOCKERHUB_USERNAME }}/blog-
frontend:latest
    region: ${{ secrets.GOOGLECLOUD_REGION }}
```

12. Save the file and commit and push your changes to the `main` branch. You will see **Deploy Blog Application** being triggered on GitHub Actions.

The following screenshot shows the result of our blog application being successfully deployed via GitHub Actions:

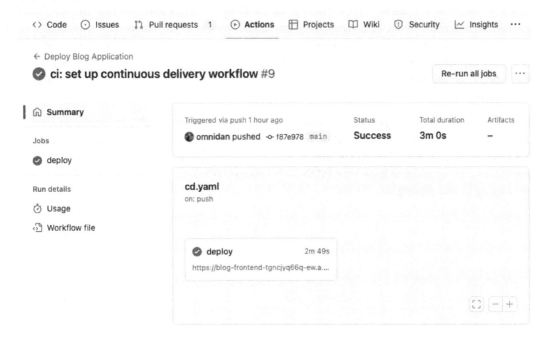

Figure 5.10 – A successful deployment of our full-stack application using GitHub Actions

You can click on the URL to open the deployed frontend and will see that it works the same way as the manually deployed version.

Congratulations! You have successfully automated the integration and deployment of your first full-stack application!

> **Note**
>
> In this book, we only created a single-stage deployment, deploying automatically directly to production. In a real-world application, you may want to define multiple stages. For example, CD could automatically deploy to a staging environment. Deploying to production could then be configured to require manual confirmation.

Summary

In this chapter, we started by learning how to create Docker images and how to instantiate local containers from them. Then, we automated this process by using Docker Compose. Next, we published our images on the Docker Hub registry to be able to deploy them on Google Cloud Run. We then manually deployed our full-stack application on Cloud Run. Finally, we learned how to set up CI/CD workflows with GitHub Actions to automate the running of the linter, tests, and deploying the blog application.

Up until now, everything in our application has been publicly accessible. With no user management, anyone can just create posts as any author. In the next chapter, *Chapter 6, Adding Authentication with JWT*, we are going to learn how to implement user accounts and authentication in our full-stack blog application. We are going to learn what **JSON Web Tokens** (**JWTs**) are and implement multiple routes for logging in and signing up.

Part 3:
Practicing Development of Full-Stack Web Applications

In this part, we are going to dive deeper into full-stack web development. We will start by adding authentication to our app using **JSON Web Tokens**. Then, we will learn how to improve the load time using server-side rendering. Next, we will learn how to optimize an app for search engines. We will also implement end-to-end tests using **Playwright** to make sure our app stays robust. Then, we will learn how to collect events, aggregate data using **MongoDB**, and create statistics to visualize the aggregated data using **Victory**. Toward the end of this part, we will learn about building a backend with a **GraphQL API** and how to interface with GraphQL on the frontend using **Apollo Client**.

This part includes the following chapters:

- *Chapter 6, Adding Authentication with JWT*
- *Chapter 7, Improving the Load Time Using Server-Side Rendering*
- *Chapter 8, Making Sure Customers Find You with Search Engine Optimization*
- *Chapter 9, Implementing End-To-End Tests Using Playwright*
- *Chapter 10, Aggregating and Visualizing Statistics Using MongoDB and Victory*
- *Chapter 11, Building a Backend with a GraphQL API*
- *Chapter 12, Interfacing with GraphQL on the Frontend Using Apollo Client*

6

Adding Authentication
with JWT

After developing and deploying our first full-stack application, we now have a way for anyone to create posts on our blog. However, since the author is an input field, anyone could enter any author, impersonating others! That's not good. In this chapter, we are going to add authentication with **JSON Web Token** (**JWT**) and functionalities to sign up and log into our application by adding additional routes using React Router.

In this chapter, we are going to cover the following main topics:

- What is JWT?
- Implementing login, signup, and authenticated routes in the backend using JWT
- Integrating login and signup in the frontend using React Router and JWT
- Advanced token handling

Technical requirements

Before we start, please install all the requirements from *Chapter 1, Preparing for Full-Stack Development*, and *Chapter 2, Getting to Know Node.js and MongoDB*.

The versions listed in those chapters are the ones used in this book. While installing a newer version should not be an issue, please note that certain steps might work differently. If you are having an issue with the code and steps provided in this book, please try using the versions mentioned in *Chapter 1* and *Chapter 2*.

You can find the code for this chapter on GitHub: `https://github.com/PacktPublishing/Modern-Full-Stack-React-Projects/tree/main/ch6`.

The CiA video for this chapter can be found at: `https://youtu.be/LloHmkgRLWk`.

What is JWT?

JWT, pronounced "jot", is an open industry standard (RFC 7519) for safely passing claims between multiple parties. Claims can be information about a certain party or object, such as the email address, user ID, and roles of a user. In our case, we will pass JWTs between our backend and frontend.

JWT is used by many products and services and is supported by third-party authentication providers, such as Auth0, Okta, and Firebase Auth. It is easy to parse JWTs as we only need to base64 decode them and parse the JSON string. After verifying the signature, we can be sure that the JWT is authentic and trust the claims within it.

JWTs consist of the following components:

- **Header**: Containing the algorithm and token type
- **Payload**: Containing the data/claims of the token
- **Signature**: For verifying that the token was created by a legit source

These three components form a JWT as they're joined into a single string, separated by a period (.), as follows:

```
header.payload.signature
```

Let's look at each component separately.

JWT header

The JWT header typically consists of a token type (in our case, JWT), specified by the `typ` property, and the algorithm used to create the signature (in our case, we will use HMAC SHA256, a SHA256 hash-based message authentication code), specified by the `alg` property. The header is defined as a JSON object, like so:

```
{
    "alg": "HS256",
    "typ": "JWT"
}
```

This JSON object is then base64 encoded and forms the first part of the JWT.

JWT payload

The main part of the JWT is the payload, which contains all claims. Claims are information about an entity (such as the user) and additional data. The JWT standard distinguishes between three types of claims:

- **Registered claims**: These are predefined claims and it's recommended that they're set. They include information about the following:

  - The issuer (`iss`), which is the entity that created the token.

  - The expiration time (`exp`), which tells us when the token expires.

  - The subject (`sub`), which tells us about the entity identified by the token (such as the user who generated the token during a login).

  - The audience (`aud`), which tells us about the intended recipients of the token.

  - The issued at time (`iat`), which tells us when the token was created.

  - The not before time (`nbf`), which specifies a time before which the token is not valid yet.

  - The JWT ID (`jti`), which provides a unique identifier for the JWT. It's used to prevent JWTs from being replayed.

> **Note**
>
> The JSON object properties defined in the JWT standard are all three-letter names to keep the JWT as compact as possible.

- **Public claims**: These are additional claims that are commonly used and shared across many services. A list of those can be found on the **Internet Assigned Numbers Authority (IANA)** website: `https://www.iana.org/assignments/jwt/jwt.xhtml`. If we want to store additional information, we should always consult this list first to see if we can use a standardized claim name.

- **Private claims**: These are custom-defined claims, which are neither registered nor public. If we need a special claim that isn't defined yet, we can make a private claim that only our services will understand.

All claims are optional, but it makes sense to at least include one claim to identify the subject, such as the `sub` registered claim.

Putting together what we've learned, we can create the following example payload:

```
{
    "sub": "1234567890",
    "name": "Daniel Bugl",
    "admin": true
}
```

In our example, the sub claim is a registered claim, the name claim is a public claim, and the admin claim is a private claim.

The payload is also base64 encoded and forms the second part of the JWT. As such, this information is publicly readable by anyone who has access to the token. Do not put secret information into the payload or header of a JWT! However, the information cannot be *changed* without invalidating the existing signature, making all claims tamper-proof. Only a backend service with access to the private key can generate a new signature to create a valid JWT.

JWT signature

The final part of a JWT is its signature. The signature is what proves that all the information that we've defined up until now has not been tampered with. The signature is created by taking the base64-encoded header and payload, joining those strings with a period symbol, and using the specified algorithm to sign it with a secret key:

```
HMACSHA256(
    base64UrlEncode(header) + "." + base64UrlEncode(payload),
    secret
)
```

Now that we've learned about the different components of a JWT, let's put this all together to create a valid JWT.

Creating a JWT

Follow these steps to create a JWT:

1. Go to the https://jwt.io/ website and scroll down to the **Debugger** section.

2. Enter our previously defined header and payload.

3. Enter full-stack as the secret.

4. The encoded JWT should update on the fly as you're changing the values.

As you can see, we have successfully created our first JWT:

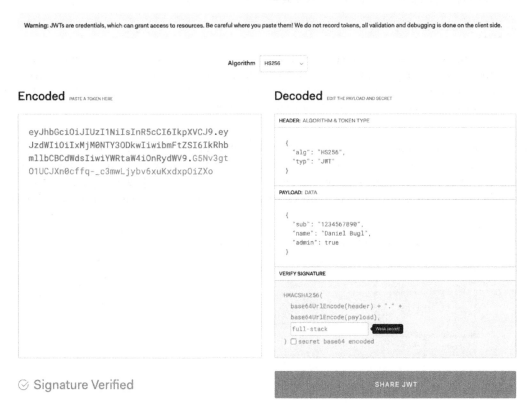

Figure 6.1 – Our first JWT, created with the jwt.io debugger

The generated JWT consists of three components, each of them base64-encoded and separated by periods. In the debugger, they are highlighted in three different colors. Try changing the base64 string in the "Encoded" section by removing some characters; you will see that the JWT is now invalid due to an "Invalid Signature" issue. Now that we've created our first JWT, let's learn how to use it.

Using JWT

In the login process, we are going to generate a JWT for the logged-in user in the backend. This JWT will be returned to the user's browser. When the user wants to access a protected route, we can send the JWT to the backend server by using the `Authorization` header with the `Bearer` schema, as follows:

```
Authorization: Bearer <token>
```

The backend can then check for this header, verify the signature of the token, and grant the user access to certain routes. By sending the token in a header instead of a cookie, we don't have to deal with CORS issues that we would have when dealing with cookies.

> **Note**
>
> Be careful not to send too much data in the header since some servers do not accept more than 8 KB in headers. This means that, for example, complex role information should not be stored in the JWT claims as it might take up too much space. Instead, this kind of information could be stored in the database associated with a user ID from the JWT.

An interesting advantage of using a JWT is that the authentication server and the actual backend for our app do not have to be the same. We could have a separate authentication service, get a JWT, and in the backend verify the signature of the JWTs to guarantee that they were generated by the authentication service. This allows us to use external services for authentication, such as Auth0, Okta, or Firebase Auth.

The following diagram shows the authorization flow for a JWT:

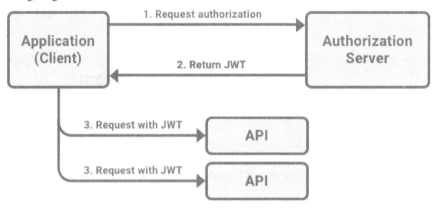

Figure 6.2 – Authorization flow for a JWT

As we can see, the application requests authorization to the authorization server, which can also be either a third-party provider, a separate service, or part of the backend service. Then, when authorization is granted (if the login details are correct), the authorization server returns a JWT. This JWT can then be used to access protected routes on APIs. Before granting access, the JWT signature is validated to ensure that it has not been tampered with.

Storing JWT

We should take great care about where we store the JWT. Local storage is *not* a good way to store authentication information such as a JWT. Cross-site scripting can be used to steal all data in local storage. For short-lived tokens, we can store them in a JavaScript runtime variable (such as a React context). For longer-term storage, we could use an `httpOnly` cookie, which has additional security guarantees.

Now that we've learned how JWT works, let's put theory into practice and implement login, signup, and authenticated routes in the backend using JWT.

Implementing login, signup, and authenticated routes in the backend using JWTs

Now that we've learned about JWTs, we'll implement them in our backend. First, we need to create a user model in our database, after which we can create routes to sign up and log into our app. Finally, we will implement authenticated routes that are only accessible with a JWT.

Creating the user model

We'll start the backend implementation by creating a user model, as follows:

1. Copy the `ch5` folder to a new `ch6` folder, as follows:

    ```
    $ cp -R ch5 ch6
    ```

2. Open the `ch6` folder in VS Code.

3. Create a new `backend/src/db/models/user.js` file and define a new `userSchema` inside it:

    ```
    import mongoose, { Schema } from 'mongoose'

    const userSchema = new Schema({
    ```

4. A user should have a required unique `username` and a required `password`:

    ```
      username: { type: String, required: true, unique: true },
      password: { type: String, required: true },
    })
    ```

5. Create and export the model:

    ```
    export const User = mongoose.model('user', userSchema)
    ```

6. At this point, let's also adjust the post model so that we can store a reference to a user ID instead of the username as the author. Edit `backend/src/db/models/post.js`, as follows:

```
author: { type: Schema.Types.ObjectId, ref: 'user',
required: true },
```

We changed the type to `ObjectId`, with a reference to the `user` model, and made `author` required (as you will need to be logged in to create a post after we add an authenticated route later in this chapter).

Making `author` required means that the unit tests will need to be adjusted, but doing so is left as an exercise for you.

Now that we've successfully created the user model, let's move on to creating the signup service so that we have a way to create new users.

Creating the signup service

When a user signs up, we need to hash the password provided by the user before storing it in the database. We should never store passwords in plaintext as that would mean that if our database gets leaked, an attacker will have access to the passwords of all users. Hashing is a one-way function that turns a string into a different string in a deterministic way. This means that, for example, if we do `hash("password1")`, we get a specific string every time we do it. However, if we do `hash("password2")`, we get a completely different string. By choosing a good hash function, we can ensure that reversing a hash is so computationally expensive that it is impossible to do in a reasonable time. When the user signs up, we can store the hash of their password. When a user then enters their password to log in, we can hash their entered password again and compare it to the hash in the database.

Let's start implementing the signup service with hashed passwords:

1. Install the `bcrypt` npm package. We are going to use this to hash the password before storing it:

```
$ cd backend
$ npm install bcrypt@5.1.1
```

2. Create a new `backend/src/services/users.js` file and import `bcrypt` and the `User` model:

```
import bcrypt from 'bcrypt'
import { User } from '../db/models/user.js'
```

3. Define a `createUser` function that takes `username` and `password` values:

```
export async function createUser({ username, password }) {
```

4. Inside this function, we use the `bcrypt.hash` function to create a hash from the plaintext password using 10 salt rounds (repeating the hashing 10 times to make it even harder to reverse it):

    ```
    const hashedPassword = await bcrypt.hash(password, 10)
    ```

5. Now, we can create a new user and store it in our database:

    ```
    const user = new User({ username, password: hashedPassword })
    return await user.save()
    }
    ```

For brevity, we won't cover creating tests for the user services. Refer to *Chapter 3, Implementing a Backend Service Using Express, Mongoose ODM, and Jest*, for information on how to create tests for your service functions. You can write similar tests to what we did for the posts service functions.

After creating the signup service, we can create the signup route.

Creating the signup route

Now, let's expose the signup service function by adding an API route for it:

1. Create a new `backend/src/routes/users.js` file and import the `createUser` service:

    ```
    import { createUser } from '../services/users.js'
    ```

2. Define a new `userRoutes` function and expose a `POST /api/v1/user/signup` route. This route creates a new user from the request body and return the username:

    ```
    export function userRoutes(app) {
      app.post('/api/v1/user/signup', async (req, res) => {
        try {
          const user = await createUser(req.body)
          return res.status(201).json({ username: user.username })
        } catch (err) {
          return res.status(400).json({
            error: 'failed to create the user, does the username
    already exist?'
          })
        }
      })
    }
    ```

In this case, we define a singular `user` route instead of calling it `users` as we are only dealing with one user at a time. To keep things simple, the error handling is very rudimentary. It would be a good idea to distinguish between the different errors that can happen and show a different error message, depending on the error.

3. Edit `backend/src/app.js` and import the `userRoutes` function:

```
import { postRoutes } from './routes/posts.js'
import { userRoutes } from './routes/users.js'
```

4. In the same file, call the `userRoutes` function after the `postRoutes` function to mount them:

```
postRoutes(app)
userRoutes(app)
```

5. Make sure the `dbserver` container is running in Docker.

6. Start the backend by running the following command in a Terminal inside the `backend/` folder:

```
$ cd backend
$ npm run dev
```

7. Now, make a request to the new `POST /api/v1/user/signup` route. You will see that creating a user works if `username` and `password` values are provided properly. Enter the following code in your browser console while the backend is running, on a blank tab or at `http://localhost:3001/`:

```
const res = await fetch('http://localhost:3001/api/v1/user/
signup', {
    method: 'POST',
    headers: { 'Content-Type': 'application/json' },
    body: JSON.stringify({ username: 'dan', password: 'hunter2'
})
})
console.log(await res.json())
```

8. If we try creating another user with the same username (by executing the same fetch again), it will fail because the `username` field is defined to be unique in Mongoose.

Now that we have successfully created our first user, let's continue by creating the login service to allow our user to log in.

Creating the login service

So far, we have only created a user in our database. As we aren't authorizing the user yet, we haven't dealt with JWTs yet. Let's start doing that now:

1. Open a new Terminal and install the `jsonwebtoken` library, which contains functions to deal with the creation and verification of JWTs:

```
$ cd backend
$ npm install jsonwebtoken@9.0.2
```

2. Edit the `backend/src/services/users.js` file and import `jwt` from the `jsonwebtoken` library:

```
import jwt from 'jsonwebtoken'
```

3. Define a new `loginUser` function, which takes a username and password:

```
export async function loginUser({ username, password }) {
```

4. Now, fetch a user with the given `username` from our database:

```
const user = await User.findOne({ username })
if (!user) {
  throw new Error('invalid username!')
}
```

5. Then, use `bcrypt.compare` to compare the entered password to the hashed password from the database:

```
const isPasswordCorrect = await bcrypt.compare(password, user.
password)
if (!isPasswordCorrect) {
  throw new Error('invalid password!')
}
```

6. If the user correctly enters a username and password, we use `jwt.sign()` to create a new JWT and sign it with a secret. For the secret, we use an environment variable:

```
const token = jwt.sign({ sub: user._id }, process.env.JWT_
SECRET, {
  expiresIn: '24h',
})
```

In the last argument, we also specify that our token should be valid for 24 hours.

> **Note**
>
> We are using the user ID, not the username, to identify the user. This is done to future-proof the system as the user ID is a value that will never change. In the future, we might want to add a way to change the username. It would be hard to deal with such a change if we always use the username to identify the user.

7. Lastly, we return the token:

```
return token
}
```

8. Now, we define the JWT_SECRET environment variable by editing the .env file:

    ```
    JWT_SECRET=replace-with-random-secret
    ```

    Make sure you generate a safe JWT secret for the production environment, which you never expose or use in development environments or for debugging! If you want to deploy your app to Google Cloud Run again, you would also need to add this secret as an environment variable there.

9. We'll also add one to .env.template as an example:

    ```
    JWT_SECRET=replace-with-random-secret
    ```

After successfully creating a login service to create and sign JWTs, we can create the login route.

Creating the login route

We still need to expose the login service as an API route for users to be able to log in. Let's do that now:

1. Edit the backend/src/routes/users.js file and import the loginUser function:

    ```
    import { createUser, loginUser } from '../services/users.js'
    ```

2. Add a new POST /api/v1/user/login route inside the userRoutes function, where we call the loginUser function and return the token:

    ```
    app.post('/api/v1/user/login', async (req, res) => {
      try {
        const token = await loginUser(req.body)
        return res.status(200).send({ token })
      } catch (err) {
        return res.status(400).send({
          error: 'login failed, did you enter the correct
    username/password?'
        })
      }
    })
    ```

3. If the backend is not running anymore, start it again. Then, make a request to /api/v1/user/login to test it out by entering the following code in your browser console:

    ```
    const res = await fetch('http://localhost:3001/api/v1/user/
    login', {
        method: 'POST',
        headers: { 'Content-Type': 'application/json' },
        body: JSON.stringify({ username: 'dan', password: 'hunter2'
    ```

```
    })
    })
    console.log(await res.json())
```

4. We have successfully created a valid JWT! To verify that the JWT is valid, we can paste it into the debugger at `https://jwt.io/`. Make sure that you also change the secret in the **Verify Signature** section on the page, as shown in the following screenshot:

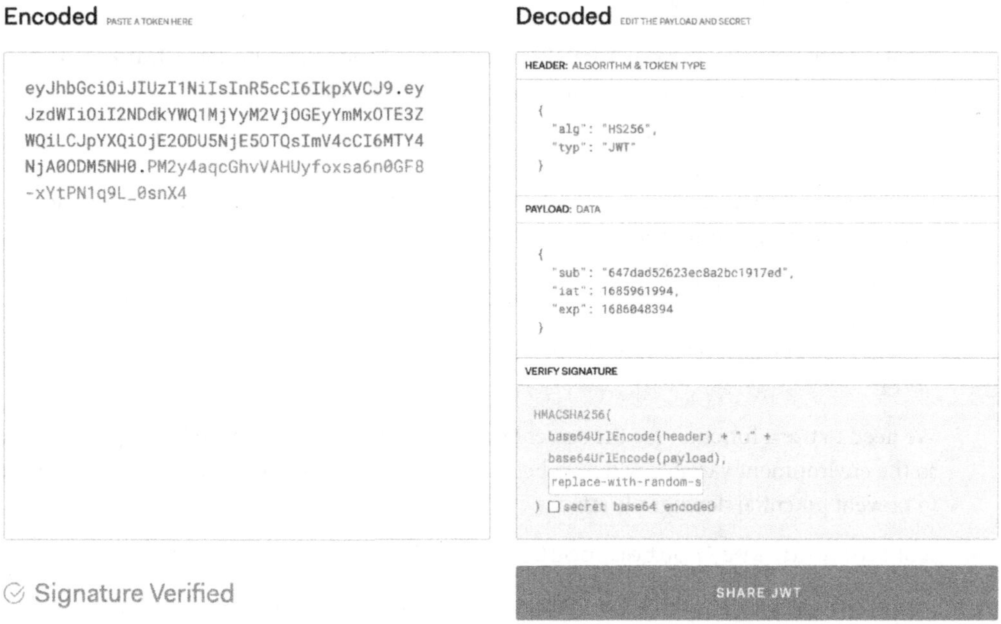

Encoded PASTE A TOKEN HERE

Decoded EDIT THE PAYLOAD AND SECRET

```
eyJhbGciOiJIUzI1NiIsInR5cCI6IkpXVCJ9.ey
JzdWIiOiI2NDdkYWQ1MjYyM2VjOGEyYmMxOTE3Z
WQiLCJpYXQiOjE2ODU5NjE5OTQsImV4cCI6MTY4
NjA0ODM5NH0.PM2y4aqcGhvVAHUyfoxsa6n0GF8
-xYtPN1q9L_0snX4
```

HEADER: ALGORITHM & TOKEN TYPE

```
{
    "alg": "HS256",
    "typ": "JWT"
}
```

PAYLOAD: DATA

```
{
    "sub": "647dad52623ec8a2bc1917ed",
    "iat": 1685961994,
    "exp": 1686048394
}
```

VERIFY SIGNATURE

```
HMACSHA256(
    base64UrlEncode(header) + "." +
    base64UrlEncode(payload),
    replace-with-random-s
) □ secret base64 encoded
```

⊘ Signature Verified

SHARE JWT

Figure 6.3 – Verifying the JWT created from the login service

> **Note**
>
> When copying the token from the JSON response in your browser, make sure that you are copying the full string value, and not the truncated one (with ... in the middle of the string). Otherwise, the JWT might not decode properly in the debugger.

After successfully logging our user in and creating a token for them, we can now protect certain routes and make sure that only logged-in users can access them.

Defining authenticated routes

Now that we have successfully created a valid JWT, we can start protecting routes. To do so, we are going to use the express-jwt library, as follows:

1. Install the express-jwt npm package:

    ```
    $ cd backend
    $ npm install express-jwt@8.4.1
    ```

2. Create a new backend/src/middleware folder. Inside it, create a new backend/src/middleware/jwt.js file and import expressjwt there:

    ```
    import { expressjwt } from 'express-jwt'
    ```

3. Create and export a requireAuth middleware by using the expressjwt function and your secret and algorithm settings:

    ```
    export const requireAuth = expressjwt({
      secret: () => process.env.JWT_SECRET,
      algorithms: ['HS256'],
    })
    ```

    We need to use a function for the secret because dotenv isn't initialized at import time yet, so the environment variable will only be available later. Specifying the algorithms is required to prevent potential downgrade attacks.

4. Edit backend/src/routes/posts.js and import the requireAuth middleware:

    ```
    import { requireAuth } from '../middleware/jwt.js'
    ```

5. Add the middleware to the create route. Middleware in Express can be added to specific routes by passing it as a second argument to the function, as follows:

    ```
    app.post('/api/v1/posts', requireAuth, async (req, res) => {
    ```

6. Repeat the same for the edit route:

    ```
    app.patch('/api/v1/posts/:id', requireAuth, async (req, res)
    => {
    ```

7. Now, do this for the delete route:

    ```
    app.delete('/api/v1/posts/:id', requireAuth, async (req, res)
    => {
    ```

8. Try accessing the routes without being logged in. You will see that they fail with a **401 Unauthorized** status. Execute the following code into your browser console:

```
const res = await fetch('http://localhost:3001/api/v1/posts', {
    method: 'POST',
    headers: {
        'Content-Type': 'application/json'
    },
    body: JSON.stringify({ title: 'Test Post' })
})
console.log(await res.json())
```

You can see the results of executing the code in the following screenshot:

```
> fetch('http://localhost:3001/api/v1/posts', {
      method: 'POST',
      headers: {
          'Content-Type': 'application/json'
      },
      body: JSON.stringify({ title: 'Test Post' })
  })
    .then(res => res.json())
    .then(console.log)
<  ▶ Promise {<pending>}
```

```
⊗  ▶ POST http://localhost:3001/api/v1/posts 401 (Unauthorized)          VM899:1 ⊕
⊗  ▶ Uncaught (in promise) SyntaxError: Unexpected token '<', "          VM900:1
   <!DOCTYPE "... is not valid JSON
```

```
> fetch('http://localhost:3001/api/v1/posts', {
      method: 'POST',
      headers: {
          'Content-Type': 'application/json',
          'Authorization': 'Bearer
  eyJhbGciOiJIUzI1NiIsInR5cCI6IkpXVCJ9.eyJzdWIiOiI2NDdkYWQ1MjYyM2VjOGEyYmMxOTTE
  3ZWQiLCJpYXQiOjE2ODU5NjE5OTQsImV4cCI6MTY4NjA0ODM5NH0.PM2y4aqcGhvVAHUyfoxsa6n
  0GF8-xYtPN1q9L_0snX4'
      },
      body: JSON.stringify({ title: 'Test Post' })
  })
    .then(res => res.json())
    .then(console.log)
<  ▶ Promise {<pending>}
   ▶ {title: 'Test Post', tags: Array(0), _id: '647dd5a928f9824089ee712f', creat
     edAt: '2023-06-05T12:31:37.512Z', updatedAt: '2023-06-05T12:31:37.512Z', …}
```

Figure 6.4 – Attempting to access a protected route without a JWT and then with a JWT

> **Note**
> Instead of using the `express-jwt` library, we could also manually extract the token from the `Authorization` header and use the `jwt.verify` function from the `jsonwebtoken` library to verify it.

The routes are protected now, but we aren't considering which user accessed them. Let's do that now by accessing the currently logged-in user from the token.

Accessing the currently logged-in user

After adding authenticated routes, we successfully protected some routes so that they can only be accessed by logged-in users. However, it's still possible to edit posts of other users or create posts under a different username. Let's change that:

1. Edit the `backend/src/services/posts.js` file and add a `userId` argument to the `createPost` function, *removing* `author` from the object:

    ```
    export async function createPost(userId, { title, author,
    contents, tags }) {
    ```

2. Instead of setting the author through the request body, we will set the author to the ID of the logged-in user:

    ```
        const post = new Post({ title, author: userId, contents, tags
    })
    ```

3. We adjust the `updatePost` and `deletePost` functions similarly (adding the `userId` argument, removing the `author` argument, and removing the author variable from the `$set` object), ensuring that the currently logged-in user is the author of the post:

    ```
    export async function updatePost(userId, postId, { title,
    author, contents, tags }) {
      return await Post.findOneAndUpdate(
        { _id: postId, author: userId },
        { $set: { title, author, contents, tags } },
        { new: true },
      )
    }


    export async function deletePost(userId, postId) {
      return await Post.deleteOne({ _id: postId, author: userId })
    }
    ```

In our case, we simply fetch a post with the given ID and an author as the current user. We could still extend this code to first fetch the post with the given ID, check if it exists (if not, return a **404 Not Found** error), and if it does exist, verify that the author is the currently logged-in user (if not, return a **403 Forbidden** error).

> **Note**
>
> This is a breaking API change and requires changing the tests. For brevity, we will not go through adjusting the tests step by step here, so this is left as an exercise for you.

4. Edit the `backend/src/routes/posts.js` file and use the `req.auth.sub` variable to pass the user ID to the `createPost` function:

    ```
    const post = await createPost(req.auth.sub, req.body)
    ```

5. Do the same for the `updatePost` function:

    ```
    const post = await updatePost(req.auth.sub, req.params.id,
    req.body)
    ```

6. Also, do this for the `deletePost` function:

    ```
    const { deletedCount } = await deletePost(req.auth.sub, req.
    params.id)
    ```

7. Try creating a new post; you will see that it is created by the user identified in the JWT. You can do this by executing the following code in the browser console (don't forget to replace `<TOKEN>` with your previously generated JWT):

    ```
    const res = await fetch('http://localhost:3001/api/v1/posts', {
        method: 'POST',
        headers: {
            'Content-Type': 'application/json',
            'Authorization': 'Bearer <TOKEN>'
        },
        body: JSON.stringify({ title: 'Test Post' })
    })
    console.log(await res.json())
    ```

Editing and deleting your posts is also possible, but not for posts from other users anymore!

> **Info**
>
> The `express-jwt` middleware stores all decoded claims from the JWT in a `req.auth` object. So, we can access any claims made when creating our JWT here. Of course, the middleware validates the JWT signature against the defined secret first, to ensure that it received an authentic JWT.

Now that we've set up the login, signup, and authenticated routes, let's continue by integrating login and signup in the frontend.

Integrating login and signup in the frontend using React Router and JWT

Now that we have successfully implemented authorization in the backend, let's start extending the frontend with signup and login pages and connecting them to the backend. First, we are going to learn how to implement multiple pages in a React app using React Router. Then, we are going to implement the signup UI and connect it to the backend. Afterward, we are going to implement a login UI, store the token in the frontend, and set up automatic redirects when we are successfully logged in. Finally, we are going to update the code for creating posts to pass the token in the Authorization header and properly access our authenticated route.

Let's get started with the frontend integration by setting up React Router.

Using React Router to implement multiple routes

React Router is a library that allows us to manage routing in our app by defining multiple pages on different routes, just like what we have done in Express for API routes, but for the frontend! Let's set up React Router:

1. Install the `react-router-dom` library in the frontend project (the root of the `ch6` folder, not inside the `backend` folder):

    ```
    $ npm install react-router-dom@6.21.0
    ```

2. Edit `src/App.jsx` and import the `createBrowserRouter` function and `RouterProvider` component:

    ```
    import { createBrowserRouter, RouterProvider } from 'react-
    router-dom'
    ```

3. Create a new `router` and define the routes. First, we'll define an index route for rendering our `Blog` component:

    ```
    const router = createBrowserRouter([
      {
    ```

```
        path: '/',
        element: <Blog />,
    },
])
```

4. Then, in the `App` component, replace the `<Blog>` component with `<RouterProvider>`, as follows:

```
export function App() {
    return (
        <QueryClientProvider client={queryClient}>
            <RouterProvider router={router} />
        </QueryClientProvider>
    )
}
```

5. Start the frontend by running the following command in the root of the `ch6` folder:

```
$ npm run dev
```

6. The blog should render the same way as before, but now, we can start defining new routes! You can verify that React Router is working by going to a page that we did not define – for example, `http://localhost:5173/test`. React Router will display the default 404 page, as shown in the following screenshot:

Unexpected Application Error!

404 Not Found

 Hey developer 🖐

You can provide a way better UX than this when your app throws errors by providing your own `ErrorBoundary` or `errorElement` prop on your route.

Figure 6.5 – The default 404 page provided by React Router

Now that we have successfully set up React Router, we can move on to creating the signup page.

Creating the signup page

We will start by updating our folder structure so that it supports multiple pages. Then, we will implement a `Signup` component and define a `/signup` route to link to it. Follow these steps:

1. Create a new `src/pages/` folder.

2. Move the `src/Blog.jsx` file into the `src/pages/` folder. When VS Code asks you to update all imports, select **Yes**. Alternatively, update the import in `src/App.jsx`, as follows:

    ```
    import { Blog } from './pages/Blog.jsx'
    ```

3. Create a new `src/api/users.js` file and define an API function for the `signup` route, as follows:

    ```
    export const signup = async ({ username, password }) => {
      const res = await fetch(`${import.meta.env.VITE_BACKEND_URL}/
    user/signup`, {
        method: 'POST',
        headers: { 'Content-Type': 'application/json' },
        body: JSON.stringify({ username, password }),
      })
      if (!res.ok) throw new Error('failed to sign up')
      return await res.json()
    }
    ```

    We are checking for `res.ok` here, which will be `false` when the response status code is an error code, such as `400`.

4. Create a new `src/pages/Signup.jsx` file, import the `useState`, `useMutation`, and `useNavigate` hooks from `react-router-dom`, as well as the `signup` function, and define a `Signup` component there:

    ```
    import { useState } from 'react'
    import { useMutation } from '@tanstack/react-query'
    import { useNavigate } from 'react-router-dom'

    import { signup } from '../api/users.js'

    export function Signup() {
    ```

5. In this component, we first create state hooks for the `username` and `password` fields:

    ```
    const [username, setUsername] = useState('')
    const [password, setPassword] = useState('')
    ```

6. Then, we use the `useNavigate` hook to get a function to navigate to a different route:

```
const navigate = useNavigate()
```

7. We also define a `useMutation` hook to send the `signup` request. On success, we navigate to the `/login` route, which we will define soon:

```
const signupMutation = useMutation({
  mutationFn: () => signup({ username, password }),
  onSuccess: () => navigate('/login'),
  onError: () => alert('failed to sign up!'),
})
```

In case of an error, we could also use the `signupMutation.isError` state and the response from the backend to show a more nicely formatted error message.

8. Then, we define a function to handle the submission of the form, as we did for the `CreatePost` component:

```
const handleSubmit = (e) => {
  e.preventDefault()
  signupMutation.mutate()
}
```

9. Now, we create a simple form to enter a username, password, and a button to submit the request, similar to the `CreatePost` component:

```
return (
  <form onSubmit={handleSubmit}>
    <div>
      <label htmlFor='create-username'>Username: </label>
      <input
        type='text'
        name='create-username'
        id='create-username'
        value={username}
        onChange={(e) => setUsername(e.target.value)}
      />
    </div>
    <br />
    <div>
      <label htmlFor='create-password'>Password: </label>
      <input
        type='password'
        name='create-password'
        id='create-password'
```

```
              value={password}
              onChange={(e) => setPassword(e.target.value)}
          />
        </div>
        <br />
        <input
          type='submit'
          value={signupMutation.isPending ? 'Signing up...' :
'Sign Up'}
          disabled={!username || !password || signupMutation.
isPending}
        />
      </form>
    )
}
```

10. Edit `src/App.jsx` and import the `Signup` page component:

```
import { Signup } from './pages/Signup.jsx'
```

11. Add a new `/signup` route that points to the `Signup` page component:

```
const router = createBrowserRouter([
  {
    path: '/',
    element: <Blog />,
  },
  {
    path: '/signup',
    element: <Signup />,
  },
])
```

After defining the signup page, we still need a way to link to it. Let's add the link now.

Linking to other routes using the Link component

Now that we have multiple pages in our blog app, we need to link between them. To do this, we can use the `Link` component provided by React Router. We could also use a normal link by using `<a href="">`, but that would cause a full page refresh. The `Link` component uses client-side routing and thus avoids doing a full refresh of the page. Instead, it immediately renders the new component on the client side.

Follow these steps to create a link from the index page to the signup page:

1. Create a new `src/components/Header.jsx` file and import the `Link` component from `react-router-dom`:

    ```
    import { Link } from 'react-router-dom'
    ```

2. Define a component and return the `Link` component to define a link to the signup route, as follows:

    ```
    export function Header() {
      return (
        <div>
          <Link to='/signup'>Sign Up</Link>
        </div>
      )
    }
    ```

3. Edit `src/pages/Blog.jsx` and import the `Header` component:

    ```
    import { Header } from '../components/Header.jsx'
    ```

4. Then, render the `Header` component in the `Blog` component:

    ```
    return (
      <div style={{ padding: 8 }}>
        <Header />
        <br />
        <hr />
        <br />
        <CreatePost />
    ```

5. Edit `src/pages/Signup.jsx` and import the `Link` component:

    ```
    import { useNavigate, Link } from 'react-router-dom'
    ```

6. Add the `Link` component to link back to the index page:

    ```
    return (
      <form onSubmit={handleSubmit}>
        <Link to='/'>Back to main page</Link>
        <hr />
        <br />
    ```

Now that we've successfully linked our signup page, let's continue by creating the login page.

Creating the login page and storing the JWT

Now that we have successfully defined the signup page, we can create the login page. However, first, we need to come up with a way to store the JWT. We shouldn't store it in local storage as a potential attacker can steal the token from there (through, for example, script injection). In a **single-page application (SPA)**, where we have no page reloads, a safe and simple way to store the token is to store it in the runtime using a React context. Let's do that now:

1. Create a new `src/contexts/` folder. Inside it, create a `src/contexts/AuthContext.jsx` file and import the `createContext`, `useState`, and `useContext` functions from `react`:

    ```
    import { createContext, useState, useContext } from 'react'
    import PropTypes from 'prop-types'
    ```

2. Then, define the following context:

    ```
    export const AuthContext = createContext({
      token: null,
      setToken: () => {},
    })
    ```

3. Next, define an `AuthContextProvider` component that provides the context with a state hook:

    ```
    export const AuthContextProvider = ({ children }) => {
      const [token, setToken] = useState(null)
      return (
        <AuthContext.Provider value={{ token, setToken }}>
          {children}
        </AuthContext.Provider>
      )
    }

    AuthContextProvider.propTypes = {
      children: PropTypes.element.isRequired,
    }
    ```

4. Also, define a hook to use the context with a `useState`-like API:

    ```
    export function useAuth() {
      const { token, setToken } = useContext(AuthContext)
      return [token, setToken]
    }
    ```

5. Edit `src/App.jsx` and import `AuthContextProvider`:

    ```
    import { AuthContextProvider } from './contexts/AuthContext.jsx'
    ```

6. Wrap `RouterProvider` with `AuthContextProvider` to make it available to all pages:

    ```
    <AuthContextProvider>
        <RouterProvider router={router} />
    </AuthContextProvider>
    ```

7. Edit `src/api/users.js` and define a new login function:

    ```
    export const login = async ({ username, password }) => {
      const res = await fetch(`${import.meta.env.VITE_BACKEND_URL}/
    user/login`, {
        method: 'POST',
        headers: { 'Content-Type': 'application/json' },
        body: JSON.stringify({ username, password }),
      })
      if (!res.ok) throw new Error('failed to login')
      return await res.json()
    }
    ```

8. Copy over the `src/pages/Signup.jsx` file to a new `src/pages/Login.jsx` file and adjust the import and component name. Also, add a new import for the `useAuth` hook:

    ```
    import { login } from '../api/users.js'
    import { useAuth } from '../contexts/AuthContext.jsx'

    export function Login() {
    ```

9. Next, edit `src/pages/Login.jsx`, add the `useAuth` hook, adjust the `signupMutation` to call login, set the token, and navigate to the index page upon successfully logging in:

    ```
    const [, setToken] = useAuth()

    const loginMutation = useMutation({
      mutationFn: () => login({ username, password }),
      onSuccess: (data) => {
        setToken(data.token)
        navigate('/')
      },
      onError: () => alert('failed to login!'),
    })

    const handleSubmit = (e) => {
      e.preventDefault()
    ```

```
        loginMutation.mutate()
    }
```

10. Adjust the submit button, as follows:

```
        <input
          type='submit'
          value={loginMutation.isPending ? 'Logging in...' : 'Log
    In'}
          disabled={!username || !password || loginMutation.
    isPending}
        />
```

11. Edit src/App.jsx and import the Login page:

```
    import { Login } from './pages/Login.jsx'
```

12. Lastly, define the /login route, as follows:

```
    {
      path: '/login',
      element: <Login />,
    },
```

With that, our signup and login pages are working properly, but we still need to link to the login page and show the currently logged-in user on the index page. Let's do that now.

Using the stored JWT and implementing a simple logout

In this section, we are going to check if the user is logged in already by checking if there is a valid JWT stored in the context. Then, we are going to use the auth context hook to log our user out again by simply removing the token from it. This is not a full logout as the JWT is still technically valid. For a full logout, we would have to invalidate the token in the backend (for example, by blacklisting that token in the authentication service database). This process is called **token revocation**.

Let's start using the stored JWT and implement a simple logout:

1. Install the jwt-decode library in the root of our project (the frontend):

```
    $ npm install jwt-decode@4.0.0
```

2. Edit src/components/Header.jsx and import the jwtDecode function and the useAuth hook:

```
    import { jwtDecode } from 'jwt-decode'
    import { useAuth } from '../contexts/AuthContext.jsx'
```

3. Get the token from the `useAuth` hook in the `Header` component:

```
export function Header() {
  const [token, setToken] = useAuth()
```

4. Add a check for if the token is properly set. If it is, parse the token and render the user ID from it:

```
if (token) {
  const { sub } = jwtDecode(token)
  return (
    <div>
      Logged in as <b>{sub}</b>
```

> **Note**
>
> In this case, we are only decoding the token in one place. If this functionality is used in multiple places, it would make sense to abstract the decoding into a separate hook.

5. Additionally, we'll show a button to log out here, which just resets the token:

```
      <br />
      <button onClick={() => setToken(null)}>Logout</button>
    </div>
  )
}
```

6. While we're at it, let's also add a link to the login page to the header, if the user isn't logged in yet:

```
return (
  <div>
    <Link to='/login'>Log In</Link> | <Link to='/signup'>Sign Up</Link>
  </div>
)
```

Congratulations! We have successfully implemented a simple JWT user authentication flow. However, you may have noticed that all the users in our blog appear as their user ID, not with their username. Let's change that.

Fetching the usernames

To show the usernames instead of the user IDs, we are going to create a `User` component that will fetch user information from an endpoint in our backend, which we are going to create now. For now, we will only show the username, but in the future, this feature could be used to fetch other information, such as the avatar or full name of the user.

Implementing the backend endpoint

Let's get started by implementing the backend endpoint for fetching user information:

1. Edit `backend/src/services/users.js` and add a new function to get user information by `id`. As a fallback, we return the user ID if we can't find a matching user:

    ```
    export async function getUserInfoById(userId) {
      try {
        const user = await User.findById(userId)
        if (!user) return { username: userId }
        return { username: user.username }
      } catch (err) {
        return { username: userId }
      }
    }
    ```

    We specifically make sure we only return the username here, to avoid leaking the password or other sensitive user information!

2. Edit `backend/src/routes/users.js` and import the newly defined function there:

    ```
    import { createUser, loginUser, getUserInfoById } from '../
    services/users.js'
    ```

3. Then, define a new route inside the `userRoutes` function, which will get a user with a specific ID. For this route, we use the plural `users` as we are dealing with multiple users here:

    ```
    app.get('/api/v1/users/:id', async (req, res) => {
      const userInfo = await getUserInfoById(req.params.id)
      return res.status(200).send(userInfo)
    })
    ```

4. Since we are already working on the backend, let's also change the existing `author` filter so that it works with usernames. Edit `backend/src/services/posts.js` and import the `User` model:

    ```
    import { User } from '../db/models/user.js'
    ```

5. Refactor the `listPostsByAuthor` function by finding a user with the given username, then listing all posts by the user ID (if one was found):

    ```
    export async function listPostsByAuthor(authorUsername, options)
    {
      const user = await User.findOne({ username: authorUsername })
      if (!user) return []
      return await listPosts({ author: user._id }, options)
    }
    ```

Now that we have an endpoint that returns user information for a given user ID, let's use it in the frontend!

Implementing a User component to fetch and render the username

In the frontend, we are going to create a component that will fetch and render the username. React Query helps us a lot here because we don't need to worry about fetching the same user IDs multiple times – it will cache the result for us and instantly return it, instead of making another request.

Follow these steps to implement a `User` component:

1. First, we need to define the API function. Edit `src/api/users.js` and add a function to get the user info by `id`:

   ```
   export const getUserInfo = async (id) => {
     const res = await fetch(`${import.meta.env.VITE_BACKEND_URL}/
   users/${id}`, {
       method: 'GET',
       headers: { 'Content-Type': 'application/json' },
     })
     return await res.json()
   }
   ```

2. Create a new `src/components/User.jsx` file and import `useQuery`, `PropTypes`, and the API function:

   ```
   import { useQuery } from '@tanstack/react-query'
   import PropTypes from 'prop-types'
   import { getUserInfo } from '../api/users.js'
   ```

3. Now, define the component and get the user info via the query hook:

   ```
   export function User({ id }) {
     const userInfoQuery = useQuery({
       queryKey: ['users', id],
       queryFn: () => getUserInfo(id),
     })
     const userInfo = userInfoQuery.data ?? {}
   ```

4. We render the username if available and fall back to the ID otherwise:

   ```
   return <strong>{userInfo?.username ?? id}</strong>
   }
   ```

5. Lastly, we define the prop types for the component:

```
User.propTypes = {
  id: PropTypes.string.isRequired,
}
```

6. Now, we can make use of the newly created component and import it in `src/components/Header.jsx`:

```
import { User } from './User.jsx'
```

7. Then, we can edit the existing code to render the `User` component instead of directly rendering the user ID:

```
Logged in as <User id={sub} />
```

8. Next, we repeat the same process for `src/components/Post.jsx` and import the `User` component:

```
import { User } from './User.jsx'
```

9. Then, we adjust the code to render the `User` component:

```
Written by <User id={author} />
```

Now, our usernames will all render properly again, as shown in the following screenshot:

Logged in as **dan**
Logout

Figure 6.6 – Properly fetching and showing the username

Now that usernames show up properly, we need to do one more thing: send the JWT header when creating posts.

Sending the JWT header when creating posts

When creating a post, we don't need to send the author anymore. Instead, we need to send the JWT with the `Authentication` header.

Let's refactor the code so that we can do this:

1. Edit `src/api/posts.jsx` and adjust the `createPost` function so that it accepts a JWT as the first argument, which is then passed on inside an `Authentication` header:

    ```
    export const createPost = async (token, post) => {
      const res = await fetch(`${import.meta.env.VITE_BACKEND_URL}/
    posts`, {
        method: 'POST',
        headers: {
          'Content-Type': 'application/json',
          Authorization: `Bearer ${token}`,
        },
        body: JSON.stringify(post),
      })
      return await res.json()
    }
    ```

2. Edit `src/components/CreatePost.jsx` and import the `useAuth` hook:

    ```
    import { useAuth } from '../contexts/AuthContext.jsx'
    ```

3. Get the JWT from the `useAuth` hook inside the component:

    ```
    export function CreatePost() {
      const [token] = useAuth()
    ```

4. *Remove* the `author` state:

    ```
    const [author, setAuthor] = useState('')
    ```

5. Also, *remove* the `author` state from the `createPost` function and instead pass in the `token` state as the first argument:

    ```
    mutationFn: () => createPost(token, { title, author,
    contents }),
    ```

6. Before rendering the component, check if the user is logged in by checking if a token exists. If the user is not logged in, we tell them to log in first:

    ```
    if (!token) return <div>Please log in to create new posts.</
    div>

    return (
      <form onSubmit={handleSubmit}>
    ```

7. *Remove* the following code to remove the `author` field:

```
<br />
<div>
  <label htmlFor='create-author'>Author: </label>
  <input
    type='text'
    name='create-author'
    id='create-author'
    value={author}
    onChange={ (e) => setAuthor (e.target.value) }
  />
</div>
```

Now, creating a post works successfully again! It stores the user ID of the currently logged-in user in the database as the author and resolves it to the username when showing the post.

Next, we'll learn about advanced token handling.

Advanced token handling

You may have noticed that our simple authentication solution is still missing some features that a fully-fledged solution should have, such as the following:

- Using asymmetric keys for the tokens so that we can verify the authenticity (using the public key) without exposing our secret (the private key) to all services. Up until now, we have been using a symmetric key, which means that we need the same secret to generate and verify a JWT.

- Storing tokens in safe `httpOnly` cookies so that they can be accessed again, even when the page is refreshed or closed.

- Invalidating tokens after logging out on the backend.

Implementing these things requires a lot of effort manually, so it is best practice to use an authentication solution such as Auth0 or Firebase Auth. These solutions work similarly to our simple JWT implementation, but they provide an external authentication service to create and handle the tokens for us. This chapter intended to introduce how those providers work behind the scenes so that you can easily understand and integrate any of the providers as you see fit in your projects.

So far, all users have been considered equal, with everyone being allowed to create posts, but only update and delete their own posts. For a public blog, it would be good to have a way for administrators to delete other people's posts to moderate the content on the platform. A good way to add roles is to store and fetch them from the database. While adding roles in the JWT is technically possible, it has some downsides, such as the need to invalidate existing tokens and create a new token when the roles change.

Summary

In this chapter, we learned how JWTs work in depth. First, we learned about the theory of authentication and JWTs, and how to manually create them. Then, we implemented login, signup, and authenticated routes in the backend. Next, we integrated these routes in the frontend by creating new pages and routing between them using React Router. Finally, we wrapped up this chapter by learning about advanced token handling and giving pointers on more things to learn about authentication and role management.

In the next chapter, *Chapter 7, Improving the Load Time Using Server-Side Rendering*, we are going to learn how to implement server-side rendering to improve the initial load time of our blog. We are already doing a lot of requests on the first load (fetching all blog posts, then the usernames of each author). We can bundle them together by doing this on the backend.

7

Improving the Load Time Using Server-Side Rendering

After implementing authentication using JWTs, let's focus on optimizing the performance of our blog app. We are going to start by benchmarking the current load time of our application and learn about various metrics to consider. Then, we are going to learn how to render React components and fetch data on the server. At the end of this chapter, we are going to briefly cover advanced server-side rendering concepts.

In this chapter, we are going to cover the following main topics:

- Benchmarking the load time of our application
- Rendering React components on the server
- Server-side data fetching
- Advanced server-side rendering

Technical requirements

Before we start, please install all requirements mentioned in *Chapter 1*, *Preparing For Full-Stack Development*, and *Chapter 2*, *Getting to Know Node.js and MongoDB*.

The versions listed in those chapters are the ones used in the book. While installing a newer version should not be an issue, please note that certain steps might work differently on a newer version. If you are having an issue with the code and steps provided in this book, please try using the versions mentioned in *Chapters 1* and *2*.

You can find the code for this chapter on GitHub: `https://github.com/PacktPublishing/Modern-Full-Stack-React-Projects/tree/main/ch7`.

The CiA video for this chapter can be found at: `https://youtu.be/O0lmicibYWQ`.

Benchmarking the load time of our application

Before we can get started improving the load time, we first must learn about the metrics to benchmark the performance of our application. The main metrics for measuring the performance of web applications are called **Core Web Vitals**, and they are as follows:

- **First Contentful Paint (FCP)**: This measures the loading performance of an app by reporting the time until the first image or text block is rendered on the page. A good target would be to get this metric below 1.8 seconds.

- **Largest Contentful Paint (LCP)**: This measures the loading performance of an app by reporting the time until the largest image or text block is visible within the viewport. A good target would be to get this metric below 2.5 seconds.

- **Total Blocking Time (TBT)**: This measures the interactivity of an app by reporting the time between the FCP and a user being able to interact with the page. A good target would be to get this metric below 200 milliseconds.

- **Cumulative Layout Shift (CLS)**: This measures the visual stability of an app by reporting unexpected movement on the page during loading, such as a link first being loaded on the top of the page, but then getting pushed further down to the bottom when other elements load. While this metric does not directly measure the actual performance of the app, it is still an important metric to consider, as it can lead to annoying the users when they attempt to click on something, but the layout shifts.

All these metrics can be measured by using the open-source **Lighthouse** tool, which is also available from the Google Chrome DevTools under the **Lighthouse** panel. Let's get started benchmarking our app now:

1. Copy the ch6 folder to a new ch7 folder, as follows:

    ```
    $ cp -R ch6 ch7
    ```

2. Open the ch7 folder in VS Code, open a Terminal, and run the frontend with the following command:

    ```
    $ npm run dev
    ```

3. Make sure the dbserver container is running in Docker.

4. Open a new Terminal and run the backend with the following command:

    ```
    $ cd backend
    $ npm run dev
    ```

5. Go to http://localhost:5173 in Google Chrome and open the inspector (right-click and then press **Inspect**).

> **Note**
>
> It would be best to do this in an incognito tab so that extensions do not interfere with the measurements.

6. Open the **Lighthouse** tab (it might be hidden by the >> menu). It should look as follows:

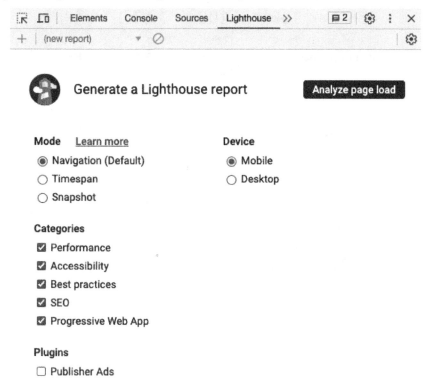

Figure 7.1 – The Lighthouse tab in Google Chrome DevTools

7. In the **Lighthouse** tab, leave all options as their default settings and click on the **Analyze page load** button.

    Lighthouse will start analyzing the website and give a report with metrics such as **First Contentful Paint**, **Largest Contentful Paint**, **Total Blocking Time**, and **Cumulative Layout Shift**. As we can see, our app already performs quite well in terms of TBT and CLS but performs particularly badly in terms of FCP and LCP. See the following screenshot for reference:

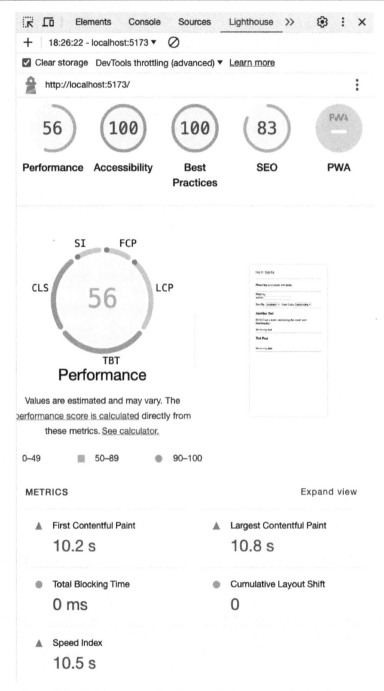

Figure 7.2 – Lighthouse results when analyzing our app in development
mode (while hovering the cursor over the performance score)

There are two reasons why the paint takes so long. Firstly, we are running the server in dev mode, which generally makes everything slower. Additionally, we are rendering everything on the client side, which means that the browser first must download and execute our JavaScript code before it can start rendering the interface. Let's statically build our frontend and benchmark again now:

1. Install the `serve` tool globally with the following command, which is a tool that runs a simple web server:

    ```
    $ npm install -g serve
    ```

2. Build the frontend with this command (execute it in the root of our project):

    ```
    $ npm run build
    ```

3. Statically serve our app by running the following command:

    ```
    $ serve dist/
    ```

4. Open `http://localhost:3000` in Google Chrome and run Lighthouse again (you may have to clear the old reports or click the list in the top left and select (**new report**) to analyze again).

    You should see the results of the new benchmark on the statically served frontend, which is closer to how it would be served in production. You can see an example of the results in the following screenshot:

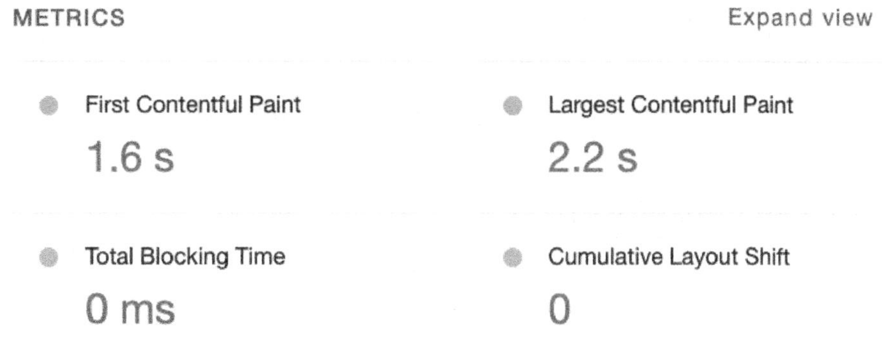

    METRICS   Expand view

    ● First Contentful Paint   ● Largest Contentful Paint

    1.6 s   2.2 s

    ● Total Blocking Time   ● Cumulative Layout Shift

    0 ms   0

Figure 7.3 – Lighthouse report results on our statically built app

Now, the results are pretty good! However, it could still be improved further. Additionally, **Core Web Vitals** do not take into account the cascading requests to get the author usernames. While the first and largest contentful paints are fast in our app, the author names are not even loaded yet at that point. In addition to the Lighthouse report, we can also take a look at the **Network** tab to further debug the performance of our app, as follows:

1. In DevTools, go to the **Network** tab.

2. Refresh the page while the tab is open. You will see a waterfall diagram and the measured time to make requests, as shown in the following screenshot:

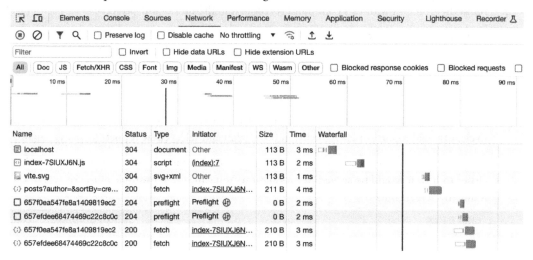

Figure 7.4 – The waterfall diagram on the Network tab

But the times are extremely low (all below 10 ms). This is because our backend is running locally, so there is no network delay. This is not a realistic scenario. In production, we would have latency on every request that we make, so we would first have to wait for the blog posts to be pulled, then fetch the names of authors for each author separately. We can use the DevTools to simulate a slower network connection; let's do that now:

1. At the top of the **Network** tab, click on the **No throttling** dropdown.

2. Select the **Slow 3G** preset. See the following screenshot for reference:

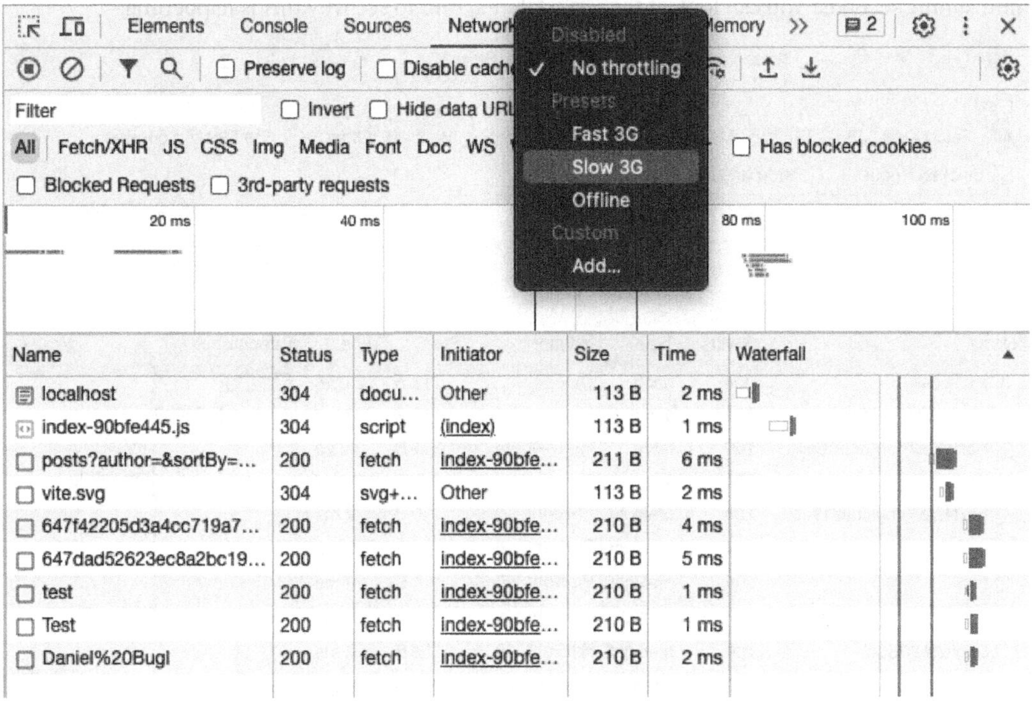
Elements
Console
Sources
Network
Memory
Disabled
No throttling
Presets
Fast 3G
Slow 3G
Offline
Custom
Add...
Preserve log
Disable cache
Filter
Invert
Hide data URLs
All
Fetch/XHR
JS
CSS
Img
Media
Font
Doc
WS
Has blocked cookies
Blocked Requests
3rd-party requests
20 ms
40 ms
80 ms
100 ms
Name
Status
Type
Initiator
Size
Time
Waterfall
localhost 304 docu... Other 113 B 2 ms
index-90bfe445.js 304 script (index) 113 B 1 ms
posts?author=&sortBy=... 200 fetch index-90bfe... 211 B 6 ms
vite.svg 304 svg+... Other 113 B 2 ms
647f42205d3a4cc719a7... 200 fetch index-90bfe... 210 B 4 ms
647dad52623ec8a2bc19... 200 fetch index-90bfe... 210 B 5 ms
test 200 fetch index-90bfe... 210 B 1 ms
Test 200 fetch index-90bfe... 210 B 1 ms
Daniel%20Bugl 200 fetch index-90bfe... 210 B 2 ms

Figure 7.5 – Simulating slow networks in Google Chrome DevTools

> **Note**
>
> Lighthouse has a form of throttling built in, which is like the network throttling we are using here, but not the same. While the network throttling in DevTools is a fixed delay added to all requests, the throttling in Lighthouse attempts to simulate a more realistic scenario by adjusting the throttling based on the data observed in the initial unthrottled load.

3. Refresh the page. You will now see the app slowly loading the main layout, then a list of all posts, and finally resolving the author IDs to usernames.

This is how our page would load on slow networks. Now, the overall time to finish loading our app is almost nine seconds! You can look at the waterfall diagram to see why this is happening:

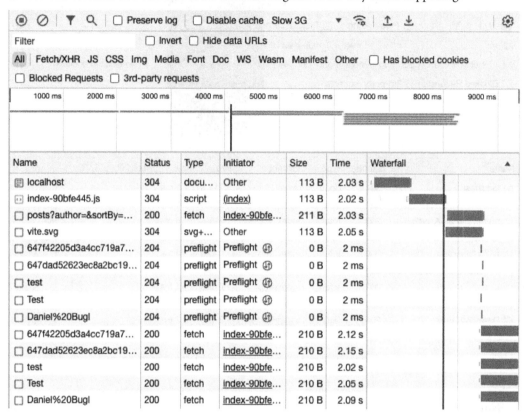

Figure 7.6 – Checking the waterfall diagram with Slow 3G throttling on

The issue in our app is that the requests are cascading. First, the HTML document loads, which then loads the JavaScript file for our app. This JavaScript file is then executed and starts rendering the layout and fetching the list of posts. After the posts are loaded, multiple requests are made in parallel to resolve the author names. As each request takes a bit over two seconds on our simulated slow network, we end up with a total load time of over eight seconds.

Now that we have learned how to benchmark a web application and found a performance bottleneck in our app (the cascading requests), let's learn how to improve the performance!

Rendering React components on the server

In the previous section, we identified cascading requests as the problem for our bad performance on slow connections. Possible solutions to this problem are as follows:

- **Bundled requests**: Fetch everything on the server and then serve everything at once to the client in a single request. This would solve the cascading requests when fetching author names, but not the initial waiting time between the HTML page being loaded and the JavaScript executing to start fetching the data. With a latency of two seconds per request, that's still four seconds added (two seconds for loading the JavaScript and two seconds for making the request) after the HTML is fetched.

- **Server-side rendering**: Render the initial user interface with all data on the server and serve it instead of the initial HTML that just contains a URL to the JavaScript file. This would mean that no additional requests are needed to fetch the data or JavaScript and we can show the blog posts right away. Another advantage of this approach is that it allows for caching the results, so, we only need to regenerate the page on the server when a blog post gets added. A downside of this approach is that it puts more strain on the server, especially when the pages are complex to render.

In cases where data does not change so frequently or the same data is accessed by all users, server-side rendering is beneficial. In cases where data frequently changes or is personalized to each user, it might make more sense to bundle the requests into one by making a new route or using a system that can aggregate requests, such as GraphQL, which we will learn more about later in this book, in *Chapter 11, Building a Backend With a GraphQL API*. In this chapter, however, we will focus on the server-side rendering approach.

Let's have a look at the differences between server-side rendering as opposed to client-side rendering:

- In **client-side rendering**, the browser downloads a minimal HTML page, which, most of the time, only contains information on where to download a JavaScript bundle, which contains all the code that will render the app.

- In **server-side rendering**, the React components are rendered on the server and served as HTML to the browser. This ensures that the app can be rendered immediately. The JavaScript bundle can be loaded later.

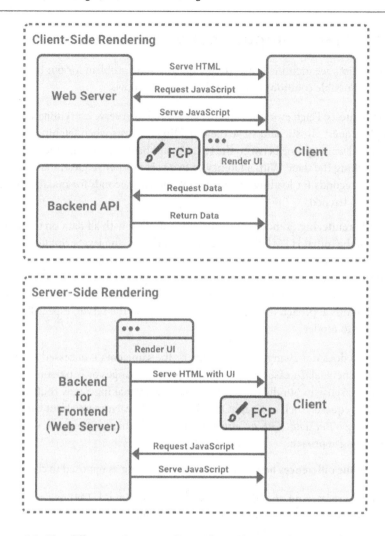

Figure 7.7 – The differences between client-side rendering and server-side rendering

It is also possible to combine the two into **isomorphic rendering**. This involves rendering the initial page on the server side, and then continuing to render changes on the client side. Isomorphic rendering combines the best of both worlds.

In addition to the performance improvements, server-side rendering is also good for **search engine optimization** (**SEO**), because search engine crawlers do not need to run JavaScript to see the page. We are going to learn more about SEO in the next chapter, *Chapter 8, Making Sure Customers Find You With Search Engine Optimization*.

Now that we have learned about server-side rendering, let's get started implementing it in our frontend, as follows:

- Setting up the server

- Defining the server-side entry point

- Defining the client-side entry point

- Updating `index.html` and `package.json`

- Making React Router work with server-side rendering

Let's start by setting up the server.

Setting up the server

Before we can get started with server-side rendering, we need to set up some boilerplate for running an Express server in tandem with Vite, so that we do not lose the benefits of Vite, such as hot reloading. Let's follow these steps to set up the server:

1. Install the `express` and `dotenv` dependencies in the root of our project (the frontend); we are going to use them to create a small web server to serve our server-side rendered page:

   ```
   $ npm install express@4.18.2 dotenv@16.3.1
   ```

2. Edit `.eslintrc.json` and add the `node` env, as we are going to add server-side code to our frontend now:

   ```
   "env": {
       "browser": true,
       "node": true
   },
   ```

3. Create a new `server.js` file in the `ch7` folder, and import the `fs`, `path`, `url`, `express`, and `dotenv` dependencies:

   ```
   import fs from 'fs'
   import path from 'path'
   import { fileURLToPath } from 'url'

   import express from 'express'
   import dotenv from 'dotenv'
   dotenv.config()
   ```

4. Save the current path in a variable to be used later to reference other files in our project, using the ESM-compatible `import.meta.url` variable, which contains a `file://` URL to our project:

```
const __dirname = path.dirname(fileURLToPath(import.meta.url))
```

We convert this URL to a regular path here.

5. Define a new `createDevServer` function, where we will create a Vite dev server with hot reloading and server-side rendering:

```
async function createDevServer() {
```

6. Inside this function, we first define the Express app:

```
const app = express()
```

7. Then, import and create a Vite dev server. We use the dynamic `import` syntax here so that we don't need to import Vite when we define the production server later:

```
const vite = await (
  await import('vite')
).createServer({
  server: { middlewareMode: true },
  appType: 'custom',
})
app.use(vite.middlewares)
```

Middleware mode runs Vite as a middleware in an existing Express server. Setting `appType` as `custom` disables Vite's own serving logic so that we can control which HTML will be served.

8. Now, define a route that matches all paths and start by loading the `index.html` file:

```
app.use('*', async (req, res, next) => {
  try {
    const templateHtml = fs.readFileSync(
      path.resolve(__dirname, 'index.html'),
      'utf-8',
    )
```

Make sure to load it in UTF-8 mode to support various languages and emojis in `index.html`.

9. Next, inject the Vite hot-module-replacement client to allow for hot reloading:

```
const template = await vite.transformIndexHtml(
  req.originalUrl,
  templateHtml
)
```

10. Load the entry point file for our server-side rendered app, which we will define in the next step:

```
        const { render } = await vite.ssrLoadModule('/src/entry-
    server.jsx')
```

The `ssrLoadModule` function in Vite automatically transforms the ESM source code so that it is usable in Node.js. This means we can hot-reload the entry point file without having to run a manual build.

11. Render the app using React. We will define the `render` function later in the server-side entry point. For now, we just call the function:

```
        const appHtml = await render()
```

12. Insert the rendered HTML from our app into the HTML template by matching a placeholder string, which we will define later in the `index.html` file:

```
        const html = template.replace(`<!--ssr-outlet-->`,
    appHtml)
```

13. Return a `200 OK` response with the final HTML contents:

```
        res.status(200).set({ 'Content-Type': 'text/html'
    }).end(html)
```

14. To wrap up the server creation, catch all errors and let Vite fix the stack trace, mapping source files in the stack trace back to the actual source code. Then, return the created Express app:

```
      } catch (e) {
        vite.ssrFixStacktrace(e)
        next(e)
      }
    })

    return app
  }
```

15. Lastly, execute the `createDevServer` function and make the app listen on a defined port:

```
const app = await createDevServer()
app.listen(process.env.PORT, () =>
  console.log(
    `ssr dev server running on http://localhost:${process.env.
  PORT}`,
  ),
)
```

16. Let's not forget to define the PORT environment variable in the .env file. Edit the .env file and add the PORT environment variable, as follows:

```
VITE_BACKEND_URL="http://localhost:3001/api/v1"
PORT=5173
```

Now that we have successfully created the Express server with Vite integration, we continue by implementing the server-side entry point.

Defining the server-side entry point

The server-side entry point will use ReactDOMServer to render our React components on the server. We need to distinguish this entry point from the client-side entry point because not everything React can do is supported on the server side. Specifically, some hooks such as effect hooks will not run on the server side. Also, we will have to handle the router differently on the server side, but more on that later.

Now, let's get started defining the server-side entry point:

1. First, create a new src/entry-server.jsx file and import ReactDOMServer and the App component:

```
import ReactDOMServer from 'react-dom/server
import { App } from './App.jsx'
```

2. Define and export the render function, which returns the App component using the ReactDOMServer.renderToString function:

```
export async function render() {
  return ReactDOMServer.renderToString(
    <App />,
  )
}
```

After defining the server-side entry point, we are going to continue by defining the client-side entry point.

Defining the client-side entry point

The client-side entry point uses regular ReactDOM to render our React components. However, we need to let React know to make use of the already server-side rendered DOM. Instead of rendering, we **hydrate** the existing DOM. Like when adding water to plants, hydration makes the DOM "come alive" by adding all React functionality to the server-side rendered static DOM.

Follow these steps to define the client-side entry point:

1. Rename the existing src/main.jsx file to src/entry-client.jsx.

2. Replace the createRoot function with the hydrateRoot function, as follows:

```
ReactDOM.hydrateRoot(
  document.getElementById('root'),
  <React.StrictMode>
    <App />
  </React.StrictMode>,
)
```

The hydrateRoot function accepts the component as a second argument, and does not require us to call .render().

Now that we have defined both entry points, let's update index.html and package.json.

Updating index.html and package.json

We still need to add the placeholder string to the index.html file and adjust package.json to execute our custom server instead of the vite command directly. Let's do that now:

1. Edit index.html and add a placeholder where the server-rendered HTML will be injected:

```
<div id="root"><!--ssr-outlet--></div>
```

2. Adjust the module import to point to the client-side entry point:

```
<script type="module" src="/src/entry-client.jsx"></script>
```

3. Now, edit package.json and replace the dev script with the following:

```
"dev": "node server",
```

4. Additionally, replace the build command with commands to build the server and client:

```
"build": "npm run build:client && npm run build:server",
"build:client": "vite build --outDir dist/client",
"build:server": "vite build --outDir dist/server --ssr src/
entry-server.jsx",
```

Our setup is now ready for server-side rendering. However, when you start the server, you will immediately notice that React Router does not work with our current setup. Let's fix that now.

Making React Router work with server-side rendering

To make React Router work with server-side rendering, we need to use `StaticRouter` on the server side and `BrowserRouter` on the client side. We can reuse the same route definitions for both sides. Let's get started refactoring our code to make React Router work on the server side:

1. Edit `src/App.jsx` and *remove* the router-related imports (the highlighted lines) from it:

```
import { QueryClient, QueryClientProvider } from '@tanstack/
react-query'
import { createBrowserRouter, RouterProvider } from 'react-
router-dom'

import { AuthContextProvider } from './contexts/AuthContext.jsx'
import { Blog } from './pages/Blog.jsx'
import { Signup } from './pages/Signup.jsx'
import { Login } from './pages/Login.jsx'
```

2. Import `PropTypes`, as we will need it later:

```
import PropTypes from 'prop-types'
```

3. Next, *remove* the following route definitions from it; we will put them in a new file soon:

```
const router = createBrowserRouter([
  {
    path: '/',
    element: <Blog />,
  },
  {
    path: '/signup',
    element: <Signup />,
  },
  {
    path: '/login',
    element: <Login />,
  },
])
```

4. Adjust the function to accept `children` and replace `RouterProvider` with `{children}`:

```
export function App({ children }) {
  return (
    <QueryClientProvider client={queryClient}>
      <AuthContextProvider>
        {children}
```

```
      </AuthContextProvider>
      </QueryClientProvider>
  )
  }
```

5. We also need to add the `propTypes` definitions for the App component now:

```
App.propTypes = {
  children: PropTypes.element.isRequired,
}
```

6. Create a new `src/routes.jsx` file and import the previously removed imports there:

```
import { Blog } from './pages/Blog.jsx'
import { Signup } from './pages/Signup.jsx'
import { Login } from './pages/Login.jsx'
```

7. Then, add the route definitions and export them:

```
export const routes = [
  {
    path: '/',
    element: <Blog />,
  },
  {
    path: '/signup',
    element: <Signup />,
  },
  {
    path: '/login',
    element: <Login />,
  },
]
```

Now that we have refactored our app structure in a way where we can reuse the routes on the client-side and server-side entry points, let's redefine the router in the client entry point.

Defining the client-side router

Follow these steps to re-define the router in the client entry point:

1. Edit `src/entry-client.jsx` and import `RouterProvider`, the `createBrowserRouter` function, and `routes`:

```
import React from 'react'
import ReactDOM from 'react-dom/client'
```

```
import { createBrowserRouter, RouterProvider } from 'react-
router-dom'
import { App } from './App.jsx'
import { routes } from './routes.jsx'
```

2. Then, create a new browser router based on the `routes` definition:

```
const router = createBrowserRouter(routes)
```

3. Adjust the `render` function to render `App` with `RouterProvider`:

```
ReactDOM.hydrateRoot(
  document.getElementById('root'),
  <React.StrictMode>
    <App>
      <RouterProvider router={router} />
    </App>
  </React.StrictMode>,
)
```

Next, let's define the **server-side router**.

Mapping the Express request to a Fetch request

On the server side, we will get an Express request, which we first need to convert to a Fetch request, so that React Router can understand it. Let's do that now:

1. Create a new `src/request.js` file and define a `createFetchRequest` function there, which takes an Express request as an argument:

```
export function createFetchRequest(req) {
```

2. First, define the `origin` for the request and build the URL:

```
const origin = `${req.protocol}://${req.get('host')}`
const url = new URL(req.originalUrl || req.url, origin)
```

We need to use `req.originalUrl` first (if available), to take into account the Vite middleware potentially changing the URL.

3. Then, we define a new `AbortController` to handle when the request is closed:

```
const controller = new AbortController()
req.on('close', () => controller.abort())
```

4. Next, we map the Express request `headers` to Fetch headers:

```
const headers = new Headers()

for (const [key, values] of Object.entries(req.headers)) {
  if (!values) continue
  if (Array.isArray(values)) {
    for (const value of values) {
      headers.append(key, value)
    }
  } else {
    headers.set(key, values)
  }
}
```

5. Now, we can build the `init` object for the Fetch request, which consists of `method`, `headers`, and `AbortController`:

```
const init = {
  method: req.method,
  headers,
  signal: controller.signal,
}
```

6. If our request was not a GET or HEAD request, we also get `body`, so, let's add that to the Fetch request, too:

```
if (req.method !== 'GET' && req.method !== 'HEAD') {
  init.body = req.body
}
```

7. Finally, let's create the Fetch `Request` object from our extracted information:

```
  return new Request(url.href, init)
}
```

Now that we have a utility function to convert an Express request to a Fetch request, we can make use of it to define the server-side router.

Defining the server-side router

The server-side router works very similarly to the client-side router, except that we are getting the request info from Express instead of the page, and using StaticRouter, because the route cannot change on the server side. Follow these steps to define the server-side router:

1. Edit src/entry-server.jsx and import StaticRouterProvider and the createStaticHandler and createStaticRouter functions. Also, import the routes definition and the createFetchRequest function we just defined:

   ```
   import ReactDOMServer from 'react-dom/server'
   import {
     createStaticHandler,
     createStaticRouter,
     StaticRouterProvider,
   } from 'react-router-dom/server'
   import { App } from './App.jsx'
   import { routes } from './routes.jsx'
   import { createFetchRequest } from './request.js'
   ```

2. Define a static handler for the routes:

   ```
   const handler = createStaticHandler(routes)
   ```

3. Adjust the render function to accept an Express request object and then create a Fetch request from it using our previously defined function:

   ```
   export async function render(req) {
     const fetchRequest = createFetchRequest(req)
   ```

4. We can now use this converted request to pass it to our static handler, which creates context for the route, allowing React Router to see which route we are trying to access and with which parameters:

   ```
   const context = await handler.query(fetchRequest)
   ```

5. From the routes defined by the handler and the context, we can create a static router:

   ```
   const router = createStaticRouter(handler.dataRoutes, context)
   ```

6. Finally, we can adjust the rendering to render the static router and our refactored App structure:

   ```
   return ReactDOMServer.renderToString(
     <App>
       <StaticRouterProvider router={router} context={context} />
     </App>,
   ```

```
        )
    }
```

7. There's still one more thing left to do. We need to pass the Express request to the `render()` function of the server-side entry point. Edit the following line in the `server.js` file:

    ```
    const appHtml = await render(req)
    ```

8. If the frontend and backend are already running, make sure to quit them.

9. Start the frontend, as follows:

    ```
    $ npm run dev
    ```

10. Also, start the backend in a separate Terminal:

    ```
    $ cd backend
    $ npm run dev
    ```

The frontend will now output `ssr dev server running on http://localhost:5173` and successfully server-side render all our pages! You can verify that it is server-side rendered by opening the DevTools, clicking on the cog icon in the top right, scrolling down in the **Settings | Preferences** pane to the **Debugger** section, and checking the box for **Disable JavaScript**, as follows:

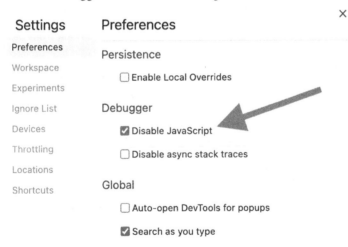

Figure 7.8 – Disabling JavaScript in the DevTools

Now, refresh the page, and you will see that part of the app still gets rendered. Only the top part of the app is fully rendered by the server side right now. The posts list is not rendered on the server side yet. This is because the `useQuery` hooks internally use an effect hook to fetch data after the component has mounted. As such, they do not work with server-side rendering. However, we can still get data fetching working with server-side rendering. Let's learn about that in the next section.

Server-side data fetching

As we have seen, data fetching does not work out of the box on the server side. There are two approaches for server-side data fetching with React Query:

- **Initial data approach**: Use the `initialData` option in the `useQuery` hook to pass prefetched data in. This approach is enough for fetching a list of posts but would be tricky for fetching deeply nested data, such as the usernames of each author.

- **Hydration approach**: This allows us to prefetch any requests and store the result by their query key and prefetch any request on the server side, even if it is deeply nested within the app, without having to pass the prefetched data down using props or a context.

We are first going to use the `initialData` option to fetch the list of blog posts, and then extend our solution to the hydration approach so that we can get a feeling for how both approaches work and what their pros and cons are.

Using initial data

React Router allows us to define **loaders** in routes, which we can use to fetch data on the server side and client side when the route is loaded. We can then pass the data fetched from the loaders into the `Blog` component and the `useQuery` hook via the `initialData` option. Let's do that now:

1. Edit `src/routes.jsx` and import the `useLoaderData` hook from `react-router-dom` and the `getPosts` function:

    ```
    import { useLoaderData } from 'react-router-dom'
    import { Blog } from './pages/Blog.jsx'
    import { Signup } from './pages/Signup.jsx'
    import { Login } from './pages/Login.jsx'
    import { getPosts } from './api/posts.js'
    ```

2. Adjust the route to define a `loader` function, in which we simply call the `getPosts` function. We can then define a `Component()` method in which we use the `useLoaderData` hook to get the data from the loader, and pass it into the `Blog` component, as follows:

    ```
    export const routes = [
      {
        path: '/',
        loader: getPosts,
        Component() {
          const posts = useLoaderData()
          return <Blog initialData={posts} />
        },
      },
    ```

3. Edit `src/pages/Blog.jsx` and import `PropTypes` there, so that we can define a new prop for the component later:

```
import PropTypes from 'prop-types'
```

4. Then, add the `initialData` prop to the `Blog` component:

```
export function Blog({ initialData }) {
```

5. Pass the `initialData` prop into the `useQuery` hook, as follows:

```
const postsQuery = useQuery({
  queryKey: ['posts', { author, sortBy, sortOrder }],
  queryFn: () => getPosts({ author, sortBy, sortOrder }),
  initialData,
})
```

6. Lastly, define `propTypes` for the `Blog` component:

```
Blog.propTypes = {
  initialData: PropTypes.shape(PostList.propTypes.posts),
}
```

Refresh the frontend page (with JavaScript disabled) and it will now show the post list, but without resolving the author usernames. As we can see, the initial data approach is quite simple. However, if we wanted to fetch the usernames of all authors, we would have to store them somewhere and then pass them down into the user components using either props or a context, both of which would be quite tedious and would not scale well if we need to make more requests later. Thankfully, there is another, more advanced approach, which we are going to learn about now.

Using hydration

With the hydration approach, we create a query client to prefetch any requests we want to make, and then dehydrate it, pass it to the component using a loader, and hydrate it again there. Using this approach, we can simply make any query and store it using a query key. If a component uses the same query key, it will be able to render the results on the server side. Let's implement the hydration approach now:

1. Edit `src/routes.jsx` and import `QueryClient`, the `dehydrate` function, and the `Hydrate` component from React Query:

```
import { QueryClient, dehydrate, HydrationBoundary } from '@
tanstack/react-query'
```

2. Also, import the `getUserInfo` function, as we are going to fetch usernames too now:

```
import { getUserInfo } from './api/users.js'
```

3. Adjust the loader; we are now going to create a query client there:

```
{
    path: '/',
    loader: async () => {
        const queryClient = new QueryClient()
```

4. Then, we simulate the getPosts request from the Blog component by passing in the same default arguments to it as the component would:

```
        const author = ''
        const sortBy = 'createdAt'
        const sortOrder = 'descending'
        const posts = await getPosts({ author, sortBy, sortOrder
})
```

> **Note**
>
> This duplication of default arguments is a bit problematic. However, with our current server-side rendering solution, the data fetching and component rendering are too separated to properly share the code between them. A more sophisticated server-side rendering solution, such as Next.js or Remix, can deal with this pattern better.

5. Now, we can call queryClient.prefetchQuery, with the same query key as the one that will be used by the useQuery hook in the component, to prefetch the results of the query:

```
        await queryClient.prefetchQuery({
            queryKey: ['posts', { author, sortBy, sortOrder }],
            queryFn: () => posts,
        })
```

6. Next, we use the fetched posts array to get a unique list of author IDs from them:

```
        const uniqueAuthors = posts
            .map((post) => post.author)
            .filter((value, index, array) => array.indexOf(value)
=== index)
```

7. We now loop through all author IDs and prefetch their information:

```
        for (const userId of uniqueAuthors) {
            await queryClient.prefetchQuery({
                queryKey: ['users', userId],
                queryFn: () => getUserInfo(userId),
            })
        }
```

8. Now that we have prefetched all the necessary data, we need to call dehydrate on queryClient to return it in a serializable format:

```
return dehydrate(queryClient)
},
```

9. In the Component () method, we get this dehydrated state and use the Hydrate component to hydrate it again. This hydration process makes the data accessible to the server-side rendered query client:

```
Component() {
  const dehydratedState = useLoaderData()
  return (
    <HydrationBoundary state={dehydratedState}>
      <Blog />
    </HydrationBoundary>
  )
},
},
```

10. Finally, we can revert the src/pages/Blog.jsx component to the previous state. We start by *removing* the PropTypes import:

```
import PropTypes from 'prop-types'
```

11. Then, we *remove* the initialData prop:

```
export function Blog({ initialData }) {
```

12. We also *remove* it in the useQuery hook:

```
const postsQuery = useQuery({
  queryKey: ['posts', { author, sortBy, sortOrder }],
  queryFn: () => getPosts({ author, sortBy, sortOrder }),
  initialData,
})
```

13. Lastly, we *remove* the propTypes definition:

```
Blog.propTypes = {
  initialData: PropTypes.shape(PostList.propTypes),
}
```

14. Quit the frontend via *Ctrl* + *C*, then restart it as follows:

```
$ npm run dev
```

15. Refresh the page and you will see that the full blog post list, including all author names, is properly rendered on the server side now, even with JavaScript disabled!

Let's do another benchmark to see how the performance has improved:

1. Open the Chrome DevTools.

2. Enable JavaScript again by going to the cog wheel, **Settings | Preferences**, and unchecking **Disable JavaScript**.

3. Go to the **Lighthouse** tab. Click on **Analyze page load** to generate a new report.

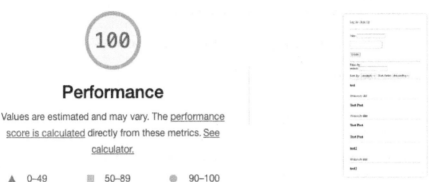

METRICS   Expand view

● First Contentful Paint   ● Largest Contentful Paint
0.7 s   0.7 s

● Total Blocking Time   ● Cumulative Layout Shift
0 ms   0

● Speed Index
0.7 s

Figure 7.9 – The Lighthouse Performance score of the server-side rendered app with the dev server

The FCP and LCP times are almost half of the previously reported times from client-side rendering in production mode. Looking at the waterfall diagram in the **Network** tab, we can now see that there is only one request to fetch the initial page.

Let's now wrap up the chapter by learning about advanced server-side rendering.

Advanced server-side rendering

In the previous sections, we have successfully created a server that can do server-side rendering with hot reloading, which is very useful for development but will worsen the performance in production. Let's create another server function for a production server now, which will build files, use compression, and not load Vite middleware for hot reloading. Follow these steps to create the production server:

1. In the root of our project, install the `compression` dependency with the following command:

    ```
    $ npm install compression@1.7.4
    ```

2. Edit `server.js` and define a new function for the production server, above the `createDevServer` function:

    ```
    async function createProdServer() {
    ```

3. In this function, we define a new Express app and use the `compression` package and the `serve-static` package to serve our client:

    ```
    const app = express()

    app.use((await import('compression')).default())
    app.use(
      (await import('serve-static')).default(
        path.resolve(__dirname, 'dist/client'),
        {
          index: false,
        },
      ),
    )
    ```

4. Then, we define a route that catches all paths again, this time loading the template from the built files in the `dist/` folder:

    ```
    app.use('*', async (req, res, next) => {
      try {
        let template = fs.readFileSync(
          path.resolve(__dirname, 'dist/client/index.html'),
          'utf-8',
        )
    ```

5. We also directly import and render the server-side entry point now:

```
const render = (await import('./dist/server/entry-server.
js')).render
```

6. As before, we render the React app, replace the placeholder in `index.html` with the rendered app, and return the resulting HTML:

```
const appHtml = await render(req)
const html = template.replace(`<!--ssr-outlet-->`,
appHtml)
res.status(200).set({ 'Content-Type': 'text/html'
}).end(html)
```

7. For the error handling, we simply pass it on to the next middleware now and return the app:

```
} catch (e) {
next(e)
}
})

return app
}
```

8. At the bottom of the `server.js` file, where we created the dev server, we now do a check for the NODE_ENV environment variable and use it to decide whether to start the production server or the development server:

```
if (process.env.NODE_ENV === 'production') {
const app = await createProdServer()
app.listen(process.env.PORT, () =>
console.log(
`ssr production server running on http://
localhost:${process.env.PORT}`,
),
)
} else {
const app = await createDevServer()
app.listen(process.env.PORT, () =>
console.log(
`ssr dev server running on http://localhost:${process.env.
PORT}`,
),
)
}
```

9. Install the `cross-env` package, as follows:

    ```
    $ npm install cross-env@7.0.3
    ```

10. Edit `package.json` and add a `start` script, which starts the server in production mode:

    ```
    "start": "cross-env NODE_ENV=production node server",
    ```

11. Quit the frontend dev server, build, and start the production server:

    ```
    $ npm run build
    $ npm start
    ```

As we can see, our server still serves the app just fine, but now we are not in development mode anymore, so we do not have hot reloading available. This wraps up our implementation of server-side rendering! As you can imagine, the server-side rendering implementation in this chapter is somewhat basic, and there are still multiple things we would need to handle:

- Redirects and proper HTTP status codes

- Static-site generation (caching resulting HTML pages so we don't have to server-side render them again every time)

- Better data fetching functionality

- Better code splitting between the server and client

- Better handling of environment variables between the server and client

To solve these issues, it is better to use a fully-fledged server-side rendering implementation in a web framework, such as Next.js or Remix. These frameworks already provide ways to do server-side rendering, data fetching, and routing out of the box, and do not require us to manually get everything to work in tandem. We are going to learn more about Next.js in *Chapter 16, Getting Started with Next.js*.

Summary

In this chapter, we first learned how to benchmark web applications using Lighthouse and Chrome DevTools. We also learned about useful metrics for such benchmarks, called Core Web Vitals. Then, we learned about rendering React components on the server and the differences between client-side rendering and server-side rendering. Next, we implemented server-side rendering for our app using Vite and React Router. Then, we implemented server-side data fetching using React Query. We then benchmarked our app again and saw an improvement in the performance of more than 40%. Lastly, we learned about getting our server-side rendering server ready for production and concepts that a more sophisticated server-side rendering framework needs to deal with.

In the next chapter, *Chapter 8, Making Sure Customers Find You with Search Engine Optimization*, we are going to learn how to make our web app more accessible to search engine crawlers, increasing the SEO score that we saw in the Lighthouse report. We are going to add meta tags to have more information about our web app and add integrations for various social media sites.

8

Making Sure Customers Find You with Search Engine Optimization

When we optimized the performance of our blog in the previous chapter, you may have noticed that the Lighthouse report also includes a **Search Engine Optimization** (**SEO**) score, which our app scored relatively low on. This score tells us how optimized our app is for being indexed properly and found by search engines such as Google or Bing. After successfully developing a working blog app, of course, we want our blog to be found by users. In this chapter, we are going to learn the basics of SEO and how to optimize the SEO score for our React application. Then, we are going to learn how to create meta tags for easier integration on various social media sites.

In this chapter, we are going to cover the following main topics:

- Optimizing an application for search engines
- Improving social media embeds

Technical requirements

Before we start, please install all requirements from *Chapter 1, Preparing For Full-Stack Development*, and *Chapter 2, Getting to Know Node.js and MongoDB*.

The versions listed in those chapters are the ones used in the book. While installing a newer version should not be an issue, please note that certain steps might work differently on a newer version. If you are having an issue with the code and steps provided in this book, please try using the versions mentioned in *Chapters 1* and *2*.

You can find the code for this chapter on GitHub: `https://github.com/PacktPublishing/Modern-Full-Stack-React-Projects/tree/main/ch8`.

The CiA video for this chapter can be found at: `https://youtu.be/1xN310MMTbY`

If you cloned the full repository for the book, Husky may not find the `.git` directory when running `npm install`. In that case, just run `git init` in the root of the corresponding chapter folder.

Optimizing an application for search engines

Before we get started optimizing our app for search engines, let's briefly learn how search engines work. Search engines work by storing information about websites in an index. The **index** contains the location, content, and meta information of websites. Adding or updating pages in the index is called indexing and done by a crawler. A **crawler** is an automated software that fetches websites and indexes them. It is called a crawler because it follows further links on the website to find more websites. More advanced crawlers, such as the **Googlebot**, can also detect whether JavaScript is required to render the contents of a website and even render it.

The following graphic visualizes how a search engine crawler works:

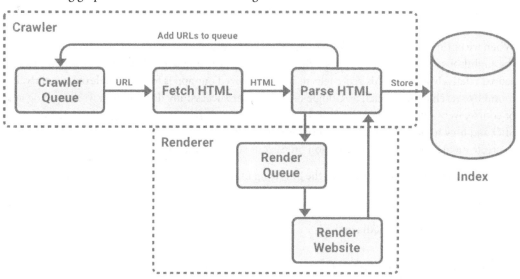

Figure 8.1 – Visualization of how a search engine crawler works

As we can see, a search crawler has a queue containing URLs that it needs to crawl and index. It then visits the URLs one by one, fetches the HTML and, if it is an advanced crawler, detects whether it needs to execute JavaScript to render the content. In that case, the URL is added to a render queue and the rendered HTML is passed back into the crawler later. Then, the crawler extracts all the links to other pages and adds them to the queue. Finally, the parsed content is added to the index.

To see whether a website is already indexed by a search engine, most search engines provide a `site:` operator, which can be used to check whether a URL is already indexed by it. For example, `site:wikipedia.org` shows various URLs on Wikipedia that are already indexed. If your website is not indexed yet, you can submit it to tools such as the **Google Search Console**. The Google Search Console also has a detailed overview of the indexing status and any problems with indexing. However, it is not necessary to submit our site for it to be found, because most search engines automatically crawl the web and will eventually find our website.

If your website still does not get indexed, this might be because it is improperly configured. First, you need to create a `robots.txt` file to specify whether search engines are allowed to crawl parts of your website, and which parts they are allowed to crawl.

> **Note**
>
> The `robots.txt` should not be used to hide web pages from Google search results. Instead, it is used to reduce traffic from crawlers on unimportant or similar pages. If you want to completely hide web pages from Google search results, either password-protect them, or use the `noindex` meta tag.

Next, you need to make sure the contents of your website are visible to the crawler. Server-side rendering can help here by allowing crawlers to view the contents of your website without running JavaScript. Additionally, adding meta information using special HTML tags helps crawlers to get additional information about your website. For small websites, pages need to be linked properly or add a manual sitemap. For larger websites, such as a blog with many posts, a sitemap should always be defined. Finally, having good performance, fast load times, and a good user experience makes your website rank higher on search engines.

We have already added server-side rendering to speed up crawling by serving content immediately without relying on JavaScript to render it. Now, let's further optimize our app for search engines. We start by creating a `robots.txt` file.

Creating a robots.txt file

First, let's ensure that crawlers are explicitly allowed to access our app and index all pages on it. To do so, we need to create a `robots.txt` file, which crawlers will read to find out which pages they are allowed to access (if any). Follow these steps to create a `robots.txt` file that allows access for all crawlers to all pages:

1. Copy the ch7 folder to a new ch8 folder, as follows:

   ```
   $ cp -R ch7 ch8
   ```

2. Open the ch8 folder in VS Code.

3. Create a new `public/robots.txt` file in the root of our project.

4. Open the newly created file and enter the following contents to allow all crawlers to index all pages:

    ```
    User-agent: *
    Allow: /
    ```

    The `robots.txt` works by defining blocks, each block being defined by matching a user agent. The user agent can match various crawlers, such as `Googlebot` for Google, or you can use `*` to match all crawlers. After the user agent, one or multiple `Allow` and/or `Disallow` statements can be made, that decide which paths a crawler is allowed or not allowed to access. In our case, we are allowing access to all paths. Additionally, a `Sitemap` can be specified, but we'll see more on that later in the *Creating a sitemap* subsection.

5. Open a Terminal pane and start the frontend by running the following command:

    ```
    $ npm run dev
    ```

6. Open another Terminal pane and start the backend by running the following commands:

    ```
    $ cd backend
    $ npm run dev
    ```

7. Go to `http://localhost:5173/robots.txt` in your browser to see the `robots.txt` file being served properly.

Now that we have successfully allowed crawlers to access our app, we should improve our URL structure. Let's do that by creating separate pages for each post.

Creating separate pages for posts

At the moment, it is not possible to view only a single post in our blog app, we can only view the list of all posts. That is not good for SEO, as it means a search engine will always link to the index page, which might already contain different articles than what the user was searching for. Let's refactor our app a bit to only show post titles and authors on the main page, and then link to separate pages for each blog post:

1. Edit `src/components/Post.jsx` to allow displaying a single full post while displaying a smaller version of the post in the list, with a link to the full version. First, we import the `Link` component from `react-router-dom`:

    ```
    import { Link } from 'react-router-dom'
    ```

2. Then, we add an `_id` prop and a `fullPost` prop to the `Post` component. The `fullPost` prop will be set to `false` by default (when displayed in the post list) and set to `true` when using it in the single-post page:

```
export function Post({
  title,
  contents,
  author,
  _id,
  fullPost = false,
}) {
```

3. We make some adjustments to the component to show a link to the single-post page if we are not on a single-post page yet:

```
{fullPost ? (
  <h3>{title}</h3>
) : (
  <Link to={`/posts/${_id}`}>
    <h3>{title}</h3>
  </Link>
)}
```

4. Additionally, we only show the contents of the blog post on a single-post page, and adjust the spacing of the author info accordingly:

```
{fullPost && <div>{contents}</div>}
{author && (
  <em>
    {fullPost && <br />}
    Written by <User id={author} />
  </em>
)}
```

5. Adjust the prop types to add the newly defined props:

```
Post.propTypes = {
  title: PropTypes.string.isRequired,
  contents: PropTypes.string,
  author: PropTypes.string,
  _id: PropTypes.string.isRequired,
  fullPost: PropTypes.bool,
}
```

6. Edit `src/api/posts.js` and add a new function to get a single post by `id`:

```
export const getPostById = async (postId) => {
  const res = await fetch(`${import.meta.env.VITE_BACKEND_URL}/
posts/${postId}`)
  return await res.json()
}
```

7. Create a new `src/pages/ViewPost.jsx` file, and start by importing all the components and functions that we are going to need:

```
import { Link } from 'react-router-dom'
import PropTypes from 'prop-types'
import { useQuery } from '@tanstack/react-query'
import { Header } from '../components/Header.jsx'
import { Post } from '../components/Post.jsx'
import { getPostById } from '../api/posts.js'
```

8. Then, define a component that accepts a `postId` as props:

```
export function ViewPost({ postId }) {
```

9. In the component, we use a query hook to fetch a single post by `id`:

```
const postQuery = useQuery({
  queryKey: ['post', postId],
  queryFn: () => getPostById(postId),
})
const post = postQuery.data
```

10. Next, render the header and a link back to the main page:

```
return (
  <div style={{ padding: 8 }}>
    <Header />
    <br />
    <hr />
    <Link to='/'>Back to main page</Link>
    <br />
    <hr />
```

11. Then, if we managed to fetch a post with the given ID, render a post with the `fullPost` prop set. Otherwise, we show a `not found` message:

```
    {post ? <Post {...post} fullPost /> : `Post with id
${postId} not found.`}
  </div>
```

```
    )
  }
```

12. Lastly, define the prop types for the `ViewPost` component:

```
ViewPost.propTypes = {
  postId: PropTypes.string.isRequired,
}
```

13. Edit `src/routes.jsx` and import the `ViewPost` component and the `getPostById` function (for server-side rendering):

```
import { ViewPost } from './pages/ViewPost.jsx'
import { getPosts, getPostById } from './api/posts.js'
```

14. Define a new `/posts/:postId` route for viewing a single post. In the loader, we fetch the single blog post and an author, if it has one. We then return the dehydrated state and the post ID:

```
{
    path: '/posts/:postId',
    loader: async ({ params }) => {
      const postId = params.postId

      const queryClient = new QueryClient()

      const post = await getPostById(postId)
      await queryClient.prefetchQuery({
        queryKey: ['post', postId],
        queryFn: () => post,
      })

      if (post?.author) {
        await queryClient.prefetchQuery({
          queryKey: ['users', post.author],
          queryFn: () =>
            getUserInfo(post.author),
        })
      }

      return { dehydratedState: dehydrate(queryClient), postId }
    },
```

15. Define a `Component` method for the route, where we get `dehydratedState` and `postId` and pass them on to the `ViewPost` component, as follows:

```
Component() {
  const { dehydratedState, postId } = useLoaderData()
  return (
    <HydrationBoundary state={dehydratedState}>
      <ViewPost postId={postId} />
    </HydrationBoundary>
  )
},
},
```

16. Go to `http://localhost:5173/` in your browser and you will see that all blog posts in the list now have a link in their title. Click on the link to see the full blog post, as shown in the following screenshot:

Logged in as **DanielBugl**

Logout

Back to main page

Making Sure Customers Find You With Search Engine Optimization

When developing a web application, it is important to make it not only easily accessible for users, but also for search engine crawlers and embeddable on social media sites. In this chapter, we are first going to learn how to optimize your React application for search engines. Then, we are going to learn how to create meta tags for integration on various social media sites.

*Written by **DanielBugl***

Figure 8.2 – Viewing a single blog post on a separate page

Now our blog app is already much more organized, as we do not see the full contents of all blog posts on the main page. We only see the title and author now and can then decide whether the article is interesting to us or not. Furthermore, a search engine can provide separate entries for each blog post, making it easier to find posts on our app. There is still room for improvement with the URL structure though, as it currently only contains the post ID. Let's introduce more meaningful URLs in the next step.

Creating meaningful URLs (slugs)

Websites often put keywords in the URLs to make it easier for users to see what they will be opening just by looking at the URL. Keywords in URLs are also a ranking factor for search engines, albeit a not-so-strong one. The strongest one is always good content. Nevertheless, having a good URL structure improves the user experience. For example, if the link is `/posts/64a42dfd6a7b7ab47009f5e3/making-sure-customers-find-you-with-search-engine-optimization` instead of just `/posts/64a42dfd6a7b7ab47009f5e3`, it is already clear from the URL alone what content they will find on the page. Such keywords in the URL are called a URL slug, named after "slugs" in journalism, which refers to using short descriptions of articles as internal names. Let's get started introducing slugs on our post pages:

1. Edit `src/routes.jsx` and adjust the path to allow for optionally including a slug:

    ```
    path: '/posts/:postId/:slug?',
    ```

> **Note**
>
> We are not doing any checks on whether the slug is correct or not. In fact, this is not really necessary, and many pages do not do this. As long as we have a correct ID, we can render the blog post. We only need to make sure that the links to the page all include the correct slug. However, we could additionally add a `<link>` element with the `rel="canonical"` attribute to a page, specifying the canonical page with the correct slug. This would tell crawlers not to index duplicate pages when incorrect slugs are used.

2. In the root of our project, install the `slug` npm package, which contains a function to properly slugify a title:

    ```
    $ npm install slug@8.2.3
    ```

    This package already handles unicode and returns URL-safe strings. So, we do not need to worry about sanitizing the `title` string ourselves.

3. Edit `src/components/Post.jsx` and import the `slug` function:

    ```
    import slug from 'slug'
    ```

4. Then, adjust the link to the blog post by adding the slug, as follows:

    ```
    <Link to={`/posts/${_id}/${slug(title)}`}>
    ```

5. Now, when we open a link from the list, the URL will look as follows:

    ```
    http://localhost:5173/posts/64a42dfd6a7b7ab47009f5e3/
    making-sure-customers-find-you-with-search-engine-
    optimization
    ```

Now we have human readable URLs for our blog posts! However, you might have noticed that the title is still **Vite + React** on all pages of our app. Let's change that now by introducing dynamic titles and including the blog post title in the page title.

Adding dynamic titles

The title of a page is even more important for SEO than keywords in the URL, as that is the title that will be shown in the search results in most cases. So, we should choose our title wisely, and if we have dynamic content (like in our blog), we should also dynamically adjust the title to fit the content. We can use the React Helmet library to facilitate changes in the <head> section of the HTML document. This library allows us to render a special `Helmet` component. The children of this component will replace existing tags in the <head> section. Follow these steps to use React Helmet to dynamically set the title:

1. First of all, let's change the general title of our app, as it is still **Vite + React**. Edit `index.html` in the root of our project and change the title. We are going to call our blog app `Full-Stack React Blog`:

    ```
    <title>Full-Stack React Blog</title>
    ```

2. In the root of our project, install the `react-helmet-async` dependency to be able to dynamically change the title:

    ```
    $ npm install react-helmet-async@1.3.0
    ```

> **Note**
>
> React Helmet Async is a fork of the original React Helmet that adds support for newer React versions.

3. Edit `src/pages/ViewPost.jsx` and import the `Helmet` component from `react-helmet-async`:

    ```
    import { Helmet } from 'react-helmet-async'
    ```

4. Render the `Helmet` component and define the `<title>` tag inside it, as follows:

    ```
    return (
      <div style={{ padding: 8 }}>
        {post && (
          <Helmet>
            <title>{post.title} | Full-Stack React Blog</title>
          </Helmet>
        )}
    ```

5. Edit `src/pages/Blog.jsx` and import `Helmet`:

    ```
    import { Helmet } from 'react-helmet-async'
    ```

6. Then, reset the title to `Full-Stack React Blog` in the `Blog` component:

    ```
    return (
      <div style={{ padding: 8 }}>
        <Helmet>
          <title>Full-Stack React Blog</title>
        </Helmet>
    ```

7. Edit `src/App.jsx` and import the `HelmetProvider`:

    ```
    import { HelmetProvider } from 'react-helmet-async'
    ```

8. Then, adjust the App component to render `HelmetProvider`:

    ```
    export function App({ children }) {
      return (
        <HelmetProvider>
          <QueryClientProvider client={queryClient}>
            <AuthContextProvider>
              {children}
            </AuthContextProvider>
          </QueryClientProvider>
        </HelmetProvider>
      )
    }
    ```

9. Click on a single post in the app and you will see that the title now updates to include the post title!

Now that we have successfully set a dynamic title, let's pay some attention to other important information in the `<head>` section, the **meta tags**.

Adding other meta tags

Meta tags, as the name tells us, contain meta information about a page. Besides the title, we can set meta information such as a short description, or information on how the browser should render a website. In this section, we will cover the most important SEO-relevant meta tags, starting with the description meta tag.

Description meta tag

The description meta tag contains a short description of the contents of the page. Similarly to the title tag, we can also dynamically set this tag, as follows:

1. Edit `src/pages/Blog.jsx` and add the following generic description `<meta>` tag:

    ```
    <Helmet>
      <title>Full-Stack React Blog</title>
      <meta
        name='description'
        content='A blog full of articles about full-stack
    React development.'
      />
    </Helmet>
    ```

    Now, let's add a dynamic meta description tag for each blog post. The meta description should have between 50 and 160 characters, and since we do not have a short summary of our blog posts, let's just use the full contents and truncate them after 160 characters. Of course, it would be even better to let authors add a short summary when creating posts, but for simplicity, we just truncate the description here.

2. Edit the `src/pages/ViewPost.jsx` file and define a simple function to truncate a string:

    ```
    function truncate(str, max = 160) {
      if (!str) return str
      if (str.length > max) {
        return str.slice(0, max - 3) + '...'
      } else {
        return str
      }
    }
    ```

    We limit the string to 160 characters, and if it's above 160, we truncate it to 157 characters and add three dots at the end.

3. Add the truncated content as a meta description tag to the `Helmet` component, as follows:

    ```
    {post && (
      <Helmet>
        <title>{post.title} | Full-Stack React Blog</title>
        <meta name='description' content={truncate(post.
    contents)} />
    ```

After adding the description meta tag, let's learn about other meta tags that could be used.

Robots meta tag

The `robots` meta tag tells crawlers whether and how they should crawl web pages. It can be used in addition to `robots.txt`, but we should only use it if we want to dynamically restrict the way a certain page is crawled. It looks as follows:

```
<meta name="robots" content="index, follow">
```

The `index` keyword tells crawlers to index the page, the `follow` keyword tells crawlers to crawl further links on the page. The `index` and `follow` keywords can be toggled off by using `noindex` and `nofollow`, respectively.

Viewport meta tag

Another important meta tag to add is the viewport tag, which tells the browser (and crawlers) that your website is mobile friendly. See the following example of how the meta tag affects how pages are rendered on mobile:

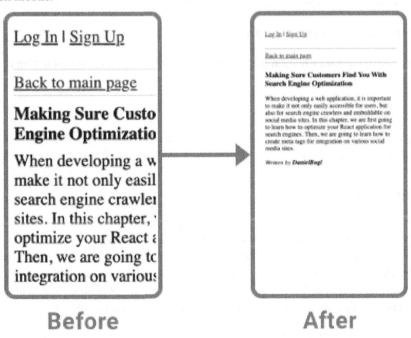

Figure 8.3 – A blog post rendering before and after adding the viewport meta tag

Vite already added this meta tag automatically for us in the index.html template it provided. You can see it by looking at the index.html file:

```
<meta name="viewport" content="width=device-width, initial-scale=1.0" />
```

After learning about the viewport tag, we continue by learning about the charset meta tag.

Charset meta tag

The charset meta tag tells the browser and crawlers about the character encoding of the web page. Usually, you want to set this to UTF-8 to ensure all Unicode characters are rendered properly. Again, Vite already added this meta tag automatically for us:

```
<meta charset="UTF-8" />
```

Now that we have learned about the relevant meta tags, let's move on to creating a sitemap, which helps crawlers find all the pages on our app more easily.

Other relevant meta information

There is additional meta information that can be relevant for a website, such as setting the language in the <html> tag, as follows:

```
<html lang="en">
```

Setting a favicon also improves the search snippet, which is what users see when deciding whether they should click on a link.

Creating a sitemap

A sitemap contains a list of URLs that are part of an app, so that crawlers can easily detect new content and crawl the app more efficiently. It also makes sure that all content is found, which is especially important for content-based apps with a large number of pages/posts. Usually, sitemaps are provided in XML format. They are not mandatory for SEO, but will make it easier and faster for crawlers to pick up content on your app. As we have dynamic content on our blog app, we should also create a dynamic sitemap. Follow these steps to create a dynamic sitemap for our blog app:

1. First, we are going to need a base URL for our (deployed) frontend to prefix all paths on our sitemap with. For now, we are simply going to set this to our localhost URL, but in production, this environment variable should be changed to the proper base URL of the app. Edit .env in the root of our project and add a FRONTEND_URL environment variable:

    ```
    FRONTEND_URL="http://localhost:5173"
    ```

2. Create a new `generateSitemap.js` file in the root of our project, start by importing the `slug` function and `dotenv`:

```
import slug from 'slug'
import dotenv from 'dotenv'
dotenv.config()
```

3. Then, save the previously created environment variable in a `baseUrl` variable:

```
const baseUrl = process.env.FRONTEND_URL
```

4. Now, define an `async` function to generate a sitemap. In this function, we start by fetching a list of blog posts, as we want each blog post to be part of the sitemap:

```
export async function generateSitemap() {
  const postsRequest = await fetch(`${process.env.VITE_BACKEND_
URL}/posts`)
  const posts = await postsRequest.json()
```

5. Next, we return a string containing the XML for the sitemap. We start by defining the XML header and a `<urlset>` tag:

```
  return `<?xml version="1.0" encoding="UTF-8"?>
<urlset xmlns="http://www.sitemaps.org/schemas/sitemap/0.9">
```

6. Inside the `<urlset>` tag, we can use `<url>` tags with `<loc>` tags to link to various pages. We first list all the static pages:

```
    <url>
        <loc>${baseUrl}</loc>
    </url>
    <url>
        <loc>${baseUrl}/signup</loc>
    </url>
    <url>
        <loc>${baseUrl}/login</loc>
    </url>
```

7. Then, we loop over all posts that we fetched from the backend and generate a `<url>` tag for each of them, constructing the URLs from the post ID and the slug:

```
    ${posts
      .map(
        (post) => `
    <url>
        <loc>${baseUrl}/posts/${post._id}/${slug(post.title)}</
loc>
```

8. We can also optionally specify a `<lastmod>` tag, telling the crawler when the content was last modified:

```
<lastmod>${post.updatedAt ?? post.createdAt}</lastmod>
```

9. Lastly, we join all generated `<url>` tags together into a single string and close the `<urlset>` tag:

```
    </url>`,
      )
        .join('')}
  </urlset>`
}
```

Now that we have a function to dynamically generate a sitemap, we still need to include a route to it in our server.

10. Edit `server.js` and import the `generateSitemap` function there:

```
import { generateSitemap } from './generateSitemap.js'
```

11. Then, go to the first `app.use('*')` declaration inside the `createProdServer` function and check whether the URL is `/sitemap.xml`. If yes, generate the sitemap and return it as XML:

```
app.use('*', async (req, res, next) => {
  if (req.originalUrl === '/sitemap.xml') {
    const sitemap = await generateSitemap()
    return res
      .status(200)
      .set({ 'Content-Type': 'application/xml' })
      .end(sitemap)
  }
}
```

> **Note**
>
> In a more sophisticated setup, we could cache the generated sitemap either on our Express server, our own web server, or a separate caching service.

12. We do the same change as in the previous step for the second `app.use('*')` declaration inside the `createDevServer` function.

13. Restart the server and go to `http://localhost:5173/sitemap.xml` to see the sitemap being dynamically generated, with links to all created posts and their last modified timestamps.

14. We can now link to the sitemap in the `robots.txt` file. As an example, we are going to set the URL to localhost. In a production app, you would adjust this URL to point to the sitemap on the URL of the deployed application. Edit `public/robots.txt` and add the following line:

```
Sitemap: http://localhost:5173/sitemap.xml
```

Now that we have successfully implemented measures to improve our app for search engines, let's take a look at our SEO score in the Lighthouse report:

Figure 8.4 – Our Lighthouse SEO score is now 100!

As we can see, our SEO score is now 100 (from 91 before). This might only seem like a slight improvement, but the Lighthouse report only takes into account basic checks, such as having a title, description, viewport tag, and a `robots.txt` file. We have done much more to optimize the user experience for visitors and search engines, such as improving the URL structure and adding dynamic titles and descriptions.

We could still further optimize our app by serving static assets via a **Content Delivery Network** (**CDN**) and using responsive images (serving images in different sizes to optimize performance on slower connections and avoid loading the full-size images). However, that is outside the scope of this book.

To wrap up this chapter, we are going to take a look at improving embeds on social media sites.

Improving social media embeds

We have already added the important meta tags for search engines. However, social media websites, such as Facebook and X (formerly Twitter), read additional meta tags to improve the embedding of your app on their sites and apps. Most social networks use a standard called Open Graph Meta Tags, which was originally created at Facebook. These tags can contain additional information on the type of page, a special title, the description, and an image for embedding the page on a social media website.

Open Graph meta tags

The **Open Graph** (**OG**) meta tags have four generic properties that every page can have:

- `og:type`: Describes the type of the page; specific types may have additional properties
- `og:title`: Describes the title of the page as it should appear on embeds
- `og:image`: An URL to an image that should be used for the embed
- `og:url`: An URL to a link that should be used for the embed

The og:type meta tag describes the type of content available on the page. It tells the social media sites how the embed should be formatted. Among others, the following values are possible:

- website: The default value, a basic embed
- article: This is for news and blog posts, and has additional parameters for published_time, modified_time, author, section, and tag
- profile: For user profiles, with additional parameters for first_name, last_name, username, and gender
- book: For books, with additional parameters for author, isbn, release_date, and tag
- music types: This includes music.song, music.album, music.playlist, and music.radio_station, each of them having different additional parameters
- video types: This includes video.movie, video.episode, video.tv_show, and video.other, each of them having different additional parameters

A full description of the OG meta tags and all possible values can be found on their official website: https://ogp.me/.

> **Info**
>
> Most social media sites support OG meta tags for embeds. However, some websites, including X (formerly Twitter), have their own meta tags, which take priority over OG meta tags, if provided. X can still read OG meta tags though, so it is enough to only provide those.

Now, we are going to focus on the article type, as we are developing a blog application, so we can use this type to provide better embeds for the blog posts.

Using the OG article meta tags

As we have learned, the article type allows us to include meta information about the published time, modified time, and author of an article on our page. Let's do this now for our single-post page:

1. Edit src/pages/ViewPost.jsx and import the getUserInfo API function, as we will need to resolve the author name for the corresponding meta tag:

   ```
   import { getUserInfo } from '../api/users.js'
   ```

2. Inside the `ViewPost` component after we fetch the post, fetch the author name. We make sure to only do this call if the `post?.author` attribute exists by using the `enabled` option of the `useQuery` hook:

```
const userInfoQuery = useQuery({
  queryKey: ['users', post?.author],
  queryFn: () => getUserInfo(post?.author),
  enabled: Boolean(post?.author),
})
const userInfo = userInfoQuery.data ?? {}
```

3. Inside the `Helmet` component, we define the `og:type` tag as `article` and define the title, published time, and modified time:

```
{post && (
  <Helmet>
    <title>{post.title} | Full-Stack React Blog</title>
    <meta name='description' content={truncate(post.
contents)} />
    <meta property='og:type' content='article' />
    <meta property='og:title' content={post.title} />
    <meta property='og:article:published_time'
content={post.createdAt} />
    <meta property='og:article:modified_time'
content={post.updatedAt} />
```

4. Then, we set the `og:article:author` to the resolved username:

```
    <meta property='og:article:author' content={userInfo.
username} />
```

5. Lastly, we loop through the tags (if there are none, we default to an empty array) and define a meta tag for each tag:

```
    {(post.tags ?? []).map((tag) => (
      <meta key={tag} property='og:article:tag'
content={tag} />
    ))}
  </Helmet>
)}
```

Arrays in OG meta tags work by redefining the same property multiple times.

Now that we have successfully added meta tags, our blog app is optimized for search engines and social media sites!

Summary

In this chapter, we first briefly learned how search engines work. Then, we created a `robots.txt` file, along with separate pages for each blog post, to better optimize our blog for search engines. Next, we created meaningful URLs (slugs) and set dynamic titles and meta tags. Then, we created a sitemap and evaluated the SEO score of our blog after all optimizations. Finally, we learned how social media embeds work and which meta tags can be used to improve embeds for articles, such as blog posts.

In the next chapter, *Chapter 9, Implementing End-to-End Tests Using Playwright*, we are going to learn how to write end-to-end tests for our user interface by setting up Playwright. Then, we are going to write some frontend tests for our blog application.

9

Implementing End-to-End Tests Using Playwright

In the previous chapters, we have written unit tests for our backend using Jest. Now, we are going to learn how to write and run end-to-end tests on our user interface using Playwright. First, we set up Playwright in our project and VS Code to allow for running frontend tests. Then, we are going to write some frontend tests for our application. Next, we are going to learn about reusing test setups with fixtures. Finally, we are going to learn how to view test reports and run Playwright in CI using GitHub Actions.

In this chapter, we are going to cover the following main topics:

- Setting up Playwright for end-to-end testing
- Writing and running end-to-end tests
- Reusable test setups using fixtures
- Viewing test reports and running in CI

Technical requirements

Before we start, please install all requirements from *Chapter 1, Preparing for Full-Stack Development*, and *Chapter 2, Getting to Know Node.js and MongoDB*.

The versions listed in those chapters are the ones used throughout the book. While installing a newer version should not be an issue, please note that certain steps might work differently on a newer version. If you are having an issue with the code and steps provided in this book, please try using the versions mentioned in the *Technical requirements* section of *Chapters 1* and *2*.

You can find the code for this chapter on GitHub: `https://github.com/PacktPublishing/Modern-Full-Stack-React-Projects/tree/main/ch9`.

If you cloned the full repository for the book, Husky may not find the `.git` directory when running `npm install`. In that case, just run `git init` in the root of the corresponding chapter folder.

The CiA link for this chapter can be found at: `https://youtu.be/WjwEwUR8g2c`

Setting up Playwright for end-to-end testing

Playwright is a test runner to facilitate end-to-end testing on various web rendering engines, such as Chromium (Chrome, Edge, Opera, etc.), WebKit (Safari), and Firefox. It can run tests on Windows, Linux, and macOS, locally or on CI. There are two ways of running Playwright:

- **Headed**: Opens a browser window where it can be seen what Playwright is doing
- **Headless**: Runs the rendering engine in the background and only displays the results of the tests in the Terminal or a generated test report

In this chapter, we are going to explore both ways of running Playwright. Let's now install Playwright in our project.

Installing Playwright

To install Playwright, we can use `npm init playwright`, which runs a command that installs Playwright, creates a folder for end-to-end tests for us, adds a GitHub Actions workflow to run tests in CI, and installs Playwright browsers so it can run tests in various engines. Follow these steps to install Playwright:

1. Copy the existing `ch8` folder to a new `ch9` folder, as follows:

   ```
   $ cp -R ch8 ch9
   ```

2. Open the `ch9` folder in VS Code and open a new Terminal.

3. Run the following command:

   ```
   $ npm init playwright@1.17.131
   ```

> **Note**
>
> Usually, it is a good idea to install the latest version here by running `npm init playwright@latest`. However, to make sure the instructions in this book are reproducible even when new versions with breaking changes are released, we pin the version here.

4. When asked if you want to proceed with installing the `create-playwright` package, press *Return/Enter* to confirm it. Then select **JavaScript**. As for the directory name, keep the `tests` default name and press *Return/Enter* to confirm it. Type `y` to add a GitHub Actions workflow. Type `y` again to install Playwright browsers. It will now take a while to download and install the different browser engines.

5. We need to adjust some files to make Playwright work with ES modules. Edit `playwright.config.js` and change the line with the `require()` import at the beginning of the file to the following:

    ```
    import { defineConfig, devices } from '@playwright/test'
    ```

6. Also, change the export from `module.exports` to the following:

    ```
    export default defineConfig({
    ```

7. *Delete* the `tests-examples/` folder and the `tests/example.spec.js` file.

After installing Playwright, we need to prepare our backend for end-to-end testing, so let's do that now.

Preparing the backend for end-to-end testing

To prepare the backend for end-to-end testing, we need to start an instance of the backend with the in-memory MongoDB server, similarly to what we did for the Jest tests. Let's do that now:

1. Create a new `backend/src/e2e.js` file. Inside it, import `dotenv`, `globalSetup`, and the app and `initDatabase` functions:

    ```
    import dotenv from 'dotenv'
    dotenv.config()

    import globalSetup from './test/globalSetup.js'
    import { app } from './app.js'
    import { initDatabase } from './db/init.js'
    ```

2. Then, define a new `async` function to run a testing server:

    ```
    async function runTestingServer() {
    ```

3. Inside this function, we first run the `globalSetup` function, which runs an in-memory MongoDB server. Then, we initialize the database and run the Express app:

    ```
    await globalSetup()
    await initDatabase()
    const PORT = process.env.PORT
    app.listen(PORT)
    console.info(`TESTING express server running on http://
    localhost:${PORT}`)
    }
    ```

4. Finally, we run the defined function:

    ```
    runTestingServer()
    ```

5. Edit `backend/package.json` and add a new script to run the `e2e.js` file:

    ```
    "e2e": „node src/e2e.js",
    ```

6. In the root of the project, install `concurrently`, a tool to run two commands in parallel:

    $ npm install --save-dev concurrently@8.2.2

    We are going to use this tool to run the backend and frontend in parallel.

7. Edit `package.json` in the root of the project and define an `e2e` script that will run `e2e:client` and `e2e:server` scripts in parallel:

    ```
    "e2e": "concurrently \"npm run e2e:client\" \"npm run
    e2e:server\"",
    ```

8. Now, define the `e2e:client` script, in which we just run the prebuilt frontend:

    ```
    "e2e:client": "npm run build && npm run start",
    ```

    For performance reasons, we do not run the dev server. Otherwise, we would be slowing down our end-to-end tests. We could omit the build script here, but then we must remember to build our frontend after making changes before running tests, and we must do this in CI as well. Alternatively, when running the tests locally, especially when we are only running certain tests and not all of them, we could run the dev server instead of building.

9. Then, we define the `e2e:server` script, which runs the `e2e` script in the `backend` folder:

    ```
    "e2e:server": "cd backend/ && npm run e2e",
    ```

10. Edit `playwright.config.js` and set the `baseURL` by changing the following line:

    ```
    use: {
        /* Base URL to use in actions like `await page.goto('/')`.
    */
        baseURL: 'http://localhost:5173',
    ```

11. Finally, edit `playwright.config.js` and *replace* the `webServer` config at the bottom of the file with the following:

    ```
    webServer: {
      command: 'npm run e2e',
      url: 'http://localhost:5173',
    },
    ```

Now that we have successfully set up Playwright and prepared the backend for end-to-end testing, let's get started writing and running end-to-end tests!

Writing and running end-to-end tests

We are now going to write and run our first end-to-end test with Playwright. Let's start with a simple test, which just verifies that we have properly optimized our title for search engines. Follow these steps to write and run your first end-to-end test:

1. Create a new `tests/seo.spec.js` file. Inside this file, we are going to check whether the title of our page is set properly.

2. Inside this newly created file, first import the `test` and `expect` functions from `@playwright/test`:

    ```
    import { test, expect } from '@playwright/test'
    ```

3. Then, we define a test in which we check whether the title of the blog is set properly:

    ```
    test('has title', async ({ page }) => {
    ```

    As you can see, the `test` function is similar to how we defined tests in Jest. Playwright additionally allows us to access special contexts in our test, called **fixtures**. The `page` fixture is the most essential fixture in Playwright and allows us to access browser features and interact with a page.

4. Inside the test, we first navigate to the URL of our frontend by using the `page.goto` function:

    ```
    await page.goto('/')
    ```

5. Then, we use the `expect` function to check whether the page displays the correct title:

    ```
    await expect(page).toHaveTitle('Full-Stack React Blog')
    })
    ```

    As we can see, the syntax of Playwright is very similar to Jest. We also have an `expect` function to make assertions, such as the page having a certain title.

6. Before running the tests, make sure the `dbserver` Docker container is running.

7. We can now run this test by opening a new Terminal and executing the following command:

    ```
    $ npx playwright test
    ```

Make sure you are in the root of our project (`ch9` folder), and not inside the `backend` folder, when running this command!

You will see that Playwright runs our test three times (on Chromium, Firefox, and Webkit) and that all of them passed successfully. The following screenshot shows the result of running Playwright in the command line:

```
→ ~/D/F/ch9 ⫤ main± > npx playwright test


Running 3 tests using 3 workers
  3 passed (15.4s)

To open last HTML report run:

  npx playwright show-report
```

Figure 9.1 – Running our first test in Playwright!

Now that we have successfully executed our test, let's move on to running tests using the VS Code extension.

Using the VS Code extension

Instead of manually running all tests via the command line, we can also run specific tests (or all tests) using a VS Code extension, similar to what we did for Jest. Additionally, the extension also allows us to get a visual overview of which tests are succeeding (or not), allows us to inspect tests while running in a browser, and can even record our interactions in the browser and generate tests from it!

Let's start by setting up the VS Code extension and running our test from it:

1. Open the **Extensions** tab in VS Code and search for `Playwright`.
2. Click the **Install** button to install **Playwright Test for VS Code** by Microsoft.
3. Click on the **Testing** tab in VS Code (the flask icon), which we also used for the Jest extension. Here, you will now see **Jest** and **Playwright** in the list.
4. Expand the **Playwright | tests** path, click on **seo.spec.js** to load the file, and then click on the **Play** icon next to **seo.spec.js** to run the test.

As we can see in the following screenshot, the test was executed successfully, and all tests are passing:

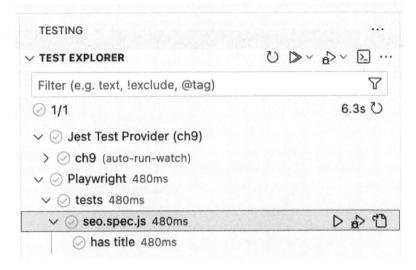

Figure 9.2 – Our playwright test successfully running from the VS Code extension!

Now that we have successfully run the tests in the VS Code extension in headless mode, let's move on to running them in headed mode, where we show what Playwright is doing in the browser while running tests.

Showing the browser while running tests

The Playwright VS Code extension also has a useful **Show browser** option, which opens the browser while running the tests. This allows us to debug tests or the frontend while the tests are running. Let's try it out now:

1. On the bottom of the **Testing** sidebar, check the **Show browser** box at the bottom of the sidebar and run the test again.

   A browser window will open and run the test. However, our test is very quick and simple, so it runs within a short amount of time and there is not much to see.

2. To better inspect the test, we can use the trace viewer. Check **Show trace viewer** at the bottom of the **Testing** sidebar and run the test again. You will see the following window open:

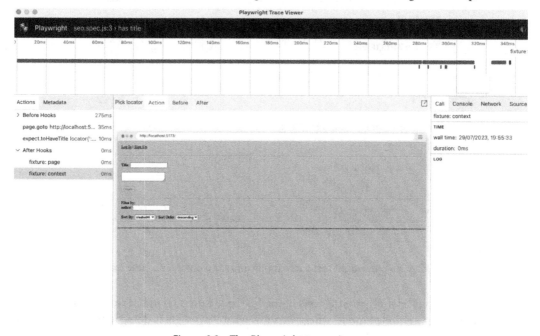

Figure 9.3 – The Playwright trace viewer

As we can see, the Playwright trace viewer shows us that the test ran `page.goto` and then `expect.toHaveTitle`. It also shows the state of the app at each step of the test. In our case, we only have one step though. This feature is especially useful when developing larger and more complex tests.

> **Note**
>
> It is also possible to run Playwright in UI mode, which opens the Playwright app in a separate window that allows us to run the tests separately and look at them being executed, similar to using the **Show trace viewer** function in the VS Code extension. You can run Playwright in UI mode by executing the following command: `npx playwright test --ui`

Now that we have learned about using the extension to run tests, we can move on to a very useful feature of the extension: recording actions to create a new test. Let's do that now.

Recording a test

The Playwright extension can also record new tests. Let's now create a new test for the signup page by using the test recording functionality of the VS Code extension:

1. Unlike running a Playwright test, the test recorder does not automatically start our frontend and backend, so we need to start them manually first. Open a new Terminal and execute the following command:

    ```
    $ npm run e2e
    ```

2. In the bottom section of the **Testing** sidebar, click on **Record new**. A browser window should open.

3. In the browser window, navigate to the frontend by pasting `http://localhost:5173/` into the URL bar.

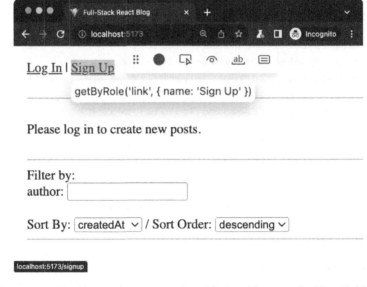

Figure 9.4 – The Playwright test recorder while hovering over the "Sign Up" link

4. Then, click on the **Sign Up** link. The sign-up page should open.

5. On this new page, enter a username and password; for example, `test` and `test`. Then press the **Sign Up** button.

6. You will get redirected to the login page. Now, log in with the same username and password as before.

7. You will get redirected to the main page and will be logged in as **test**. You can now close the browser window. You will see that inside VS Code you now have a new `test-1.spec.ts` file containing all the actions we just did in the browser!

8. Save the file and quit the `e2e` script running the backend and frontend. You will now see the `test-1.spec.ts` file in the **Testing** sidebar. If you try running the test, you will notice that it gets stuck on the login part, because our test currently does not wait for the redirect to the login page.

While recording tests is a useful feature to speed up writing end-to-end tests, it cannot always write functioning tests for us. We now need to clean up our recorded test and add assertions to it.

For reference, here is the full code generated by the Playwright test recorder:

```
import { test, expect } from '@playwright/test'

test('test', async ({ page }) => {
  await page.goto('http://localhost:5173/')
  await page.getByRole('link', { name: 'Sign Up' }).click()
  await page.getByLabel('Username:').click()
  await page.getByLabel('Username:').fill('test')
  await page.getByLabel('Password:').click()
  await page.getByLabel('Password:').fill('test')
  await page.getByRole('button', { name: 'Sign Up' }).click()
  await page.getByLabel('Username:').click()
  await page.getByLabel('Username:').fill('test')
  await page.getByLabel('Password:').click()
  await page.getByLabel('Password:').fill('test')
  await page.getByRole('button', { name: 'Log In' }).click()
})
```

Now that we have recorded a test, let's clean it up to make it run properly.

Cleaning up and finalizing the recorded test

If you have a look at the test, you will see that it has all the actions we performed in the browser, but it does not verify that we have been successfully logged in. It also does not wait for pages to finish loading and some matchers do not match the proper text. Let's fix those problems now:

1. Rename `tests/test-1.spec.ts` to `tests/auth.spec.js`.

2. Edit `tests/auth.spec.js` and rename the test to `allows sign up and log in`:

    ```
    test('allows sign up and log in', async ({ page }) => {
    ```

3. We need to define a unique username to be able to run our test multiple times without having to restart the backend to clear the MongoDB memory server:

    ```
    const testUser = 'test' + Date.now()
    ```

> **Note**
>
> It is important to not sign up twice with the same username, as the in-memory MongoDB database is reused for all the tests. Make sure that tests can run independently from each other and do not rely on data from other test files, as the test files could run in any order. Only the order within a single test file is guaranteed. Using `Date.now()` returns the current time in milliseconds and is mostly collision-safe as long as we do not run too many tests in parallel. For a more collision-safe solution, you could use a UUID generator instead.

4. Change the `page.goto()` URL to `/` to ensure it uses the `baseURL` we set up earlier:

    ```
    await page.goto('/')
    ```

5. Fill in the generated username when signing up:

    ```
    await page.getByLabel('Username:').fill(testUser)
    ```

6. After the click on the **Sign Up** button, wait for the URL to update by using the following function:

    ```
    await page.getByRole('button', { name: 'Sign Up' }).click()
    await page.waitForURL('**/login')
    ```

    Waiting for the next page to load is necessary because the recording does not support page-loading detection right now and it would otherwise fire the commands on the old page or during the redirect, which would cause the test to fail.

7. For the login, we also fill in the generated username:

    ```
    await page.getByLabel('Username:').fill(testUser)
    ```

8. After that, make the test click on on the **Log In** button and wait for the URL to update again:

    ```
    await page.getByRole('button', { name: 'Log In' }).click()
    await page.waitForURL('**/')
    ```

9. To more easily match the `Header` React component, edit `src/components/Header.jsx` and turn the `<div>` elements into `<nav>` elements:

    ```
    export function Header() {
      const [token, setToken] = useAuth()

      if (token) {
        const { sub } = jwtDecode(token)
        return (
          <nav>
            Logged in as <User id={sub} />
            <br />
            <button onClick={() => setToken(null)}>Logout</button>
    ```

```
        </nav>
    )
  }

  return (
    <nav>
      <Link to='/login'>Log In</Link> | <Link to='/signup'>Sign
Up</Link>
      </nav>
  )
}
```

10. At the end of the test, we now add an assertion that checks whether the Header (<nav> element) contains the text **Logged in as** and the generated username:

```
await expect(page.locator('nav')).toContainText('Logged in as
' + testUser)
})
```

Using toContainText instead of toHaveText ensures that the text does not have to be exactly the provided string. In our case, the **Logout** text is also part of the <nav> element, so the full text would be **Logged in as testXXXXLogout**.

11. Run the test either using the VS Code extension or by running the npx playwright test command in the Terminal (whichever you prefer), and you will see that it passes successfully now!

Note

If the test does not execute successfully, you might have accidentally recorded some additional actions and not cleaned them up properly. Compare your test to the code example provided by this book to make sure the test is properly defined and cleaned.

Now that we know how defining basic tests works in Playwright, let's learn about reusable test setups using fixtures.

Reusable test setups using fixtures

After creating the authentication test, you might be thinking: what if I want to define a test for creating a new post now? We would have to first sign up, then log in, then create the post. This is quite tedious and the more complex our tests get; the more tedious defining tests would get. Fortunately, Playwright has a solution for these kinds of problems. Playwright introduces a concept called fixtures, which are contexts for the test that can contain reusable functions. For example, we could define an auth fixture to provide sign-up and log-in functions to all tests.

When we used Jest, we were using before/after hooks to prepare the common environment for multiple tests. Fixtures have some advantages over before/after hooks. Mainly, they encapsulate setup and teardown in the same place and are reusable between test files, composable, and more flexible. Additionally, fixtures are provided *on demand*, which means that Playwright will only set up the fixtures necessary for running a certain test.

Playwright also includes some fixtures out of the box, which we are going to learn about now.

Overview of built-in fixtures

Playwright comes with some built-in fixtures, one of which we have already learned about: the page fixture. We are now going to briefly introduce the most important built-in fixtures Playwright provides out of the box:

- browser: Allows controlling browser features, such as opening a new page

- browserName: Contains the name of the browser that is currently running the test

- page: By far the most important built-in fixture, used to control interactions with the page, visiting URLs, matching elements, doing actions, and much more

- context: An isolated context for the current test run

- request: Used to make API requests from Playwright

Now that we have learned about the built-in fixtures Playwright provides, let's continue by defining our own fixture.

Writing our own fixture

Signing up and logging in are common actions that we will need to do often in our end-to-end tests, so they are the perfect case for creating a fixture. Follow these steps to create a new auth fixture:

1. Create a new tests/fixtures/ folder.

2. Inside it, create a new tests/fixtures/AuthFixture.js file, where we define an AuthFixture class:

    ```
    export class AuthFixture {
    ```

3. This class will receive the page fixture in the constructor:

    ```
    constructor(page) {
      this.page = page
    }
    ```

4. Define a `signUpAndLogIn` method, which follows the actions from the auth test to generate a unique username, then sign up and log in the user:

```
async signUpAndLogIn() {
    const testUser = 'test' + Date.now()
    await this.page.goto('/signup')
    await this.page.getByLabel('Username:').fill(testUser)
    await this.page.getByLabel('Password:').fill('password')
    await this.page.getByRole('button', { name: 'Sign Up'
}).click()
    await this.page.waitForURL('**/login')
    await this.page.getByLabel('Username:').fill(testUser)
    await this.page.getByLabel('Password:').fill('password')
    await this.page.getByRole('button', { name: 'Log In'
}).click()
    await this.page.waitForURL('**/')
    return testUser
    }
}
```

5. Create a new `tests/fixtures/index.js` file. Inside it, import the `test` function from Playwright (renaming it to `baseTest`) and the `AuthFixture` we just defined:

```
import { test as baseTest } from '@playwright/test'
import { AuthFixture } from './AuthFixture.js'
```

6. Then, define and export a new `test` function, extending the `baseTest` function from Playwright by defining a new `auth` fixture inside it:

```
export const test = baseTest.extend({
  auth: async ({ page }, use) => {
    const authFixture = new AuthFixture(page)
    await use(authFixture)
  },
})
```

> **Tip**
>
> It is also possible to do additional setup of the fixture context before calling the `use()` function, and additional breakdown after calling it. This can be used to, for example, create a set of example posts before executing tests and deleting them again afterward. If the backend had a way to delete a user, creating a temporary user and deleting the created username again after using the fixture would be a better option to deal with the issue of username collisions.

7. Additionally, re-export the `expect` function from Playwright to make it easier to import from our fixtures:

```
export { expect } from '@playwright/test'
```

Now that we have defined our custom fixture, let's use it while creating a new test!

Using custom fixtures

We are now going to define an end-to-end test for creating a new post. To create a post, we need to be logged in so we can use our `auth` fixture for preparing the environment. Follow these steps to define the new test and use our custom fixture:

1. Create a new `tests/create-post.spec.js` file. To use the custom fixture, we now need to import the `test` and `expect` functions from the `fixtures/index.js` file:

```
import { test, expect } from './fixtures/index.js'
```

2. Define a new test to verify that post creation works, using the `page` and `auth` fixtures:

```
test('allows creating a new post', async ({ page, auth }) => {
```

3. We can now use the `signUpAndLogIn` method from our custom `auth` fixture to create and log in a new user:

```
    const testUser = await auth.signUpAndLogIn()
})
```

4. We can make use of Playwright code generation again to record our test. First, save the file and execute the `create-post.spec.js` test with **Show browser** enabled.

5. Then, create a new line after the `auth.signUpAndLogIn` function is called and press **Record at cursor**.

6. Now we can record actions from the already opened browser window (which is also already logged in, because the fixture methods were called already!). Click into the title field and enter `Test Post` as the post title, then press *Tab* to go to the next field, enter `Hello World!` as the post content, then press *Tab* again and press *Return/Enter* to create a new post.

Note

The post does not actually get created, because Playwright closes the backend right after it finishes running it, so at the time of recording, the backend is already shut down. If you want to record with the backend running, explore the `webServer.reuseExistingServer` setting in `playwright.config.js`.

---

7. Go back to the file, and you will see that all actions were properly recorded! The following code should have been recorded:

```
await page.getByLabel('Title:').click()
await page.getByLabel('Title:').fill('Test Post')
await page.getByLabel('Title:').press('Tab')
await page.locator('textarea').fill('Hello World!')
await page.locator('textarea').press('Tab')
await page.getByRole('button', { name: 'Create'
}).press('Enter')
```

8. Now, we just need to add a check whether the post was created successfully:

```
await expect(page.getByText(`Test PostWritten by
${testUser}`)).toBeVisible()
})
```

As we are controlling the test environment, it is enough to check that the text **Test PostWritten by testXXX** (without a space between "Post" and "Written") is visible on the page. This will tell us that the post was created in the list.

9. Run the test, and you will see that it passes successfully!

We could create additional fixtures for handling posts (creating, editing, deleting) and use these to, for example, verify that the link to a single post works properly and adjusts the title accordingly. However, extending end-to-end tests like that is similar to what we have already done and is thus left as an exercise for you.

Viewing test reports and running in CI

After successfully creating some end-to-end tests for our blog application, let's wrap up the chapter by learning how to view HTML test reports and how to run Playwright in CI.

Viewing an HTML report

Playwright automatically generates HTML reports of test runs. We can generate these by executing the following command to run all tests:

```
$ npx playwright test
```

Then, run the following command to serve and view the HTML report of the last run:

```
$ npx playwright show-report
```

The report should open in a new browser window, and look as follows:

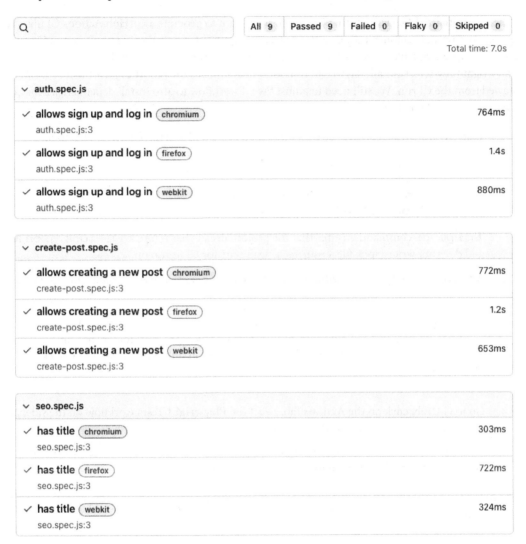

Figure 9.5 – An HTML test report generated by Playwright

As we can see, our three tests were successfully run on all three browsers. Click on one of the test runs to view all executed test steps in detail.

Running Playwright tests in CI

When we initialized Playwright, we were asked if we want to generate a GitHub Actions CI file. We agreed, so Playwright automatically generated a CI configuration for us in the `.github/workflows/playwright.yml` file. This workflow checks out the repository, installs all dependencies, installs Playwright browsers, runs all Playwright tests, and then uploads the report as an artifact so it can be viewed from the CI run. We still need to adjust the CI workflow to also install dependencies for our backend, so let's do that now:

1. Edit `.github/workflows/playwright.yml` and add the following step to it:

    ```
    - name: Install dependencies
      run: npm ci
    - name: Install backend dependencies
      run: cd backend/ && npm ci
    ```

    The `npm ci` command ensures that the project already has a `package-lock.json` file and does not write a lock file, ensuring a clean state for CI to run on.

2. Add, commit, and push everything to a GitHub repository to see Playwright running in CI.

> **Note**
>
> Make sure to create a new repository from just the contents of the ch9 folder (not the whole `Full-Stack-React-Projects` folder!), otherwise GitHub Actions will not detect the `.github` folder.

3. Go to GitHub, click on the **Actions** tab, select the **Playwright Tests** workflow on the sidebar, and then click on the latest workflow run.

4. At the bottom of the run, there is an **Artifacts** section, which contains a `playwright-report` object that can be downloaded to view the HTML report.

The following screenshot shows the Playwright tests running in GitHub Actions, with the report provided as an artifact:

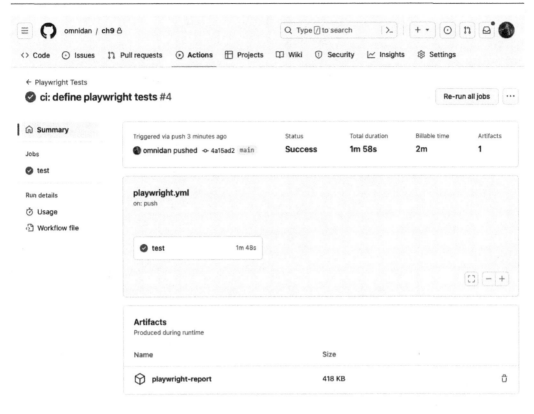

Figure 9.6 – Playwright running in GitHub Actions

As we can see, running Playwright in CI by using the provided template is simple and straightforward.

Summary

In this chapter, we learned about using Playwright for end-to-end testing. We first set up Playwright in our project and prepared our backend for end-to-end testing. Then, we wrote and ran our first test. Next, we learned about fixtures to make reusable test contexts. Finally, we viewed the generated HTML report and set up CI to run Playwright, generate a report, and save it as an artifact in the pipeline.

In the next chapter, *Chapter 10, Aggregating and Visualizing Statistics Using MongoDB and Victory*, we are going to learn how to aggregate data using MongoDB and expose this aggregated data via a backend. Then, we are going to consume the aggregated data in the frontend and visualize it using Victory with various visualization types.

10

Aggregating and Visualizing Statistics Using MongoDB and Victory

In this chapter, we are going to learn how to collect, aggregate, and visualize statistics for our blog application using MongoDB and Victory. We start out by learning how we can collect events from users viewing blog posts. Then, we randomly generate some events to have a dataset to work with. We use this dataset to learn how to aggregate data with MongoDB and generate summary statistics, such as the number of views per post, or the average session duration on a post. This kind of information will help authors know how well their posts are doing. Finally, we create some graphs to visualize these aggregated statistics using the Victory library.

In this chapter, we are going to cover the following main topics:

- Collecting and simulating events
- Aggregating data with MongoDB
- Implementing data aggregation in the backend
- Integrating and visualizing data on the frontend using Victory

Technical requirements

Before we start, please install all requirements from *Chapter 1*, *Preparing for Full-Stack Development*, and *Chapter 2*, *Getting to Know Node.js and MongoDB*.

The versions listed in those chapters are the ones used in the book. While installing a newer version should not be an issue, please note that certain steps might work differently on a newer version. If you are having an issue with the code and steps provided in this book, please try using the versions mentioned in *Chapters 1* and *2*.

You can find the code for this chapter on GitHub: `https://github.com/PacktPublishing/Modern-Full-Stack-React-Projects/tree/main/ch10`.

If you cloned the full repository for the book, Husky may not find the `.git` directory when running `npm install`. In that case, just run `git init` in the root of the corresponding chapter folder.

The CiA video for this chapter can be found at: `https://youtu.be/DmSq2P_IQQs`.

Collecting and simulating events

Before we can get started aggregating and visualizing statistics, we first need to collect (and later simulate) events, which we are going to use to create the statistics. We will start by thinking about which data we want to collect, and which data would be useful for us. We will focus on post views for now, so we would like to show the following statistics per post:

- Total number of views on a post
- Daily views on a post
- Daily average viewing duration on a post

Let's start by creating the database model for events that will allow us to show these statistics.

Creating the event model

To create these statistics, we need to collect events from users. Events will contain a reference to a post, a session ID to track events from the same viewing, an action (started viewing, ended viewing), and a date of when the event happened.

Let's get started defining the database model for events:

1. Copy the existing `ch9` folder to a new `ch10` folder, as follows:

    ```
    $ cp -R ch9 ch10
    ```

2. Open the `ch10` folder in VS Code.

3. Create a new backend/src/db/models/event.js file. Inside this file, define a schema that contains a reference to a post:

```
import mongoose, { Schema } from 'mongoose'

const eventsSchema = new Schema(
  {
    post: { type: Schema.Types.ObjectId, ref: 'post', required:
true },
```

4. Then define a session, action, and date:

```
    session: { type: String, required: true },
    action: { type: String, required: true },
    date: { type: Date, required: true },
  },
  { timestamps: true },
)
```

5. Finally, export the model:

```
export const Event = mongoose.model('events', eventsSchema)
```

Now that we have defined the database model, let's continue by defining a service function and route to track events.

Defining a service function and route to track events

Now that we have successfully defined our database model for events, let's create a service function and route to track new events, as follows:

1. To generate session IDs, we are going to use the uuid library, which generates **universally unique identifiers (UUIDs)** for us. Install it by running the following commands:

```
$ cd backend/
$ npm install uuid@9.0.1
```

2. Create a new backend/src/services/events.js file. Inside it, import the v4 function from uuid and the Event model and define a function to create a new event document, as follows:

```
import { v4 as uuidv4 } from 'uuid'
import { Event } from '../db/models/event.js'

export async function trackEvent({
  postId,
  action,
```

```
    session = uuidv4(),
    date = Date.now(),
}) {
    const event = new Event({ post: postId, action, session, date
})
    return await event.save()
}
```

In the arguments to the function, we set the default session ID to a randomly generated UUID and the date to the current date.

3. Create a new backend/src/routes/events.js file. Inside it, import the trackEvent function and the getPostById function:

```
import { trackEvent } from '../services/events.js'
import { getPostById } from '../services/posts.js'
```

4. Define a new POST /api/v1/events route, in which we get the postId, session, and action from the body:

```
export function eventRoutes(app) {
    app.post('/api/v1/events', async (req, res) => {
        try {
            const { postId, session, action } = req.body
```

5. Then, we check whether a post with the given ID exists in the database. If not, we return a 400 Bad Request status code:

```
            const post = await getPostById(postId)
            if (post === null) return res.status(400).end()
```

6. If the post exists, we get the session ID and use the trackEvent function to create a new event:

```
            const event = await trackEvent({ postId, session, action
})
            return res.json({ session: event.session })
        } catch (err) {
            console.error('error tracking action', err)
            return res.status(500).end()
        }
    })
}
```

7. Edit backend/src/app.js and import eventRoutes:

```
import { eventRoutes } from './routes/events.js'
```

8. Then mount the routes to the app:

```
postRoutes(app)
userRoutes(app)
eventRoutes(app)
```

9. Start the backend as follows (and keep it running for future development):

```
$ cd backend/
$ npm run dev
```

Now that we have successfully defined a backend route to track events, let's implement event collection on the frontend.

Collecting events on the frontend

After defining the route, let's create the API function for the frontend and define a way to track when a user started and ended viewing a post. Follow these steps to collect events on the frontend:

1. Create a new `src/api/events.js` file and define a `postTrackEvent` function, which takes an event object and sends it to the previously defined route:

```
export const postTrackEvent = (event) =>
  fetch(`${import.meta.env.VITE_BACKEND_URL}/events`, {
    method: 'POST',
    headers: {
      'Content-Type': 'application/json',
    },
    body: JSON.stringify(event),
  }).then((res) => res.json())
```

2. Edit `src/pages/ViewPost.jsx` and import the `useEffect`, `useState`, and `useMutation` hooks:

```
import { useEffect, useState } from 'react'
import { useQuery, useMutation } from '@tanstack/react-query'
```

3. Additionally, import the `postTrackEvent` API function:

```
import { postTrackEvent } from '../api/events.js'
```

4. Now, inside the `ViewPost` function, define a new state hook to store the session ID, and a mutation to track the events. When an event is successfully tracked, we get a session ID from the backend. We store this in the state hook:

```
const [session, setSession] = useState()
const trackEventMutation = useMutation({
```

```
        mutationFn: (action) => postTrackEvent({ postId, action,
    session }),
        onSuccess: (data) => setSession(data?.session),
    })
```

5. Then, define a new effect hook in which we track a `startView` event a second after the user opened the post (to prevent tracking accidental events, such as from quick refreshes), and an `endView` event when the effect hook unmounts. We give it no dependencies to ensure the effect hook is only triggered when the page mounts and unmounts:

```
useEffect(() => {
  let timeout = setTimeout(() => {
    trackEventMutation.mutate('startView')
    timeout = null
  }, 1000)
  return () => {
    if (timeout) clearTimeout(timeout)
    else trackEventMutation.mutate('endView')
  }
}, [])
```

6. Start the frontend as follows (and keep it running for future development):

```
$ npm run dev
```

Make sure to run this command in the root of the `ch10` folder, not inside the `backend` folder.

If you now open a post in your browser and take a look at the **Network** tab of the inspector, you will see that after a second, the `startView` event is tracked. When we navigate away from the page, the `endView` event is tracked.

Let's now move on to simulating events so that we have more data to aggregate and visualize later.

Simulating events

Simulating events is a great way to generate sample data to be used for testing the aggregations and visualizations. In our simulation, we first clear all current users from the database and then create a set of sample users. We repeat the same process for posts, and then for events, simulating that a random user creates a post and that someone views a random post for a random amount of time.

Follow these steps to implement a simulation:

1. First of all, we should change the database to avoid losing any data we previously created in the other chapters. Edit `backend/.env` and change the following line from `blog` to `blog-simulated`:

```
DATABASE_URL=mongodb://localhost:27017/blog-simulated
```

2. Now, create a new `backend/simulateEvents.js` file, in which we import `dotenv`, the `initDatabase` function, and all the relevant models and service functions:

```
import dotenv from 'dotenv'
dotenv.config()

import { initDatabase } from './src/db/init.js'
import { Post } from './src/db/models/post.js'
import { User } from './src/db/models/user.js'
import { Event } from './src/db/models/event.js'
import { createUser } from './src/services/users.js'
import { createPost } from './src/services/posts.js'
import { trackEvent } from './src/services/events.js'
```

3. Define a start time for the simulation, which here is set to 30 days ago (30 days * 24 hours * 60 minutes * 60 seconds * 1000 milliseconds), and an end time, which is now:

```
const simulationStart = Date.now() - 1000 * 60 * 60 * 24 * 30
const simulationEnd = Date.now()
```

4. We also define the number of users, posts, and views to simulate:

```
const simulatedUsers = 5
const simulatedPosts = 10
const simulatedViews = 10000
```

5. Then, define the `simulateEvents` function, in which we first initialize the database:

```
async function simulateEvents() {
  const connection = await initDatabase()
```

6. Next, *delete* all existing users and create new users by initializing an empty array with the number of users to be simulated and mapping over it:

```
await User.deleteMany({})
const createdUsers = await Promise.all(
  Array(simulatedUsers)
    .fill(null)
    .map(
      async (_, u) =>
        await createUser({
          username: `user-${u}`,
          password: `password-${u}`,
        }),
    ),
```

```
  )
  console.log(`created ${createdUsers.length} users`)
```

> **Info**
>
> The `Array(X)` function can be used to create an array with X entries, which then needs to be filled with an initial value before it can be iterated over.

7. Now, repeat the same process for posts:

```
  await Post.deleteMany({})
  const createdPosts = await Promise.all(
    Array(simulatedPosts)
      .fill(null)
      .map(async (_, p) => {
        const randomUser =
          createdUsers[Math.floor(Math.random() *
simulatedUsers)]
        return await createPost(randomUser._id, {
          title: `Test Post ${p}`,
          contents: `This is a test post ${p}`,
        })
      }),
  )
  console.log(`created ${createdPosts.length} posts`)
```

> **Info**
>
> We use `Math.floor(Math.random() * maxNumber)` to create a random integer between 0 and maxNumber (non-inclusive), which is perfect to be used for indexing an array.

8. Lastly, we repeat the same for events:

```
  await Event.deleteMany({})
  const createdViews = await Promise.all(
    Array(simulatedViews)
      .fill(null)
      .map(async () => {
        const randomPost =
          createdPosts[Math.floor(Math.random() *
simulatedPosts)]
```

9. Here, we start the session at a random time within the defined simulation dates:

```
const sessionStart =
    simulationStart + Math.random() * (simulationEnd -
simulationStart)
```

10. And we end it randomly after 0 to 5 minutes:

```
const sessionEnd =
    sessionStart + 1000 * Math.floor(Math.random() * 60 *
5)
```

11. Now, we simulate the event collection, first by creating a `startView` event:

```
const event = await trackEvent({
    postId: randomPost._id,
    action: 'startView',
    date: new Date(sessionStart),
})
```

12. And then we simulate an `endView` event, where we use the session ID returned from the first event:

```
await trackEvent({
    postId: randomPost._id,
    session: event.session,
    action: 'endView',
    date: new Date(sessionEnd),
})
}),
)
console.log(`successfully simulated ${createdViews.length}
views`)
```

13. Lastly, we disconnect from the database and call the function:

```
await connection.disconnect()
}

simulateEvents()
```

14. Our simulation is now ready to be used! Execute the following command to start it:

```
$ cd backend/
$ node simulateEvents.js
```

You will see that the simulation first creates 5 users, then 10 posts, and finally simulates 10,000 views.

In the next section, we are going to use this dataset to try out some aggregations with MongoDB!

Aggregating data with MongoDB

Sometimes, we do not just want to simply retrieve data from the database, but instead, we want to create some statistics from the data by combining and summarizing it. This process is called **data aggregation**, and it can help us understand more about the data. For example, we can count the total number of views per post, get the number of daily views per post, or calculate the average session duration when viewing a post.

MongoDB supports a special aggregation syntax using the `.aggregate()` function on a collection. Using this aggregation functionality from MongoDB allows us to efficiently query and process documents. The operations it provides are similar to what can be done with **Structured Query Language (SQL)** queries. Mainly, we are going to use the following aggregation operations:

- `$match`: Used to filter documents
- `$group`: Used to group documents by a certain property
- `$project`: Used to map properties to different properties, or process them
- `$sort`: Used to sort documents

> **Info**
>
> MongoDB provides many more advanced aggregation operations, all of which can be found in their documentation (https://www.mongodb.com/docs/manual/aggregation/). They are also constantly adding more operations to make aggregation even more powerful.

The `aggregate` function works by providing an array of objects, each of which defines a **stage** of the **aggregation pipeline**. We are going to learn more about aggregations in this chapter by using them in practice.

Getting the total number of views per post

The first aggregation that we are going to define is a way to get the total number of views per post. For such an aggregation, we are going to need `$match` to filter all `startView` actions (otherwise we would be counting views twice, because there is also an `endView` action for each blog post view), and `$group` to group the results by post ID and then return the number of documents using `$count`.

Follow these steps to create your first aggregation pipeline:

1. Create a new `backend/playground/` folder for our playground scripts.

2. Click on the MongoDB extension (the leaf icon) in the VS Code sidebar.

3. Connect to the database, then expand the **Playgrounds** section (if it is not expanded already), and click on the **Create New Playground** button.

    A new file will open up with some code already predefined for us. *Delete* all predefined code, as we are going to *replace* it with our own.

4. First, define the `use` and `db` globals, which the MongoDB Playground provides for us:

    ```
    /* global use, db */
    ```

5. Then, use the `blog-simulated` database:

    ```
    use('blog-simulated')
    ```

6. Now, execute the following aggregation function:

    ```
    db.getCollection('events').aggregate([
    ```

7. The first stage of the pipeline will be matching all `startView` actions:

    ```
        {
            $match: { action: 'startView' },
        },
    ```

8. Then, we group by post. The `$group` stage requires us to define an `_id`, which contains the property to be grouped by. We need to use the `$` operator to resolve the variable to be used, so `$post` will access the `event.post` property (which contains a post ID):

    ```
        {
            $group: {
              _id: '$post',
              views: { $count: {} },
            },
        },
    ])
    ```

9. Save the script as a `backend/playground/views-per-post.mongodb.js` file.

10. Click on the **Play** icon at the top right to run the script. A new tab will open with the results of the aggregation:

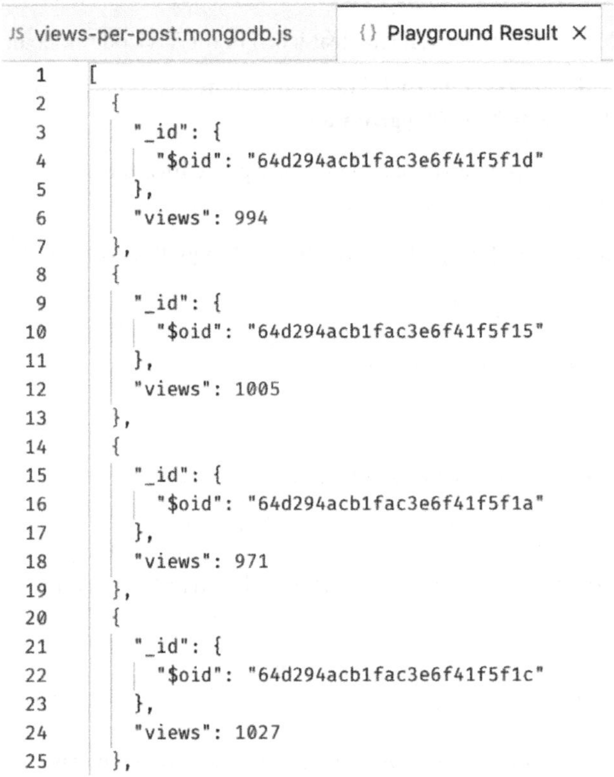

```
JS views-per-post.mongodb.js          {} Playground Result  X

1    [
2       {
3          "_id": {
4             "$oid": "64d294acb1fac3e6f41f5f1d"
5          },
6          "views": 994
7       },
8       {
9          "_id": {
10            "$oid": "64d294acb1fac3e6f41f5f15"
11         },
12         "views": 1005
13      },
14      {
15         "_id": {
16            "$oid": "64d294acb1fac3e6f41f5f1a"
17         },
18         "views": 971
19      },
20      {
21         "_id": {
22            "$oid": "64d294acb1fac3e6f41f5f1c"
23         },
24         "views": 1027
25      },
```

Figure 10.1 – Our first MongoDB aggregation result!

After creating and executing our first simple aggregation, let's continue practicing by writing more advanced aggregations.

Getting the number of daily views per post

Now that we are already familiar with the general process of writing MongoDB aggregations, let's try writing a bit more complicated aggregation: getting the number of daily views per post. Follow these steps to create it:

1. Create a new playground file, as before, with the following aggregation function:

```
/* global use, db */
use('blog-simulated')
db.getCollection('events').aggregate([
```

2. Again, we first match only the `startView` actions:

```
{
    $match: { action: 'startView' },
},
```

3. Then we use `$project` to keep the `post` property, and define a new `day` property, which uses the `$dateTrunc` function to simplify the `date` property to only cover days (instead of containing the full timestamp):

```
{
    $project: {
        post: '$post',
        day: { $dateTrunc: { date: '$date', unit: 'day' } },
    },
},
```

An important thing to keep in mind with `$project` is that only properties that are listed here will be passed on to further stages in the pipeline, so we need to list all properties that we are still going to need later here!

4. Finally, we use `$group` to group the documents by `post` and `day` by passing an object to the `_id` property. We use `$count` again to count the number of documents in each group:

```
{
    $group: {
        _id: { post: '$post', day: '$day' },
        views: { $count: {} },
    },
},
])
```

5. Save the script as a `backend/playground/views-per-post-per-day.mongodb.js` file.

6. Run this script by clicking on the **Play** button and you will see that we are now getting a list of documents grouped by post and day, and the corresponding number of views of a certain post on a certain day:

```
{} Playground Result  ×
1    [
2        {
3            "_id": {
4                "post": {
5                    "$oid": "65c8ef3599c4fdd0c066ed74"
6                },
7                "day": {
8                    "$date": "2024-01-30T00:00:00Z"
9                }
10           },
11           "views": 36
12       },
13       {
14           "_id": {
15               "post": {
16                   "$oid": "65c8ef3599c4fdd0c066ed72"
17               },
18               "day": {
19                   "$date": "2024-01-12T00:00:00Z"
20               }
21           },
22           "views": 7
23       },
```

Figure 10.2 – Showing the number of views per post per day

After getting the number of daily views per post, let's continue practicing by calculating the average session duration.

Calculating the average session duration

As you may remember, we are first sending a `startView` action, and then later an `endView` action, both of which have a separate `date`. Let's use aggregations to group these two actions together into a single document, and then compute the duration of a session:

1. Create a new playground file, and start writing an aggregation that first creates some new properties using `$project`, and keeps the `session` property, as we will need it later:

```
/* global use, db */
use('blog-simulated')
db.getCollection('events').aggregate([
  {
    $project: {
      session: '$session',
```

```
        startDate: {
            $cond: [{ $eq: ['$action', 'startView'] }, '$date',
    undefined],
          },
          endDate: { $cond: [{ $eq: ['$action', 'endView'] },
    '$date', undefined] },
        },
    },
```

Here, we are using the $cond operator to create a conditional (kind of like a ternary/if statement). It accepts an array with three elements: the first being a condition, the next a result if the condition matches, and lastly, a result if the condition does not match. In our case, we check whether the action property is startView (using the $eq operator). If true, then we set the date to the startDate property. Otherwise, we do not define the startDate property. Similarly, if the action is endView, we create an endDate property.

2. Now, we can group the documents by the session ID and select the lowest start date and the highest end date of a session:

```
    {
      $group: {
        _id: '$session',
        startDate: { $min: '$startDate' },
        endDate: { $max: '$endDate' },
      },
    },
```

There should only be one startView and endView action per session anyway, but we cannot guarantee this, so we need to aggregate them down into a single value!

3. Finally, we use $project again to rename the _id property to session, and calculate the duration by subtracting the startDate from the endDate:

```
    {
      $project: {
        session: '$_id',
        duration: { $subtract: ['$endDate', '$startDate'] },
      },
    },
  ])
```

4. Save the script as a backend/playground/session-duration.mongodb.js file.

5. Run the script and you will see a list of documents with a session ID and a corresponding duration in milliseconds:

```
{} Playground Result  ×

1    [
2      {
3        "_id": "546c319f-45f3-4a8b-8115-ec3298aef3eb",
4        "session": "546c319f-45f3-4a8b-8115-ec3298aef3eb",
5        "duration": 35000
6      },
7      {
8        "_id": "e0adff0d-2dad-4137-8b40-0480e0a71a5e",
9        "session": "e0adff0d-2dad-4137-8b40-0480e0a71a5e",
10       "duration": 78000
11     },
12     {
13       "_id": "cde9dff5-7403-4725-a3b9-945d5e433b33",
14       "session": "cde9dff5-7403-4725-a3b9-945d5e433b33",
15       "duration": 85000
16     },
```

Figure 10.3 – Aggregation result of the session durations

Now that we are more familiar with how data aggregation works in MongoDB, let's implement similar aggregations in our backend!

Implementing data aggregation in the backend

For our backend, we are going to use very similar aggregation pipelines. However, we need to adjust them slightly, as we always want to get the data for a single post only. As such, we will first be using $match to filter our documents. This also ensures that the aggregation stays fast, even if we have millions of events in our database, because we are first filtering down to all events of a single post!

Defining aggregation service functions

Follow these steps to implement the aggregation functions in the backend:

1. Edit `backend/src/services/events.js` and define a new function to get the total number of views for a post. In this case, we can simplify our code by using the `countDocuments` function instead of the aggregate function:

```
export async function getTotalViews(postId) {
  return {
```

```
        views: await Event.countDocuments({ post: postId, action:
    'startView' }),
      }
    }
```

2. Next, define a new function to get the daily views of a post with a given ID. We now use the `$match` operation to only get the `startView` actions of a certain post:

```
export async function getDailyViews(postId) {
  return await Event.aggregate([
    {
      $match: {
        post: postId,
        action: 'startView',
      },
    },
```

3. Then, we use the `$group` operation in combination with `$dateTrunc` to get the views per day, just like we did before in the MongoDB Playground script:

```
    {
      $group: {
        _id: {
          $dateTrunc: { date: '$date', unit: 'day' },
        },
        views: { $count: {} },
      },
    },
```

4. Lastly, we use the `$sort` operation to sort the resulting documents by `_id` (which contains the day):

```
    {
      $sort: { _id: 1 },
    },
  ])
}
```

5. For the last function, we use our session duration aggregation, but extend it a little bit to give the average duration per day. Again, we first need to match a post ID:

```
export async function getDailyDurations(postId) {
  return await Event.aggregate([
    {
      $match: {
        post: postId,
```

```
        },
      },
```

6. Then, we use the same `$project` and `$group` operations to get the `session`, `startDate`, and `endDate`, just like we did before:

```
    {
      $project: {
        session: '$session',
        startDate: {
          $cond: [{ $eq: ['$action', 'startView'] }, '$date',
    undefined],
        },
        endDate: {
          $cond: [{ $eq: ['$action', 'endView'] }, '$date',
    undefined],
        },
      },
    },
    {
      $group: {
        _id: '$session',
        startDate: { $min: '$startDate' },
        endDate: { $max: '$endDate' },
      },
    },
```

7. Now, we use the `$project` operation to get `day` from our `startDate`, like we did in the previous aggregation where we got the number of daily views of a post:

```
    {
      $project: {
        day: { $dateTrunc: { date: '$startDate', unit: 'day' }
    },
        duration: { $subtract: ['$endDate', '$startDate'] },
      },
    },
```

8. We group the results per day, and calculate the average duration of a day:

```
    {
      $group: {
        _id: '$day',
        averageDuration: { $avg: '$duration' },
      },
    },
```

9. Finally, we sort the results per day:

```
    {
      $sort: { _id: 1 },
    },
  ])
}
```

As we can see, aggregation pipelines are extremely powerful and allow us to do a lot of data processing directly in the database! In the next section, we are going to create routes for these aggregation functions.

Defining the routes

Defining the routes is pretty straightforward; we simply check whether a post with the given ID exists, and if it does, we return the results from the corresponding aggregation service function. Let's start defining the routes:

1. Edit `backend/src/routes/events.js` and import the `getTotalViews`, `getDailyViews`, and `getDailyDurations` functions:

```
import {
  trackEvent,
  getTotalViews,
  getDailyViews,
  getDailyDurations,
} from '../services/events.js'
```

2. Next, inside the `eventRoutes` function, define a new route for getting the total number of views of a post, as follows:

```
  app.get('/api/v1/events/totalViews/:postId', async (req, res)
=> {
    try {
      const { postId } = req.params
      const post = await getPostById(postId)
      if (post === null) return res.status(400).end()
      const stats = await getTotalViews(post._id)
      return res.json(stats)
    } catch (err) {
      console.error('error getting stats', err)
      return res.status(500).end()
    }
  })
```

3. Then define a similar route for the number of daily views of a post:

```
app.get('/api/v1/events/dailyViews/:postId', async (req, res)
=> {
  try {
    const { postId } = req.params
    const post = await getPostById(postId)
    if (post === null) return res.status(400).end()
    const stats = await getDailyViews(post._id)
    return res.json(stats)
  } catch (err) {
    console.error('error getting stats', err)
    return res.status(500).end()
  }
})
```

4. And finally, define a route for the daily average viewing duration of a post:

```
app.get('/api/v1/events/dailyDurations/:postId', async (req,
res) => {
  try {
    const { postId } = req.params
    const post = await getPostById(postId)
    if (post === null) return res.status(400).end()
    const stats = await getDailyDurations(post._id)
    return res.json(stats)
  } catch (err) {
    console.error('error getting stats', err)
    return res.status(500).end()
  }
})
```

Now that we have successfully defined routes for our aggregation functions, it's time to integrate them into the frontend and start visualizing the data we have been simulating and collecting!

Integrating and visualizing data on the frontend using Victory

In this final section, we are going to integrate the aggregation endpoints we previously defined. Then, we are going to introduce the Victory library in the frontend to create graphs to visualize our aggregated data!

Integrating the aggregation API

First of all, we need to integrate the API routes in the frontend, as follows:

1. Edit the `src/api/events.js` file and add three new API functions to get the total views, daily views, and daily durations of a post:

```
export const getTotalViews = (postId) =>
  fetch(`${import.meta.env.VITE_BACKEND_URL}/events/
totalViews/${postId}`).then(
    (res) => res.json(),
  )

export const getDailyViews = (postId) =>
  fetch(`${import.meta.env.VITE_BACKEND_URL}/events/
dailyViews/${postId}`).then(
    (res) => res.json(),
  )

export const getDailyDurations = (postId) =>
  fetch(
    `${import.meta.env.VITE_BACKEND_URL}/events/
dailyDurations/${postId}`,
  ).then((res) => res.json())
```

2. Create a new `src/components/PostStats.jsx` file, in which we are going to query these new API routes. Start by importing `useQuery`, `PropTypes`, and the three API functions:

```
import { useQuery } from '@tanstack/react-query'
import PropTypes from 'prop-types'
import {
  getTotalViews,
  getDailyViews,
  getDailyDurations,
} from '../api/events.js'
```

3. Define a new component that takes a `postId` and fetches all the stats that we aggregated on the backend using query hooks:

```
export function PostStats({ postId }) {
  const totalViews = useQuery({
    queryKey: ['totalViews', postId],
    queryFn: () => getTotalViews(postId),
  })
  const dailyViews = useQuery({
    queryKey: ['dailyViews', postId],
```

```
      queryFn: () => getDailyViews(postId),
    })
    const dailyDurations = useQuery({
      queryKey: ['dailyDurations', postId],
      queryFn: () => getDailyDurations(postId),
    })
```

4. While the stats are loading, we display a simple loading message:

```
    if (
      totalViews.isLoading ||
      dailyViews.isLoading ||
      dailyDurations.isLoading
    ) {
      return <div>loading stats...</div>
    }
```

5. Once the stats are finished loading, we can display them. For now, we simply display the total number of views and the JSON responses from the other two API requests:

```
    return (
      <div>
        <b>{totalViews.data?.views} total views</b>
        <pre>{JSON.stringify(dailyViews.data)}</pre>
        <pre>{JSON.stringify(dailyDurations.data)}</pre>
      </div>
    )
  }
```

6. We still need to define the prop types for this component, as follows:

```
  PostStats.propTypes = {
    postId: PropTypes.string.isRequired,
  }
```

7. Now we can render the `PostStats` component in our `ViewPost` page component. Edit `src/pages/ViewPost.jsx` and import the `PostStats` component there:

```
  import { PostStats } from '../components/PostStats.jsx'
```

8. Then, at the bottom of the component, render the stats as follows:

```
        {post ? (
          <div>
            <Post {...post} fullPost />
            <hr />
```

```
            <PostStats postId={postId} />
          </div>
      ) : (
          `Post with id ${postId} not found.`
      )}
    </div>
  )
}
```

If you open a post on the frontend now (you may need to refresh the frontend if you see an error), you will see that all the stats are properly fetched! Now, all that's left to do is visualize the daily stats using Victory!

Visualizing data using Victory

Victory is a React library that provides modular components that can be used to create charts and all kinds of data visualizations. It even supports interactive visualization tools, such as brushing and grouping (where you, for example, select a certain section of a graph to more closely inspect it on other graphs). In this chapter, we are only going to scratch the surface of what Victory can do, as data visualization in React is a big topic on its own.

You can find more information about Victory on their official website: `https://commerce.nearform.com/open-source/victory/`

Creating a bar chart

Let's get started visualizing our data using Victory now:

1. Install the library by executing the following command in the root of the project:

   ```
   $ npm install victory@36.9.1
   ```

2. Edit `src/components/PostStats.jsx` and import the following components from Victory:

   ```
   import {
     VictoryChart,
     VictoryTooltip,
     VictoryBar,
     VictoryLine,
     VictoryVoronoiContainer,
   } from 'victory'
   ```

3. *Replace* the <pre> tags at the end of the component with the following charts, starting with the daily views chart:

```
return (
  <div>
    <b>{totalViews.data?.views} total views</b>
    <div style={{ width: 512 }}>
      <h3>Daily Views</h3>
      <VictoryChart domainPadding={16}>
```

The VictoryChart component is a wrapper, used to combine all elements of a Victory chart. We set domainPadding to 16 pixels, which is a padding inside of the graph. It makes sure that the lines and bar charts do not stick to the edges of the graph, making it look slightly better.

4. Then, define a bar chart with VictoryBar, using VictoryTooltip to display the labels:

```
<VictoryBar
  labelComponent={<VictoryTooltip />}
```

The tooltip looks like this:

Figure 10.4 – A tooltip on a bar chart in Victory

5. Now we get to the most important part, the data. Here, we map over our dailyViews data returned by the query hook to bring it into a format that Victory understands:

```
data={dailyViews.data?.map((d) => ({
```

6. We map the _id property to the x-axis value (parsing it as a date), and the views property to the y-axis value:

```
x: new Date(d._id),
y: d.views,
```

7. Then we create a label, where we turn the day into a local date string and then show the number of views on the given day:

```
label: `${new Date(d._id).toLocaleDateString()}:
${d.views} views`,
})))}
```

```
          />
        </VictoryChart>
      </div>
    </div>
  )
}
```

We have successfully created our first visualization using Victory! The chart will now look as follows:

Daily Views

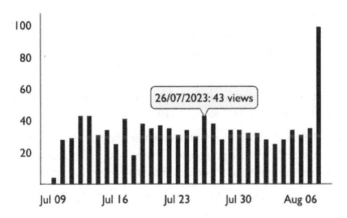

Figure 10.5 – Our first chart in Victory – a bar chart!

As you can see, Victory automatically formatted the dates for us and adjusted the axes to fit our chart into the allotted space!

Let's visualize the daily average viewing duration next.

Creating a line chart

Creating a line chart in Victory is pretty similar to creating a bar chart, with one exception: the tooltips. In line charts, we cannot use tooltips directly, as lines could theoretically be continuous (not discrete blocks of data), so it is unclear where to place the tooltip. Instead, we use a **Voronoi container** for displaying tooltips on line charts in Victory. The name Voronoi comes from mathematics, where a Voronoi diagram partitions a region into multiple sections. In simple terms, the Voronoi container makes an intersection between the mouse position and the line chart, gets the data from that intersection point, and then displays a tooltip there.

With that in mind, let's now get started creating the line chart for the daily average viewing duration:

1. Edit `src/components/PostStats.jsx` and continue where we left off with the other chart, adding a new `VictoryChart` after the container of the bar chart:

```
      </VictoryChart>
    </div>
    <div style={{ width: 512 }}>
      <h4>Daily Average Viewing Duration</h4>
      <VictoryChart
        domainPadding={16}
```

2. In the `VictoryChart` component, we now define `containerComponent`, which will contain our `VictoryVoronoiContainer`:

```
        containerComponent={
          <VictoryVoronoiContainer
            voronoiDimension='x'
```

We defined it to only intersect with the values on the x-axis, meaning that the mouse pointer will only intersect with the days on our chart.

3. We can now define labels for our container, using the `datum` property to get the data entry that intersects with the mouse pointer to create a label. Our label should display the current date and the viewing duration in minutes, fixed to two decimal points:

```
            labels={({ datum }) =>
                `${datum.x.toLocaleDateString()}:
  ${datum.y.toFixed(2)} minutes`
            }
```

4. Again, we use `VictoryTooltip` to display these labels:

```
            labelComponent={<VictoryTooltip />}
          />
        }
      >
```

5. Now we can finally define the `VictoryLine` chart, in which we map the data again, parsing dates and dividing the average duration to convert it from milliseconds to minutes:

```
        <VictoryLine
          data={dailyDurations.data?.map((d) => ({
            x: new Date(d._id),
            y: d.averageDuration / (60 * 1000),
          }))}
        />
```

```
        </VictoryChart>
      </div>
    </div>
  )
}
```

As you can see, the rest was pretty simple and similar to creating the bar chart! It looks as follows:

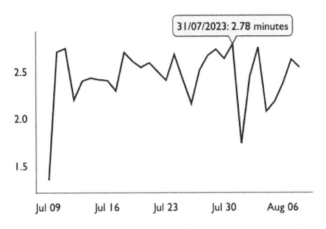

Daily Average Viewing Duration

Figure 10.6 – A line chart using Victory, displaying the daily average viewing duration of a post!

As you can see, Victory is a pretty powerful library for creating charts with React, and we have only scratched the surface of what it can do! You can still customize the theme of the charts and create all sorts of complex visualizations. In this chapter, however, we focused on the most essential and widely used charts: bar and line charts.

Summary

In this chapter, we learned about tracking events using our backend and frontend. Then, we simulated events to be used as a sample dataset for our aggregations and visualizations. Next, we learned how to aggregate data with MongoDB using the MongoDB Playground. Then, we implemented data aggregation functions in our backend. Finally, we integrated and visualized the data on the frontend using Victory.

In the next chapter, *Chapter 11, Building a Backend with a GraphQL API*, we are going to learn how to use an alternative to REST, called GraphQL, to query deeply nested objects more easily.

11

Building a Backend with a GraphQL API

Up until now, we have only been interfacing with REST APIs. For more complex APIs that have deeply nested objects, we can use GraphQL to allow selective access to certain parts of large objects. In this chapter, we are first going to learn what GraphQL is and when it is useful. Then, we are going to experiment with making GraphQL queries and mutations. After that, we are going to implement GraphQL in a backend. Finally, we are going to briefly cover advanced GraphQL concepts.

In this chapter, we are going to cover the following main topics:

- What is GraphQL?
- Implementing a GraphQL API in a backend
- Implementing GraphQL authentication and mutations
- Overview of advanced GraphQL concepts

Technical requirements

Before we start, please install all requirements from *Chapter 1, Preparing for Full-Stack Development*, and *Chapter 2, Getting to Know Node.js and MongoDB*.

The versions listed in those chapters are the ones used in the book. While installing a newer version should not be an issue, please note that certain steps might work differently on a newer version. If you are having an issue with the code and steps provided in this book, please try using the versions mentioned in *Chapters 1* and *2*.

You can find the code for this chapter on GitHub: `https://github.com/PacktPublishing/Modern-Full-Stack-React-Projects/tree/main/ch11`.

If you cloned the full repository for the book, Husky may not find the `.git` directory when running `npm install`. In that case, just run `git init` in the root of the corresponding chapter folder.

The CiA video for this chapter can be found at: `https://youtu.be/6gP0uM-XaVo`.

What is GraphQL?

Before we start learning how to use GraphQL, let's first focus on what GraphQL is. Like REST, it is a way to query APIs. However, it is also much more than that. GraphQL includes a server-side runtime for executing queries and a type system to define your data. It works with many database engines and can be integrated into your existing backend.

GraphQL services are created by defining types (such as a `User` type), fields on types (such as a `username` field), and functions to resolve values of fields. Let's assume we have defined the following `User` type with a function to get a username:

```
type User {
  username: String
}

function User_username(user) {
  return user.getUsername()
}
```

We could then define a `Query` type and a function to get the current user:

```
type Query {
  currentUser: User
}

function Query_currentUser(req) {
  return req.auth.user
}
```

> **Info**
>
> The `Query` type is a special type that defines the "entry point" into the GraphQL schema. It allows us to define which fields are allowed to be queried using the GraphQL API.

Now that we have defined types with fields and functions to resolve those fields, we can make a GraphQL query to get the username of the current user. GraphQL queries look like JavaScript objects, but they only list the field names that you want to query. The GraphQL API will then return a JavaScript object that has the same structure as the query, but with the values filled in. Let's find out how a query to get the username of the current user would look like:

```
{
  currentUser {
```

```
    username
  }
}
```

That query would then return a JSON result that looks like this:

```
{
  "data": {
    "currentUser": {
      "username": "dan"
    }
  }
}
```

As you can see, the result has the same shape as the query. This is one of the essential concepts of GraphQL: the client can specifically ask for the fields that it needs, and the server will return exactly those fields. If we need more data about a user, we can just add new fields to the type and query.

GraphQL validates queries and results against the defined types. This ensures that we do not break the contract between the client and server. The GraphQL types serve as that contract between the client and server. After validating the query, it is executed by a GraphQL server, which then returns a result that looks exactly like the shape requested by the query. Each requested field executes a function on the server. These functions are called **resolvers**.

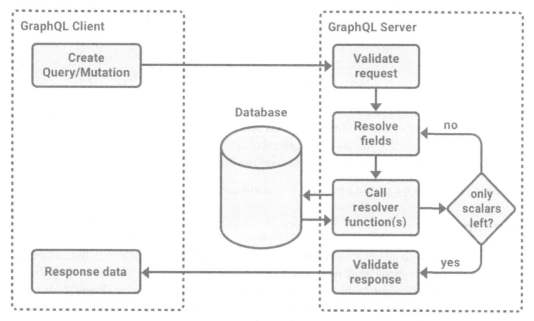

Figure 11.1 – Interaction between GraphQL client and server

Types and queries can also be deeply nested. For example, a user could have a field that returns all the posts that this user is an author of. We can then make a sub-selection of fields in those post objects as well. This works for objects within objects and even arrays of objects within objects, in multiple nesting levels. GraphQL will keep resolving fields until only simple values (scalars), such as strings and numbers are left. For example, the following query could fetch the IDs and titles of all posts that the current user created:

```
{
  currentUser {
    username
    posts {
      id
      title
    }
  }
}
```

Additionally, GraphQL allows us to define arguments for fields, which will be passed to the functions that resolve our fields. We can use arguments to, for example, get all posts with a certain tag. In GraphQL we can pass arguments to any field, even when they are deeply nested. Arguments can even be passed to single value fields, for instance, to transform a value. For example, the following query would get a post by ID and return the post title:

```
{
  postById(id: "1234") {
    title
  }
}
```

GraphQL is especially useful if you build the backend yourself or with it in mind, as it can allow for patterns where deeply nested and interconnected data can be queried easily. However, if there are existing REST backends that you are not in control of, it is usually not worth it to add GraphQL as a separate, independent layer, due to its schema-based restrictions.

Having learned about queries, let's move on to mutations.

Mutations

In REST, any request could cause a side effect (such as writing data to the database). But, as we have learned, GET requests should only return data, and should not cause such side effects. Only POST/PUT/PATCH/DELETE requests should cause data in the database to change. In GraphQL, there is a similar concept: theoretically, any field function could cause the database state to change. However, in GraphQL, we define a mutation instead of a query to explicitly state that we want to change the database state. Besides being defined with the mutation keyword, mutations have the same structure as queries. There is one difference, though: queries fetch fields in parallel, while mutations run in series, executing the first field function first, then the next, and so on. This behavior ensures that we do not end up with race conditions in mutations.

> **Info**
>
> In addition to the built-in `Query` type, there is also a `Mutation` type to define the allowed mutation fields.

Now that we have learned the basics of what GraphQL is and how it works, let's get started using it in practice by implementing GraphQL in our blog application backend!

Implementing a GraphQL API in a backend

We are now going to set up GraphQL in our existing blog application backend in addition to the REST API. Doing so will allow us to see how GraphQL compares to and differs from a REST API. Follow these steps to get started setting up GraphQL on the backend:

1. Copy the existing `ch10` folder to a new `ch11` folder, as follows:

   ```
   $ cp -R ch10 ch11
   ```

2. Open the `ch11` folder in VS Code.

3. First, let's install a VS Code extension to add GraphQL language support. Go to the **Extensions** tab and search for the `GraphQL.vscode-graphql` extension developed by the GraphQL Foundation. Install the extension.

4. Next, install the `graphql` and `@apollo/server` libraries in the backend using the following commands:

   ```
   $ cd backend/
   $ npm install graphql@16.8.1 @apollo/server@4.10.0
   ```

   Apollo Server is a production-ready GraphQL server implementation that supports multiple backend web frameworks, including Express.

5. Create a new `backend/src/graphql/` folder. Inside it, create a `backend/src/graphql/query.js` file, inside which we define a Query schema, which is the entry point of our GraphQL API (listing all supported queries for our backend), as follows:

   ```
   export const querySchema = `#graphql
     type Query {
       test: String
     }
   ```

It is important to add a `#graphql` directive at the beginning of the template string, so that the string is recognized as GraphQL syntax and properly highlighted in a code editor. Inside our schema, we defined a `test` field, for which we define a resolver now.

6. Define a `queryResolver` object which contains a function to resolve the `test` field to a static string:

```
export const queryResolver = {
  Query: {
    test: () => {
      return 'Hello World from GraphQL!'
    },
  },
}
```

7. Create a new `backend/src/graphql/index.js` file and import the `querySchema` and `queryResolver` there:

```
import { querySchema, queryResolver } from './query.js'
```

8. Then, export an array called `typeDefs`, which includes all schemas (for now, only the query schema) and an array called `resolvers`, which contains all resolvers (for now, only the query resolver):

```
export const typeDefs = [querySchema]
export const resolvers = [queryResolver]
```

9. Edit `backend/src/app.js` and import `ApolloServer` and `expressMiddleware` from the `@apollo/server` library:

```
import { ApolloServer } from '@apollo/server'
import { expressMiddleware } from '@apollo/server/express4'
```

10. Then, import `typeDefs` and `resolvers`:

```
import { typeDefs, resolvers } from './graphql/index.js'
```

11. After all other middleware and before the route definitions, create a new Apollo server using the schema type definitions and defined resolvers:

```
const apolloServer = new ApolloServer({
  typeDefs,
  resolvers,
})
```

12. Then, after the server is ready, mount `expressMiddleware` to a `/graphql` route, as follows:

```
apolloServer
  .start()
  .then(() => app.use('/graphql',
expressMiddleware(apolloServer)))
```

13. Start the backend in development mode by running the following command:

```
$ npm run dev
```

14. Go to `http://localhost:3001/graphql` in your browser; you should see the Apollo interface to input a query on the left side, and the results on the right side.

15. Remove all comments from the editor on the left and input the following GraphQL query:

```
query ExampleQuery {
  test
}
```

16. Press the **Play** button to run the query, and you will see the following result:

Figure 11.2 – Successful execution of our first GraphQL query!

As you can see, our query for the `test` field returns our previously defined static string!

After implementing a basic field, let's implement some fields that access our service functions and retrieve data from MongoDB.

Implementing fields that query posts

Follow these steps to implement the fields to query posts:

1. Edit `backend/src/graphql/query.js` and import the relevant service functions:

```
import {
  getPostById,
  listAllPosts,
```

```
      listPostsByAuthor,
      listPostsByTag,
    } from '../services/posts.js'
```

2. Adjust the schema to include a `posts` field, which returns an array of posts:

```
export const querySchema = `#graphql
  type Query {
    test: String
    posts: [Post!]!
```

In GraphQL, the `[Type]` syntax means that something is an array of `Type`. We will define the `Post` type later. `Type!` is the non-null modifier and means that a type is not null (required), so `[Type!]` means that each element is a `Type`, and not `null` (the array can still be empty, though). `[Type!]!` means that the array will always exist and never be `null` (but the array can still be empty).

3. Additionally, define fields for querying posts by `author` and `tag`, both of which accept a required argument:

```
    postsByAuthor(username: String!): [Post!]!
    postsByTag(tag: String!): [Post!]!
```

4. Lastly, define a field to query a post by `id`:

```
    postById(id: ID!): Post
  }
```

5. Now that we have defined the schema, we still need to provide resolvers for all those fields. Thanks to our service functions, this is quite straightforward: we can simply call our service functions with the relevant arguments in `async` functions, as follows:

```
export const queryResolver = {
  Query: {
    test: () => {
      return 'Hello World from GraphQL!'
    },
    posts: async () => {
      return await listAllPosts()
    },
    postsByAuthor: async (parent, { username }) => {
      return await listPostsByAuthor(username)
    },
    postsByTag: async (parent, { tag }) => {
      return await listPostsByTag(tag)
```

```
        },
        postById: async (parent, { id }) => {
          return await getPostById(id)
        },
      },
    }
```

The resolver functions always receive the `parent` object as the first argument and an object with all arguments as a second argument.

Now we have successfully defined fields to query posts. However, the `Post` type is not defined yet, so our GraphQL queries will not work yet. Let's do that next.

Defining the Post type

After defining the `Query` type, we continue by defining the `Post` type, as follows:

1. Create a new `backend/src/graphql/post.js` file, where we import the `getUserInfoById` function to resolve the author of a post later:

    ```
    import { getUserInfoById } from '../services/users.js'
    ```

2. Then, define `postSchema`. Note that `Post` consists of `id`, `title`, `author`, `contents`, `tags`, and the `createdAt` and `updatedAt` timestamps:

    ```
    export const postSchema = `#graphql
      type Post {
        id: ID!
        title: String!
        author: User
        contents: String
        tags: [String!]
        createdAt: Float
        updatedAt: Float
      }
    ```

In this case, we use `[String!]` for the tags, and not `[String!]!`, because the `tags` field can also be non-existent/null.

The `createdAt` and `updatedAt` timestamps are too large to fit into a 32-bit signed integer, so their type needs to be `Float` instead of `Int`.

3. Next, define a resolver for the `author` field that gets the user using the service function:

```
export const postResolver = {
  Post: {
    author: async (post) => {
      return await getUserInfoById(post.author)
    },
  },
}
```

The resolvers for getting posts are already part of the `Query` schema, so we do not need to define how to get a post here. GraphQL knows that the query fields return `Post` arrays and then allows us to resolve further fields on the posts.

4. Edit `backend/src/graphql/index.js` and add the `postSchema` and `postResolver`:

```
import { querySchema, queryResolver } from './query.js'
import { postSchema, postResolver } from './post.js'

export const typeDefs = [querySchema, postSchema]
export const resolvers = [queryResolver, postResolver]
```

After defining the `Post` type, let's continue with the `User` type.

Defining the User type

When defining the `Post` type, we used the `User` type to define the author of a post. However, we have not defined the `User` type yet. Let's do that now:

1. Create a new `backend/src/graphql/user.js` file and import the `listPostsByAuthor` function here, as we are going to add a way to resolve the posts of a user when getting a user object, to show how GraphQL can deal with deeply nested relations:

```
import { listPostsByAuthor } from '../services/posts.js'
```

2. Define `userSchema`. Each `User` in our GraphQL schema has `username` and a `posts` field, in which we will resolve all posts that the user has written:

```
export const userSchema = `#graphql
  type User {
    username: String!
    posts: [Post!]!
  }
```

> **Info**
>
> We do not specify any other properties here, as we are only returning the username in our `getUserInfoById` service function. If we wanted to get the user ID here too, we would have to return it from that function. We are not just returning the full user object, as that could be a potential security vulnerability, exposing internal data such as the password (or billing info in some apps).

3. Next, define `userResolver`, which gets all posts from the current user:

```
export const userResolver = {
  User: {
    posts: async (user) => {
      return await listPostsByAuthor(user.username)
    },
  },
}
```

4. Edit `backend/src/graphql/index.js` and add the `userSchema` and `userResolver`:

```
import { querySchema, queryResolver } from './query.js'
import { postSchema, postResolver } from './post.js'
import { userSchema, userResolver } from './user.js'

export const typeDefs = [querySchema, postSchema, userSchema]
export const resolvers = [queryResolver, postResolver,
userResolver]
```

After defining the `User` type, let's try out some deeply nested queries!

Trying out deeply nested queries

Now that we have successfully defined our GraphQL schemas and resolvers, we can start querying our database using GraphQL!

For example, we can now get a full list of all posts, with their ID, title, and the username of the author, as follows:

```
query GetPostsOverview {
  posts {
    id
    title
    author {
      username
    }
  }
}
```

Execute the preceding query in the Apollo interface. As we can see, the query gets all posts, selects `id`, `title`, and `author` for each post, and then resolves `username` for each `author` instance. This query allows us to get all the data we need on the overview page in a single request, and we do not need to make separate requests to resolve the author usernames anymore!

> **Info**
>
> We did not specify the `password` field on the `User` type, so GraphQL will not allow us to access it, even if the resolver function returns a user object that contains the password.

Now, let's try out a query that gets a post by ID and then finds other posts by the same author. This could be used to, for example, recommend other articles to view from the same author after someone has finished reading a post:

1. We can automatically generate a query in the Apollo interface by clearing the contents of the **Operation** textbox and then selecting **Query** from **Root Types** in the **Documentation** sidebar on the left. Now click on the + button next to the `postById` field on the left, which automatically defines a query variable for us, which looks as follows:

    ```
    query PostById($postByIdId: ID!) {
      postById(id: $postByIdId) {
    ```

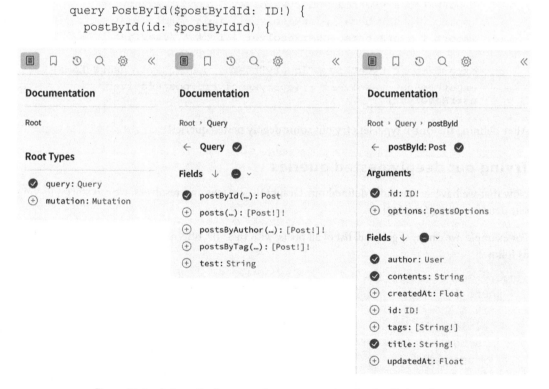

Figure 11.3 – Automatically generating a query using the Apollo interface

2. Within the post, we can now get the `title`, `contents`, and `author` values of the post:

    ```
    title
    contents
    author {
    ```

3. Inside the `author` field, we get `username` and the IDs and titles of their posts:

    ```
    username
    posts {
      id
      title
    }
      }
    }
    ```

4. At the bottom of the Apollo interface, there is a **Variables** section, which we need to fill with an ID that exists in our database:

    ```
    {
      "postByIdId": "<ENTER ID FROM DATABASE>"
    }
    ```

5. Run the query, and you will see that the post and author are resolved, and all posts written by that same author are also listed properly, as shown in the following screenshot:

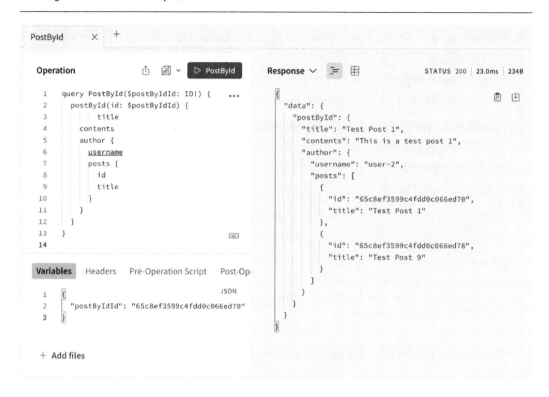

Figure 11.4 – Running deeply nested queries in GraphQL

Next, let's learn how to provide arguments to fields by defining input types.

Implementing input types

We have already learned how to define regular types in GraphQL, but what if we have a common way to provide arguments to fields? For example, the options to query posts are always the same (`sortBy` and `sortOrder`). We cannot use a regular type for this, instead, we need to define an input type. Follow these steps to implement query options in GraphQL:

1. Edit `backend/src/graphql/query.js` and define an input type in the schema:

    ```
    export const querySchema = `#graphql
      input PostsOptions {
        sortBy: String
        sortOrder: String
      }
    ```

2. Then, use the input type as an argument to fields, as follows:

```
type Query {
  test: String
  posts(options: PostsOptions): [Post!]!
  postsByAuthor(username: String!, options: PostsOptions):
[Post!]!
  postsByTag(tag: String!, options: PostsOptions): [Post!]!
  postById(id: ID!, options: PostsOptions): Post
}
```

3. Now, edit the resolvers to pass on `options` to the service functions:

```
posts: async (parent, { options }) => {
  return await listAllPosts(options)
},
postsByAuthor: async (parent, { username, options }) => {
  return await listPostsByAuthor(username, options)
},
postsByTag: async (parent, { tag, options }) => {
  return await listPostsByTag(tag, options)
},
```

4. Try out the following query to see whether the posts are sorted properly:

```
query SortedPosts($options: PostsOptions) {
  posts(options: $options) {
    id
    title
    createdAt
    updatedAt
  }
}
```

5. Set the following variables:

```
{
  "options": {
    "sortBy": "updatedAt",
    "sortOrder": "ascending"
  }
}
```

6. Run the query by pressing the **Play** button, and you should see that the response is sorted by the updatedAt timestamp ascending!

Now that we have successfully implemented functionality to query our database using GraphQL, let's move on to implementing a way to create a new post using GraphQL Mutations.

Implementing GraphQL authentication and mutations

We are now going to implement a way to create new posts using GraphQL. To define fields that change the database state, we need to create them under the mutation type. Before we can do that, however, we first need to implement authentication in GraphQL, so that we can access the currently logged-in user when creating a post.

Adding authentication to GraphQL

Because we are using GraphQL with Express, we can use any Express middleware with GraphQL and pass it to our resolvers as context. As such, we can use the existing express-jwt middleware to parse the JWT. Let's get started adding authentication to GraphQL now:

1. Our current configuration of the requireAuth middleware ensures that the user is logged in and throws an error if they are not. However, this is an issue when passing the auth context to GraphQL, because not all queries require authentication. We are now going to create a new optionalAuth middleware that does not require credentials to process a request. Edit backend/src/middleware/jwt.js and define the following new middleware:

    ```
    export const optionalAuth = expressjwt({
      secret: () => process.env.JWT_SECRET,
      algorithms: ['HS256'],
      credentialsRequired: false,
    })
    ```

2. Now, edit backend/src/app.js and import the optionalAuth middleware there:

    ```
    import { optionalAuth } from './middleware/jwt.js'
    ```

3. Edit the app.use() call where we defined the /graphql route and add the optionalAuth middleware to it, similarly to how we did it for routes:

    ```
    apolloServer.start().then(() =>
      app.use(
        '/graphql',
        optionalAuth,
    ```

4. Then, add a second argument to the Apollo `expressMiddleware`, defining a `context` function that provides `req.auth` to the GraphQL resolvers as context:

```
expressMiddleware(apolloServer, {
  context: async ({ req }) => {
    return { auth: req.auth }
  },
}),
  ),
)
```

Next, let's move on to implementing mutations in GraphQL.

Implementing mutations

Now that we have added authentication to GraphQL, we can define our mutations. Follow these steps to create mutations for signup, login, and creating posts:

1. Create a new `backend/src/graphql/mutation.js` file and import `GraphQLError` (for throwing an `UNAUTHORIZED` error when the user is not logged in), as well as the `createUser`, `loginUser`, and `createPost` functions:

```
import { GraphQLError } from 'graphql'
import { createUser, loginUser } from '../services/users.js'
import { createPost } from '../services/posts.js'
```

2. Define `mutationSchema`, in which we first define fields to sign up and log in users. The `signupUser` field returns a user object, and the `loginUser` field returns a JWT:

```
export const mutationSchema = `#graphql
type Mutation {
      signupUser(username: String!, password: String!): User
      loginUser(username: String!, password: String!): String
```

3. Then, define a field to create a new post from some given `title`, `contents` (optional), and `tags` (optional). It returns a newly created post:

```
      createPost(title: String!, contents: String, tags:
[String]): Post
    }
```

4. Define the resolver, in which we first define the `signupUser` and `loginUser` fields, which are quite straightforward:

```
export const mutationResolver = {
  Mutation: {
    signupUser: async (parent, { username, password }) => {
      return await createUser({ username, password })
    },
    loginUser: async (parent, { username, password }) => {
      return await loginUser({ username, password })
    },
```

5. Next, we define the `createPost` field. Here, we first access the arguments passed to the field, and as a third argument to the resolver function, we get the context we created earlier:

```
    createPost: async (parent, { title, contents, tags }, { auth
}) => {
```

6. If the user is not logged in, the `auth` context will be `null`. We throw an error in that case and do not create a new post:

```
      if (!auth) {
        throw new GraphQLError(
          'You need to be authenticated to perform this
action.',
          {
            extensions: {
              code: 'UNAUTHORIZED',
            },
          },
        )
      }
```

7. Otherwise, we use `auth.sub` (which contains the user ID) and the provided arguments to create a new post:

```
      return await createPost(auth.sub, { title, contents, tags
})
    },
  },
}
```

8. Edit `backend/src/graphql/index.js` and add the `mutationSchema` and `mutationResolver`:

```
import { querySchema, queryResolver } from './query.js'
import { postSchema, postResolver } from './post.js'
```

```
import { userSchema, userResolver } from './user.js'
import { mutationSchema, mutationResolver } from './mutation.js'

export const typeDefs = [querySchema, postSchema, userSchema,
mutationSchema]
export const resolvers = [
  queryResolver,
  postResolver,
  userResolver,
  mutationResolver,
]
```

After implementing mutations, let's learn how to use them.

Using mutations

After defining the possible mutations, we can use them by running them in the Apollo interface. Follow these steps to first sign up a user, then log them in, and finally create a post – all using GraphQL:

1. Go to `http://localhost:3001/graphql` to view the Apollo interface. Define a new mutation that signs up a user with a given username and password, and returns the username if the signup was successful:

    ```
    mutation SignupUser($username: String!, $password: String!) {
      signupUser(username: $username, password: $password) {
        username
      }
    }
    ```

> **Tip**
>
> You can use the **Documentation** section on the left by going back to **Root Types**, clicking on **Mutation**, and then clicking on the + icon next to **signupUser**. Then, click on the + icon next to the **username** field. This will automatically create the preceding code.

2. Edit the variables at the bottom and enter a username and password:

    ```
    {
      "username": "graphql",
      "password": "gql"
    }
    ```

3. Execute the `SignupUser` mutation by pressing the play button.

4. Next, create a new mutation to log in a user:

    ```
    mutation LoginUser($username: String!, $password: String!) {
      loginUser(username: $username, password: $password)
    }
    ```

5. Enter the same variables as before and press the play button, the response contains a JWT. Copy and store the JWT somewhere for later use.

6. Define a new mutation to create a post. This mutation returns `Post`, so we can get the `id`, `title`, and `username` values for `author`:

    ```
    mutation CreatePost($title: String!, $contents: String, $tags:
    [String]) {
      createPost(title: $title, contents: $contents, tags: $tags) {
        id
        title
        author {
          username
        }
      }
    }
    ```

    This is an example of where GraphQL really shines. We can resolve the username of the author after creating the post to see whether it was really created with the correct user, because we can access the resolvers defined for `Post`, even in mutations! As you can see, GraphQL is very flexible.

7. Enter the following variables:

    ```
    {
      "title": "GraphQL Post",
      "contents": "This is posted from GraphQL!"
    }
    ```

8. Select the **Headers** tab, press the **New header** button, enter `Authorization` for header key, and `Bearer <Paste previously copied JWT here>` for value. Then press the **Play** button to submit the mutation.

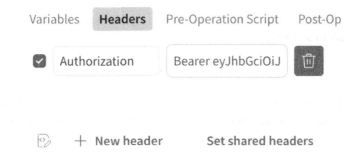

Figure 11.5 – Adding the Authorization header in the Apollo interface

9. In the response, you can see that the post was successfully created, and the author is set and resolved correctly!

Having implemented GraphQL queries and mutations for our blog applications, let's wrap up the chapter by giving an overview of advanced GraphQL concepts.

Overview of advanced GraphQL concepts

Out of the box, GraphQL comes with a set of scalar types:

- `Int`: A signed 32-bit integer

- `Float`: A signed double-precision floating-point value

- `String`: A UTF-8 encoded character sequence

- `Boolean`: Can be true or false

- `ID`: A unique identifier, serialized as a `String`, but meant to signify that it is not human readable

GraphQL also allows the definition of enums, which are a special kind of scalar. They are restricted to certain values. For example, we could have the following enum to distinguish different types of posts:

```
enum PostType {
  UNPUBLISHED,
  UNLISTED,
  PUBLIC
}
```

In Apollo, enums will be handled as strings that can only have certain values, but this may be different in other GraphQL implementations.

Many GraphQL implementations also allow defining custom scalar types. Apollo, for example, supports the definition of custom scalar types.

Fragments

When the same kind of fields are regularly accessed, we can create a fragment to simplify and standardize access to them. For example, if we often resolve users, and users have fields such as `username`, `profilePicture`, `fullName`, and `biography`, we could create the following fragment:

```
fragment UserInfo on User {
  username
  profilePicture
  fullName
  biography
}
```

This fragment can then be used in queries. For example, see this snippet:

```
{
  posts {
    author {
      ...UserInfo
    }
  }
}
```

Fragments are especially useful when the same kind of field structure is used multiple times in the same query. For example, if an author had `followedBy` and `follows` fields, we could resolve all users like this:

```
{
  posts {
    author {
      ...UserInfo
      followedBy {
        ...UserInfo
      }
      follows {
        ...UserInfo
      }
    }
  }
}
```

Introspection

Introspection allows us to query the defined schemas themselves to get a feeling for the data that the server can provide for us. It is essentially querying the schemas defined by the GraphQL server. We can use the __schema field to get all schemas. A schema consists of types, which have name values.

For example, we can use the following query to get all types defined by our server:

```
{
  __schema {
    types {
      name
    }
  }
}
```

If you execute this query on our server, you will get (among other types) our defined Query, Post, User, and Mutation types.

Introspection queries are very powerful, and you can get a lot of information about the possible queries and mutations from it. Actually, the Apollo interface uses introspection to render the **Documentation** sidebar and to auto-complete fields for us!

Summary

In this chapter, we learned what GraphQL is and how it can be more flexible than REST while requiring less boilerplate code, especially when querying deeply nested objects. Then, we implemented GraphQL in our backend and created various types, queries, and mutations. We also learned how to integrate JWT authentication in GraphQL. Finally, we wrapped up the chapter by learning about advanced concepts, such as the type system, fragments, and introspection.

In the next chapter, *Chapter 12, Interfacing with GraphQL on the Frontend Using Apollo Client*, we are going to learn how to access and integrate GraphQL in our frontend using React and the Apollo Client library.

12

Interfacing with GraphQL on the Frontend Using Apollo Client

After successfully implementing a GraphQL backend using Apollo Server in the previous chapter, we are now going to interface with our new GraphQL API on the frontend using Apollo Client. Apollo Client is a library that makes it easier and more convenient to interact with GraphQL APIs. We'll start by replacing the fetching of the post list with GraphQL queries, then resolve the author usernames without needing extra queries, showing the power of GraphQL. Next, we'll add variables to the query to allow setting filters and sorting options. Finally, we'll learn how to use mutations on the frontend.

In this chapter, we are going to cover the following main topics:

- Setting up Apollo Client and making our first query
- Using variables in GraphQL queries
- Using mutations on the frontend

Technical requirements

Before we start, please install all requirements from *Chapter 1*, *Preparing For Full-Stack Development*, and *Chapter 2*, *Getting to Know Node.js and MongoDB*.

The versions listed in those chapters are the ones used in the book. While installing a newer version should not be an issue, please note that certain steps might work differently on a newer version. If there is an issue with the code and steps provided in this book, please try using the versions mentioned in *Chapters 1* and *2*.

You can find the code for this chapter on GitHub: `https://github.com/PacktPublishing/Modern-Full-Stack-React-Projects/tree/main/ch12`.

The CiA video for this chapter can be found at: `https://youtu.be/Gl_5i9DR_xA`.

If you cloned the full repository for the book, Husky may not find the `.git` directory when running `npm install`. In that case, just run `git init` in the root of the corresponding chapter folder.

Setting up Apollo Client and making our first query

Before we can get started making GraphQL queries on the frontend, we first need to set up Apollo Client. **Apollo Client** is the frontend counterpart to Apollo Server, which we have already been using on the backend. While it is not required to use Apollo Client (we could also simply make a POST request to the `/graphql` endpoint), Apollo Client makes interacting with GraphQL much easier and more convenient. It also includes additional features, such as caching, out of the box.

Follow these steps to set up Apollo Client:

1. Copy the existing `ch11` folder to a new `ch12` folder, as follows:

    ```
    $ cp -R ch11 ch12
    ```

2. Open the `ch12` folder in VS Code.

3. Install the `@apollo/client` and `graphql` dependencies:

    ```
    $ npm install @apollo/client@3.9.5 graphql@16.8.1
    ```

4. Edit `.env` and add a new environment variable, pointing to the endpoint for our GraphQL server:

    ```
    VITE_GRAPHQL_URL="http://localhost:3001/graphql"
    ```

5. Edit `src/App.jsx` and import `ApolloClient`, `InMemoryCache`, and `ApolloProvider` from the `@apollo/client` package:

    ```
    import { ApolloProvider } from '@apollo/client/react/index.js'
    import { ApolloClient, InMemoryCache } from '@apollo/client/
    core/index.js'
    ```

    At the time of writing, there is an issue with ESM imports in Apollo Client, so we need to import directly from the `index.js` files.

6. Create a new instance of Apollo Client, pointing to the GraphQL endpoint and using `InMemoryCache`:

    ```
    const apolloClient = new ApolloClient({
      uri: import.meta.env.VITE_GRAPHQL_URL,
      cache: new InMemoryCache(),
    })
    ```

7. Adjust the App component to add `ApolloProvider`, providing the Apollo Client context to our whole app:

```
export function App({ children }) {
  return (
    <HelmetProvider>
      <ApolloProvider client={apolloClient}>
        <QueryClientProvider client={queryClient}>
          <AuthContextProvider>{children}</AuthContextProvider>
        </QueryClientProvider>
      </ApolloProvider>
    </HelmetProvider>
  )
}
```

8. We are also going to create a GraphQL config file now so that the VS Code GraphQL extension can autocomplete and validate queries for us. Create a new `graphql.config.json` file in the root of the project, with the following contents:

```
{
  "schema": "http://localhost:3001/graphql",
  "documents": "src/api/graphql/**/*.{js,jsx}"
}
```

The `schema` defines the URL to the GraphQL endpoint, and `documents` defines where to find files that contain GraphQL queries. We are going to put the GraphQL queries in the `src/api/graphql/` folder later.

9. Make sure Docker and the database container are running, then start the backend, as follows:

```
$ cd backend/
$ npm run dev
```

Keep the backend running throughout this chapter, so that the GraphQL extension can access the GraphQL endpoint.

10. Restart the VS Code GraphQL extension. You can do so by accessing the VS Code command palette (*Ctrl* + *Shift* + *P* on Windows/Linux and *Cmd* + *Shift* + *P* on macOS) and typing in `GraphQL: Manual Restart`.

Querying posts from the frontend using GraphQL

Now that Apollo Client is set up and ready to be used, let's define our first GraphQL query: a simple query to fetch all posts.

Follow these steps to define the query and use it in our app:

1. Create a new `src/api/graphql/` folder, where we will put our GraphQL queries.

2. Inside this folder, create a new `src/api/graphql/posts.js` file.

3. In the `src/api/graphql/posts.js` file, import the `gql` function from `@apollo/client`:

   ```
   import { gql } from '@apollo/client/core/index.js'
   ```

4. Define a new `GET_POSTS` query, which retrieves all the relevant properties for a post (except the author, which will come later):

   ```
   export const GET_POSTS = gql`
     query getPosts {
       posts {
         id
         title
         contents
         tags
         updatedAt
         createdAt
       }
     }
   ```

You should see that the GraphQL extension is offering us autocomplete options for the types we defined in our backend! If we enter the wrong field name, it will also warn us that this field does not exist on the type.

5. Edit `src/pages/Blog.jsx` and import the `useQuery` hook from `@apollo/client`:

   ```
   import { useQuery as useGraphQLQuery } from '@apollo/client/
   react/index.js'
   ```

We renamed the `useQuery` hook from Apollo Client to `useGraphQLQuery` to avoid confusion with the `useQuery` hook from TanStack React Query.

6. Import the previously defined `GET_POSTS` query:

   ```
   import { GET_POSTS } from '../api/graphql/posts.js'
   ```

7. *Remove* the imports to `useQuery` and `getPosts`:

   ```
   import { useQuery } from '@tanstack/react-query'
   import { getPosts } from '../api/posts.js'
   ```

8. *Remove* the existing useQuery hook:

```
const postsQuery = useQuery({
  queryKey: ['posts', { author, sortBy, sortOrder }],
  queryFn: () => getPosts({ author, sortBy, sortOrder }),
})
const posts = postsQuery.data ?? []
```

9. *Replace* it with the following hook:

```
const postsQuery = useGraphQLQuery(GET_POSTS)
const posts = postsQuery.data?.posts ?? []
```

10. Make sure you are in the root of the project, then run the frontend as follows:

```
$ npm run dev
```

Now, open the frontend on http://localhost:5173/ and you will see that the post titles are properly shown. However, the links to posts do not work and there is an error in the console. There is a slight difference in the results from GraphQL and the REST API: the REST API returns the ID of posts as an _id property, while GraphQL returns them as an id property.

Let's adjust our code to accommodate this change now:

1. Edit src/components/Post.jsx and change the _id prop to id:

```
export function Post({
  title,
  contents,
  author,
  id,
})
```

2. Also, update the variable name where it is used:

```
<Link to={`/posts/${id}/${slug(title)}`}>
```

3. Make sure to update propTypes as well:

```
Post.propTypes = {
  title: PropTypes.string.isRequired,
  contents: PropTypes.string,
  author: PropTypes.string,
  id: PropTypes.string.isRequired,
```

4. Now that the prop is changed, edit `src/pages/ViewPost.jsx` and pass in the new prop, as follows:

```
{post ? (
  <Post {...post} id={postId} fullPost />
) : (
  `Post with id ${postId} not found.`
)}
```

After saving all files, the frontend should refresh and properly render the list of all posts with working links. Now all that's left to do to restore the original functionality is to show the author usernames.

Resolving author usernames in a single query

Instead of resolving each author username separately, we can now get them all at once in a single query, thanks to the power of GraphQL! Let's make use of this power to refactor our code a bit to make it simpler and improve the performance:

1. Start by editing the GraphQL query in `src/api/graphql/posts.js`, adding the `author.username` field, as follows:

```
export const GET_POSTS = gql`
  query getPosts {
    posts {
      author {
        username
      }
```

2. Then, edit the `src/components/User.jsx` component. *Replace* the whole component with the following, simpler component:

```
import PropTypes from 'prop-types'

export function User({ username }) {
  return <b>{username}</b>
}

User.propTypes = {
  username: PropTypes.string.isRequired,
}
```

It is not necessary to fetch the user info here anymore, as we can directly display the username from the GraphQL response.

3. Next, edit `src/components/Post.jsx` and pass the whole `author` object to the `User` component, as follows:

```
Written by <User {...author} />
```

4. We also need to adjust `propTypes` now to accept a full `author` object for the `Post` component, instead of a user ID:

```
author: PropTypes.shape(User.propTypes),
```

5. Edit `src/pages/ViewPost.jsx` and pass the whole `author` object to the `Post` component:

```
<Post {...post} id={postId} author={userInfo} fullPost
/>
```

Thankfully, we are already resolving the username for the meta tags on this page, so we do not need to make an additional query here either.

6. However, in `Header`, we do need to make an additional query to resolve the username when a user is logged in.

Edit `src/components/Header.jsx` and import the `useQuery` hook and the `getUserInfo` API function:

```
import { useQuery } from '@tanstack/react-query'
import { getUserInfo } from '../api/users.js'
```

7. Then, adjust the component to get the user ID from the token (the `sub` field of the JWT) and make a query for the user info:

```
export function Header() {
  const [token, setToken] = useAuth()

  const { sub } = token ? jwtDecode(token) : {}
  const userInfoQuery = useQuery({
    queryKey: ['users', sub],
    queryFn: () => getUserInfo(sub),
    enabled: Boolean(sub),
  })
  const userInfo = userInfoQuery.data
```

8. Lastly, we check whether we were able to resolve the query for user info (instead of just checking for `token`). If so, we pass the user info to the `User` component:

```
if (token && userInfo) {
  return (
    <nav>
      Logged in as <User {...userInfo} />
```

We also removed the token decoding here, like we already did earlier.

Now we are using GraphQL to fetch the list of posts and resolve the author usernames in one single request! However, the filters and sorting do not work anymore, as we are not passing this information to the GraphQL query yet.

In the next section, we are going to introduce variables for filtering and sorting our GraphQL queries.

Using variables in GraphQL queries

To add support for filters and sorting, we need to add variables to our GraphQL query. We can then fill in these variables when executing the query.

Follow these steps to add variables to the query:

1. Edit `src/api/graphql/posts.js` and adjust the query to accept an `$options` variable:

    ```
    export const GET_POSTS = gql`
      query getPosts($options: PostsOptions) {
    ```

2. Then, pass the `$options` variable to the `posts` resolver, for which we already implemented an `options` argument in the previous chapter:

    ```
    posts(options: $options) {
    ```

3. Now, we just need to pass the options when executing the query. Edit `src/pages/Blog.jsx` and pass the variable, as follows:

    ```
    const postsQuery = useGraphQLQuery(GET_POSTS, {
      variables: { options: { sortBy, sortOrder } },
    })
    ```

4. Go to the blog frontend and change the sort order to ascending to see the variable in action!

Using fragments to reuse parts of queries

Now that sorting is working, we just need to add filtering by author. To do this, we need to add a second query for `postsByAuthor`. As you can imagine, this query should return the same fields as the `posts` query. We can make use of a fragment to reuse the fields for both queries, as follows:

1. Edit `src/api/graphql/posts.js` and define a new fragment in GraphQL that contains all the fields that we need from a post:

    ```
    export const POST_FIELDS = gql`
      fragment PostFields on Post {
        id
        title
        contents
    ```

```
      tags
      updatedAt
      createdAt
      author {
        username
      }
    }
  }
```

The fragment is defined by giving it a name (PostFields) and specifying which type it can be used on (on Post). Then, all fields from the specified type can be queried in the fragment.

2. To use the fragment, we first have to include its definition in the GET_POSTS query:

```
export const GET_POSTS = gql`
  ${POST_FIELDS}
  query getPosts($options: PostsOptions) {
```

3. Now, instead of listing all fields manually, we can use the fragment:

```
    posts(options: $options) {
      ...PostFields
    }
  }
```

The syntax for using a fragment is like object destructuring in JavaScript, where all properties defined in an object are spread into another object.

> **Note**
>
> Sometimes the VS Code GraphQL extension needs to be restarted to be able to detect fragments properly. You can do so by accessing the VS Code command palette (*Ctrl* + *Shift* + *P* on Windows/ Linux and *Cmd* + *Shift* + *P* on macOS) and typing in GraphQL: Manual Restart.

4. Next, we define a second query, where we query posts by author, and get all necessary fields with the fragment:

```
export const GET_POSTS_BY_AUTHOR = gql`
  ${POST_FIELDS}
  query getPostsByAuthor($author: String!, $options:
PostsOptions) {
    postsByAuthor(username: $author, options: $options) {
      ...PostFields
    }
  }
```

We defined the `$author` variable as required for this query (by using an exclamation mark after the type). We need to do this because the `postsByAuthor` field also requires the first argument (`username`) to be set.

5. Edit `src/pages/Blog.jsx` and import the newly defined query:

    ```
    import { GET_POSTS, GET_POSTS_BY_AUTHOR } from '../api/graphql/
    posts.js'
    ```

6. Then, adjust the hook to use the `GET_POSTS_BY_AUTHOR` query if `author` is defined:

    ```
    const postsQuery = useGraphQLQuery(author ? GET_POSTS_BY_
    AUTHOR : GET_POSTS, {
    ```

7. Pass the `author` variable to the query:

    ```
    variables: { author, options: { sortBy, sortOrder } },
    })
    ```

8. Lastly, we need to adjust how we select the results because the `postsByAuthor` field from the `GET_POSTS_BY_AUTHOR` query will return the results in `data.postsByAuthor`, while the `GET_POSTS` query uses the `posts` field, which returns results in `data.posts`. As there is no case where both fields are returned at once, we can simply do the following:

    ```
    const posts = postsQuery.data?.postsByAuthor ?? postsQuery.
    data?.posts ?? []
    ```

9. Go to the frontend and try filtering by author. The filter works again now!

As we can see, fragments are very useful for reusing the same fields for multiple queries! Now that our post list is fully refactored to use GraphQL, let's move on to using mutations on the frontend, allowing us to migrate the signup, login, and create post functionalities to GraphQL.

Using mutations on the frontend

As we learned in the previous chapter, mutations in GraphQL are used to change the state of the backend (similar to `POST` requests in REST). We are now going to implement mutations for signing up and logging in to our app.

Follow these steps:

1. Create a new `src/api/graphql/users.js` file and import `gql`:

    ```
    import { gql } from '@apollo/client/core/index.js'
    ```

2. Then, define a new `SIGNUP_USER` mutation, which takes a username and a password and calls the `signupUser` mutation field:

    ```
    export const SIGNUP_USER = gql`
      mutation signupUser($username: String!, $password: String!) {
        signupUser(username: $username, password: $password) {
          username
        }
      }
    ```

3. Edit `src/pages/Signup.jsx` and *replace* the current `useMutation` hook from TanStack React Query with the one from Apollo Client. As we did before for `useQuery`, we are also going to rename this hook to `useGraphQLMutation` to avoid confusion:

    ```
    import { useMutation as useGraphQLMutation } from '@apollo/
    client/react/index.js'
    ```

4. Additionally, *replace* the import of the `signup` function with an import of the `SIGNUP_USER` mutation:

    ```
    import { SIGNUP_USER } from '../api/graphql/users.js'
    ```

5. *Replace* the existing mutation hook with the following:

    ```
    const [signupUser, { loading }] = useGraphQLMutation(SIGNUP_
    USER, {
        variables: { username, password },
        onCompleted: () => navigate('/login'),
        onError: () => alert('failed to sign up!'),
    })
    ```

    As can be seen, the Apollo Client mutation hook has a slightly different API than the TanStack React Query mutation hook. It returns an array with a function to call the mutation, and an object with the loading state, error state, and data. Similar to the `useGraphQLQuery` hook, it also accepts the mutation as the first argument and an object with variables as the second argument. Moreover, the `onSuccess` function is called `onCompleted` in Apollo Client.

6. Change the `handleSubmit` function as follows:

    ```
    const handleSubmit = (e) => {
      e.preventDefault()
      signupUser()
    }
    ```

7. Lastly, change the submit button as follows:

```
<input
  type='submit'
  value={loading ? 'Signing up...' : 'Sign Up'}
  disabled={!username || !password || loading}
/>
```

Now the signup functionality is successfully migrated to GraphQL. Next, let's migrate the login functionality.

Migrating login to GraphQL

Refactoring the login functionality to GraphQL is very similar to the signup functionality, so let's quickly go through the steps:

1. Edit `src/api/graphql/users.js` and define a mutation for logging in:

```
export const LOGIN_USER = gql`
  mutation loginUser($username: String!, $password: String!) {
    loginUser(username: $username, password: $password)
  }
```

2. Edit `src/pages/Login.jsx` and *replace* the imports to TanStack React Query and the `login` function with the following:

```
import { useMutation as useGraphQLMutation } from '@apollo/
client/react/index.js'
import { LOGIN_USER } from '../api/graphql/users.js'
```

3. Update the hook as well:

```
const [loginUser, { loading }] = useGraphQLMutation(LOGIN_
USER, {
  variables: { username, password },
  onCompleted: (data) => {
    setToken(data.loginUser)
    navigate('/')
  },
  onError: () => alert('failed to login!'),
})
```

4. Update the `handleSubmit` function:

```
const handleSubmit = (e) => {
  e.preventDefault()
  loginUser()
}
```

5. Finally, update the submit button:

```
<input
  type='submit'
  value={loading ? 'Logging in...' : 'Log In'}
  disabled={!username || !password || loading}
/>
```

Now that signup and login are using GraphQL mutations, let's move on to migrating the create post functionality to GraphQL.

Migrating create post to GraphQL

The create post functionality is a bit trickier to implement, as it requires us to be logged in (which means that we need to send the JWT header), and invalidate the post list queries, so that the list gets updated after creating a new post.

Now let's get started on implementing this with Apollo Client:

1. First, let's define the mutation. Edit `src/api/graphql/posts.js` and add the following code:

```
export const CREATE_POST = gql`
  mutation createPost($title: String!, $contents: String, $tags:
[String!]) {
    createPost(title: $title, contents: $contents, tags: $tags)
{
      id
      title
    }
  }
`
```

For this mutation, we are going to use the response to get the `id` and `title` of the created post. We are going to make use of this data to show a link to the post upon successful creation.

2. Then, edit `src/components/CreatePost.jsx` and *replace* the TanStack React Query import with an import of the mutation hook:

```
import { useMutation as useGraphQLMutation } from '@apollo/
client/react/index.js'
```

3. Also, import the `Link` component and `slug` function to show a link to the created post:

    ```
    import { Link } from 'react-router-dom'
    import slug from 'slug'
    ```

4. *Replace* the import of the `createPost` function with imports of the `CREATE_POST` mutation and the `GET_POSTS` and `GET_POSTS_BY_AUTHOR` queries. We are going to use these query definitions to make Apollo Client re-fetch them for us later:

    ```
    import {
      CREATE_POST,
      GET_POSTS,
      GET_POSTS_BY_AUTHOR,
    } from '../api/graphql/posts.js'
    ```

5. *Replace* the existing query client and mutation hooks with the following GraphQL mutation, where we pass the `title` and `contents` variables:

    ```
    const [createPost, { loading, data }] =
    useGraphQLMutation(CREATE_POST, {
        variables: { title, contents },
    ```

6. Next, we provide the JWT header as `context` to the mutation:

    ```
    context: { headers: { Authorization: `Bearer ${token}` } },
    ```

7. Then, we provide a `refetchQueries` option to the mutation, telling Apollo Client to re-fetch certain queries after the mutation was called:

    ```
    refetchQueries: [GET_POSTS, GET_POSTS_BY_AUTHOR],
    })
    ```

> **Note**
>
> As re-fetching after a mutation is a common operation, Apollo Client provides a simple way to do this in the mutation hook. Simply pass all queries that should be re-fetched there, and Apollo Client will take care of it.

8. Adjust the `handleSubmit` function:

    ```
    const handleSubmit = (e) => {
      e.preventDefault()
      createPost()
    }
    ```

9. Adjust the submit button:

```
<input
  type='submit'
  value={loading ? 'Creating...' : 'Create'}
  disabled={!title || loading}
/>
```

10. Lastly, we are going to change the success message, showing a link to the created post:

```
{data?.createPost ? (
  <>
    <br />
    Post{' '}
    <Link
      to={`/posts/${data.createPost.id}/${slug(data.
createPost.title)}`}
    >
      {data.createPost.title}
    </Link>{' '}
    created successfully!
  </>
) : null}
```

Because of the way types and resolvers work in GraphQL, it easily allows us to access fields from the result of a mutation, the same way as if we were fetching a single post. For example, we could even tell GraphQL to fetch the username of the author of the created post here!

11. Try creating a new post, and you will see that the success message now shows a link to the created post, and the post list automatically re-fetches for us!

The following screenshot shows a new post being successfully created, showing the link to the new post in the success message, and the new post in the post list (automatically re-fetched by Apollo Client):

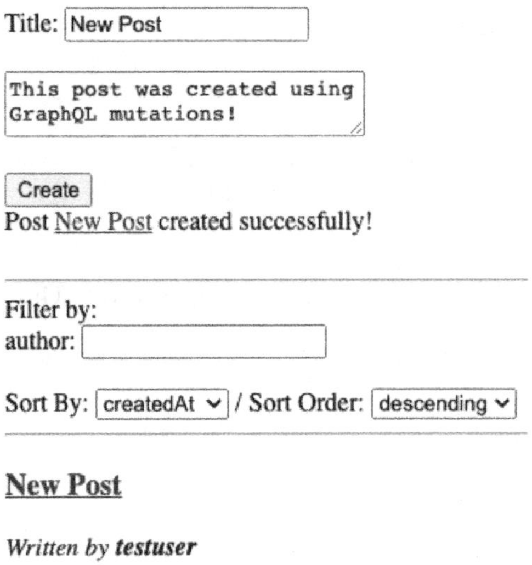

Title: [New Post]

```
This post was created using
GraphQL mutations!
```

[Create]
Post New Post created successfully!

Filter by:
author: [   ]

Sort By: [createdAt ▾] / Sort Order: [descending ▾]

New Post

Written by **testuser**

Figure 12.1: Creating a post using GraphQL mutations, with a re-fetching post list

Now that we have successfully implemented creating posts with GraphQL, our blog app is fully connected to our GraphQL server.

There are many more advanced concepts in GraphQL that we have not covered yet in this book, such as advanced re-fetching, subscriptions (getting real-time updates from the GraphQL server), error handling, suspense, pagination, and caching. The GraphQL chapters in this book only serve as an introduction to GraphQL.

If you wish to learn more about GraphQL and Apollo, I recommend checking out the extensive Apollo docs (`https://www.apollographql.com/docs/`), which contain detailed information and hands-on examples about using Apollo Server and Apollo Client.

Summary

In this chapter, we connected our previously created GraphQL backend to the frontend using Apollo Client. We started by setting up Apollo Client and making a GraphQL query to fetch all posts. Then, we improved the performance of the post list by fetching author usernames in a single request, leveraging the power of GraphQL.

Next, we introduced variables in our query and re-implemented sorting and filtering by author. We also introduced fragments in our queries to reuse the same fields. Lastly, we implemented GraphQL mutations in the frontend to sign up, log in, and create posts. We also learned about re-fetching queries in Apollo Client along the way and briefly mentioned advanced concepts of GraphQL and Apollo.

In the next chapter, *Chapter 13, Building a Backend Based on Event-Driven Architecture Using Express and Socket.IO*, we are going to depart from traditional full-stack architectures and build a new app using a special kind of full-stack architecture: an event-based application.

Part 4:
Exploring an Event-Based
Full-Stack Architecture

In this part of the book, we will depart from traditional full-stack architectures and explore a special kind of full-stack architecture: **event-based applications**. Examples of event-based applications are apps that deal with real-time data, such as collaborative applications (e.g., Google Docs, online whiteboard, etc.) or financial applications (e.g., Kraken crypto exchange). We are first going to develop an event-based backend using **Express** and **Socket.IO**. Then, we are going to create a frontend to consume and send events. Lastly, we will add persistence and functionality to replay events to our app using **MongoDB**.

This part includes the following chapters:

- *Chapter 13, Building an Event-Based Backend Using Express and Socket.IO*
- *Chapter 14, Creating a Frontend to Consume and Send Events*
- *Chapter 15, Adding Persistence to Socket.IO Using MongoDB*

13

Building an Event-Based Backend Using Express and Socket.IO

In this chapter, we will learn about event-based applications and the tradeoffs of using such an architecture versus a more traditional one. Then, we are going to learn about WebSockets and how they work. Afterward, we are going to implement a backend using Socket.IO and Express. Finally, we are going to learn how to integrate authentication by using JWT with Socket.IO.

In this chapter, we are going to cover the following main topics:

- What are event-based applications?
- Setting up Socket.IO
- Creating a backend for a chat app using Socket.IO
- Adding authentication by integrating JWT with Socket.IO

Technical requirements

Before we start, please install all the requirements from *Chapter 1, Preparing For Full-Stack Development*, and *Chapter 2, Getting to Know Node.js and MongoDB.*

The versions listed in those chapters are the ones used in this book. While installing a newer version should not be an issue, please note that certain steps might work differently. If you are having an issue with the code and steps provided in this book, please try using the versions mentioned in *Chapters 1* and *2*.

You can find the code for this chapter on GitHub: `https://github.com/PacktPublishing/Modern-Full-Stack-React-Projects/tree/main/ch13`.

If you cloned the full repository for this book, Husky may not find the `.git` directory when running `npm install`. In that case, just run `git init` in the root of the corresponding chapter folder.

The CiA video for this chapter can be found at: `https://youtu.be/kHGvkopIHf4`.

What are event-based applications?

In contrast to traditional web applications, where we have a request-response pattern, in event-based applications, we are dealing with events. The server and client stay connected and each side can send events, which the other side listens to and reacts to.

The following diagram shows the difference between implementing a chat app in a request-response pattern versus an event-based pattern:

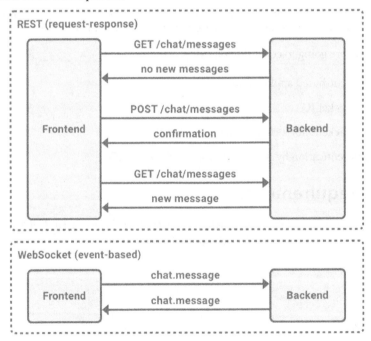

Figure 13.1 – A chat app implementation with request-response and event-based patterns

For example, to implement a chat application in a request-response pattern, we would need to regularly send a request to a `GET /chat/messages` endpoint to refresh the list of messages sent in a chat room. This process of periodically sending requests is called short polling. To send a chat message, we would make a request to `POST /chat/messages`. In an event-based pattern, we could instead send a `chat.message` event from the client to the server, which then sends a `chat.message` event to all connected users. The clients then listen to `chat.message` events and display the messages as they come in; no periodic requests are required!

Of course, each pattern comes with its advantages and disadvantages:

- REST/request-response:

  - Good for when data does not change frequently

  - Responses can be cached easily

  - Requests are stateless, making it easy to scale backends

  - Bad at real-time updates (requires periodic polling)

  - More overhead per request (bad when sending many short responses)

- WebSockets/event-based:

  - Good for applications that require frequent updates

  - More efficient because a persistent connection between the client and server is re-used for multiple requests

  - Less overhead per request

  - There might be connection issues with (corporate) proxies

  - They are stateful, which can make it harder to scale an app

As we can see, for fetching data that does not change so frequently (and can be cached), such as blog posts, a request-response pattern fits better. For applications where data is frequently changing, such as a chat room, an event-based pattern fits better.

What are WebSockets?

The WebSocket API is a browser feature that allows web applications to create an open connection between the client and the server, similar to Unix-style sockets. With WebSockets, communication can happen in both directions at the same time. This is in contrast to HTTP requests, where both parties can communicate, but not simultaneously.

WebSockets use HTTP to establish a connection between the client and the server, and then upgrade the protocol from HTTP to the WebSocket protocol. While both HTTP and WebSockets depend on the **Transmission Control Protocol (TCP)**, they are distinct protocols on the application layer (Layer 7) of the **Open Systems Interconnection (OSI)** model.

A connection to a WebSocket is established by sending an HTTP request with the `Upgrade: websocket` header and other parameters to establish a secure WebSocket connection. The server then responds with an `HTTP 101 Switching Protocols` response code and information to establish the connection. Then, the client and server continue talking on the WebSocket protocol.

What is Socket.IO?

Socket.IO is an implementation of an event-based server and client library. In most cases, it establishes a connection to the server using a WebSocket. If a WebSocket connection is not possible (due to lacking browser support or firewall settings), Socket.IO can also fall back to HTTP long-polling. However, Socket.IO isn't a pure WebSocket implementation as it adds additional metadata to each packet. It only uses WebSockets internally to transmit data.

In addition to providing a way to send events between the client and server, Socket.IO offers the following features over plain WebSockets:

- **Fallback to HTTP long-polling**: This occurs if the WebSocket connection cannot be established. This can be especially useful for companies using proxies or firewalls that block WebSocket connections.

- **Automatic reconnection**: If the WebSocket connection is interrupted.

- **Buffering packets**: When the client gets disconnected, packets can be re-sent again automatically upon reconnection.

- **Acknowledgments**: A convenient way to send events in a request-response pattern, which can sometimes be useful even in event-based applications.

- **Broadcasting**: Sending an event to all (or a subset of all) connected clients.

- **Multiplexing**: Socket.IO implements namespaces, which can be used to create "channels" that only certain users can send events to and receive events from, such as an "admin-only channel."

Now that we have learned the essentials of what Socket.IO is, let's dive deeper into how the connection and emitting/receiving events work.

Connecting to Socket.IO

The following diagram shows how a connection is established with Socket.IO:

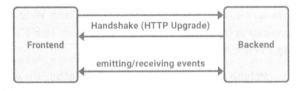

Figure 13.2 – Establishing a connection with Socket.IO

First, Socket.IO sends a handshake from the client (on the frontend) to the server (on the backend), which can contain information to authenticate with the server, or query parameters to provide additional information when establishing the connection.

If a connection via WebSockets cannot be established, Socket.IO connects to the server via HTTP long polling, which means making a request to the server that is kept active until an event occurs, at which point the server sends a response to the request. This allows waiting for events without having to periodically make a request to see if there are any new events. Of course, this is not as performant as WebSockets, but it is a good fallback for when WebSockets aren't available.

Emitting and receiving events

Once connected to Socket.IO, we can start **emitting** (sending) and receiving events. Events are handled by registering event handler functions, which are called when a certain type of event is received by either the client or the server. Both the client and the server can emit and receive events. Additionally, events can be **broadcast** from the server to multiple clients. The following diagram shows an example of how events are emitted and received in a chat application:

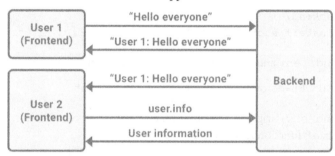

Figure 13.3 – Emitting and receiving events with Socket.IO

As we can see, **User 1** sends a **Hello everyone** message, which the server (backend) then broadcasts to all other clients (frontend). In this case, the message gets broadcast back to **User 1**, as well as to **User 2**.

If we want to restrict the clients that receive certain events, Socket.IO allows the creation of **rooms**. Clients can join a room, and on the server, we can also broadcast events to only specific rooms. This concept can be used for chat rooms, but also for collaborating on a specific project (such as editing a document together in real time).

In addition to emitting and receiving events asynchronously, Socket.IO offers a way to send an event that expects a response via **acknowledgments**. These can be used to model request-response patterns in Socket.IO. For example, we could request information about a certain user using a `user.info` event and synchronously wait for the server response (acknowledgment). We can see this in the preceding diagram, where **User 2** requests information about a certain user, and then gets a response containing the user's information.

Now that we've learned about event-based applications, WebSockets, and Socket.IO, let's put this theory into practice and set up Socket.IO.

Setting up Socket.IO

To set up the Socket.IO server, we are going to base our code on what we had in *Chapter 6, Adding Authentication and Roles with JWT*, as it already includes some boilerplate for a backend and frontend with JWT authentication. Later in this chapter, in the *Adding authentication by integrating JWT with Socket.IO* section, we are going to make use of JWT to add authentication to Socket.IO:

1. Copy the existing ch6 folder to a new ch13 folder, as follows:

    ```
    $ cp -R ch6 ch13
    ```

2. Open the ch13 folder in VS Code.

3. Now, we can start setting up Socket.IO. First, install the socket.io package in the backend folder by running the following commands:

    ```
    $ cd backend/
    $ npm install socket.io@4.7.2
    ```

4. Edit backend/.env and change DATABASE_URL so that it points to a new chat database:

    ```
    DATABASE_URL=mongodb://localhost:27017/chat
    ```

5. Edit backend/src/app.js and import the createServer function from node:http and the Server function from socket.io:

    ```
    import { createServer } from 'node:http'
    import { Server } from 'socket.io'
    ```

    We are going to need to create a node:http server as we cannot directly connect Socket.IO to Express. Instead, Socket.IO attaches to a node:http server.

6. Thankfully, Express can also be easily attached to a node:http server. Edit backend/src/app.js and, before app is exported, create a new node:http server from the Express app, as follows:

    ```
    const server = createServer(app)
    ```

7. Now, create a new Socket.IO server from the node:http server:

    ```
    const io = new Server(server, {
      cors: {
        origin: '*',
      },
    })
    ```

> **Warning**
>
> Setting the origin to * makes it possible for phishing sites to imitate your website and send requests to your backend. In production, the origin should be set to the deployed URL of your frontend.

8. We can use the Socket.IO server to listen to connections from clients and print a message:

    ```
    io.on('connection', (socket) => {
        console.log('user connected:', socket.id)
    ```

9. The active client connection can be tracked by using the `socket` object. For example, we can listen to disconnect events from the client like so:

    ```
    socket.on('disconnect', () => {
        console.log('user disconnected:', socket.id)
    })
    })
    ```

10. Lastly, change the export so that it uses the `node:http` server instead of the Express app directly:

    ```
    export { server as app }
    ```

11. Start the backend by running the following commands:

    ```
    $ cd backend/
    $ npm run dev
    ```

    Don't forget to get Docker and the database container up and running before starting the backend. Keep the backend running for the rest of this chapter.

Now that we have set up a simple Socket.IO server, let's continue by setting up the client.

Setting up a simple Socket.IO client

We are going to use the existing frontend for now. In the next chapter, *Chapter 14, Creating a Frontend to Consume and Send Events*, we are going to remove the blog components and create a new React frontend for our chat app. Let's start setting up a simple Socket.IO client:

1. In the root of the project, install the `socket.io-client` package for the frontend by running the following command:

    ```
    $ npm install socket.io-client@4.7.2
    ```

    Make sure that you aren't in the `backend` folder anymore!

2. Edit `src/App.jsx` and import the `io` function from `socket.io-client`:

    ```
    import { io } from 'socket.io-client'
    ```

3. Define a new instance of the Socket.IO client by using the `io` function and passing a hostname and port:

    ```
    const socket = io(import.meta.env.VITE_SOCKET_HOST)
    ```

    Here, we will be passing `localhost:3001` through an environment variable. We cannot pass the HTTP URL here as Socket.IO will try to connect to the hostname and port using WebSockets.

4. Listen to the `connect` event and print out a message if we successfully connected to the Socket.IO server:

    ```
    socket.on('connect', () => {
      console.log('connected to socket.io as', socket.id)
    })
    ```

5. Additionally, listen to the `connect_error` event and log an error message in case connecting to the Socket.IO server failed:

    ```
    socket.on('connect_error', (err) => {
      console.error('socket.io connect error:', err)
    })
    ```

6. Edit `.env` and add the following environment variable:

    ```
    VITE_SOCKET_HOST="localhost:3001"
    ```

7. Run the frontend, as follows:

    $ npm run dev

8. Now, open the frontend in your browser by going to `http://localhost:5173/`. Keep the frontend running for the rest of this chapter.

You will see a message stating **connected to socket.io** in the browser console. In the server output, you will see that the client connected successfully. Try refreshing the page to see it disconnecting and connecting again (with a new socket ID):

```
successfully connected to database: mongodb://localhost:27017/ch3
express server running on http://localhost:3001
user connected: 8cOlseEPbgQ8d4AzAAAB
user disconnected: 8cOlseEPbgQ8d4AzAAAB
user connected: rmGIXt3HV8S1qusRAAAD
```

Figure 13.4 – Seeing the Socket.IO client connect to and disconnect from our server

Now that we have successfully set up a Socket.IO server, let's continue by creating a backend for a chat app using Socket.IO.

Creating a backend for a chat app using Socket.IO

We can now start implementing a chat app using Socket.IO. We will be developing the following functionality for our chat app:

- **Emitting** events to send chat messages from the client to the server
- **Broadcasting** chat messages from the server to all clients
- Joining **rooms** to send messages in
- Using **acknowledgments** to get information about a user

Let's get started!

Emitting events to send chat messages from the client to the server

We'll start by **emitting** a chat.message event from the client to the server. For now, we are going to emit this event right after connecting. Later, we are going to integrate this into a frontend. Follow these steps to send chat messages from the client and receive them on the server:

1. Edit backend/src/app.js and *cut/remove* the following code:

    ```
    io.on('connection', (socket) => {
      console.log('user connected:', socket.id)
      socket.on('disconnect', () => {
        console.log('user disconnected:', socket.id)
      })
    })
    ```

2. Create a new backend/src/socket.js file, define a handleSocket function there, and paste the following code inside it:

    ```
    export function handleSocket(io) {
      io.on('connection', (socket) => {
        console.log('user connected:', socket.id)
        socket.on('disconnect', () => {
          console.log('user disconnected:', socket.id)
        })
    ```

3. Now, add a new listener that listens to the chat.message event and logs the message sent from the client:

    ```
    socket.on('chat.message', (message) => {
      console.log(`${socket.id}: ${message}`)
    })
    ```

```
    })
  }
```

4. Edit `backend/src/app.js` and import the `handleSocket` function:

    ```
    import { handleSocket } from './socket.js'
    ```

5. Once the Socket.IO server has been created, call the `handleSocket` function:

    ```
    const io = new Server(server, {
      cors: {
        origin: '*',
      },
    })
    handleSocket(io)
    ```

6. Edit `src/App.jsx` and emit a `chat.message` event with some text, as follows:

    ```
    socket.on('connect', () => {
      console.log('connected to socket.io as', socket.id)
      socket.emit('chat.message', 'hello from client')
    })
    ```

> **Info**
>
> Socket.IO allows us to send any kind of serializable data structures in an event, not just strings! For example, it is possible to send objects and arrays.

The backend and frontend should automatically refresh and the server will log the following message:

```
XXmWHjA_5zew70VIAAAM: hello from client
```

If not, make sure you (re-)start the backend and frontend and refresh the page manually.

As you can see, it is quite simple to send and receive events asynchronously in real time using Socket.IO.

Broadcasting chat messages from the server to all clients

Now that the backend server can receive messages from a client, we need to **broadcast** the messages to all other clients so that others can see the chat messages that were sent. Let's do that now:

1. Edit `backend/src/socket.js` and extend the `chat.message` event listener so that it calls `io.emit` and sends the chat message to everyone:

    ```
    socket.on('chat.message', (message) => {
      console.log(`${socket.id}: ${message}`)
      io.emit('chat.message', {
    ```

```
        username: socket.id,
        message,
      })
    })
```

> **Note**
>
> Alternatively, you can use `socket.broadcast.emit` to send an event to every client except the one that sent the message.

2. We also need to add a listener for chat messages on the client side. This works the same way as on the server. Edit `src/App.jsx` and add the following event listener:

    ```
    socket.on('chat.message', (msg) => {
      console.log(`${msg.username}: ${msg.message}`)
    })
    ```

3. Now, you should see the message being logged on the server and the client. Try opening a second window; you will see messages from both clients in your browser!

```
connected to socket.io as ewy3yhSnl_59fGhbAAAJ          App.jsx:13

ewy3yhSnl_59fGhbAAAJ: hello from client                 App.jsx:17

mYE_P9IrsqFOmVzaAAAL: hello from client                 App.jsx:17
```

Figure 13.5 – Receiving messages from another client

Joining rooms to send messages in

While having a working chat where messages get relayed to everyone is nice, often, we don't want to broadcast our messages to everyone. Instead, we might want to only send messages to a certain group of people. To facilitate this, Socket.IO provides **rooms**. Rooms can be used to group clients together so that events are only sent to all other clients in the room. This feature can be used to create chat rooms, but also for collaborating on a project together (by creating a new room for each project). Let's learn how rooms can be used in Socket.IO:

1. Socket.IO allows us to pass a query string during the handshake. We can access this query string to get the room that the client wants to join. Edit `backend/src/socket.js` and get the room from the handshake query:

    ```
    io.on('connection', (socket) => {
      console.log('user connected:', socket.id)
      const room = socket.handshake.query?.room ?? 'public'
    ```

2. Now, use `socket.join` to join the client into the selected room:

```
socket.join(room)
console.log(socket.id, 'joined room:', room)
```

3. Then, inside the `chat.message` handler, use `.to(room)` to make sure chat messages from that client are only sent to a certain room:

```
io.to(room).emit('chat.message', {
  username: socket.id,
  message,
})
```

4. In the client, we need to pass a query string to tell the server which room we would like to join. Edit `src/App.jsx`, as follows:

```
const socket = io(import.meta.env.VITE_SOCKET_HOST, {
  query: window.location.search.substring(1),
})
```

The Socket.IO query string is a URL query string, so we can simply pass the query string of the current page to it (without ? at the beginning of the string).

5. Open `http://localhost:5173/` and `http://localhost:5173/?room=test` in two separate browser windows and send messages from both. You will see that the message from the second window doesn't get sent to the first window. However, if you open another window with the `?room=test` query string and send a message there, you will see the message being forwarded to the second window (but not the first).

As we can see, we can use rooms to have more fine-grained control over which clients receive certain events. As the server controls which rooms a client joins, we can also add permission checks before allowing a client to join a room.

Using acknowledgments to get information about a user

As we have seen, events are a great way to send asynchronous messages. Sometimes, however, we want a more traditional synchronous request-response API, like we had with REST. In Socket.IO, we can implement synchronous events by using **acknowledgments**. We can use acknowledgments to, for example, get more information about a user in the current chat room. For now, we are only going to return the rooms that the user is in. Later, when we add authentication, we are going to fetch the user object from the database here. Let's get started implementing acknowledgments:

1. Edit `backend/src/socket.js` and define a new event listener:

```
socket.on('user.info', async (socketId, callback) => {
```

Note how we are passing a callback function as the last argument. This is what makes the event an acknowledgment.

2. In this event listener, we are going to fetch all sockets in the room with the ID of our socket:

```
const sockets = await io.in(socketId).fetchSockets()
```

Internally, Socket.IO creates a room for each connected socket, to make it possible to send events to a single socket.

> **Note**
>
> We could directly access the sockets of the current instance, but that wouldn't work anymore when we scale our service to multiple instances in a cluster. To make it work even in a cluster, we need to use the room functionality to get a socket by ID.

3. Now, we must check if we found a socket with the given ID. If not, we return `null`:

```
if (sockets.length === 0) return callback(null)
```

4. Otherwise, we return the socket ID and a list of rooms that the user is in:

```
const socket = sockets[0]
const userInfo = {
  socketId,
  rooms: Array.from(socket.rooms),
}
return callback(userInfo)
})
```

5. Now, we can emit the `user.info` event on the client. Edit `src/App.jsx` and start by making the `connect` event listener an `async` function:

```
socket.on('connect', async () => {
  console.log('connected to socket.io as', socket.id)
  socket.emit('chat.message', 'hello from client')
```

6. To emit an event with an acknowledgment, we can use the `emitWithAck` function, which returns a Promise that we can `await`:

```
  const userInfo = await socket.emitWithAck('user.info', socket.
id)
  console.log('user info', userInfo)
})
```

7. After saving the code, go to the browser window; you will see the user's information being logged in the console:

```
connected to socket.io as 3i1MTX28X7H8xtXYAAAB

3i1MTX28X7H8xtXYAAAB: hello from client

user info
▼ {socketId: '3i1MTX28X7H8xtXYAAAB', rooms: Array(2)} ⓘ
  ▶ rooms: (2) ['3i1MTX28X7H8xtXYAAAB', 'public']
    socketId: "3i1MTX28X7H8xtXYAAAB"
```

Figure 13.6 – Getting user information with an acknowledgment

Now that we have learned how to send various kinds of events, let's get into a more advanced topic: authentication with Socket.IO.

Adding authentication by integrating JWT with Socket.IO

So far, all chat messages have been sent with the socket ID as the "username." This is not a very good way to identify users in a chat room. To fix this, we are going to introduce user accounts by authenticating sockets with JWT. Follow these steps to implement JWT with Socket.IO:

1. Edit `backend/src/socket.js` and import `jwt` from the `jsonwebtoken` package and `getUserInfoById` from our service functions:

    ```
    import jwt from 'jsonwebtoken'
    import { getUserInfoById } from './services/users.js'
    ```

2. Inside the `handleSocket` function, define a new Socket.IO middleware by using `io.use()`. Middleware in Socket.IO works similarly to middleware in Express – we define a function that runs before requests are processed, as follows:

    ```
    export function handleSocket(io) {
      io.use((socket, next) => {
    ```

3. Inside this function, we check if the token was sent via the `auth` object (similar to how we passed `room` earlier via the query string). If no token was passed, we pass an error to the `next()` function and cause the connection to fail:

    ```
    if (!socket.handshake.auth?.token) {
        return next(new Error('Authentication failed: no token
    provided'))
      }
    ```

> **Note**
>
> It is important not to pass a JWT via the query string since this is part of the URL. It is exposed in the browser address bar and thus potentially stored in the browser history, where it could be extracted by a potential attacker. Instead, the `auth` object is sent via the request payload during the handshake, which is not exposed in the address bar.

4. Otherwise, we call `jwt.verify` to verify the token by using the existing `JWT_SECRET` environment variable:

```
jwt.verify(
  socket.handshake.auth.token,
  process.env.JWT_SECRET,
```

5. If the token is invalid, we once again return an error in the `next()` function:

```
async (err, decodedToken) => {
  if (err) {
    return next(new Error('Authentication failed: invalid
token'))
  }
```

6. Otherwise, we save the decoded token to `socket.auth`:

```
socket.auth = decodedToken
```

7. Additionally, we fetch the user information from the database and, for convenience, store it in `socket.user`:

```
socket.user = await getUserInfoById(socket.auth.sub)
    return next()
  },
  )
})
```

> **Note**
>
> Make sure that `next()` is always called in Socket.IO middleware. Otherwise, Socket.IO will keep the connection open until it is closed after a given timeout.

8. The `user` object contains a `username` value. Now, we can *replace* the socket ID in the chat message with the username:

```
socket.on('chat.message', (message) => {
  console.log(`${socket.id}: ${message}`)
  io.to(room).emit('chat.message', {
    username: socket.user.username,
```

```
        message,
    })
})
```

9. We can also return the user information from the `user.info` event:

```
const userInfo = {
  socketId,
  rooms: Array.from(socket.rooms),
  user: socket.user,
}
```

10. We still need to send the auth object from the client side, edit `src/App.jsx`, and get the token from `localStorage`, as follows:

```
const socket = io(import.meta.env.VITE_SOCKET_HOST, {
  query: window.location.search.substring(1),
  auth: {
    token: window.localStorage.getItem('token'),
  },
})
```

Note

For simplicity, we store and read the JWT in `localStorage` for this example. However, it is not a good idea to store a JWT like this in production as `localStorage` could be read by an attacker if they find a way to inject JavaScript. A better way to store a JWT would be by using a cookie with the `Secure`, `HttpOnly`, and `SameSite="Strict"` attributes.

---

11. Now that the server side is set up, we can try logging in on the client. Initially, we are going to see an error message:

```
❌ ▶ socket.io connect error: Error: Authentication failed: no  App.jsx:24
    token provided
        at Socket2.onpacket (socket.js:466:29)
        at Emitter.emit (index.mjs:136:20)
        at manager.js:204:18
```

Figure 13.7 – An error message from Socket.IO because no JWT was provided

12. To get a token, we can sign up and log in normally using the existing blog frontend. Then, we can check the **Network** tab of the inspector to find the `/login` request with a token inside the response:

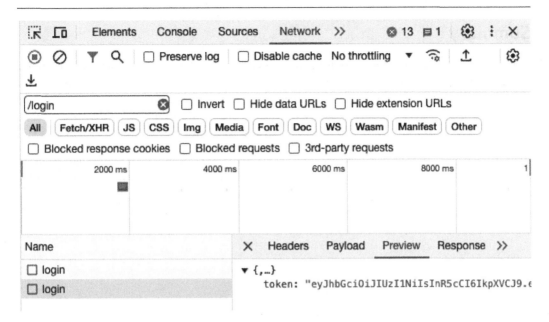

Figure 13.8 – Copying the JWT from the Network tab

13. Copy this token and add it to `localStorage` by running `localStorage.setItem('token', '<JWT>')` in the browser console (replacing `<JWT>` with the copied token). Upon refreshing the page, it should work! As we can see, when logged in with two different users, we can see their messages with their respective usernames:

```
connected to socket.io as BVasO4Ss1_UsnVY3AAAN          App.jsx:17

test: hello from client                                 App.jsx:28

user info                                               App.jsx:20
▶ {socketId: 'BVasO4Ss1_UsnVY3AAAN', rooms: Array(2), user: {…}}

daniel: hello from client                               App.jsx:28
```

Figure 13.9 – Receiving messages from different users

Our chat backend is now fully functional! In the next chapter, we are going to create a frontend to complete our chat app.

Summary

In this chapter, we learned about event-based applications, WebSockets, and Socket.IO. Then, we set up Socket.IO on the backend (server) and frontend (client). Afterward, we learned how to send messages between the server and client, how to join rooms, and how to broadcast messages. We also used acknowledgments to get information about a user in a request-response pattern with Socket. IO. Finally, we implemented authentication using JWT in Socket.IO, finalizing our chat app backend.

In the next chapter, *Chapter 14, Creating a Frontend to Consume and Send Events*, we are going to create a frontend for our chat app, which is going to interact with the backend we created in this chapter.

14

Creating a Frontend to Consume and Send Events

After successfully creating a Socket.IO backend in the previous chapter, and doing our first experiments with the Socket.IO client, let's now focus on implementing a frontend to connect to the backend and consume and send events.

We are first going to clean up our project by removing files from the previously created blog app. Then, we are going to implement a React Context to initialize and store our Socket.IO instance, making use of the existing `AuthProvider` to provide the token for authenticating with the backend. After that, we are going to implement an interface for our chat app and a way to send chat messages, as well as displaying received chat messages. Finally, we are going to implement chat commands with acknowledgments to show which rooms we are currently in.

In this chapter, we are going to cover the following main topics:

- Integrating the Socket.IO client with React
- Implementing chat functionality
- Implementing chat commands with acknowledgments

Technical requirements

Before we start, please install all the requirements from *Chapter 1, Preparing for Full-Stack Development,* and *Chapter 2, Getting to Know Node.js and MongoDB.*

The versions listed in those chapters are the ones used in the book. While installing a newer version should not be an issue, please note that certain steps might work differently on a newer version. If you have an issue with the code and steps provided in this book, please try using the versions listed in *Chapters 1* and *2.*

You can find the code for this chapter on GitHub: `https://github.com/PacktPublishing/Modern-Full-Stack-React-Projects/tree/main/ch14`.

If you cloned the full repository for the book, Husky may not find the `.git` directory when running `npm install`. In that case, just run `git init` in the root of the corresponding chapter folder.

The CiA video for this chapter can be found at: `https://youtu.be/d_TZK6S_XDU`.

Integrating the Socket.IO client with React

Let's start by cleaning up the project and deleting all old files copied over from the blog app. Then, we are going to set up a Socket.IO context to make it easier to initialize and use Socket.IO in React components. Finally, we are going to create our first component that utilizes this context to show the status of our Socket.IO connection.

Cleaning up the project

Let's first delete the folders and files from the blog application we created earlier:

1. Copy the existing `ch13` folder to a new `ch14` folder, as follows:

    ```
    $ cp -R ch13 ch14
    ```

2. Open the `ch14` folder in VS Code.

3. *Delete* the following folders and files, as they were only required for the blog application backend:

    - `backend/src/__tests__/`
    - `backend/src/example.js`
    - `backend/src/db/models/post.js`
    - `backend/src/routes/posts.js`
    - `backend/src/services/posts.js`

4. In `backend/src/app.js`, *remove* the following import:

    ```
    import postRoutes from './routes/posts.js'
    ```

5. Also, *remove* `postRoutes`:

    ```
    postRoutes(app)
    ```

6. *Delete* the following folders and files, as they were only required for the blog application frontend:

- `src/api/posts.js`
- `src/components/CreatePost.jsx`
- `src/components/Post.jsx`
- `src/components/PostFilter.jsx`
- `src/components/PostList.jsx`
- `src/components/PostSorting.jsx`
- `src/pages/Blog.jsx`

Now that we have cleaned up our project, let's get started with implementing a Socket.IO context for our new chat app.

Creating a Socket.IO context

Up until now, we have been initializing the Socket.IO client instance in the `src/App.jsx` component. However, doing this has some downsides:

- To access the socket in other components, we would need to pass it down via props.
- We can only have one socket connection for the whole app.
- It is not possible to get the token dynamically from `AuthContext`, requiring us to store the token in local storage instead.
- Our app requires a full refresh to be able to load the new token and connect with it.
- We still try to connect and get an error when not logged in.

To solve these issues, we can instead create a Socket.IO context. We can then use the provider component to do the following:

- Connect to Socket.IO only when the token is available in `AuthContext`.
- Store the status of the Socket.IO connection and use it within components to, for example, only show the chat interface when logged in.
- Store the error object and display errors in the user interface.

The following diagram shows how the status of our connection will be tracked:

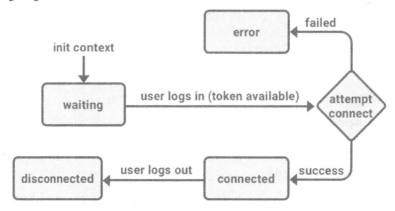

Figure 14.1 – The different states of the connection

As can be seen, the socket connection is initially waiting for the user to log in. Once the token is available, we attempt to establish a socket connection. If successful, the status changes to connected, otherwise to error. If the socket disconnects (for example, when the internet connection is lost), the state is set to disconnected.

Now, let's get started with creating a Socket.IO context:

1. Create a new src/contexts/SocketIOContext.jsx file.

2. Inside this file, import the following functions from react, socket.io-client, and prop-types:

    ```
    import { createContext, useState, useContext, useEffect } from
    'react'
    import { io } from 'socket.io-client'
    import PropTypes from 'prop-types'
    ```

3. Additionally, import the useAuth hook from AuthContext to get the current token:

    ```
    import { useAuth } from './AuthContext.jsx'
    ```

4. Now, define a React Context with some initial values for socket, status and error:

    ```
    export const SocketIOContext = createContext({
      socket: null,
      status: 'waiting',
      error: null,
    })
    ```

5. Next, define a provider component, in which we first create state hooks for the different values of the context:

```
export const SocketIOContextProvider = ({ children }) => {
  const [socket, setSocket] = useState(null)
  const [status, setStatus] = useState('waiting')
  const [error, setError] = useState(null)
```

6. Then, use the `useAuth` hook to get the JWT (if available):

```
const [token] = useAuth()
```

7. Create an effect hook that checks whether the token is available, and if so, attempts to connect to the Socket.IO backend:

```
useEffect(() => {
  if (token) {
    const socket = io(import.meta.env.VITE_SOCKET_HOST, {
      query: window.location.search.substring(1),
      auth: { token },
    })
```

Just like before, we pass the host, the `query` string, and the `auth` object. However, now we get the token from the `useAuth` hook instead of local storage.

8. Create handlers for the `connect`, `connect_error`, and `disconnect` events and set the `status` string and the `error` object, respectively:

```
socket.on('connect', () => {
  setStatus('connected')
  setError(null)
})
socket.on('connect_error', (err) => {
  setStatus('error')
  setError(err)
})
socket.on('disconnect', () => setStatus('disconnected'))
```

9. Set the `socket` object and list all necessary dependencies for the effect hook:

```
    setSocket(socket)
  }
}, [token, setSocket, setStatus, setError])
```

10. Now we can return the provider, passing all values from the state hooks to it:

```
return (
  <SocketIOContext.Provider value={{ socket, status, error }}>
    {children}
  </SocketIOContext.Provider>
)
}
```

11. Finally, we set `PropTypes` for the context provider component and define a `useSocket` hook that will simply return the whole context:

```
SocketIOContextProvider.propTypes = {
  children: PropTypes.element.isRequired,
}

export function useSocket() {
  return useContext(SocketIOContext)
}
```

Now that we have a context to initialize our Socket.IO client, let's hook it up and display the status of the socket connection.

Hooking up the context and displaying the status

We can now remove the code to connect to Socket.IO from the `App` component and use the provider instead, as follows:

1. Edit `src/App.jsx` and *remove* the following import:

```
import { io } from 'socket.io-client'
```

2. Add an import to `SocketIOContextProvider`:

```
import { SocketIOContextProvider } from './contexts/
SocketIOContext.jsx'
```

3. Then, *remove* the following code related to the Socket.IO connection:

```
const socket = io(import.meta.env.VITE_SOCKET_HOST, {
  query: window.location.search.substring(1),
  auth: {
    token: window.localStorage.getItem('token'),
  },
})

socket.on('connect', async () => {
```

```
  console.log('connected to socket.io as', socket.id)
  socket.emit('chat.message', 'hello from client')
  const userInfo = await socket.emitWithAck('user.info', socket.
id)
  console.log('user info', userInfo)
})

socket.on('connect_error', (err) => {
  console.error('socket.io connect error:', err)
})

socket.on('chat.message', (message) => {
  console.log(message)
})
```

4. Inside the App component, render the context provider:

```
export function App() {
  return (
    <QueryClientProvider client={queryClient}>
      <AuthContextProvider>
        <SocketIOContextProvider>
          <RouterProvider router={router} />
        </SocketIOContextProvider>
      </AuthContextProvider>
    </QueryClientProvider>
  )
}
```

After hooking up the Socket.IO context, let's move on to creating a Status component to display the status.

Creating a Status component

Now, let's create a Status component to display the current status of the socket:

1. Create a new src/components/Status.jsx file.

2. Inside it, import the useSocket hook from our SocketIOContext:

```
import { useSocket } from '../contexts/SocketIOContext.jsx'
```

3. Define a Status component, in which we get the status string and error object from the hook:

```
export function Status() {
  const { status, error } = useSocket()
```

4.   Render the socket status:

```
return (
  <div>
    Socket status: <b>{status}</b>
```

5.   If we have an `error` object, we can additionally display the error message now:

```
    {error && <i> - {error.message}</i>}
  </div>
)
}
```

Now that we have a `Status` component, let's create a `Chat` page component, where we render the `Header` and `Status` components.

Creating a Chat page component

We previously had a `Blog` page for our blog app, which we deleted earlier in this chapter. Let's now create a new `Chat` page component for our chat app:

1.   Create a new `src/pages/Chat.jsx` file.

2.   Inside it, import the `Header` component (which we are going to reuse from the `Blog` app) and the `Status` component:

```
import { Header } from '../components/Header.jsx'
import { Status } from '../components/Status.jsx'
```

3.   Render a `Chat` component in which we display the `Header` and `Status` components:

```
export function Chat() {
  return (
    <div style={{ padding: 8 }}>
      <Header />
      <br />
      <hr />
      <br />
      <Status />
    </div>
  )
}
```

4.   Edit `src/App.jsx` and locate the following import:

```
import { Blog } from './pages/Blog.jsx'
```

Replace it with an import to the Chat component:

```
import { Chat } from './pages/Chat.jsx'
```

5. Finally, *replace* the `<Blog />` component in the main path in our router with the `<Chat />` component:

```
const router = createBrowserRouter([
  {
    path: '/',
    element: <Chat />,
  },
```

Starting and testing our chat app frontend

We can now start and test out our chat app frontend:

1. Run the frontend, as follows:

```
$ npm run dev
```

2. Run the backend, as follows (make sure Docker and the database container are running!):

```
$ cd backend/
$ npm run dev
```

3. Now go to `http://localhost:5173/` and you should see the following interface:

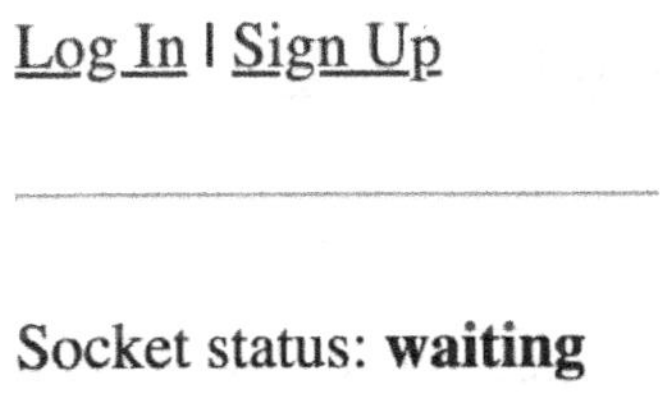

<u>Log In</u> I <u>Sign Up</u>

Socket status: **waiting**

Figure 14.2 – Socket connection waiting for user to be logged in

4. Log in (create a new user if you do not have one yet), and the socket should connect successfully:

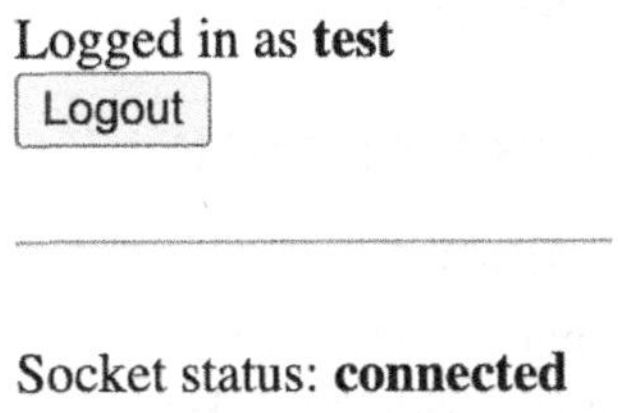

Logged in as **test**

Logout

Socket status: **connected**

Figure 14.3 – Socket connected after user is logged in

Disconnecting socket on logout

You may have noticed that when pressing **Logout**, the socket stays connected. Let's fix that now, by disconnecting the socket when logging out:

1. Edit `src/components/Header.jsx` and import the `useSocket` hook:

    ```
    import { useSocket } from '../contexts/SocketIOContext.jsx'
    ```

2. Get the socket from the `useSocket` hook, as follows:

    ```
    export function Header() {
      const [token, setToken] = useAuth()
      const { socket } = useSocket()
    ```

3. Define a new `handleLogout` function, which disconnects the socket and resets the token:

    ```
    const handleLogout = () => {
      socket.disconnect()
      setToken(null)
    }
    ```

4. Lastly, set the `onClick` handler to the `handleLogout` function:

    ```
    <button onClick={handleLogout}>Logout</button>
    ```

Now, when you log out, the socket will be disconnected, as can be seen in the following screenshot:

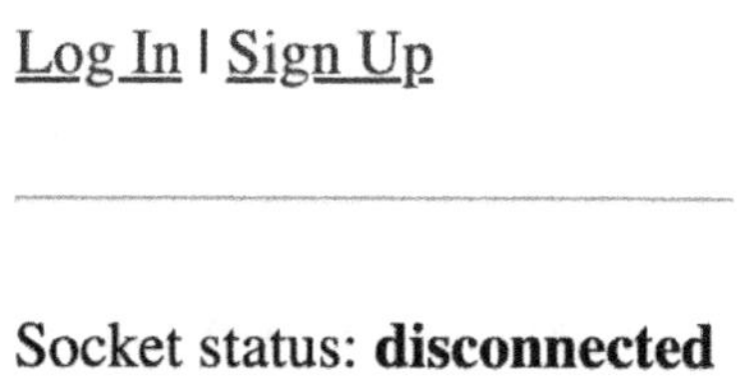

<u>Log In</u> | <u>Sign Up</u>

Socket status: **disconnected**

Figure 14.4 – Socket disconnected after logging out

Now that the Socket.IO client is successfully integrated with our React frontend, we can continue by implementing chat functionality in the frontend.

Implementing chat functionality

We are now going to implement functionality to send and receive messages in our chat app. First, we are going to implement all the components that we need. Then, we are going to create a `useChat` hook to implement the logic to interface with the socket connection and provide functions to send/receive messages. Lastly, we are going to put it all together by creating a chat room.

Implementing the chat components

We are going to implement the following chat components:

- ChatMessage: To display chat messages

- EnterMessage: A field to enter new messages and a button to send them

Implementing the ChatMessage component

Let's start by implementing the ChatMessage component:

1. Create a new src/components/ChatMessage.jsx file, which will render a chat message.

2. Import PropTypes and define a new function with username and message props:

```
import PropTypes from 'prop-types'

export function ChatMessage({ username, message }) {
```

3. Render the username in bold and the message next to it:

```
return (
  <div>
    <b>{username}</b>: {message}
  </div>
)
}
```

4. Define the prop types, as follows:

```
ChatMessage.propTypes = {
  username: PropTypes.string.isRequired,
  message: PropTypes.string.isRequired,
}
```

Implementing the EnterMessage component

Now, let's create the EnterMessage component, which will allow users to send a new chat message:

1. Create a new src/components/EnterMessage.jsx file.

2. Import the useState hook and PropTypes:

```
import { useState } from 'react'
import PropTypes from 'prop-types'
```

3. Define a new EnterMessage component, which receives an onSend function as props:

```
export function EnterMessage({ onSend }) {
```

4. We store the current state of the message entered:

```
const [message, setMessage] = useState('')
```

5. Then, we define a function to handle sending the request and clearing the field afterward:

```
function handleSend(e) {
  e.preventDefault()
  onSend(message)
  setMessage('')
}
```

> **Reminder**
>
> Because we are submitting a form using a submit button, we need to call e.preventDefault() to prevent the form from refreshing the page.

6. Render a form with an input field to enter the message and a button to send it:

```
return (
  <form onSubmit={handleSend}>
    <input
      type='text'
      value={message}
      onChange={(e) => setMessage(e.target.value)}
    />
    <input type='submit' value='Send' />
  </form>
)
}
```

7. Define the prop types, as follows:

```
EnterMessage.propTypes = {
  onSend: PropTypes.func.isRequired,
}
```

Implementing a useChat hook

To bundle all the logic together, we are going to implement a useChat hook, which is going to deal with sending and receiving messages, as well as storing all current messages in a state hook. Follow these steps to implement it:

1. Create a new src/hooks/ folder. Inside it, create a new src/hooks/useChat.js file.

2. Import the `useState` and `useEffect` hooks from React:

    ```
    import { useState, useEffect } from 'react'
    ```

3. Import the `useSocket` hook from our context:

    ```
    import { useSocket } from '../contexts/SocketIOContext.jsx'
    ```

4. Define a new `useChat` function, where we get the socket from the `useSocket` hook, and define a state hook to store an array of messages:

    ```
    export function useChat() {
        const { socket } = useSocket()
        const [messages, setMessages] = useState([])
    ```

5. Next, define a `receiveMessage` function, which appends a new message to the array:

    ```
    function receiveMessage(message) {
        setMessages((messages) => [...messages, message])
    }
    ```

6. Now, create an effect hook, in which we create a listener using `socket.on`:

    ```
    useEffect(() => {
        socket.on('chat.message', receiveMessage)
    ```

7. We need to make sure to remove the listener again using `socket.off` when the effect hook unmounts, otherwise we might end up with multiple listeners when the component re-renders or unmounts:

    ```
        return () => socket.off('chat.message', receiveMessage)
    }, [])
    ```

8. Now, receiving messages should work fine. Let's move on to sending messages. To do this, we create a `sendMessage` function, which uses `socket.emit` to send the message:

    ```
    function sendMessage(message) {
        socket.emit('chat.message', message)
    }
    ```

9. Lastly, return the `messages` array and the `sendMessage` function so that we can use them in our components:

    ```
    return { messages, sendMessage }
    }
    ```

Now that we have successfully implemented the `useChat` hook, let's use it!

Implementing the ChatRoom component

Finally, we can put it all together and implement a ChatRoom component. Follow these steps to get started:

1. Create a new `src/components/ChatRoom.jsx` file.

2. Import the `useChat` hook and the `EnterMessage` and `ChatMessage` components:

    ```
    import { useChat } from '../hooks/useChat.js'
    import { EnterMessage } from './EnterMessage.jsx'
    import { ChatMessage } from './ChatMessage.jsx'
    ```

3. Define a new component, which gets the `messages` array and the `sendMessage` function from the `useChat` hook:

    ```
    export function ChatRoom() {
      const { messages, sendMessage } = useChat()
    ```

4. Then, render the list of messages as `ChatMessage` components:

    ```
    return (
      <div>
        {messages.map((message, index) => (
          <ChatMessage key={index} {...message} />
        ))}
    ```

5. Next, render the `EnterMessage` component and pass the `sendMessage` function as the `onSend` prop:

    ```
        <EnterMessage onSend={sendMessage} />
      </div>
    )
    }
    ```

6. Edit `src/pages/Chat.jsx` and import the `ChatRoom` component and the `useSocket` hook:

    ```
    import { ChatRoom } from '../components/ChatRoom.jsx'
    import { useSocket } from '../contexts/SocketIOContext.jsx'
    ```

7. Get the status from the `useSocket` hook in the `Chat` page component:

    ```
    export function Chat() {
      const { status } = useSocket()
    ```

8. If the status is `connected`, we show the `ChatRoom` component:

```
return (
  <div style={{ padding: 8 }}>
    <Header />
    <br />
    <hr />
    <br />
    <Status />
    <br />
    <hr />
    <br />
    {status === 'connected' && <ChatRoom />}
```

9. Now, go to `http://localhost:5173/` in your browser and log in with a username and password. The socket connects and the chat room is rendered. Enter a chat message and send it by pressing *Return/Enter* or by clicking the **Send** button. You will see that the message is received and displayed!

10. Open a second browser window and log in with a second user. Send another message there. You will see that the message is received by both users, as can be seen in the following screenshot:

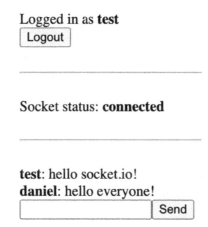

Figure 14.5 – Sending and receiving messages from different users

Now that we have a basic chat app working, let's explore how we could implement chat commands using acknowledgments.

Implementing chat commands with acknowledgments

In addition to sending and receiving messages, chat apps often offer a way to send commands to the client and/or server. For example, we could send a /clear command to clear our local messages list. Or we could send a /rooms command to get a list of rooms that we are in. Follow these steps to implement chat commands:

1. Edit src/hooks/useChat.js and adjust the sendMessage function inside it. First, let's make it an async function:

   ```
   async function sendMessage(message) {
   ```

2. *Replace* the contents of the function with the following. We first check whether the message starts with a slash (/). If so, then we get the command by removing the slash and use a switch statement:

   ```
   if (message.startsWith('/')) {
     const command = message.substring(1)
     switch (command) {
   ```

3. For the clear command, we simply set the array of messages to an empty array:

   ```
   case 'clear':
     setMessages([])
     break
   ```

4. For the rooms command, we get the user info by using socket.emitWithAck and our own socket.id:

   ```
   case 'rooms': {
     const userInfo = await socket.emitWithAck('user.info',
   socket.id)
   ```

5. Then, we get the list of rooms, filtering out our own room (with the name of our socket.id) that we automatically join in Socket.IO:

   ```
   const rooms = userInfo.rooms.filter((room) => room !==
   socket.id)
   ```

6. We reuse the receiveMessage function to send a message from the server, telling us the rooms that we are in:

   ```
   receiveMessage({
     message: `You are in: ${rooms.join(', ')}`,
   })
   break
   }
   ```

Note that we are not sending a username here, just a message. We will have to adapt the `ChatMessage` component to accommodate that later.

7. If we receive any other command, we show an error message:

```
default:
  receiveMessage({
    message: `Unknown command: ${command}`,
  })
  break
}
```

8. Otherwise (if the message did not start with a slash), we simply emit the chat message, as before:

```
} else {
  socket.emit('chat.message', message)
}
}
```

9. Finally, edit `src/components/ChatMessage.jsx` and adapt the component to render a system message if no username was given:

```
export function ChatMessage({ username, message }) {
  return (
    <div>
      {username ? (
        <span>
          <b>{username}</b>: {message}
        </span>
      ) : (
        <i>{message}</i>
      )}
    </div>
  )
}
```

10. Do not forget to adjust `PropTypes` to make the username optional (by *removing* `.isRequired` from the `username` prop):

```
ChatMessage.propTypes = {
  username: PropTypes.string,
```

11. Go to `http://localhost:5173/` in your browser and try sending a couple messages. Then, type `/clear` and you will see all messages were cleared. Next, type `/rooms` to get the list of rooms that you are in, as you can see in the following screenshot:

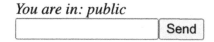

Figure 14.6 – Sending the /rooms command

> **Note**
>
> Joining different rooms currently does not work due to the query parameter getting cleared after logging in. In the next chapter, we are going to refactor the chat app and implement a `/join` command to join a different room.

Summary

In this chapter, we implemented a frontend for our chat app backend. We started by integrating the Socket. IO client with React by making a context and a custom hook for it. Then, we used `AuthProvider` to get the token to authenticate a user when connecting to the socket. After that, we displayed the status of our socket. Then, we implemented a chat app interface to send and receive messages. Finally, we implemented chat commands by using acknowledgments to get the rooms that we are in.

In the next chapter, *Chapter 15, Adding Persistence to Socket.IO Using MongoDB*, we are going to learn how to store and replay previously sent messages using MongoDB with Socket.IO.

15

Adding Persistence to Socket.IO Using MongoDB

Now that we have implemented a Socket.IO backend and frontend, let's spend some time integrating it with the MongoDB database by temporarily storing messages in the database and replaying them when a new user joins, so that users can see the chat history after they join. Additionally, we will refactor our chat app to be ready for future expansions and maintenance. Finally, we will test out the new structure by implementing new commands to join and switch rooms.

In this chapter, we are going to cover the following main topics:

- Storing and replaying messages using MongoDB
- Refactoring the app to be more extensible
- Implementing commands to join and switch rooms

Technical requirements

Before we start, please install all requirements from *Chapter 1, Preparing for Full Stack Development*, and *Chapter 2, Getting to Know Node.js and MongoDB*.

The versions listed in those chapters are the ones used in the book. While installing a newer version should not be an issue, please note that certain steps might work differently on a newer version. If you are having an issue with the code and steps provided in this book, please try using the versions mentioned in *Chapters 1* and *2*.

You can find the code for this chapter on GitHub: `https://github.com/PacktPublishing/` `Modern-Full-Stack-React-Projects/tree/main/ch15`.

If you cloned the full repository for the book, Husky may not find the `.git` directory when running `npm install`. In that case, just run `git init` in the root of the corresponding chapter folder.

The CiA video for this chapter can be found at: `https://youtu.be/Mi7Wj_jxjhM`.

Storing and replaying messages using MongoDB

Currently, if a new user joins the chat, they will not see any messages until someone actively sends messages. As such, new users will not be able to participate well in ongoing discussions. To solve this issue, we can store messages in the database and replay them when a user joins.

Creating the Mongoose schema

Follow these steps to create a Mongoose schema for storing chat messages:

1. Copy the existing ch14 folder to a new ch15 folder, as follows:

    ```
    $ cp -R ch14 ch15
    ```

2. Open the new ch15 folder in VS Code.

3. Create a new backend/src/db/models/message.js file.

4. Inside it, define a new messageSchema, which we are going to use to store chat messages in the database:

    ```
    import mongoose, { Schema } from 'mongoose'

    const messageSchema = new Schema({
    ```

5. The message schema should contain username (person who sent the message), message, a room that it was sent in, and a sent date for when the message was sent:

    ```
      username: { type: String, required: true },
      message: { type: String, required: true },
      room: { type: String, required: true },
      sent: { type: Date, expires: 5 * 60, default: Date.now,
    required: true },
    })
    ```

    For the sent date, we specify expires to make the messages automatically expire after 5 minutes (5 * 60 seconds). This ensures that our database does not get cluttered with lots of chat messages. We also set the default value to Date.now so that all messages are by default tagged as being sent at the current time.

> **Info**
>
> MongoDB only actually checks for data expiration once a minute, so the expired documents might persist for up to a minute past their defined expiration time.

6.   Create a model from the schema and export it:

```
export const Message = mongoose.model('message', messageSchema)
```

After creating the Mongoose schema and model, let's move on to creating the service functions for dealing with chat messages.

Creating the service functions

We need to create service functions to save a new message in the database and to get all messages sent in a given room, sorted by sent date, showing the oldest messages first. Follow these steps to implement the service functions:

1.   Create a new backend/src/services/messages.js file.

2.   Inside it, import the Message model:

```
import { Message } from '../db/models/message.js'
```

3.   Then, define a function to create a new Message object in the database:

```
export async function createMessage({ username, message, room })
{
    const messageDoc = new Message({ username, message, room })
    return await messageDoc.save()
}
```

4.   Also, define a function to get all messages from a certain room, listing the oldest messages first:

```
export async function getMessagesByRoom(room) {
    return await Message.find({ room }).sort({ sent: 1 })
}
```

Next, we are going to use these service functions in our chat server.

Storing and replaying messages

Now that we have all the functions, we need to implement storing and replaying messages in our chat server. Follow these steps to implement the functionality:

1.   Edit backend/src/socket.js and import the service functions we defined earlier:

```
import { createMessage, getMessagesByRoom } from './services/
messages.js'
```

2. When a new user connects, get all messages from the current room, and send (replay) them to the user using `socket.emit`:

```
export function handleSocket(io) {
  io.on('connection', async (socket) => {
    const room = socket.handshake.query?.room ?? 'public'
    socket.join(room)
    console.log(socket.id, 'joined room:', room)

    const messages = await getMessagesByRoom(room)
    messages.forEach(({ username, message }) =>
      socket.emit('chat.message', { username, message }),
    )
```

3. Additionally, when a user sends a message, store it in the database:

```
socket.on('chat.message', (message) => {
  console.log(`${socket.id}: ${message}`)
  io.to(room).emit('chat.message', {
    username: socket.user.username,
    message,
  })
  createMessage({ username: socket.user.username, message,
room })
})
```

4. Start the frontend server as follows:

```
$ npm run dev
```

5. Then, start the backend server (do not forget to start the Docker container for the database!):

```
$ cd backend/
$ npm run dev
```

6. Go to `http://localhost:5173/`, log in and send some messages. Then, open a new tab, log in with a different user, and you will see the messages sent earlier get replayed:

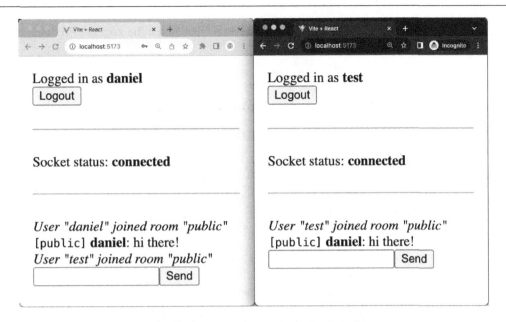

Figure 15.1 – Successfully replaying stored messages

> **Note**
>
> The screenshot in *Figure 15.1* is from a later version of the app, where we show messages when a user joins a room (we are going to implement these messages later in this chapter). Here, we use these messages to show that replaying works when the user joins after a message was sent.

If you wait 5 minutes and then join the chat again, you will see that the existing messages have expired and are not replayed anymore.

Now, let's make it clearer which messages were replayed in the user interface.

Visually distinguishing replayed messages

Currently, it looks like the other user sent the message right after we joined. It is not clear that the message was replayed from the server. To solve this issue, we can visually distinguish replayed messages by, for example, making them slightly grayer. Let's do that now, as follows:

1. Edit `backend/src/socket.js` and add a `replayed` flag to the replayed messages:

    ```
    const messages = await getMessagesByRoom(room)
    messages.forEach(({ username, message }) =>
       socket.emit('chat.message', { username, message, replayed:
    true }),
       )
    ```

2. Now, edit `src/components/ChatMessage.jsx`, and if the `replayed` flag was set, display the messages with a lower opacity:

    ```
    export function ChatMessage({ username, message, replayed }) {
      return (
        <div style={{ opacity: replayed ? 0.5 : 1.0 }}>
    ```

3. Do not forget to update `propTypes` and add the `replayed` flag:

    ```
    ChatMessage.propTypes = {
      username: PropTypes.string,
      message: PropTypes.string.isRequired,
      replayed: PropTypes.bool,
    }
    ```

4. Go to `http://localhost:5173/` again and repeat the same procedure (sending messages from one user, then logging in with a different user in another tab), and you will see that replayed messages are now easy to distinguish from new messages:

Figure 15.2 – Replayed messages are now displayed in a lighter color

Now that we have successfully stored our message history in the database, let's focus a bit on refactoring the chat app to make it more extensible and maintainable in the future.

Refactoring the app to be more extensible

For the refactoring, we will start by defining service functions for all chat functionality that our server provides.

Defining service functions

Follow these steps to get started defining service functions for the chat functionality:

1. Create a new `backend/src/services/chat.js` file.

2. Inside it, import the service functions related to messages:

    ```
    import { createMessage, getMessagesByRoom } from './messages.js'
    ```

3. Define a new function to send a private message directly to a user:

    ```
    export function sendPrivateMessage(
      socket,
      { username, room, message, replayed },
    ) {
      socket.emit('chat.message', { username, message, room,
    replayed })
    }
    ```

    Private messages will be used to, for example, replay messages to a specific user, and are not stored in the database.

4. Also, define a function to send a system message:

    ```
    export function sendSystemMessage(io, { room, message }) {
      io.to(room).emit('chat.message', { message, room })
    }
    ```

    System messages will be used to, for example, announce that a user joined a room. We also do not want to store these in the database.

5. Then, define a function to send a public message:

    ```
    export function sendPublicMessage(io, { username, room, message
    }) {
      io.to(room).emit('chat.message', { username, message, room })
      createMessage({ username, message, room })
    }
    ```

    Public messages will be used to send regular chat messages to a room. These messages are stored in the database so that we can replay them later.

6. We also define a new function to join a given `socket` to a `room`:

```
export async function joinRoom(io, socket, { room }) {
  socket.join(room)
```

7. Inside this function, send a system message telling everyone in the room that someone joined:

```
sendSystemMessage(io, {
  room,
  message: `User "${socket.user.username}" joined room
"${room}"`,
})
```

8. Then, replay all messages that were sent to the room privately to the user that just joined it:

```
const messages = await getMessagesByRoom(room)
messages.forEach(({ username, message }) =>
  sendPrivateMessage(socket, { username, message, room,
replayed: true })
  )
}
```

9. Lastly, define a service function to get the user info from the `socketId`. We simply copy and paste the code we have previously had in `backend/src/socket.js` here:

```
export async function getUserInfoBySocketId(io, socketId) {
  const sockets = await io.in(socketId).fetchSockets()
  if (sockets.length === 0) return null
  const socket = sockets[0]
  const userInfo = {
    socketId,
    rooms: Array.from(socket.rooms),
    user: socket.user,
  }
  return userInfo
}
```

Now that we have created the service functions for the chat functionality, let's use them in the Socket.IO server.

Refactoring the Socket.IO server to use the service functions

Now that we have defined service functions, let's refactor the chat server code to use them. Follow these steps to do so:

1. Open backend/`src/socket.js` and find the following import:

    ```
    import { createMessage, getMessagesByRoom } from './services/
    messages.js'
    ```

    Replace the preceding import with the following import to the new chat service functions:

    ```
    import {
      joinRoom,
      sendPublicMessage,
      getUserInfoBySocketId,
    } from './services/chat.js'
    ```

2. *Replace* the whole handleSocket function with the following new code. When a connection is made, we automatically join the public room using the joinRoom service function:

    ```
    export function handleSocket(io) {
      io.on('connection', (socket) => {
        joinRoom(io, socket, { room: 'public' })
    ```

3. Then, define a listener for the chat.message event and send it to the given room by using the sendPublicMessage service function:

    ```
        socket.on('chat.message', (room, message) =>
          sendPublicMessage(io, { username: socket.user.username,
      room, message }),
        )
    ```

> **Note**
>
> We changed the signature of the chat.message event to require passing a room now, so that we can implement a better way to deal with multiple rooms later. Later, we need to make sure to adjust the client code to accommodate this.

4. Next, define a listener for the user.info event, in which we use the async service function getUserInfoBySocketId and return the result of it in callback to turn this event into an acknowledgment:

    ```
        socket.on('user.info', async (socketId, callback) =>
          callback(await getUserInfoBySocketId(io, socketId)),
        )
      })
    ```

5. Finally, we can re-use the authentication middleware from before:

```
io.use((socket, next) => {
  if (!socket.handshake.auth?.token) {
    return next(new Error('Authentication failed: no token
provided'))
  }
  jwt.verify(
    socket.handshake.auth.token,
    process.env.JWT_SECRET,
    async (err, decodedToken) => {
      if (err) {
        return next(new Error('Authentication failed: invalid
token'))
      }
      socket.auth = decodedToken
      socket.user = await getUserInfoById(socket.auth.sub)
      return next()
    },
  )
})
}
```

Now that our chat server is refactored, let's continue with refactoring the client-side code.

Refactoring the client-side code

Now that our server-side code uses service functions to encapsulate the functionality of the chat app, let's do a similar refactoring of the client-side code by extracting client-side commands into separate functions, as follows:

1. Edit `src/hooks/useChat.js` and within the `useChat` hook, define a new function to clear the messages:

```
function clearMessages() {
  setMessages([])
}
```

2. Then, define an `async` function to get all rooms that the user is in:

```
async function getRooms() {
  const userInfo = await socket.emitWithAck('user.info',
socket.id)
  const rooms = userInfo.rooms.filter((room) => room !==
socket.id)
```

```
        return rooms
    }
```

3. We can now use these functions in the `sendMessage` function, as follows:

```
async function sendMessage(message) {
  if (message.startsWith('/')) {
    const command = message.substring(1)
    switch (command) {
      case 'clear':
        clearMessages()
        break
      case 'rooms': {
        const rooms = await getRooms()
        receiveMessage({
          message: `You are in: ${rooms.join(', ')}`,
        })
        break
      }
```

4. Lastly, we adjust the `chat.message` event to send `room` in addition to `message`. For now, we always send messages to the `'public'` room:

```
      default:
        receiveMessage({
          message: `Unknown command: ${command}`,
        })
        break
    }
  } else {
    socket.emit('chat.message', 'public', message)
  }
}
```

In the next section, we will expand this to be able to switch between different rooms.

5. Go to `http://localhost:5173/` and verify that the chat app still works the same way as before.

Now that we have successfully refactored our chat app to be more extensible, let's test out the flexibility of the new structure by implementing new commands to join and switch rooms.

Implementing commands to join and switch rooms

Let's now test out the new structure by implementing commands to join and switch rooms on the chat app, as follows:

1. Edit `backend/src/socket.js` and define a new listener below the `chat.message` listener, which will call the `joinRoom` service function when we receive a `chat.join` event from the client:

    ```
    socket.on('chat.join', (room) => joinRoom(io, socket, { room
    }))
    ```

    As we can see, having a `joinRoom` service function makes it really simple to reuse the code to join a new room here. It already sends a system message telling everyone that someone joined the room, just like it does when the user joins the `public` room by default upon connection.

2. Edit `src/components/ChatMessage.jsx` and display `room`:

    ```
    export function ChatMessage({ room, username, message, replayed
    }) {
      return (
        <div style={{ opacity: replayed ? 0.5 : 1.0 }}>
          {username ? (
            <span>
              <code>[{room}]</code> <b>{username}</b>: {message}
            </span>
    ```

3. Add the `room` prop to the `propTypes` definition:

    ```
    ChatMessage.propTypes = {
      username: PropTypes.string,
      message: PropTypes.string.isRequired,
      replayed: PropTypes.bool,
      room: PropTypes.string,
    }
    ```

4. Now, edit `src/hooks/useChat.js` and define a state hook to store the room we are currently in:

    ```
    export function useChat() {
      const { socket } = useSocket()
      const [messages, setMessages] = useState([])
      const [currentRoom, setCurrentRoom] = useState('public')
    ```

    By default, we are in the `public` room.

5. Define a new function to switch rooms:

```
function switchRoom(room) {
  setCurrentRoom(room)
}
```

At the moment, we are only calling `setCurrentRoom` here, but we might want to extend this function later, so it is good practice to abstract it in advance into a separate function.

6. Define a new function to join a room by sending the `chat.join` event and switching the current room:

```
function joinRoom(room) {
  socket.emit('chat.join', room)
  switchRoom(room)
}
```

7. Change the `sendMessage` function to accept arguments for commands, as follows:

```
async function sendMessage(message) {
  if (message.startsWith('/')) {
    const [command, ...args] = message.substring(1).split(' ')
    switch (command) {
```

We can now send commands such as `/join <room-name>` and the room name will be stored in `args[0]`.

8. Define a new command to join a room, in which we first check whether arguments were passed to the command:

```
      case 'join': {
        if (args.length === 0) {
          return receiveMessage({
            message: 'Please provide a room name: /join
<room>',
          })
        }
```

9. Then, we ensure that we have not already joined the room by using the `getRooms` function:

```
        const room = args[0]
        const rooms = await getRooms()
        if (rooms.includes(room)) {
          return receiveMessage({
            message: `You are already in room "${room}".`,
          })
        }
```

10. Finally, we can join the room by using the `joinRoom` function:

```
joinRoom(room)
break
}
```

11. Similarly, we can implement the `/switch` command as follows:

```
case 'switch': {
    if (args.length === 0) {
        return receiveMessage({
            message: 'Please provide a room name: /switch
<room>',
        })
    }
    const room = args[0]
    const rooms = await getRooms()
    if (!rooms.includes(room)) {
        return receiveMessage({
            message: `You are not in room "${room}". Type "/
join ${room}" to join it first.`,
        })
    }
    switchRoom(room)
    receiveMessage({
        message: `Switched to room "${room}".`,
    })
    break
}
```

In this case, we are checking whether the user is in the room already. If not, we tell them that they must join the room first before switching to it.

12. Adjust the `chat.message` event to send to the `currentRoom`, as follows:

```
} else {
    socket.emit('chat.message', currentRoom, message)
}
```

13. Go to `http://localhost:5173/`, send a message to the public room, then join the `react` room by executing the `/join react` command. Send a different message to that room.

14. Open another browser window, log in with a different user, and you will see that the first message from the `public` room gets replayed. However, we do not see the message from the `react` room, because we have not joined it yet!

15. Now, in the second browser window, call `/join react` as well. You will see that the second message gets replayed now.

16. Try using `/switch public` to switch back to the `public` room and send another message there. You will see that both clients receive it because they are both in the `public` room.

The result of these actions can be seen in the following screenshot:

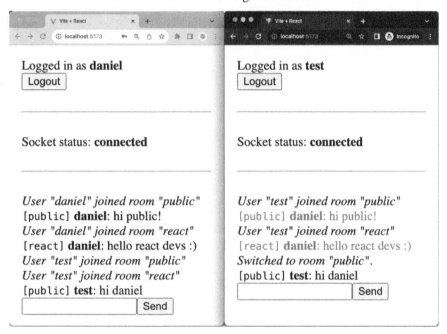

Figure 15.3 – Chatting in different rooms

Summary

In this chapter, we first connected our chat app to the database by storing messages in MongoDB. We also learned how to make documents expire after a certain amount of time. Then, we implemented functionality to replay messages when a new user joins the chat. Next, we spent some time refactoring the chat app to make it more extensible and maintainable in the future. Finally, we implemented ways to join new rooms and switch between rooms.

Up until now, we have only been using libraries to develop our apps. In the next chapter, *Chapter 16, Getting Started with Next.js*, we will learn how to use a full-stack React framework for developing apps. Frameworks, such as Next.js, provide more structure for our apps and offer us a lot of features, such as server-side rendering, out of the box.

Part 5: Advancing to Enterprise-Ready Full-Stack Applications

In this part, we will introduce **Next.js** as an enterprise-ready full-stack application framework. We will learn how it works and what its advantages are over using **React** alone. Then, we will create an app using Next.js and the new **App Router** paradigm. After that, we will introduce **React Server Components** and **Server Actions** as a way to directly interface with the database, without requiring a REST or GraphQL API. Then, we will dive deeper into the Next.js framework and learn about **caching**, **API routes**, adding metadata, and how to optimally load images and fonts. Next, we will learn how to deploy a Next.js app using **Vercel** and a custom deployment setup using **Docker**. Finally, we give an overview and briefly cover various advanced topics in full-stack development that have not been covered in this book yet. This includes concepts such as maintaining large-scale projects, optimizing the bundle size, an overview of UI libraries, and advanced state management solutions.

This part includes the following chapters:

- *Chapter 16, Getting Started with Next.js*
- *Chapter 17, Introducing React Server Components*
- *Chapter 18, Advanced Next.js Concepts and Optimizations*
- *Chapter 19, Deploying a Next.js App*
- *Chapter 20, Diving Deeper into Full-Stack Development*

16

Getting Started with Next.js

Up until now, we have been using various libraries and tools to develop full-stack web applications. Now, we introduce Next.js as an enterprise-ready full-stack web application framework for React. Next.js combines all the functions and tools you need for full-stack web development in one package. In this book, we use Next.js because it is currently the most popular framework supporting all new React features, such as React Server Components and Server Actions, which are the future of full-stack React development. However, there are other frameworks for full-stack React, such as Remix, which have recently also started supporting the new React features.

In this chapter, we will learn how Next.js works and what its advantages are. Then, we will re-create our blog project in Next.js to highlight the differences between using a simple bundler such as Vite, and a full framework such as Next.js. Along the way, we will learn how the Next.js App Router works. Finally, we are going to re-create our (static) blog app by creating components and pages and then defining links between them.

In this chapter, we are going to cover the following main topics:

- What is Next.js?
- Setting up Next.js
- Introducing the App Router
- Creating static components and pages

Technical requirements

Before we start, please install all the requirements from *Chapter 1, Preparing for Full-Stack Development*, and *Chapter 2, Getting to Know Node.js and MongoDB*.

The versions listed in those chapters are the ones used in the book. While installing a newer version should not be an issue, please note that certain steps might work differently on a newer version. If you are having an issue with the code and steps provided in this book, please try using the versions mentioned in *Chapters 1* and *2*.

You can find the code for this chapter on GitHub: `https://github.com/PacktPublishing/Modern-Full-Stack-React-Projects/tree/main/ch16`.

The CiA video for this chapter can be found at: `https://youtu.be/jQFCZqCspoc`.

What is Next.js?

Next.js is a React framework that puts together everything you need to create a full-stack web application with React. Its main features are as follows:

- Good developer experience out of the box, including hot module reloading, error handling, and more.
- File-based routing and nested layouts, route handlers to define API endpoints, all from Next.js.
- **Internationalization (i18n)** support in routing, allowing us to create internationalized routes.
- Enhanced server-side and client-side data fetching with caching out of the box.
- Middleware to run code before requests are completed.
- Options to run API endpoints on serverless runtimes.
- Out-of-the-box support for static generation of pages.
- Dynamic streaming of components when they are needed, allowing us to show an initial page quickly, and then load other components later.
- Advanced client and server rendering, allowing us to not only render React components on the server side (**server-side rendering (SSR)**) but also make use of **React Server Components**, which allow us to render React components exclusively on the server without sending additional JavaScript to the client.
- **Server Actions** to progressively enhance forms and actions sent from the client to the server, allowing us to submit forms even without JavaScript on the client.
- Built-in optimizations for images, fonts, and scripts to improve Core Web Vitals.
- Additionally, Next.js provides a platform to easily deploy our apps on – Vercel.

All in all, Next.js puts together everything we have learned about full-stack development throughout this book, refines each concept and makes it more advanced and customizable, and provides all of that in one single package. We are now going to re-create the blog application from earlier chapters, but from scratch with Next.js. Doing so will allow us to see the differences between developing an app with and without a full-stack framework.

Setting up Next.js

We are now going to set up a new project using the `create-next-app` tool, which sets up everything automatically for us. Follow these steps to get started:

1. Open a new Terminal window. Make sure you are outside of any project folders. Run the following command to create a new folder and initialize a Next.js project there:

   ```
   $ npx create-next-app@14.1.0
   ```

2. When asked if it's **Ok to proceed?**, press y and confirm by pressing *Return/Enter*.

3. Give the project a name, such as `ch16`.

4. Answer the questions as follows:

   - **Would you like to use TypeScript?**: No

   - **Would you like to use ESLint?**: Yes

   - **Would you like to use Tailwind CSS?**: No

   - **Would you like to use `src/` directory?**: Yes

   - **Would you like to use App Router?**: Yes

   - **Would you like to customize the default import alias?**: No

5. After answering all the questions, a new Next.js app will be created in the `ch16` folder. The output should look as follows:

```
● → ~/D/Full-Stack-React-Projects ⎇ main± > npx create-next-app@14.1.0
Need to install the following packages:
create-next-app@14.1.0
Ok to proceed? (y) y
✓ What is your project named? … ch16
✓ Would you like to use TypeScript? … No / Yes
✓ Would you like to use ESLint? … No / Yes
✓ Would you like to use Tailwind CSS? … No / Yes
✓ Would you like to use `src/` directory? … No / Yes
✓ Would you like to use App Router? (recommended) … No / Yes
✓ Would you like to customize the default import alias (@/*)? … No / Yes
Creating a new Next.js app in /Users/dan/Development/Full-Stack-React-Projects/ch16.

Using npm.

Initializing project with template: app


Installing dependencies:
- react
- react-dom
- next

Installing devDependencies:
- eslint
- eslint-config-next


added 305 packages, and audited 306 packages in 3s

120 packages are looking for funding
  run `npm fund` for details

found 0 vulnerabilities
Success! Created ch16 at /Users/dan/Development/Full-Stack-React-Projects/ch16
```

Figure 16.1 – Creating a new Next.js project

6. Open the newly created ch16 folder in VS Code.

7. In the new VS Code window, open a Terminal and run the project with the following command:

    ```
    $ npm run dev
    ```

8. Open http://localhost:3000 in your browser to see the Next.js app running! The app should look as follows:

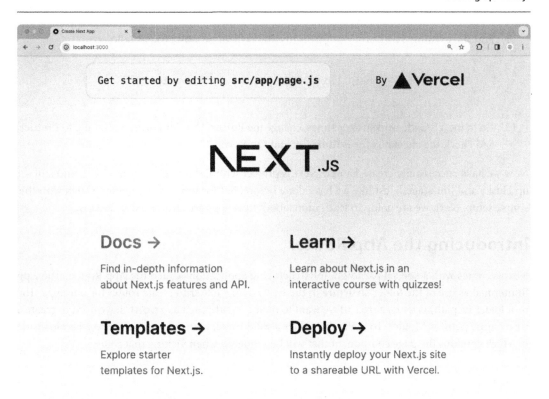

Figure 16.2 – Our newly created Next.js app running in the browser

9. Unfortunately, `create-next-app` does not set up Prettier for us, so let's quickly do that now. Install Prettier by running the following command:

```
$ npm install --save-dev prettier@2.8.4 \
  eslint-config-prettier@8.6.0
```

10. Create a new `.prettierrc.json` file in the root of the project, with the following contents:

```
{
  "trailingComma": "all",
  "tabWidth": 2,
  "printWidth": 80,
  "semi": false,
  "jsxSingleQuote": true,
  "singleQuote": true
}
```

11. Edit the existing .eslintrc.json to extend from prettier, as follows:

```
{
    "extends": ["next/core-web-vitals", "prettier"]
}
```

12. Go to the VS Code workspace settings, change the **Editor: Default Formatter** setting to **Prettier**, and check the checkbox for **Editor: Format On Save**.

Now we have successfully created a new Next.js project with ESLint and Prettier! We could still set up Husky and lint-staged, just like we have done before, but for now, we are going to stick with this simple setup. Next, we are going to learn more about how apps are structured in Next.js.

Introducing the App Router

Next.js comes with a special paradigm for structuring applications called the App Router. The App Router makes use of the folder structure in the src/app/ folder to create routes for our apps. The root folder (/ path) is src/app/. If we want to define a path, such as /posts, we need to create a src/app/posts/ folder. To make this folder a valid route, we need to put a page.js file inside it, which contains the page component that will be rendered when visiting that route.

> **Note**
>
> Alternatively, we can put a route.js file into a folder to turn it into an API route instead of rendering a page. We are going to learn more about API routes in *Chapter 18, Advanced Next. js Concepts and Optimizations*.

Additionally, Next.js allows us to define a layout.js file, which will be used as the layout for a certain path. The layout component accepts children, which can contain other layouts or pages. This flexibility allows us to define nested routes with sub-layouts.

There are other special files in the App Router paradigm, such as the error.js file, which will be rendered when there is an error on the page, and the loading.js file, which will be rendered while the page is loading (using React Suspense).

Take a look at the following example of a folder structure with the App Router:

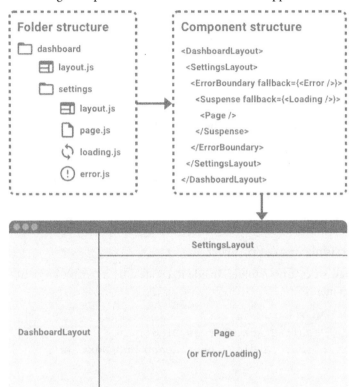

Figure 16.3 – Example of a folder structure with the App Router

In the preceding example, we have a dashboard/settings/ route, defined by the dashboard and settings folders. The dashboard folder does not have a page.js file, so going to dashboard/ will result in a 404 Not Found error. However, the dashboard folder has a layout.js file, which defines the main layout of the dashboard. The settings folder has another layout.js file, which defines the layout of the settings page on the dashboard. It also has a page.js file, which will be rendered when the dashboard/settings/ route is visited. Additionally, it has a loading.js file, which is rendered inside the settings layout, while the settings page is loading. It also contains an error.js file, which is rendered inside the settings layout if there is an error while loading the settings page.

As we can see, the App Router makes it easy to implement common use cases, such as nested routes, layouts, errors, and loading components. Let's now get started with defining the folder structure for our blog app.

Defining the folder structure

Let's recap and refine the routing structure of the blog application from previous chapters:

- / – the index page of our blog, containing a list of posts
- /login – the login page to login to an existing account
- /signup – the signup page to create a new account
- /create – a page to create a new blog post (this route is new)
- /posts/:id – a page to view a single blog post

All of these pages share a common layout with a navigation bar at the top, allowing us to navigate between the various pages of our app.

Let's now create this routing structure as a folder structure in the App Router:

1. *Delete* the existing src/app/ folder.

2. Create a new src/app/ folder. Inside it, create a src/app/layout.js file with the following contents:

```
export const metadata = {
  title: 'Full-Stack Next.js Blog',
  description: 'A blog about React and Next.js',
}


export default function RootLayout({ children }) {
  return (
    <html lang="en">
      <body>
        <main>{children}</main>
      </body>
    </html>
  )
}
```

The metadata object is a special exported object in Next.js used to provide meta tags, such as the <title> and <meta name="description"> tags.

The default export of files in the App Router needs to be the component that should be rendered for the respective layout/page.

3. Create a new src/app/page.js file, with the following placeholder contents:

```
export default function HomePage() {
  return <strong>Blog home page</strong>
}
```

4. Create a new `src/app/login/` folder. Inside it, create a `src/app/login/page.js` file with the following placeholder contents:

    ```
    export default function LoginPage() {
      return <strong>Login</strong>
    }
    ```

5. Create a new `src/app/signup/` folder. Inside it, create a `src/app/signup/page.js` file with the following placeholder contents:

    ```
    export default function SignupPage() {
      return <strong>Signup</strong>
    }
    ```

6. Create a new `src/app/create/` folder. Inside it, create a `src/app/create/page.js` file with the following placeholder contents:

    ```
    export default function CreatePostPage() {
      return <strong>CreatePost</strong>
    }
    ```

7. Create a new `src/app/posts/` folder. Inside it, create a new `src/app/posts/[id]/` folder. This is a special folder containing a route parameter `id`, which we can use when rendering the page.

8. Create a new `src/app/posts/[id]/page.js` file with the following placeholder contents:

    ```
    export default function ViewPostPage({ params }) {
      return <strong>ViewPost {params.id}</strong>
    }
    ```

    As you can see, we are getting the `id` from the `params` object provided by Next.js.

9. If it's not running anymore, start the Next.js dev server with the following command:

    $ npm run dev

10. Then go to `http://localhost:3000/` (or refresh the page) in your browser to see the main route working. Go to the different routes, such as `/login` and `/posts/123`, to see the different pages being rendered and the `route` param working!

Now that we defined the folder structure for our project, let's continue by creating static components and pages.

Creating static components and pages

For the components in our blog, we can reuse a lot of the code we wrote in previous chapters, as it is not that much different in Next.js than it is in plain React. Only specific components, such as the navigation bar, will be different, because Next.js has its own router. We are going to create most of our components in a separate `src/components/` folder. This folder will only contain React components that can be reused across multiple pages. All page and layout components will still be in `src/app/`.

> **Note**
>
> In Next.js, it is also possible to co-locate regular components with the page and layout components, which should be done in large-scale projects for components that are only used on those specific pages. In small projects, it does not really matter as much, and we can just put all our regular components in a separate folder to make them easier to distinguish from page and layout components.

Defining components

Let's now get started with creating the components for our blog app:

1. Create a new `src/components/` folder.

2. Create a new `src/components/Login.jsx` file. Inside it, define a `<form>` with a `username` field, a `password` field, and a submit button:

    ```jsx
    export function Login() {
      return (
        <form>
          <div>
            <label htmlFor='username'>Username: </label>
            <input type='text' name='username' id='username' />
          </div>
          <br />
          <div>
            <label htmlFor='password'>Password: </label>
            <input type='password' name='password' id='password' />
          </div>
          <br />
          <input type='submit' value='Log In' />
        </form>
      )
    }
    ```

> **Note**
>
> We use uncontrolled input fields (so, no `useState` hooks) here on purpose, as it is not necessary to make controlled input fields for submitting forms with Server Actions, which we are going to learn about in the next chapter, *Chapter 17, Introducing React Server Components*. However, it is important to properly define the `name` property of input fields, as that is what will be used to identify the field when the form is submitted.

3. In a similar fashion, create a new `src/components/Signup.jsx` file and define a form with the same fields:

```jsx
export function Signup() {
  return (
    <form>
      <div>
        <label htmlFor='username'>Username: </label>
        <input type='text' name='username' id='username' />
      </div>
      <br />
      <div>
        <label htmlFor='password'>Password: </label>
        <input type='password' name='password' id='password' />
      </div>
      <br />
      <input type='submit' value='Sign Up' />
    </form>
  )
}
```

4. Create a new `src/components/CreatePost.jsx` file and define a form with a required `title` input field, a `textarea` to define the `contents`, and a submit button:

```jsx
export function CreatePost() {
  return (
    <form>
      <div>
        <label htmlFor='title'>Title: </label>
        <input type='text' name='title' id='title' required />
      </div>
      <br />
      <textarea name='contents' id='contents' />
      <br />
      <br />
      <input type='submit' value='Create' />
    </form>
```

```
       )
     }
```

5. Create a new `src/components/Post.jsx` file. As an improvement over the structure from previous chapters, the `Post` component will be used in the `PostList`, and only show the `title` and `author` of a blog post, with a link to the full post:

```jsx
import PropTypes from 'prop-types'

export function Post({ _id, title, author }) {
  return (
    <article>
      <h3>{title}</h3>
      <em>
        Written by <strong>{author.username}</strong>
      </em>
    </article>
  )
}
```

6. We also need to define `propTypes`. In this case, we will use a structure similar to the result from a database query, as we will be able to directly use database results when we introduce React Server Components in the next chapter:

```jsx
Post.propTypes = {
  _id: PropTypes.string.isRequired,
  title: PropTypes.string.isRequired,
  author: PropTypes.shape({
    username: PropTypes.string.isRequired,
  }).isRequired,
  contents: PropTypes.string,
}
```

7. Create a new `src/components/PostList.jsx` file. Here, we are going to reuse the `propTypes` from the `Post` component, so let's also import the `Post` component:

```jsx
import { Fragment } from 'react'
import PropTypes from 'prop-types'
import { Post } from './Post.jsx'
```

8. Then, we define the `PostList` component, which renders each blog post with the `Post` component:

```jsx
export function PostList({ posts = [] }) {
  return (
    <div>
```

```
        {posts.map((post) => (
          <Fragment key={`post-${post._id}`}>
            <Post _id={post._id} title={post.title} author={post.
author} />
            <hr />
          </Fragment>
        ))}
      </div>
    )
}
```

> **Note**
>
> It is best practice to use a unique ID for the key prop, such as a database ID, so that React can
> keep track of items changing in a list.

9. We now define the propTypes for the PostList component by making use of the
    existing Post.propTypes:

```
PostList.propTypes = {
  posts: PropTypes.arrayOf(
    PropTypes.shape(Post.propTypes)
  ).isRequired,
}
```

10. Lastly, we create a new src/components/FullPost.jsx file, in which we display the
    full post with all its contents:

```
import PropTypes from 'prop-types'

export function FullPost({ title, contents, author }) {
  return (
    <article>
      <h3>{title}</h3>
      <div>{contents}</div>
      <br />
      <em>
        Written by <strong>{author.username}</strong>
      </em>
    </article>
  )
}
```

11. Instead of reusing `propTypes` from the `Post` component, we are redefining them here, because the `FullPost` component needs different props than the `Post` component (it does not have the `_id` prop, but instead has the `contents` prop):

```
FullPost.propTypes = {
  title: PropTypes.string.isRequired,
  author: PropTypes.shape({
    username: PropTypes.string.isRequired,
  }).isRequired,
  contents: PropTypes.string,
}
```

Now that we have defined all the components we are going to need for our blog app, let's move on to properly defining the page components.

Defining pages

After creating various components that we are going to need for our blog app, let's now replace the placeholder page components with proper pages that render the appropriate components. Follow these steps to get started:

1. Edit `src/app/login/page.js` and import the `Login` component, then render it:

```
import { Login } from '@/components/Login'

export default function LoginPage() {
  return <Login />
}
```

> **Note**
>
> Remember when we set up Next.js and were asked if we wanted to customize the default import alias? This import alias allows us to reference the `src/` folder of our project, making our imports absolute rather than relative. By default, this is done using the @ alias. So, we can now just import from `@/components/Login` to import from the `src/components/Login.jsx` file, instead of having to import from `../../components/Login.jsx`. Absolute imports with import aliases become especially useful in large projects and make it easy to re-structure projects later.

2. Edit `src/app/signup/page.js` and, in a similar fashion, import and render the `Signup` component:

```
import { Signup } from '@/components/Signup'

export default function SignupPage() {
```

```
    return <Signup />
}
```

3. Repeat the process by editing the src/app/create/page.js file as follows:

```
import { CreatePost } from '@/components/CreatePost'

export default function CreatePostPage() {
    return <CreatePost />
}
```

4. Now, edit the src/app/posts/[id]/page.js file and import the FullPost component:

```
import { FullPost } from '@/components/FullPost'
```

5. Then, define a sample post object:

```
export default function ViewPostPage({ params }) {
    const post = {
        title: `Hello Next.js (${params.id})`,
        contents: 'This will be fetched from the database later',
        author: { username: 'Daniel Bugl' },
    }
```

   To show that the param still works, we also put the id into the title.

6. Render the FullPost component, as follows:

```
    return (
        <FullPost
            title={post.title}
            contents={post.contents}
            author={post.author}
        />
    )
}
```

7. Lastly, edit src/app/page.js by importing the PostList component, creating an example posts array, and rendering the PostList component:

```
import { PostList } from '@/components/PostList'

export default function HomePage() {
    const posts = [
        { _id: '123', title: 'Hello Next.js', author: { username:
'Daniel Bugl' } },
    ]
```

```
    return <PostList posts={posts} />
}
```

8. Go to `http://localhost:3000/posts/123` to see the `FullPost` component being rendered with the `id` param in the title. Feel free to change the `id` in the URL to see how the title changes. The following screenshot shows the `FullPost` component being rendered on the `/posts/123` path:

Hello Next.js (123)

This will be fetched from the database later

Written by Daniel Bugl

Figure 16.4 – Rendering the FullPost component with a Next.js route param in the title

After successfully defining all our pages, we still need a way to navigate between them, so let's continue by adding links between pages.

Adding links between pages

As mentioned earlier in this chapter, Next.js provides its own routing solution – the App Router. The routes are defined by the folder structure in the `src/app/` directory, and they all work already. All that's left to do now is to add links between them. To do this, we need to use the `Link` component from `next/link`. Follow these steps to get started with implementing a navigation bar:

1. Create a new `src/components/Navigation.jsx` file, where we import the `Link` component and `PropTypes`:

    ```
    import Link from 'next/link'
    import PropTypes from 'prop-types'
    ```

2. Define a `UserBar` component, which will be rendered when the user is logged in and allow a user to access the **Create Post** page and log out:

```
export function UserBar({ username }) {
  return (
    <form>
      <Link href='/create'>Create Post</Link> | Logged in as{'
'}
      <strong>{username}</strong> <button>Logout</button>
    </form>
  )
}

UserBar.propTypes = {
  username: PropTypes.string.isRequired,
}
```

3. Then, define a `LoginSignupLinks` component, which will be rendered when the user is not logged in yet. It provides links to the `/login` and `/signup` pages to allow users to sign up and log in to our app:

```
export function LoginSignupLinks() {
  return (
    <div>
      <Link href='/login'>Log In</Link> | <Link href='/
signup'>Sign Up</Link>
    </div>
  )
}
```

4. Next, define a `Navigation` component, which adds a link to the home page, and then conditionally renders either the `UserBar` component, or the `LoginSignupLinks` component, depending on whether the user is logged in or not:

```
export function Navigation({ username }) {
  return (
    <>
      <Link href='/'>Home</Link>
      {username ? <UserBar username={username} /> :
<LoginSignupLinks />}
    </>
  )
}
```

```
Navigation.propTypes = {
  username: PropTypes.string,
}
```

5. Now we just need to render the `Navigation` component. To make sure it appears on all pages of our blog app, we are going to put it in the root layout. Edit `src/app/layout.js` and import the `Navigation` component:

```
import { Navigation } from '@/components/Navigation'
```

6. Then, define a sample `user` object to simulate a user being logged in:

```
export default function RootLayout({ children }) {
  const user = { username: 'dan' }
```

7. Render the `Navigation` component, as follows:

```
return (
  <html lang='en'>
    <body>
      <nav>
        <Navigation username={user?.username} />
      </nav>
      <br />
      <main>{children}</main>
    </body>
  </html>
)
}
```

8. We still need to add a link from a single post in the list to the full post page. Edit `src/components/Post.jsx` and import the `Link` component:

```
import Link from 'next/link'
```

9. Then, add a link to the title, as follows:

```
export function Post({ _id, title, author }) {
  return (
    <article>
      <h3>
        <Link href={`/posts/${_id}`}>{title}</Link>
      </h3>
```

10. Go to `http://localhost:3000/` and you will see the navigation bar being rendered with the `UserBar` component.

11. Click on the **Create Post** link to go to the corresponding page, then go back using the **Home** link. Also, try going to the full post page by clicking on the title of the blog post on the home page.

The following screenshot shows the **Home** page being rendered after we added the navigation bar:

Figure 16.5 – Our (static) blog app re-created in Next.js!

Summary

In this chapter, we first learned what Next.js is and how it can be useful for full-stack development. Then, we set up a new Next.js project and learned about the App Router paradigm. Finally, we re-created the blog app in Next.js by creating components, pages, and a navigation bar, making use of the Next.js Link component to navigate between the different pages in our app.

In the next chapter, *Chapter 17, Introducing React Server Components*, we are going to learn how to make our blog app interactive by creating React Server Components, which are components that run on the server and can, for example, execute database queries. Additionally, we are going to learn about Server Actions, which are used to submit forms, such as the Login, Signup, and Create Post forms.

17

Introducing React
Server Components

After implementing our static blog app in Next.js, it's time to introduce some interactivity to it. Instead of using the traditional pattern of writing a separate backend server, which the frontend fetches data from and makes requests to, we are going to use a new pattern called **React Server Components** (**RSCs**). This new pattern allows us to directly access the database from React components by executing certain React components (so-called server components) only on the server. Together with Server Actions (a way to call functions on the server from the client), this new pattern allows us to easily and quickly develop full-stack apps. In this chapter, we are going to learn what RSCs and Server Actions are, why they matter, what their advantages are, and how to implement them properly and securely.

In this chapter, we are going to cover the following main topics:

- What are RSCs?
- Adding a data layer to our Next.js app
- Using RSCs to fetch data from the database
- Using Server Actions to sign up, log in, and create new posts

Technical requirements

Before we start, please install all the requirements from *Chapter 1, Preparing For Full-Stack Development*, and *Chapter 2, Getting to Know Node.js and MongoDB*.

The versions listed in those chapters are the ones used in this book. While installing a newer version should not be an issue, please note that certain steps might work differently. If you are having an issue with the code and steps provided in this book, please try using the versions mentioned in *Chapters 1* and *2*.

You can find the code for this chapter on GitHub: `https://github.com/PacktPublishing/Modern-Full-Stack-React-Projects/tree/main/ch17`.

The CiA video for this chapter can be found at: `https://youtu.be/4hGZJRmZW6E`.

What are RSCs?

So far, we have been using the traditional React architecture, where all components are **client components**. We started with client-side rendering. However, there are some downsides to client-side rendering:

- The JavaScript client bundle must be downloaded from the server before the client can start rendering anything, delaying the **first contentful paint** (**FCP**) for the user.

- Data must be fetched from the server (after all JavaScript is downloaded and executed) to show anything meaningful, delaying the **first meaningful paint** (**FMP**) for the user.

- Most of the load is on the client, even for pages that are not interactive, which is especially problematic for clients with slow processors, such as low-end mobile devices or old laptops. It also uses more battery to load a heavy client-side rendered page.

- In certain cases, data is fetched sequentially (for example, loading posts first and then resolving the authors of each post), which is especially a problem for slow connections with high latency.

To solve these problems, **server-side rendering** (**SSR**) was introduced, but it still has a big downside: the initial page load can be slow due to everything being rendered on the server. This slowdown happens because of the following reasons:

- Data must be fetched from the server before any of it can be shown.

- The JavaScript client bundle must be downloaded from the server before the client can be hydrated with it. Hydration means that the page is ready to be interacted with by a user. To refresh your knowledge of how hydration works, check out *Chapter 7*.

- Hydration has to be completed on the client before anything can be interacted with.

Even when a client component is pre-rendered on the server, its code will be bundled and sent to the client for hydration. This means that client components can run on both the server (for SSR) and the client, but they need to at least be able to run on the client.

In a traditional full-stack React architecture with only client components, if we needed to access the filesystem of the server or a database, we needed to write a separate backend using Node.js and expose an API (such as a REST API). Then, this API was queried in client components, for example, using TanStack Query. These queries can also be made on the server side (as we saw in *Chapter 7, Improving the Load Time Using Server-Side Rendering*), but they need to at least be executable on the client. This means we cannot directly access the filesystem or database from a React component, even if that code could run on the server; it would be bundled and sent to the client, where running it would not work (or expose internal information, such as credentials, to the database):

Without React Server Components

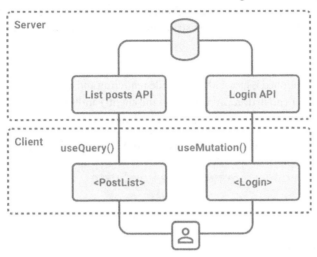

With React Server Components

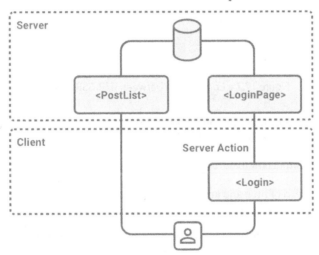

Figure 17.1 – The architecture of a full-stack app without and with RSCs

React 18 introduced a new feature called RSCs, which allows us to define components that will be solely executed on the server, with only the output sent to the client. Server components can, for example, fetch data from a database or the filesystem, and then render interactive client components, passing that data as props to them. This new feature allows for an architecture where we can more easily write a full-stack application using only React, without having to deal with the overhead of defining a REST API.

> **Note**
>
> It might still make sense to define REST APIs for certain apps, especially if the backend is developed by another team in a larger-scale project, or if it is consumed by other services and frontends.

RSCs solve the aforementioned issues with client-side rendering and SSR by allowing us to execute code exclusively on the server (no hydration needed on the client!) and selectively streaming components (so we don't have to wait for everything to pre-render before serving components to the client).

The following figure compares **client-side rendering (CSR)** with SSR and RSCs:

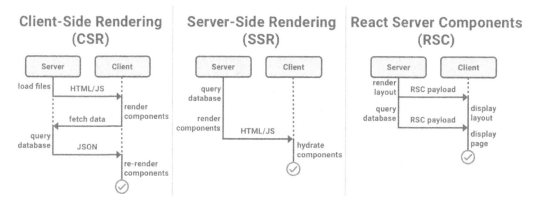

Figure 17.2 – Comparison between CSR, SSR and RSC

As you see, RSCs are not only faster overall (as a result of fewer roundtrips over the network), but they can also display the layout of an app immediately while waiting for the rest of the components to load.

Let's sum up the most important features of RSCs:

- They can run ahead of time and are excluded from the JavaScript bundle, reducing bundle size and improving performance.

- They can run either during build time (resulting in static HTML) or be executed on the fly when a request comes in. Interestingly, server components can also be exclusively executed during build time, resulting in a static HTML bundle. This can be useful for statically built CMS apps or personal blogs. RSCs also allow a mix, where the initial cache is primed with a static build, and then later revalidated through Server Actions or Webhooks. We are going to learn more about caching in *Chapter 18, Advanced Next.js Concepts and Optimizations*.

- They can pass (serializable) data to client components. Additionally, client components can still be server-side rendered to further improve performance!

- Inside a server component, other server components can be passed as props to client components, allowing for composition patterns where server components are "slotted into" interactive client components. However, all components that are imported inside client components will be considered client components; they cannot be server components anymore.

In frameworks such as Next.js, by default, a React component is considered a server component. If we want to turn it into a client component, we need to write the `"use client"` directive at the beginning of a file. We need to do this to make it possible to add interactivity (event listeners) or use state/life cycle effects and browser-only APIs.

> **Note**
>
> The `"use client"` directive defines a network boundary between server and client components. All data sent from a server component to a client component will be serialized and sent over the network. When using the `"use client"` directive in a file, all other modules that are imported into it, including child components, are considered to be part of the client bundle.

The following figure provides an overview of when to use a server component or a client component:

What do you need to do?	Server Component	Client Component
Fetch data	✓	✕
Access backend resources (directly)	✓	✕
Keep sensitive information on the server (access tokens, API keys, etc)	✓	✕
Keep large dependencies on the server (reduces client-side JavaScript)	✓	✕
Add interactivity and event listeners (onClick, onChange, etc)	✕	✓
Use state and lifecycle effects (useState, useReducer, useEffect, etc)	✕	✓
Use browser-only APIs	✕	✓
Use custom hooks that depend on state, effects, or browser-only APIs	✕	✓
Use React class components	✕	✓

Figure 17.3 – Overview of when to use server components and client components

In general, RSCs are an optimization over client components. You could simply write `"use client"` at the top of every file and be done with it, but you would be leaving all the advantages of RSCs behind! So, try to use server components whenever possible, but do not hesitate to fall back to defining something as a client component if it turns out to be too complicated to split it up into server-side and client-side parts. It can always be optimized later.

This new way of writing full-stack React applications can be hard to grasp in theory, so feel free to come back to this section again at the end of this chapter. For now, we'll move on and implement RSCs in our Next.js app as this will help us understand how the new concepts work in practice. First, we'll start by adding a data layer to our Next.js app, which will allow us to access the database from RSCs later on.

Adding a data layer to our Next.js app

In the traditional backend structure, we had the database layer, the services layer, and the routes layer. In a modern full-stack Next.js app, we don't need the routes layer of our backend because we can directly interface with it in RSCs. So, we only need to have the database layer and a data layer to provide functions that access the database. Theoretically, we could directly access the database in RSCs, but it is best practice to have specific functions that access it in certain ways. Defining such functions allows us to clearly define what data is accessible (and thus avoid accidentally leaking too much information). They are also more reusable and make it easier to unit-test and find potential vulnerabilities (for example, via a penetration test) in the data layer.

To recap, there are three main data-handling approaches:

- **HTTP APIs**: We used these in previous chapters to implement our blog app. These can be useful when separate teams are working on the backend and frontend. Due to this, this approach is recommended for existing large projects and organizations.

- **Data access layer**: This is the pattern we are going to use in this section. It is recommended for new projects that make use of the RSC architecture as it makes it easier to implement full-stack projects by separating concerns of dealing with data (and all the security challenges associated with that) and the user interface (displaying the data in React components). Dealing with each problem on its own is easier to solve and less error-prone than handling the complexity of both at once.

- **Component-level data access**: This is a pattern where the database is queried directly in RSCs. This approach can be useful for rapid prototyping and learning. However, it should not be used in a production app due to scalability issues and the potential introduction of security problems.

It is not recommended to mix these approaches, so it's better to pick one and stick to it. In our case, we are going with the "data access layer" approach as it is the safest approach for a modern RSC architecture.

Setting up the database connection

Let's start by setting up the necessary packages and initializing a database connection:

1. Copy the existing `ch16` folder to a new `ch17` folder, as follows:

   ```
   $ cp -R ch16 ch17
   ```

2. Open the `ch17` folder in VS Code and open a Terminal.

3. We are going to use a package called `server-only` to make sure code from the database and data layer are only executed on the server-side, and not accidentally imported on the client. Install it, as follows:

   ```
   $ npm install server-only@0.0.1
   ```

4. We are also going to need the `mongoose` package to connect to the database and create database schemas and models. Run the following command to install it:

   ```
   $ npm install mongoose@8.0.2
   ```

5. Create a new `src/db/` folder.

6. Inside this folder, create a new `src/db/init.js` file, in which we first import the `server-only` package to make sure the code is only executed on the server:

   ```
   import 'server-only'
   ```

7. Next, import mongoose:

   ```
   import mongoose from 'mongoose'
   ```

8. Define and export an `async` function to initialize the database:

   ```
   export async function initDatabase() {
     const connection = await mongoose.connect(process.env.
   DATABASE_URL)
     return connection
   }
   ```

9. Now, we need to define `DATABASE_URL` in a `.env` file. So, create a new `.env` file in the root of the project and add the following line:

   ```
   DATABASE_URL=mongodb://localhost:27017/blog
   ```

Now that the database connection has been set up, we can move on to creating the database models.

Creating the database models

Now, we are going to create database models for posts and users. These are going to be very similar to the ones we created for our blog app in previous chapters. Follow these steps to start creating the database models:

1. Create a new src/db/models/ folder.

2. Inside it, create a new src/db/models/user.js file, where we first import the server-only and mongoose packages:

   ```
   import 'server-only'
   import mongoose, { Schema } from 'mongoose'
   ```

3. Define userSchema, which consists of a unique required username and a required password:

   ```
   const userSchema = new Schema({
     username: { type: String, required: true, unique: true },
     password: { type: String, required: true },
   })
   ```

4. We create the Mongoose model if it has not been created yet:

   ```
   export const User = mongoose.models.user ?? mongoose.
   model('user', userSchema)
   ```

> **Note**
>
> Returning the model if it already exists and only creating a new one if it does not is necessary to avoid an OverwriteModelError issue, which happens when the model is imported (and thus redefined) multiple times.

5. Create a new src/db/models/post.js file, where we first import the server-only and mongoose packages:

   ```
   import 'server-only'
   import mongoose, { Schema } from 'mongoose'
   ```

6. Define postSchema, which consists of a required title and author (referencing the user model), and optional contents:

   ```
   const postSchema = new Schema(
     {
       title: { type: String, required: true },
       author: { type: Schema.Types.ObjectId, ref: 'user',
   required: true },
       contents: String,
   ```

```
    },
    { timestamps: true },
  )
```

7. We create the Mongoose model if it has not been created yet:

```
export const Post = mongoose.models.post ?? mongoose.
model('post', postSchema)
```

8. Create a new `src/db/models/index.js` file and re-export the models:

```
import 'server-only'
export * from './user'
export * from './post'
```

We re-export the models from this folder to ensure that we can, for example, load a post and resolve the `author` by querying the corresponding user. This would require defining the `user` model, although it is not directly used. To avoid issues like these, we simply load models from a file that defines all models upon importing them.

After defining the database models, we can define the data layer functions, which will provide various ways to access the database.

Defining data layer functions

Now that we have a database connection and schemas, let's start defining data layer functions that access the database.

Defining the posts data layer

We'll start by defining the data layer for posts. This allows us to access all the relevant functions for dealing with posts in our app:

1. Create a new `src/data/` folder.

2. Inside it, create a new `src/data/posts.js` file, where we import the `server-only` package and the `Post` model:

```
import 'server-only'
import { Post } from '@/db/models'
```

3. Define a `createPost` function that takes a `userId`, `title`, and `contents` and creates a new post:

```
export async function createPost(userId, { title, contents }) {
  const post = new Post({ author: userId, title, contents })
  return await post.save()
}
```

4. Next, define a `listAllPosts` function, which first gets all posts from the database sorted by creation date descending (showing the newest posts first):

```
export async function listAllPosts() {
  return await Post.find({})
    .sort({ createdAt: 'descending' })
```

5. Then, we must `populate` the `author` field by resolving the `user` model and getting the `username` value from it:

```
.populate('author', 'username')
```

In Mongoose, the `populate` function works like a `JOIN` statement in SQL: it takes the ID stored in the `author` field and then checks which model the ID references by looking at the `post` schema. In the `post` schema, we defined that the `author` field references the `user` schema, so Mongoose will query the `user` model for the given ID and return a user object. By providing the second argument, we specify that we only want to get the `username` value from the `user` object (the ID will always be returned anyway). This is done to avoid leaking internal information, such as the (hashed) password of a user.

6. After populating the post objects, we use `.lean()` to turn it into a plain, serializable JavaScript object:

```
.lean()
}
```

Having a serializable object is necessary to be able to pass the data from an RSC to a regular client-side component later since all data passed to the client needs to cross the network boundary, and thus needs to be serializable.

7. Lastly, we must define a `getPostById` function, which finds a single post by ID, populates the `author` field, and turns the result into a plain JavaScript object by using `lean()`:

```
export async function getPostById(postId) {
  return await Post.findById(postId)
    .populate('author', 'username')
    .lean()
}
```

Defining the data layer for users

We are now going to define the data layer for users. This will involve creating a JWT for authentication. Again, a lot of the code will be very similar to what we previously implemented for our blog app. Follow these steps to start defining the data layer for users:

1. Install bcrypt (for hashing the user password) and jsonwebtoken (for handling JWTs):

```
$ npm install bcrypt@5.1.1 jsonwebtoken@9.0.2
```

2. Create a new `src/data/users.js` file, where we import `server-only`, `bcrypt`, `jwt`, and the `User` model:

```
import 'server-only'
import bcrypt from 'bcrypt'
import jwt from 'jsonwebtoken'
import { User } from '@/db/models'
```

3. Define a `createUser` function, where we hash the given password and then create a new instance of the `User` model and save it:

```
export async function createUser({ username, password }) {
  const hashedPassword = await bcrypt.hash(password, 10)
  const user = new User({ username, password: hashedPassword })
  return await user.save()
}
```

4. Next, define a `loginUser` function, which first tries to find a user with the given username and throws an error if no user is found:

```
export async function loginUser({ username, password }) {
  const user = await User.findOne({ username })
  if (!user) {
    throw new Error('invalid username!')
  }
```

> **Note**
>
> Depending on your security requirements, you might want to consider not telling a potential attacker that a username exists and instead return a generic message such as "Invalid username or password." However, in our case, the usernames are assumed to be public information because each user is an author on the blog and their usernames are published with their articles.

5. Then, use `bcrypt` to compare the provided password against the hashed password from the database and throw an error if the password is invalid:

```
const isPasswordCorrect = await bcrypt.compare(password, user.
password)
  if (!isPasswordCorrect) {
    throw new Error('invalid password!')
  }
```

6. Lastly, generate, sign, and return a JWT:

```
const token = jwt.sign({ sub: user._id }, process.env.JWT_
SECRET, {
  expiresIn: '24h',
})
return token
}
```

7. Now, we are going to define a function to get the user information (for now, we're only going to get the username, but this could be extended later) from a user ID. If the user ID does not exist, we throw an error:

```
export async function getUserInfoById(userId) {
  const user = await User.findById(userId)
  if (!user) throw new Error('user not found!')
  return { username: user.username }
}
```

8. Next, define a function to get the user ID from a token, making sure to verify the token signature in addition to decoding the JWT, by using `jwt.verify`:

```
export function getUserIdByToken(token) {
  if (!token) return null
  const decodedToken = jwt.verify(token, process.env.JWT_SECRET)
  return decodedToken.sub
}
```

9. Finally, define a function to get the user information from a token by combining the `getUserIdByToken` and `getUserInfoById` functions:

```
export async function getUserInfoByToken(token) {
  const userId = getUserIdByToken(token)
  if (!userId) return null
  const user = await getUserInfoById(userId)
  return user
}
```

10. We still need to define the `JWT_SECRET` environment variable for our code to work. Edit `.env` and add it, as follows:

```
JWT_SECRET=replace-with-random-secret
```

> **Note**
>
> This is a very basic implementation of authentication with Next.js. For a large-scale project, it is recommended to look into a fully-fledged authentication solution, such as Auth.js (formerly next-auth), Auth0, or Supabase. Check out the Next.js docs for more information on authentication with Next.js: `https://nextjs.org/docs/app/building-your-application/authentication`.

Now that we have a data layer to access the database, we can start implementing RSCs and Server Actions, which are going to call functions from the data layer to access information from the database and render React components that display it, turning our static blog app into a fully functional blog.

Using RSCs to fetch data from the database

As we have learned, when using Next.js, React components are considered to be Server Components by default, so all page components are already executed and rendered on the server. Only if we need to use client-only functions, such as hooks or input fields, do we need to turn our components into a client component by using the `"use client"` directive. For all components that do not require user interaction, we can simply keep them as server components, and they will only be statically rendered and served as as HTML (encoded in the RSC payload) and not hydrated on the client. To the client (the browser), it will seem as if these React components don't even exist as the browser will only see static HTML code. This pattern greatly improves the performance of our web application as the client doesn't need to load JavaScript to render such components. It also reduces the bundle size because less JavaScript code is needed to load our web application.

Now, let's implement RSCs to fetch data from the database.

Fetching a list of posts

We'll start by implementing the `HomePage`, where we fetch and render a list of posts:

1. Edit `src/app/page.js` and import the `initDatabase` and `listAllPosts` functions:

    ```
    import { initDatabase } from '@/db/init'
    import { listAllPosts } from '@/data/posts'
    ```

2. Turn the `HomePage` component into an `async` function, which allows us to wait until the data is fetched before rendering the component:

    ```
    export default async function HomePage() {
    ```

3. *Replace* the sample `posts` array with the following code:

    ```
    await initDatabase()
    const posts = await listAllPosts()
    ```

Fetching a single post

Now that we can view a list of posts, let's continue by implementing the process of fetching a single post for `ViewPostPage`. Follow these steps to get started:

1. Edit `src/app/posts/[id]/page.js` and import the `notFound`, `getPostById`, and `initDatabase` functions:

```
import { notFound } from 'next/navigation'
import { getPostById } from '@/data/posts'
import { initDatabase } from '@/db/init'
```

2. Turn the page component into an `async` function:

```
export default async function ViewPostPage({ params }) {
```

3. *Replace* the sample `post` object with calls to `initDatabase` and `getPostById`:

```
await initDatabase()
const post = await getPostById(params.id)
```

If no post was found, we call the `notFound` function, which throws a `NEXT_NOT_FOUND` error and terminates the rendering of the route segment:

```
if (!post) notFound()
```

Now, we need to create a `not-found.js` file to catch the error and render a different component instead.

4. Create a new `src/app/posts/[id]/not-found.js` file, where we render a "Post not found!" message, as follows:

```
export default function ViewPostError() {
  return <strong>Post not found!</strong>
}
```

> **Tip**
>
> We can also add an `app/not-found.js` file to handle unmatched URLs for the whole application. If users access a path that is not defined by the app, the component defined in that file will be rendered instead.

5. Additionally, we can create an error component that will be rendered for any errors, such as not being able to connect to the database. Create a new `src/app/posts/[id]/error.js` file, where we render an "Error while loading the post!" message, as follows:

```
'use client'

export default function ViewPostError() {
    return <strong>Error while loading the post!</strong>
}
```

Error pages need to be client components, so we added a `'use client'` directive.

> **Info**
>
> The reason why error pages need to be client components is that they use the React `ErrorBoundary` feature, which is implemented as class components (using `componentDidCatch`). React class components cannot be server components, so we need to make the error page a client component.

6. We still need to make a small adjustment to the `Post` component because the `_id` is now actually not a string anymore; instead, it's an `ObjectId` object. Edit `src/components/Post.jsx` and change the type, as follows:

```
Post.propTypes = {
    _id: PropTypes.object.isRequired,
```

7. Make sure Docker and the MongoDB container are running properly!

8. Run the dev server, as follows:

```
$ npm run dev
```

9. Go to `http://localhost:3000` and click on one of the posts in the list; you will see that the post loads successfully. If a post does not exist (for example, if you change a single digit in the ID), the "Post not found!" message will be shown. If there was any other error (for example, an invalid ID), the "Error while loading the post!" message will be shown:

/posts/65d25393ff39b603885b6ba6 (correct id)

Home
Create Post | Logged in as **dan** [Logout]

Full-Stack React Projects

Let's become full-stack developers!

*Written by **Daniel Bugl***

/posts/65d25393ff39b603885b6ba5 (non existant id)

Home
Create Post | Logged in as **dan** [Logout]

Post not found!

/posts/65d25393ff39b603885b6ba (invalid id)

Home
Create Post | Logged in as **dan** [Logout]

Error while loading the post!

Figure 17.4 – Showing a post and the not found/error components

> **Note**
>
> If there are no posts in your database yet, either create a new post by using the blog app from earlier chapters or wait until we implement the create post functionality using Next.js at the end of this chapter.

After implementing RSCs for fetching posts, our blog app is now connected to the database. However, all it can do right now is show posts; there is no way for the user to interact with the app yet. Let's move on to making our blog app interactive by adding Server Actions to it.

Using Server Actions to sign up, log in, and create new posts

So far, we have only been fetching data from the database on the server and sending it to the client, but for user interactivity, we need to be able to send data back from the client to the server. To be able to do this, React introduced a pattern called Server Actions.

Server Actions are functions that are executed on the server side but can be triggered from the client side, for example, through a form submission. This can be done even with JavaScript disabled on the client, which will then submit the form using regular form submission. When JavaScript is enabled, the form will be progressively enhanced and not require a full refresh to submit. These functions are defined by tagging regular JavaScript functions with the `"use server"` directive, and then either importing them into a client component or passing them to a client component via props. While regular JavaScript functions cannot be passed to client components (because they aren't serializable), Server Actions can be.

> **Note**
>
> You can define a whole file to be full of Server Actions by adding the `"use server"` directive at the beginning of a file. This will tell the bundler that all functions in this file are Server Actions; it *does not* define components inside it as server components (to enforce something to be executed on the server, use the `server-only` package instead, as explained). You can then import functions from such a file in client components.

In client components, we can make use of the `useFormState` hook, which has a similar signature to `useState` but allows us to execute server actions (on the server) and get back the result on the client. The `useFormState` hook's signature looks as follows:

```
const [state, formAction] = useFormState(fn, initialState)
```

> **Note**
>
> In the React 19 release, `useFormState` hook will be renamed to `useActionState`. See `https://react.dev/reference/react/useActionState` for more information.

As we can see, we pass in a function (Server Action) and an initial state. The hook then returns the current state and a `formAction` function. The state is initially set to the initial state, and updated to the result of the Server Action after the `formAction` function is called. On the server side, the Server Action signature looks as follows:

```
function exampleServerAction(previousState, formData) {
  "use server"
  // ...do something...
}
```

As we can see, the Server Action function accepts `previousState` (which will initially be set to `initialState` from the client) and a `formData` object (which is a regular `formData` object from the XMLHttpRequest API web standard). The `formData` object contains all information submitted in form fields. This allows us to easily submit forms to perform an action on the server and return the result to the client.

Now, let's start using Server Actions to implement the signup page in our blog app.

Implementing the signup page

The first action a user needs to take to interact with the blog app is signing up, so let's start by implementing this feature. Follow these steps to get started:

1. We start by implementing the client component. Edit `src/components/Signup.jsx` and mark it as a client component, then import the `useFormState` hook and PropTypes:

    ```
    'use client'
    import { useFormState } from 'react-dom'
    import PropTypes from 'prop-types'
    ```

2. The `Signup` component now needs to accept a `signupAction`, which we are going to define on the server side later:

    ```
    export function Signup({ signupAction }) {
    ```

3. Define a `useFormState` hook, which takes a Server Action and an initial state (in our case, an empty object), and returns the current state and an action:

    ```
    const [state, formAction] = useFormState(signupAction, {})
    ```

4. Now, we can add `action` to the `<form>` tag, as follows:

```
return (
  <form action={formAction}>
```

The action will automatically be called when the form is submitted. Alternatively, Server Actions can be called by executing them like a regular async function – for example, by calling `await` `formAction()` inside an `onClick` handler function.

5. Additionally, we can show an error message below the "Sign Up" button if we get a `state.` `error` message back from the server:

```
      <input type='submit' value='Sign Up' />
      {state.error ? <strong> Error signing up: {state.error}</
strong> : null}
    </form>
  )
}
```

6. Let's not forget to define `propTypes` for the `Signup` component. `signupAction` is a function:

```
Signup.propTypes = {
  signupAction: PropTypes.func.isRequired,
}
```

7. Now, we can start implementing the actual server action. Edit `src/app/signup/page.js` and import the `redirect` function from `next/navigation` (to navigate to the login page after successfully signing up), as well as the `createUser` and `initDatabase` functions:

```
import { redirect } from 'next/navigation'
import { createUser } from '@/data/users'
import { initDatabase } from '@/db/init'
import { Signup } from '@/components/Signup'
```

8. Then, outside of the `SignupPage` component, define a new `async` function that accepts the previous state (in our case, this is the empty object we defined as the initial state, so we can ignore it) and a `formData` object:

```
async function signupAction(prevState, formData) {
```

9. We need to tag the function with the `'use server'` directive to turn it into a Server Action:

```
  'use server'
```

10. Then, we can initialize the database and attempt to create a user:

```
try {
  await initDatabase()
  await createUser({
    username: formData.get('username'),
    password: formData.get('password'),
  })
```

As you can see, Server Actions build upon existing web APIs and use the `FormData` API for form submission. We can simply call `.get()` with the `name` of the input field and it will contain the value provided in the respective input field.

11. If there is an error, we return the error message (which will then be shown in the `Signup` client component):

```
} catch (err) {
  return { error: err.message }
}
```

12. Otherwise, if everything went well, we redirect to the login page:

```
  redirect('/login')
}
```

13. After defining the Server Action, we can pass it to the `Signup` component, as follows:

```
export default function SignupPage() {
  return <Signup signupAction={signupAction} />
}
```

Alternatively, the client component could directly import the `signupAction` function from a file. So long as the function has the `'use server'` directive, it will be executed on the server. In this case, we only need the function on this specific page, so it makes more sense to define it on the page and pass it to the component.

14. Run the dev server, as follows:

```
$ npm run dev
```

15. Go to `http://localhost:3000/signup` and try entering a username and password. It should work successfully and redirect you to the login screen (the change is subtle, but the submit button changes from **Sign Up** to **Log In**).

16. Go to `http://localhost:3000/signup` again and try entering the same username. You will get the following error:

Username: `test42`

Password: `••••`

Sign Up | **Error signing up: E11000 duplicate key error collection: ch3.users index: username_1 dup key: { username: "test42" }**

Figure 17.5 – An error is shown when the username already exists

Of course, this error message is not very user-friendly, so we could do some work to improve the error messages here. But for now, this is sufficient as an example to show how Server Actions work.

As you can see, RSCs and Server Actions make implementing features that interface with the database straightforward. As an additional bonus, all Server Actions that are submitted via `<form>` even work with JavaScript disabled – try it out by repeating *Steps 15* and *16* with JavaScript disabled!

Implementing the login page and JWT handling

Now that users can sign up, we need a way for them to log in. This also means that we will need to implement functionality to create and store JWT. Now that we have more control over the server-client interaction with Next.js, we can store the JWT in a cookie instead of in memory. This means that the user session will persist even when they refresh the page.

Let's start implementing the login page and JWT handling:

1. We'll start by implementing the client component. Edit `src/components/Login.jsx` and turn it into a client component:

    ```
    'use client'
    ```

2. Then, import the `useFormState` hook and `PropTypes`:

    ```
    import { useFormState } from 'react-dom'
    import PropTypes from 'prop-types'
    ```

3. Accept `loginAction` as props. We are going to use this to define the `useFormState` hook:

    ```
    export function Login({ loginAction }) {
      const [state, formAction] = useFormState(loginAction, {})
    ```

4. Pass `formAction`, which was returned from the hook, to the `<form>` element:

    ```
    return (
      <form action={formAction}>
    ```

5. Now, we can display potential errors at the end of the component:

```
      <input type='submit' value='Log In' />
      {state.error ? <strong> Error logging in: {state.error}</
strong> : null}
    </form>
  )
}
```

6. Lastly, define `propTypes`, as follows:

```
Login.propTypes = {
  loginAction: PropTypes.func.isRequired,
}
```

7. Now, we can create the `loginAction` Server Action. Edit `src/app/login/page.js` and import the `cookies` and `redirect` functions from Next.js, as well as the `loginUser` and `initDatabase` functions from our data layer:

```
import { cookies } from 'next/headers'
import { redirect } from 'next/navigation'
import { loginUser } from '@/data/users'
import { initDatabase } from '@/db/init'
import { Login } from '@/components/Login'
```

8. Define a new `loginAction` outside of the `LoginPage` component, in which we attempt to log in with the given username and password:

```
async function loginAction(prevState, formData) {
  'use server'
  let token
  try {
    await initDatabase()
    token = await loginUser({
      username: formData.get('username'),
      password: formData.get('password'),
    })
```

9. If this fails, we return the error message:

```
  } catch (err) {
    return { error: err.message }
  }
```

10. Otherwise, we set an AUTH_TOKEN cookie with an expiry of 24 hours (the same expiry time as the JWT we created), and make it secure and httpOnly:

```
cookies().set({
  name: 'AUTH_TOKEN',
  value: token,
  path: '/',
  maxAge: 60 * 60 * 24,
  secure: true,
  httpOnly: true,
})
```

> **Note**
>
> The httpOnly attribute makes sure cookies cannot be accessed by client JavaScript, reducing the possibility of cross-site scripting attacks in our app. The secure attribute ensures that the cookie is set on the HTTPS version of the website. To improve the development experience, this doesn't apply to localhost.

11. After setting the cookie, we redirect to the home page:

```
    redirect('/')
  }
```

12. Finally, we pass the loginAction to the Login component:

```
export default function LoginPage() {
  return <Login loginAction={loginAction} />
}
```

13. Go to http://localhost:3000/login and try entering a username that doesn't exist; you will get an error. Then, try entering the same username and password that you used to sign up earlier. It should work successfully and redirect you to the home page.

Checking if the user is logged in

You may have noticed that after the user logs in, the navigation bar doesn't change. We still have to check if the user is logged in and then adjust the navigation bar accordingly. Let's do that now:

1. Edit src/app/layout.js and import the cookies function from Next.js and the getUserInfoByToken function from our data layer:

```
import { cookies } from 'next/headers'
import { getUserInfoByToken } from '@/data/users'
import { Navigation } from '@/components/Navigation'
```

2. Turn RootLayout into an async function:

    ```
    export default async function RootLayout({ children }) {
    ```

3. Get the AUTH_TOKEN cookie and pass its value to the getUserInfoByToken function to get the user object, *replacing* the sample user object we defined earlier:

    ```
    const token = cookies().get('AUTH_TOKEN')
    const user = await getUserInfoByToken(token?.value)
    ```

4. If you still have the home page open from earlier, it should hot reload automatically and show your username and the logout button.

We are already passing user?.username to the Navigation component, so that's all there is to it!

Implementing logout

Now that we can show a different navigation bar when the user is logged in, we can finally see the logout button. However, it doesn't work yet. We'll implement the logout button now:

1. Edit src/app/layout.js and define a logoutAction Server Action outside of the RootLayout component:

    ```
    async function logoutAction() {
      'use server'
    ```

2. Inside this action, we simply delete the AUTH_TOKEN cookie:

    ```
    cookies().delete('AUTH_TOKEN')
    }
    ```

3. Pass logoutAction to the Navigation component, as follows:

    ```
    <Navigation
      username={user?.username}
      logoutAction={logoutAction}
    />
    ```

4. Edit src/components/Navigation.jsx and add logoutAction to UserBar and the logout form:

    ```
    export function UserBar({ username, logoutAction }) {
      return (
        <form action={logoutAction}>
    ```

5. Add the action to propTypes of the UserBar component, as follows:

```
UserBar.propTypes = {
  username: PropTypes.string.isRequired,
  logoutAction: PropTypes.func.isRequired,
}
```

6. Then, add logoutAction as props to the Navigation component and pass it down to the UserBar component:

```
export function Navigation({ username, logoutAction }) {
  return (
    <>
      <Link href='/'>Home</Link>
      {username ? (
        <UserBar
          username={username}
          logoutAction={logoutAction}
        />
      ) : (
        <LoginSignupLinks />
      )}
    </>
  )
}
```

7. Finally, change propTypes of the Navigation component, as follows:

```
Navigation.propTypes = {
  username: PropTypes.string,
  logoutAction: PropTypes.func.isRequired,
}
```

8. Click the **Logout** button to see the navigation bar change back to show the **Log In** and **Sign Up** links.

Now, our users can finally log in and log out again successfully. Let's move on to implementing post creation.

Implementing post creation

The last feature missing in our blog app is post creation. We can use Server Actions and a JWT to authenticate the user and allow them to create a post. Follow these steps to implement post creation:

1. This time, we start by implementing the Server Action. Edit `src/app/create/page.js` and import the `cookies`, `redirect`, `createPost`, `getUserIdByToken`, and `initDatabase` functions:

    ```
    import { cookies } from 'next/headers'
    import { redirect } from 'next/navigation'
    import { createPost } from '@/data/posts'
    import { getUserIdByToken } from '@/data/users'
    import { initDatabase } from '@/db/init'
    import { CreatePost } from '@/components/CreatePost'
    ```

2. Inside the `CreatePostPage` component, get the token from the cookie:

    ```
    export default function CreatePostPage() {
      const token = cookies().get('AUTH_TOKEN')
    ```

3. Still inside the `CreatePostPage` component, define a Server Action:

    ```
    async function createPostAction(formData) {
      'use server'
    ```

    We won't be using the `useFormState` hook this time because we don't need to handle the state or result of the action on the client side. So, the Server Action does not have the `(prevState, formData)` signature and instead has a `(formData)` signature.

4. Inside the Server Action, we get the `userId` value from the token, then initialize the database connection and create a new post:

    ```
    const userId = getUserIdByToken(token?.value)
    await initDatabase()
    const post = await createPost(userId, {
      title: formData.get('title'),
      contents: formData.get('contents'),
    })
    ```

5. Lastly, we redirect to the `ViewPost` page of the newly created post:

    ```
    redirect(`/posts/${post._id}`)
    }
    ```

6. If the user isn't logged in, we can now show an error message:

```
if (!token?.value) {
    return <strong>You need to be logged in to create posts!</
strong>
}
```

7. Otherwise, we render the `CreatePost` component, passing `createPostAction` to it:

```
    return <CreatePost createPostAction={createPostAction} />
}
```

8. Now, we can adjust the `CreatePost` component. We *don't* need to turn it into a client component this time because we won't be using the `useFormState` hook. Edit `src/components/CreatePost.jsx` and import `PropTypes`:

```
import PropTypes from 'prop-types'
```

9. Then, add the `createPostAction` as props and pass it to the form element:

```
export function CreatePost({ createPostAction }) {
    return (
        <form action={createPostAction}>
```

10. Finally, define `propTypes`, as follows:

```
CreatePost.propTypes = {
    createPostAction: PropTypes.func.isRequired,
}
```

11. Go to `http://localhost:3000`, log in again, and then click the **Create Post** link. Enter a title and some contents and click the **Create** button; you should get redirected to the `ViewPost` page of the newly created blog post!

Summary

In this chapter, we learned about RSCs, why they were introduced, what their advantages are, and how they fit into our full-stack architecture. Then, we learned how to safely implement RSCs by introducing a data layer into our app. Afterward, we fetched data from our database and rendered components using RSCs. Finally, we learned about Server Actions and added interactive features to our blog app. Now, our blog app is fully functional again!

In the next chapter, *Chapter 18, Advanced Next.js Concepts and Optimizations*, we are going to dive deep into how Next.js works and how we can further optimize our app when using it. We are going to learn about caching, image and font optimizations, and how to define metadata for SEO optimization.

18

Advanced Next.js Concepts and Optimizations

Now that we've learned about the essential features of Next.js and **React Server Components** (**RSCs**), let's dive a bit deeper into the Next.js framework. In this chapter, we are going to learn how caching works in Next.js and how it can be used to optimize our applications. We are also going to learn how to implement API routes in Next.js. Then, we are going to learn how to optimize a Next.js app for search engines and social media by adding metadata. Finally, we are going to learn how to optimally load images and fonts in Next.js.

In this chapter, we are going to cover the following main topics:

- Defining API routes in Next.js
- Caching in Next.js
- **Search engine optimization** (**SEO**) with Next.js
- Optimized image and font loading in Next.js

Technical requirements

Before we start, please install all the requirements from *Chapter 1, Preparing For Full-Stack Development*, and *Chapter 2, Getting to Know Node.js and MongoDB*.

The versions listed in those chapters are the ones used in this book. While installing a newer version should not be an issue, please note that certain steps might work differently. If you are having an issue with the code and steps provided in this book, please try using the versions mentioned in *Chapter 1* and *2*.

You can find the code for this chapter on GitHub: `https://github.com/PacktPublishing/Modern-Full-Stack-React-Projects/tree/main/ch18`.

The CiA video for this chapter can be found at: `https://youtu.be/jzCRoJPGoG0`.

Defining API routes in Next.js

In the previous chapter, we used RSCs to access our database via a data layer; no API routes were needed for that! However, sometimes, it still makes sense to expose an external API. As an example, we might want to allow third-party apps to query blog posts. Thankfully, Next.js also has a feature to define API routes, called Route Handlers.

Route Handlers are also defined inside the `src/app/` directory but in a `route.js` file instead of a `page.js` file (a path can only be either a route or a page, so only one of these files should be placed inside a folder). Instead of exporting a page component, we need to export functions that handle various types of requests there. For example, to handle a GET request, we must define and export the following function:

```
export async function GET() {
```

Next.js supports the following HTTP methods for Route Handlers: GET, POST, PUT, PATCH, DELETE, HEAD, and OPTIONS. For unsupported methods, Next.js will return a 405 Method Not Allowed response.

Next.js supports the native Request (https://developer.mozilla.org/en-US/docs/Web/API/Request) and Response (https://developer.mozilla.org/en-US/docs/Web/API/Response) web APIs but extends them into NextRequest and NextResponse APIs, which make handling cookies and headers easier. We used the cookies() function from Next.js to easily create, get, and delete a cookie for the JWT in the previous chapter. The headers() function makes it easy to get headers from a request. These functions can be used in the same way in RSCs and Route Handlers.

Creating an API route for listing blog posts

Let's start by defining an API route for listing blog posts:

1. Copy the existing ch17 folder to a new ch18 folder, as follows:

    ```
    $ cp -R ch17 ch18
    ```

2. Open the ch18 folder in VS Code.

3. To make the API routes easier to distinguish from pages on our app, create a new `src/app/api/` folder.

4. Inside the `src/app/api/` folder, create a new `src/app/api/v1/` folder to make sure our API is versioned for potential changes to the API later.

5. Next, create a `src/app/api/v1/posts/` folder for the `/api/v1/posts` route.

6. Create a new `src/app/api/posts/route.js` file, where we import the `initDatabase` function and the `listAllPosts` function from the data layer:

```
import { initDatabase } from '@/db/init'
import { listAllPosts } from '@/data/posts'
```

7. Then, define and export a `GET` function. This is going to handle HTTP GET requests to the `/api/v1/posts` route:

```
export async function GET() {
```

8. Inside it, we must initialize the database and get a list of all posts:

```
await initDatabase()
const posts = await listAllPosts()
```

9. Use the `Response` web API to generate a JSON response:

```
return Response.json({ posts })
}
```

10. Make sure Docker and the MongoDB container are running properly!

11. Start the Next.js app, as follows:

```
$ npm run dev
```

12. Now, go to `http://localhost:3000/api/v1/posts` to see the posts being returned as JSON, as shown in the following figure:

Figure 18.1 – JSON response with posts generated from the Next.js Route Handler

Now, third-party apps can also get the posts via our API! Let's continue by learning more about caching in Next.js.

Caching in Next.js

So far, we have always been using Next.js in dev mode. In dev mode, most of the caching that Next.js does is turned off to make it easy for us to develop our apps with hot reloading and always up-to-date data. However, once we switch to production mode, static rendering and caching are turned on by default. Static rendering means that if a page only contains static components (such as an "About Us" or "Imprint" page, which only contains static content), it will be statically rendered and served as HTML, or as static text/JSON for routes. Additionally, Next.js will try to cache data and server-side rendered components as much as possible to keep your app performant.

Next.js has four main types of cache:

- **Data cache**: A server-side cache for storing data across user requests and deployments. This is persistent but can be revalidated.

- **Request memoization**: A server-side cache for return values of functions if they are called multiple times in a single request.

- **Full route cache**: A server-side cache of Next.js routes. This cache is persistent but can be revalidated.

- **Router cache**: A client-side cache of routes to reduce server requests on navigation, for a single user session or time-based.

The first two types of cache (data cache and request memoization) mainly apply to using the `fetch()` function on the server side to, for example, pull data from a third-party API. However, recently, it is also possible to use these two types of caches for any function by wrapping them with the `unstable_cache()` function. Despite its name, this function can already safely be used in production. It is only called "unstable" because the API might change and require code changes when new Next.js versions are released. See `https://nextjs.org/docs/app/api-reference/functions/unstable_cache` for more information.

> **Note**
>
> Alternatively, the React `cache()` function could be used to memoize return values of functions, but the Next.js `unstable_cache()` function is more flexible, allowing us to dynamically revalidate the cache via a path or tag. We are going to learn more about cache revalidation later in this section.

The full route cache is an additional cache that makes sure that when data doesn't change, we don't even need to re-render pages on the server side so that Next.js can directly return pre-rendered static HTML and the RSC payload. However, invalidating the data cache will also invalidate the corresponding full route cache and trigger a re-render.

The router cache is a client-side cache and is mainly used when the user navigates between pages, allowing us to instantly show pages that they have already visited without having to fetch them from the server again.

Additionally, if Next.js detects that a page or route only contains static content, it will pre-render and store it as static content. Static content cannot be revalidated anymore, so we need to be careful and ensure that all dynamic content on our apps is considered "dynamic" by Next.js and not accidentally detected as "static" content.

> **Note**
>
> In this book, we call this process **static rendering**. However, on other resources, it may also be called "automatic static optimization" or "static site generation."

Next.js will opt out of static rendering and consider a page or route dynamic in the following instances:

- When using a dynamic function, such as `cookies()`, `headers()`, or `searchParams`
- When setting `export const dynamic = 'force-dynamic'` or `export const revalidate = 0`
- When a Route Handler handles a non-GET request

For more in-depth information on the different types of caching, have a look at the Next.js documentation on caching: `https://nextjs.org/docs/app/building-your-application/caching`.

Now, let's explore how static rendering works in practice by looking at how our route behaves in a production build of our app.

Exploring static rendering in API routes

In this chapter, we implemented a Route Handler for getting blog posts. Now, let's explore how this route behaves in dev and production mode:

1. Edit `src/app/api/v1/posts/route.js` and add a `currentTime` value with `Date.now()` to the response, as follows:

   ```
   return Response.json({ posts, currentTime: Date.now() })
   ```

2. Refresh the page on `http://localhost:3000/api/v1/posts` a couple of times; you will see that `currentTime` is always the latest timestamp.

3. Quit the Next.js development server by using *Ctrl + C*.

4. Build the Next.js app for production and start it, as follows:

   ```
   $ npm run build
   $ npm start
   ```

5. Refresh the page on `http://localhost:3000/api/v1/posts` a couple of times. Now, `currentTime` doesn't change at all! Even if we restart the Next.js server, `currentTime` still doesn't change. The response of the GET `/api/v1/posts` route is statically rendered during build time.

Static rendering works similarly for routes and pages, so pages will also be statically rendered by default. This means that RSCs do *not* require a server, per se; they can also run during build time. We only need a Node.js server if we want to have dynamic pages/routes. This means we could, for example, create a blog or website in Next.js and export a static bundle, allowing us to host it on a simple web server.

> **Note**
>
> Exporting a Next.js app as a static bundle can be achieved by specifying the `output:` `'export'` option in the `next.config.js` file.

Interestingly, if we create a new blog post, our home page *does* get updated. However, that is only the case because `RootLayout` uses `cookies()` to check if the user is logged in, making all pages on our blog app dynamic (and thus not statically rendered). This can also be seen by looking at the output of `npm run build`:

```
● → ~/D/F/ch18  maint > npm run build

> ch16@0.1.0 build
> next build

   ▲ Next.js 14.1.0
   - Environments: .env

   Creating an optimized production build ...
 √ Compiled successfully
 √ Linting and checking validity of types
 √ Collecting page data
 √ Generating static pages (8/8)
 √ Collecting build traces
 √ Finalizing page optimization

Route (app)                              Size     First Load JS
┌ λ /                                    178 B          91.1 kB
├ λ /_not-found                          885 B          85.1 kB
├ ο /api/v1/posts                        0 B                0 B
├ λ /create                              143 B          84.3 kB
├ λ /login                               875 B            85 kB
├ λ /posts/[id]                          144 B          84.3 kB
└ λ /signup                              875 B            85 kB
+ First Load JS shared by all            84.2 kB
  ├ chunks/69-db30a0e38e2695f2.js        28.9 kB
  ├ chunks/fd9d1056-cc48c28d170fddc2.js  53.4 kB
  └ other shared chunks (total)          1.87 kB

ο  (Static)   prerendered as static content
λ  (Dynamic)  server-rendered on demand using Node.js
```

Figure 18.2 – Seeing which routes are statically and dynamically rendered in the build output

As can be seen from *Figure 18.2*, the `/api/v1/posts` route is "prerendered as static content," while all other routes are "server-rendered on demand using Node.js."

> **Note**
>
> If we wanted to statically render some pages in our blog, we would have to make sure the user bar isn't visible on those pages. For example, we could create a **route group** (https://nextjs. org/docs/app/building-your-application/routing/route-groups) for all pages that have a user bar, with a separate layout that contains the user bar. Then, we can remove the user bar from the root layout. That way, we could create, for example, an About page that is statically rendered while keeping the rest of the blog dynamic.

As we have seen, in Next.js, pages and routes are statically rendered by default (if possible). However, in the case of our API route, this is not what we want! We want to be able to dynamically fetch posts from the API. Static rendering and caching in Next.js can be confusing when we're starting out developing apps with it, but it becomes a powerful tool for keeping our apps optimized.

Now, let's learn how to properly handle the cache to make our pages and routes dynamic when they need to be while keeping them cached whenever possible.

Making the route dynamic

To make the route dynamic, we need to set the `export const dynamic = 'force-dynamic'` flag on it. Follow these steps:

1. Edit `src/app/api/v1/posts/route.js` and add the following code:

    ```
    export const dynamic = 'force-dynamic'
    ```

2. Quit the currently running Next.js server.

3. Build the Next.js app for production and start it, as follows:

    ```
    $ npm run build
    $ npm start
    ```

4. Refresh the page on `http://localhost:3000/api/v1/posts` a couple of times. Now, the API route behaves the same way as it did on the development server!

Unfortunately, we now have completely disabled the cache, so we also don't get any of the benefits of using a cache. Next, we'll learn how to turn on the cache for specific functions.

Caching functions in the data layer

To cache functions from our data layer, we can use the `unstable_cache()` function from Next.js. The `unstable_cache(fetchData, keyParts, options)` function accepts three arguments:

- `fetchData`: The first argument is the function to be called. The function can also have arguments.

- `keyParts`: The second argument is an array of unique keys that identify the function in the cache. Arguments that are passed to the function in the first argument will automatically be added to this array as well.

- `options`: The third argument is an object containing options for the cache, where we can specify `tags` to revalidate the cache later, and a `revalidate` timeout to automatically revalidate the cache after a certain number of seconds.

Now, let's enable this cache for all functions where it makes sense. Follow these steps to get started:

1. Edit `src/data/posts.js` and import the `unstable_cache()` function, aliasing it as `cache()`:

   ```
   import { unstable_cache as cache } from 'next/cache'
   ```

2. Wrap the `listAllPosts` function with `cache()`, as follows:

   ```
   export const listAllPosts = cache(
     async function listAllPosts() {
       return await Post.find({})
         .sort({ createdAt: 'descending' })
         .populate('author', 'username')
         .lean()
     },
     ['posts', 'listAllPosts'],
     { tags: ['posts'] },
   )
   ```

   As the cache key, we defined an array containing the filename (`posts`) and the function name (`listAllPosts`) to uniquely identify the function in our data layer. Additionally, we added a `posts` tag, which we are going to use later to revalidate the cache when new posts are created.

3. Next, wrap the `getPostById` function:

   ```
   export const getPostById = cache(
     async function getPostById(postId) {
       return await Post.findById(postId).populate('author',
   'username').lean()
     },
     ['posts', 'getPostById'],
   )
   ```

4.   You may notice that there is now an error when getting posts because `ObjectId` from MongoDB is getting serialized into a string by the cache. Edit `src/components/Post.jsx` and adjust `propType`, as follows:

```
Post.propTypes = {
  _id: PropTypes.string.isRequired,
```

5.   Edit `src/data/users.js` and import `unstable_cache` there:

```
import { unstable_cache as cache } from 'next/cache'
```

6.   Wrap the `getUserInfoById` function:

```
export const getUserInfoById = cache(
  async function getUserInfoById(userId) {
    const user = await User.findById(userId)
    if (!user) throw new Error('user not found!')
    return { username: user.username }
  },
  ['users', 'getUserInfoById'],
)
```

7.   Quit the currently running Next.js server.

8.   Rebuild and start the app in production. You will notice that after creating a new post, it does not update the home page (or the API route) anymore:

```
$ npm run build
$ npm start
```

That's because our posts are now cached!

9.   This cache even works in dev mode. Quit the Next.js server and start it again, as follows:

```
$ npm run dev
```

10. Create a new post; you will see that neither the home page nor the API route has the newly created post in the list.

Now that caching has been configured, let's learn how to deal with revalidating the cache (causing data in the cache to be updated).

Revalidating the cache via Server Actions

The best way of dealing with stale data is to revalidate the cache when new data comes in, for example, via Server Actions. To do this, we have two options:

- Revalidating all route segments at a specific path by using the `revalidatePath` function
- Revalidating with a specific tag (and thus potentially revalidating multiple paths) by using the `revalidateTag` function

Revalidation means that the next time data is requested from the cached function, the function will be called, and new data will be returned and cached (instead of returning previously cached data). Both functions revalidate the data cache and thus revalidate the full router cache and the client-side router cache as well.

Follow these steps to call the `revalidateTag` function after creating new posts:

1. Edit `src/app/create/page.js` and import the `revalidateTag` function:

   ```
   import { revalidateTag } from 'next/cache'
   ```

2. Inside `createPostAction`, call the `revalidateTag` function on the `posts` tag after creating the new post:

   ```
   async function createPostAction(formData) {
     'use server'
     const userId = getUserIdByToken(token?.value)
     await initDatabase()
     const post = await createPost(userId, {
       title: formData.get('title'),
       contents: formData.get('contents'),
     })
     revalidateTag('posts')
     redirect(`/posts/${post._id}`)
   }
   ```

3. Now, create a new post and go to the home page. You will see that the newly created post appears in the list! The API route will also show the newly created post now.

Revalidating the cache when data is changed via Server Actions is the most direct way of updating the cache. However, sometimes, we will be fetching data from third-party APIs, where revalidating is not possible. We'll explore this case now.

Revalidating the cache via a Webhook

If the data comes from a third-party source, we can revalidate the cache via a Webhook. Webhooks are APIs that can be used as callbacks. For example, when data changes, the third-party source calls our API endpoint to let us know that we need to re-fetch the data.

Integrating a third-party API

Before we can start implementing a Webhook, let's integrate a third-party API into our app. For this example, we are going to use the WorldTimeAPI (`https://worldtimeapi.org/`), but feel free to use any API of your choice.

Let's start implementing a page that fetches from a third-party API:

1. Create a new `src/app/time/` folder. Inside it, create a new `src/app/time/page.js` file.

2. Edit `src/app/time/page.js` and define an asynchronous page component:

    ```
    export default async function TimePage() {
    ```

3. Inside the component, fetch the current time from the WorldTimeAPI and parse the response as JSON:

    ```
    const timeRequest = await fetch('https://worldtimeapi.org/api/
    timezone/UTC')
    const time = await timeRequest.json()
    ```

4. Render the current timestamp:

    ```
    return <div>Current timestamp: {time?.datetime}</div>
    }
    ```

5. If you go to the `http://localhost:3000/time` page in your browser, you will see that it shows the current time. However, when refreshing, the time never updates. That is because requests with `fetch` are cached by default, similar to what happened after we added `unstable_cache()` to our data layer functions.

Implementing the Webhook

Now, let's create a Webhook API endpoint in our app that, when called, revalidates the cache for the third-party data:

1. Create a new `src/app/api/v1/webhook/` folder. Inside it, create a new `src/app/api/v1/webhook/route.js` file.

2. Edit `src/app/api/v1/webhook/route.js` and import the `revalidatePath` function:

    ```
    import { revalidatePath } from 'next/cache'
    ```

3. Now, define a new GET Route Handler that calls `revalidatePath` on the `/time` page and then returns a response telling us that it was successful:

```
export async function GET() {
  revalidatePath('/time')
  return Response.json({ ok: true })
}

export const dynamic = 'force-dynamic'
```

Usually, Webhooks are defined as POST Route Handlers (because they influence the state of the app), but to make it simpler to trigger the Webhook by visiting the page in our browser, we defined it as a GET Route Handler. A POST route would opt out of static rendering, but a GET route does not, so we need to specify `force-dynamic`.

4. Visit `http://localhost:3000/api/v1/webhook` in your browser, then visit `http://localhost:3000/time` again; you should see that the time has been updated! In the real world, we would be adding our Webhook URL to the interface of the third-party website that provides the API.

> **Note**
>
> Alternatively, we could add a tag to the request by passing the `next.tags` option in the `fetch()` function, as follows: `fetch('https://worldtimeapi.org/api/timezone/UTC', { next: { tags: ['time'] } })`. Then, we could revalidate the cache by calling `revalidateTag('time')`.

As we can see, revalidating the cache using Webhooks works great. However, sometimes, we cannot even add a Webhook to a third-party API. Let's explore what to do when we have no control over the third-party API.

Revalidating the cache periodically

If we have no control whatsoever over the third-party data source, we can tell Next.js to periodically revalidate the cache. Let's set that up now:

1. Edit `src/app/time/page.js` and adjust the `fetch()` function, adding the `next.revalidate` option to it:

```
const timeRequest = await fetch('https://worldtimeapi.org/api/
timezone/UTC', {
  next: { revalidate: 10 },
})
```

In this case, we told Next.js to revalidate the data cache the next time the API is requested if at least 10 seconds have passed since the last request.

> **Note**
>
> With `unstable_cache()`, we can pass the `revalidate` option in the third argument. For routes and pages, we can specify `export const revalidate = 10`, which will revalidate the corresponding route/page.

2. Refresh the `http://localhost:3000/time` page in your browser. You will see the time update. Refresh the page again; the time will not update again. If you refresh after at least 10 seconds, the time will update again.

Now that we have learned about revalidating the cache periodically, let's learn about opting out of caching.

Opting out of caching

Sometimes, you may want to opt out of caching completely for certain requests. To do this, pass the following option to the `fetch` function:

```
fetch('<URL>', { cache: 'no-store' })
```

For pages/routes, we can define `export const dynamic = 'force-dynamic'` to opt out of the full route cache (the data may still be cached though!).

Now that we've learned how to use the cache in Next.js to optimize our app, let's learn about SEO with Next.js.

SEO with Next.js

In *Chapter 8*, we learned about SEO in full-stack apps. Next.js provides functionality for SEO out of the box. Let's explore this functionality now, starting with adding dynamic titles and meta tags.

Adding dynamic titles and meta tags

In Next.js, we can statically define metadata by exporting a metadata object from a `page.js` file, or we can dynamically define metadata by exporting a `generateMetadata` function. We have already added static metadata to the root layout, as can be seen in `src/app/layout.js`:

```
export const metadata = {
  title: 'Full-Stack Next.js Blog',
  description: 'A blog about React and Next.js',
}
```

Now, let's dynamically generate metadata for our post pages:

1. Edit `src/app/posts/[id]/page.js` and define the following function outside of the page component:

    ```
    export async function generateMetadata({ params }) {
      const id = params.id
    ```

2. Fetch the post; if it does not exist, call `notFound()`:

    ```
    const post = await getPostById(id)
    if (!post) notFound()
    ```

3. Otherwise, return a title and description:

    ```
    return {
      title: `${post.title} | Full-Stack Next.js Blog`,
      description: `Written by ${post.author.username}`,
    }
    }
    ```

That's all there is to it! Next.js will set the title and meta tags appropriately for us.

> **Note**
>
> Metadata is inherited from layouts. So, it is possible to define defaults for metadata in the layout and then selectively override it for specific pages.

Now that we have successfully added a dynamic title and meta tags, let's continue by creating a `robots.txt` file so that search engines know they are allowed to index our blog app.

Creating a robots.txt file

Next.js has two ways of creating a `robots.txt` file:

*   Creating a static `robots.txt` file in `src/app/robots.txt`
*   Creating a dynamic `robots.txt` file by creating a `src/app/robots.js` script, which returns a special object that is turned into a `robots.txt` file by Next.js

> **Note**
>
> If you need a refresher on what a `robots.txt` file is and how search engines work, please check out *Chapter 8*.

We are only going to create a static `robots.txt` file as there is no need for a dynamic file for now. Follow these steps to get started:

1. Create a new `src/app/robots.txt` file.

2. Edit `src/app/robots.txt` and add the following contents to allow all crawlers to index all pages:

```
User-agent: *
Allow: /
```

Now that we have created a `robots.txt` file, let's create meaningful URLs.

Creating meaningful URLs (slugs)

Now, we are going to create slugs for our blog posts, similar to what we did in *Chapter 8*. Let's get started:

1. Rename the `src/app/posts/[id]/` folder to `src/app/posts/[...path]/`. This turns it into a catch-all route, matching everything that comes after `/posts`.

2. Edit `src/app/posts/[...path]/page.js` and adjust the code to get the first part of the URL (the id value) from the `path` param:

```
export default async function ViewPostPage({ params }) {
  await initDatabase()
  const [id] = params.path
  const post = await getPostById(id)
```

3. Also, adjust the code for the `generateMetadata` function:

```
export async function generateMetadata({ params }) {
  const [id] = params.path
```

With that, our router has been set up to accept an optional slug in the URL.

4. Install the `slug` npm package:

```
$ npm install slug@8.2.3
```

5. Edit `src/components/Post.jsx` and import the `slug` function:

```
import slug from 'slug'
```

6. Adjust the link to the blog post by adding the slug, as follows:

```
        <Link href={`/posts/${_id}/${slug(title)}`}>{title}</Link>
```

7. Open a link from the post list; you will see that the URL now contains the slug.

Now that we've made sure our URLs are meaningful, we'll wrap up this section by creating a sitemap for our blog app.

Creating a sitemap

As we learned in *Chapter 8*, a sitemap contains a list of URLs that are part of an app so that crawlers can easily detect new content and crawl the app more efficiently, making sure that all content on our blog is found.

Follow these steps to set up a dynamic sitemap in Next.js:

1. First, define a BASE_URL for our app as an environment variable. Edit .env and add the following line:

    ```
    BASE_URL=http://localhost:3000
    ```

2. Create a new src/app/sitemap.js file, where we import the initDatabase, listAllPosts, and slug functions:

    ```
    import { initDatabase } from '@/db/init'
    import { listAllPosts } from '@/data/posts'
    import slug from 'slug'
    ```

3. Define and export a new asynchronous function that will generate the sitemap:

    ```
    export default async function sitemap() {
    ```

4. First, we list all the static pages:

    ```
    const staticPages = [
      {
        url: `${process.env.BASE_URL}`,
      },
      {
        url: `${process.env.BASE_URL}/create`,
      },
      {
        url: `${process.env.BASE_URL}/login`,
      },
      {
        url: `${process.env.BASE_URL}/signup`,
      },
      {
        url: `${process.env.BASE_URL}/time`,
      },
    ]
    ```

5. Then, we get all the posts from the database:

```
await initDatabase()
const posts = await listAllPosts()
```

6. Generate an entry for each post by building the URL and adding a `lastModified` timestamp:

```
const postsPages = posts.map((post) => ({
  url: `${process.env.BASE_URL}/posts/${post._id}/${slug(post.
title)}`,
  lastModified: post.updatedAt,
}))
```

7. Finally, return `staticPages` and `postsPages` in an array:

```
  return [...staticPages, ...postsPages]
}
```

8. Go to `http://localhost:3000/sitemap.xml` in your browser; you will see that Next.js generated the XML for us from the array of objects!

> **Note**
>
> It is best practice to add the sitemap to the `robots.txt` file, but we would need to turn it into a dynamic `robots.js` file so that we can provide the full URL to the sitemap (using the `BASE_URL` environment variable). Doing this is left as an exercise for you.

Now that we've optimized our blog app for search engines, let's learn about optimized image and font loading in Next.js.

Optimized image and font loading in Next.js

Loading images and fonts in an optimized way can be tedious, but Next.js makes it very simple by providing the `Font` and `Image` components.

The Font component

Often, you'll want to use a specific font for your page to make it unique and stand out. If your font is on Google Fonts, you can have Next.js automatically self-host it for you. No requests will be sent to Google by your browser if you use this feature. Additionally, the fonts will be loaded optimally with zero layout shift.

Let's find out how Google Fonts can be self-hosted with Next.js:

1. We are going to load the `Inter` font by importing it from `next/font/google`. Edit `src/app/layout.js` and add the following import:

    ```
    import { Inter } from 'next/font/google'
    ```

2. Now, load the font, as follows:

    ```
    const inter = Inter({
      subsets: ['latin'],
      display: 'swap',
    })
    ```

    `Inter` is a variable font, so we don't need to specify the weight that we want to load. If the font isn't a variable font, don't forget to specify the weight. The `display: 'swap'` property means that the font gets an extremely small block period to be loaded. If it does not load by then, a fallback font will be used. Once the font has been loaded, it will be swapped in.

3. Specify the font in the `<html>` tag, as follows:

    ```
    <html lang='en' className={inter.className}>
    ```

4. Go to `http://localhost:3000/` in your browser; you will see that our blog app is now using the `Inter` font! See the following screenshot for reference:

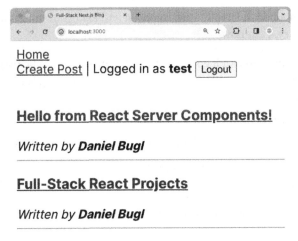

Figure 18.3 – Our blog app rendered with the Inter font

As you can see, it's very simple to use self-hosted Google Fonts with Next.js!

> **Note**
>
> If you want to use a font that is not on Google Fonts, use the `localFont` function from `next/font/local`. This allows you to load a font from a file in your project. For more information on the Font component, check out the Next.js docs: `https://nextjs.org/docs/app/building-your-application/optimizing/fonts`.

Next, we are going to learn about the `Image` component, which allows us to easily load images in an optimized way.

The Image component

Images make up a large portion of the download size of your web application, and can thus have a big impact on the **Last Contentful Paint** (**LCP**) performance. Next.js offers the `Image` component, which extends the `<img>` element by doing the following:

- Automatically serving resized images for each device and resolution
- Automatically preventing layout shift when images are loading
- Only loading images when they enter the viewport ("lazy loading"), with optional blurred placeholder images
- Offering on-demand resizing for images, even if they are stored remotely

Using the `Image` component is simple – just import it and load your images as you would with the `<img>` element. Let's try it out now:

1. Get an image to be used as a logo for your blog. Any image can be used, but make sure it is a non-vector format (such as PNG). For vector formats, resizing is not necessary, so you will not see any effect.

2. Save the image as a `src/app/logo.png` file.

3. Edit `src/app/layout.js` and import the `Image` component and the logo:

   ```
   import Image from 'next/image'
   import logo from './logo.png'
   ```

4. Above the `<nav>` element, render the `<Image>` component, as follows:

   ```
   return (
     <html lang='en' className={inter.className}>
       <body>
         <Image
           src={logo}
           alt='Full-Stack Next.js Blog Logo'
           width={500}
   ```

```
        height={47}
    />
    <nav>
        <Navigation username={user?.username}
logoutAction={logoutAction} />
    </nav>
```

It is important to specify the width and height of the image so that Next.js can infer the correct aspect ratio and prevent layout shift when the image loads in.

5. Go to `http://localhost:3000/` in your browser; you will see the logo being displayed properly! See the following screenshot for reference:

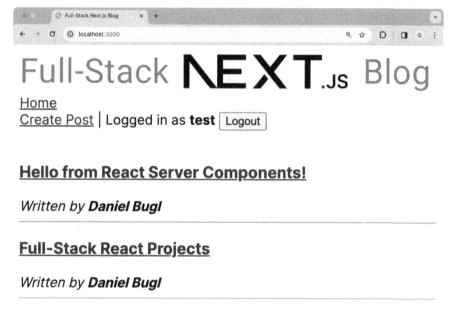

Figure 18.4 – Using the Image component to display a logo for our blog

If you inspect the image in the browser, you will see that it has the `srcset` property with different sizes provided so that the browser can choose which one to load depending on the screen resolution.

> **Note**
>
> In this example, we loaded a local image, but the `Image` component also supports loading images from a remote server, and it will still resize them properly! To use external URLs, allow the remote server by using the `images.remotePatterns` setting in the `next.config.js` file, then simply pass a URL instead of a local file to the `Image` component.

Summary

In this chapter, we learned how to define API routes in Next.js. Then, we learned about caching, how to revalidate the cache, and how to opt out of the cache. Next, we learned about SEO in Next.js by adding metadata to our pages, creating meaningful URLs, defining a `robots.txt` file, and generating a sitemap. Finally, we learned about the `Font` and `Image` components, which allowed us to load fonts and images easily and optimally in our app.

There are still many more features that Next.js offers that we have not covered yet in this book, such as the following:

- **Internationalization**: Allows us to configure the process of routing and rendering content for multiple languages
- **Middleware**: Allows us to run code before requests are completed, similar to how middleware works in Express
- **Serverless Node.js and Edge runtimes**: Allow us to scale our apps even more by not running a full Node.js server
- **Advanced routing**: Allows us to model complex routing scenarios, such as parallel routes (displaying two pages at once)

In the next chapter, *Chapter 19, Deploying a Next.js App*, we are going to learn how to deploy a Next.js app using Vercel and a custom deployment setup.

19

Deploying a Next.js App

After learning about advanced Next.js concepts, it's time to learn how to deploy a Next.js app. The easiest way to deploy Next.js apps is by using the Vercel platform, provided by the company that develops the Next.js framework. After learning how to deploy our app on the Vercel platform, we are going to learn how to create a custom deployment setup using Docker.

In this chapter, we are going to cover the following main topics:

- Deploying a Next.js app with Vercel
- Creating a custom deployment setup for Next.js apps

Technical requirements

Before we start, please install all requirements from *Chapter 1, Preparing for Full-Stack Development*, and *Chapter 2, Getting to Know Node.js and MongoDB*.

The versions listed in those chapters are the ones used in the book. While installing a newer version should not be an issue, please note that certain steps might work differently on a newer version. If you are having an issue with the code and steps provided in this book, please try using the versions mentioned in *Chapter 1* and *2*.

You can find the code for this chapter on GitHub: `https://github.com/PacktPublishing/Modern-Full-Stack-React-Projects/tree/main/ch19`.

The CiA video for this chapter can be found at: `https://youtu.be/ERBFy5mHwek`.

Deploying a Next.js app with Vercel

We are going to start by deploying our app on Vercel, a platform where we can deploy our apps for free in a simple and convenient way. Follow these steps to get started deploying our Next.js app with Vercel:

1. Copy the existing `ch18` folder to a new `ch19` folder by running the following command:

    ```
    $ cp -R ch18 ch19
    ```

2. Open the `ch19` folder in VS Code.

3. Install the Vercel CLI tool as a global package with the following command:

    ```
    $ npm install -g vercel@33.5.3
    ```

4. Run the Vercel CLI:

    ```
    $ vercel
    ```

5. You will be asked to log in to Vercel. Select either of the login methods and follow the steps provided by Vercel to log in.

6. After successfully logging in, you will be asked questions about the deployment of your project, confirm all of them with the default values provided by pressing *Enter/Return* until the Vercel CLI attempts to build your project.

```
⊗ → ~/D/F/ch19  main > vercel
Vercel CLI 33.5.3
> > No existing credentials found. Please log in:
? Log in to Vercel github
> Success! GitHub authentication complete for me@omnidan.net
? Set up and deploy "~/Development/Full-Stack-React-Projects/ch19"? [Y/n] y
? Which scope do you want to deploy to? omnidan
? Link to existing project? [y/N] n
? What's your project's name? ch19
? In which directory is your code located? ./
Local settings detected in vercel.json:
Auto-detected Project Settings (Next.js):
- Build Command: next build
- Development Command: next dev --port $PORT
- Install Command: `yarn install`, `pnpm install`, `npm install`, or `bun install`
- Output Directory: Next.js default
? Want to modify these settings? [y/N] n
⌀  Linked to omnidan/ch19 (created .vercel)
🔍  Inspect: https://vercel.com/omnidan/ch19/7PhHxuGSJog1MGxReTYY8kKZgtvj [2s]
✅  Production: https://ch19-kwlu28dbp-omnidan.vercel.app [2s]
```

Figure 19.1 – Attempting to deploy our app to Vercel

7. While the project is building, you can visit the URL provided in the CLI to see the current state of the build process (make sure you are logged in to Vercel in the same browser), as shown in the following screenshot:

Figure 19.2 – Monitoring the build process in the browser

8. Unfortunately, the build fails because the DATABASE_URL environment variable is set to mongodb://localhost:27017/blog.

We now need to adjust this environment variable in Vercel.

Setting environment variables in Vercel

Follow these steps to set up the necessary environment variables in Vercel:

1. Re-use the existing database cluster created in MongoDB Atlas or follow the steps in the *Creating a MongoDB Atlas database* section of *Chapter 5* to create a new database cluster. You should now have a connection string for your database.

2. Verify that the connection string works by executing the following command:

    ```
    $ mongosh "<connection-string>"
    ```

3. If you are re-using the existing database cluster, make sure to clear the database/collections, as the posts and users used to have a slightly different format in *Chapter 5*! Run the following commands inside the MongoDB Shell to clear the collections:

    ```
    > db.posts.drop()
    > db.users.drop()
    ```

4. Go to `https://vercel.com/` and log in with the same login provider you used earlier.

5. You should see an overview of your projects, including the `ch19` project we created earlier via the Vercel CLI, as shown in the following screenshot:

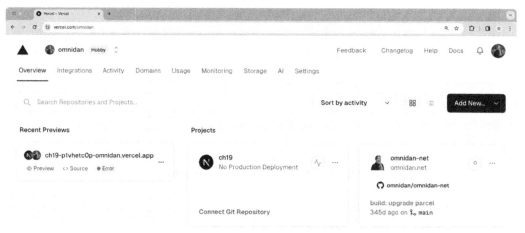

Figure 19.3 – The Vercel dashboard

6. Click on the `ch19` project, then go to the **Settings** tab, select **Environment Variables** on the sidebar, and create a new environment variable by entering DATABASE_URL as the **Key** and the previously obtained connection string as **Value**, as shown in the following screenshot:

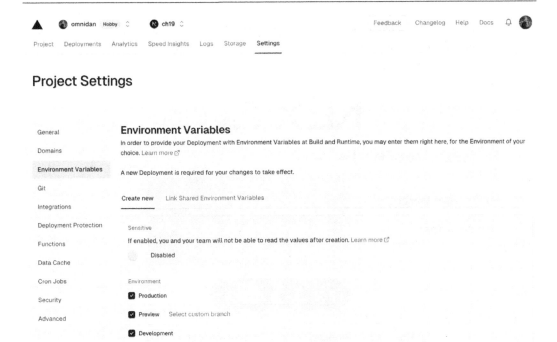

Figure 19.4 – Adding an environment variable in Vercel

> **Note**
>
> For production apps, you would also set the `JWT_SECRET` environment variable to a random secret here. Additionally, you would set the `BASE_URL` environment variable to the URL of the production deployment of your app. For example, if the public URL of your blog is going to be `https://ch19-omnidan.vercel.app/`, you would set the `BASE_URL` to that.

7. Click the **Save** button below the environment variables to save your changes.

8. Run the Vercel CLI again to attempt another deployment:

```
$ vercel
```

Alternatively, you can trigger a rebuild from the Vercel web UI.

9. You will see that it deploys successfully now, visit the **Preview** URL provided by the Vercel CLI in your browser to see our blog application loading successfully:

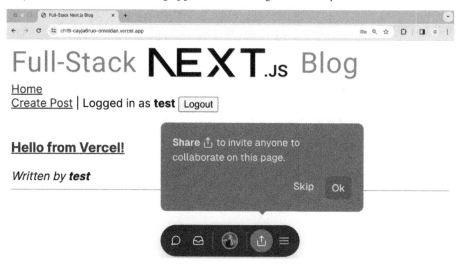

Figure 19.5 – Working "Preview" deployment of our app

Interestingly, Vercel CLI now made a **Preview** deployment for us. This is the default behavior in Vercel. It will first deploy to a **Preview** environment, where we can test everything out to make sure our app works fine. The **Preview** environment is only accessible if you are logged in via Vercel. We can also invite others to test our app here and add comments to it via the Vercel toolbar at the bottom.

10. Now that we have confirmed our app works, we can deploy it to production, as follows:

```
$ vercel --prod
```

The following screenshot shows a **Preview** and a **Production** deployment being made with the Vercel CLI:

```
● → ~/D/F/ch19  main > vercel
  Vercel CLI 33.5.3
  🔍  Inspect: https://vercel.com/omnidan/ch19/2HXmvcW1cR6TmB4yurf8kr5LpAJq [3s]
  ✅  Preview: https://ch19-cayja6ruo-omnidan.vercel.app [3s]
      To deploy to production (ch19.vercel.app), run `vercel --prod`
● → ~/D/F/ch19  main± > vercel --prod
  Vercel CLI 33.5.3
  🔍  Inspect: https://vercel.com/omnidan/ch19/3kwA6ozErmsT15heLEDChQUG3Yyj [1s]
  ✅  Production: https://ch19-f230clhd2-omnidan.vercel.app [1s]
```

Figure 19.6 – Deploying our app to "Preview" and "Production" environments with the Vercel CLI

Now our app is deployed on the **Production** environment and is accessible to anyone, without having to log in via Vercel!

> **Note**
>
> The URL provided in the Vercel CLI output is not accessible to anyone; you need to use one of the domains specified in the **Domains** section on the Vercel dashboard. The default should be `https://ch19-<vercel-username>.vercel.app/`.

As we can see, deploying our app with Vercel is very easy and convenient. However, in some cases, we want to deploy our app on our own infrastructure. Let's learn how to create a custom deployment setup for Next.js apps now.

Creating a custom deployment setup for Next.js apps

We are now going to learn how to set up a custom deployment for Next.js apps using Docker. We have already learned the basics of deploying apps using Docker in *Chapter 5*, so please refer to that chapter if anything is unclear, or if you need a refresher on Docker. Let's get started setting up our Next.js app for a Docker deployment now:

1. First, we need to change the output format for Next.js to `standalone`. This option tells Next.js to create a `.next/standalone` folder that only contains the necessary files for a production deployment, including only the necessary `node_modules`. This folder can then be deployed without having to install `node_modules` again. Edit `next.config.mjs` and adjust the config, as follows:

    ```
    /** @type {import('next').NextConfig} */
    const nextConfig = {
      output: 'standalone',
    }

    export default nextConfig
    ```

2. Now, we create a `.dockerignore` file to ignore certain files that should not be included in our image:

    ```
    node_modules
    .env*
    .vscode
    .git
    ```

3. Create a new `Dockerfile`, start by defining a `base` image from `node:20`:

    ```
    FROM node:20 AS base
    ```

4. Then, define a new image for building the app, based on the `base` image:

   ```
   FROM base AS build
   ```

5. Set the working directory to the `/app` folder and copy over the `package.json` and `package-lock.json` files:

   ```
   WORKDIR /app
   COPY package.json .
   COPY package-lock.json .
   ```

6. Now, install all dependencies, and additionally install `sharp`, which is used by Next.js to resize and optimize images in production:

   ```
   RUN npm install
   RUN npm install sharp
   ```

7. Copy over all files from our project:

   ```
   COPY . .
   ```

8. Next, define the arguments for the build process. We are going to define all environment variables here because Next.js also uses them during the build process to statically build certain routes:

   ```
   ARG DATABASE_URL
   ARG JWT_SECRET
   ARG BASE_URL
   ```

9. We can now run the `build` command, as follows:

   ```
   RUN npm run build
   ```

10. Define a new image for the final app, based on the `base` image as well:

    ```
    FROM base AS final
    ```

11. We also define the working directory:

    ```
    WORKDIR /app
    ```

12. We set up the permissions to run our app as a special `nextjs` user instead of root:

    ```
    RUN addgroup --system --gid 1001 nodejs
    RUN adduser --system --uid 1001 nextjs
    ```

13. Now, copy over the necessary files to run a standalone Next.js server from the `build` image:

```
COPY --from=build /app/public ./public
RUN mkdir -p .next
RUN chown nextjs:nodejs .next
COPY --from=build /app/.next/standalone ./
COPY --from=build /app/.next/static ./.next/static
```

14. We define the PORT, HOSTNAME, and NODE_ENV variables:

```
EXPOSE 3000
ENV PORT 3000
ENV HOSTNAME "0.0.0.0"
ENV NODE_ENV production
```

15. Then, we execute the standalone Next.js server as the `nextjs` user we defined earlier:

```
USER nextjs
CMD ["node", "server.js"]
```

16. Make sure the database server is running in a Docker container.

17. Now we can build the Docker image by running the following command:

```
$ docker build \
  -t blog-nextjs \
  --build-arg "DATABASE_URL=mongodb://host.docker.
internal:27017/blog" \
  --build-arg "JWT_SECRET=replace-with-random-secret" \
  --build-arg "BASE_URL=http://localhost:3000" \
  .
```

In the preceding command, we specified `blog-nextjs` as the name for our image and the necessary environment variables for building the image. Do not forget the dot (.) at the end of the command, as that is what specifies the build context, including where to look for the `Dockerfile`!

> **Note**
>
> You can check out the official example `Dockerfile` from Next.js for an up-to-date version: `https://github.com/vercel/next.js/blob/canary/examples/with-docker/Dockerfile`

18. Finally, run a new Docker container, as follows:

```
$ docker run \
-d \
--name blog-app \
-p 3000:3000 \
-e "DATABASE_URL=mongodb://host.docker.internal:27017/blog" \
-e "JWT_SECRET=replace-with-random-secret" \
-e "BASE_URL=http://localhost:3000" \
--restart unless-stopped \
blog-nextjs
```

In the preceding command, we specified the running of a container with the name `blog-app` in the background (daemon mode) published to port `3000`, then specified the environment variables and told Docker to restart the container if it crashes. Lastly, we specified the image name, which is `blog-nextjs` (the image we built in the previous step).

19. Visit `http://localhost:3000` and you will see the blog running successfully!

Now that we have a Docker container, we could deploy it to a cloud service (or our own server), just like we did in *Chapter 5*. While it is slightly more effort to set up a custom deployment for a Next.js app, it is still quite straightforward to do a simple setup!

For more advanced setups, such as multiple instances, you would need to set up a shared volume between the instances so the cache and optimized images can be shared (on Vercel, this is done automatically behind the scenes). However, such a setup is out of the scope of this book. You can check out the Next.js docs on self-hosting for more information on how to do this: `https://nextjs.org/docs/app/building-your-application/deploying#self-hosting`.

Summary

In this chapter, we first learned how to deploy a Next.js app using Vercel. Then, we learned how to create a custom deployment setup using Docker.

In the next and final chapter, *Chapter 20, Diving Deeper into Full-stack Development*, we are going to briefly cover various advanced full-stack development topics that have been left out of this book so far, giving you an idea of how to continue your journey of learning full-stack web development with React.

20

Diving Deeper into Full-Stack Development

After learning how to build and deploy Next.js apps, we are done with our journey into full-stack development with React. In this final chapter, I want to give you an overview and briefly cover various advanced topics that have been left out in this book. This includes concepts such as maintaining large-scale projects, optimizing the bundle size, an overview of **user interface** (**UI**) libraries, and advanced state management solutions.

In this chapter, we are going to cover the following main topics:

- Overview of other full-stack frameworks

- Overview of UI libraries

- Overview of advanced state management solutions

- Pointers on maintaining large-scale projects

> **Note**
>
> As this chapter only gives an overview of advanced topics in full-stack development with links for further reading, there are no code examples, and as such also no technical requirements for this chapter.

Overview of other full-stack frameworks

In this book, we learned about Next.js, the most popular full-stack framework for React. However, other full-stack frameworks might be of interest to you, each coming with its own pros and cons.

Before we can compare the frameworks, though, let's recap the different methods of rendering in React:

- **Client-side rendering (CSR)**: Renders components in the browser
- **Server-side rendering (SSR)**: Renders components on the server and serves the result
- **Static site generation (SSG)**: Renders components on the server and stores them as static HTML, then serves the static HTML
- **Incremental static generation (ISR)**: Does SSG on the fly and caches the result for a certain amount of time
- **Deferred site generation (DSG)**: Caches all data upon build time and when pages are re-rendered, makes use of that cached data

Additionally, many frameworks (and cloud providers) support the **Edge Runtime**, a subset of standard web APIs that are used to run code on the "edge." The "edge" in this case refers to serverless compute environments that can be deployed in many locations as close to the customer as possible. For example, if someone accesses your website from Austria, the code will run on the closest server, which may be in Austria or Germany. For someone from the United States, however, the code will run on a server in the United States. This reduces network latency and makes our app load faster.

Now, let's have a look at the different full-stack frameworks.

Next.js

We have already learned about Next.js in this book – it is the most popular full-stack web framework at the time of writing, supporting CSR, SSR, SSG, and ISR. Lately, Next.js defaults to SSG to keep your app as performant as possible, but it still offers the ability to revalidate cached pages and provide SSR when necessary.

Next.js also supports the Edge Runtime, but you have to specifically opt into using it instead of the (default) Node.js runtime. Certain features are also not available on the Edge Runtime.

You can check out Next.js here: `https://nextjs.org/`.

Remix

Remix is a full-stack framework that focuses on web standards.

Unlike Next.js, it does not offer SSG and instead focuses on improving dynamic rendering performance and integration with web infrastructure via SSR. As Remix is fully built on web standards, it does not require Node.js to run, so it can run natively on edge runtimes, such as Cloudflare Workers.

Currently, Remix does not support **React Server Components (RSCs)**, but it has its own patterns that result in the same advantages as using RSCs.

Like Next.js, it supports nested routes (with nested layouts), dynamic routing, and parallel rendering on the server. The Remix router is based on React Router, which makes it easy to understand if you have already worked with React Router. It also supports loading/error states, and a form of Server Actions.

Overall, Remix is a really good alternative to Next.js, especially if you prefer working with standard web APIs and care about edge runtime support. Its goal is to make web development simple again by relying on standards as much as possible.

You can check out Remix here: `https://remix.run/`.

Gatsby

Gatsby mainly focuses on SSG. While it can now also do SSR, the framework authors encourage using SSG as much as possible. Instead of ISR, Gatsby offers DSG, which makes data more consistent on big websites, but at the cost of potentially serving stale data.

Gatsby has recently started offering RSC support and also supports the Edge Runtime. However, like Next.js, it also depends on Node.js APIs and as such only offers a subset of its features for the Edge Runtime.

One advantage of Gatsby is its vast plugin ecosystem, allowing developers to easily integrate new features.

However, one downside of Gatsby is that it does not support nested routes with nested layouts.

While both Next.js and Remix offer support for REST and GraphQL, Gatsby focuses mainly on GraphQL, supporting REST APIs only as a second-class citizen. However, this allows Gatsby to offer plugins that easily integrate various data sources.

Overall, Gatsby can be a great framework if you mainly want SSG, the ability to integrate data from various sources, and an easy-to-learn tool. Instead of throwing all the complexity of a framework at you at once, Gatsby progressively discloses complexity through its plugin ecosystem.

You can check out Gatsby here: `https://www.gatsbyjs.com/`.

Next, we'll provide an overview of a few selected UI libraries.

Overview of UI libraries

In this book, I have purposefully left out UI libraries as they are very opinionated, constantly changing, and would make the code examples significantly longer. In this section, I would like to provide an overview of some selected UI libraries. Feel free to explore them on your own and keep an eye out for other options and new releases in this field!

Material UI (MUI)

MUI is one of the most popular component libraries for React. It supports a wide range of components, including complex components such as data tables. It also has a very extensible theming system, allowing you to adjust it to your style. However, its styling engine, at the time of writing, is incompatible with RSCs, which is something that will be improved in upcoming versions. Use MUI if you generally like its style but want to customize the colors, typography, and spacings to make it your own.

You can check out MUI here: `https://mui.com/`.

Tailwind CSS

Tailwind CSS is a utility-first CSS framework and does not require React. However, it plays well together with React, allowing you to easily style your custom components. As it is CSS-only, you can tailor the React components exactly to your needs. It also means that RSCs are fully supported because Tailwind is simply a set of CSS classes. Use Tailwind if you want to implement a fully custom style for your apps quickly and simply compared to directly using CSS.

You can check out Tailwind CSS here: `https://tailwindcss.com/`.

Tailwind UI

The makers of Tailwind CSS also provide a set of pre-made style-only components that use Tailwind CSS, called Tailwind UI. Check it out if you need inspiration for creating components with Tailwind here: `https://tailwindui.com/`.

React Aria

React Aria is a simple set of components that have great support for accessibility and internationalization out of the box. By default, the components are style-free, allowing you to build a custom design. You can also use it in combination with Tailwind. Use React Aria if you want to create a design system but do not want to deal with the challenges of creating accessible components.

You can check out React Aria here: `https://react-spectrum.adobe.com/react-aria/`.

NextUI

NextUI is an upcoming UI library using the style of Vercel (the company behind Next.js). It is built on top of Tailwind CSS but offers various components built on top of React Aria, ensuring first-class accessibility support. Like MUI, it also offers many components and is very customizable through themes. Additionally, it supports RSC because it is based on Tailwind CSS. Use NextUI if you like the style and want to customize it a bit, especially if you are developing with a framework that has RSC support.

You can check out NextUI here: `https://nextui.org/`.

Next, we'll provide an overview of advanced state management solutions.

Overview of advanced state management solutions

In this book, we focused on simple state management solutions in React, such as `useState` and contexts. However, in large-scale projects, it might make sense to use advanced state management libraries to deal with complex state. I will give an overview of some selected state management libraries here, but keep in mind that there are many more libraries out there, so feel free to check them out and decide which one fits your project best.

Recoil

Recoil is a state management library for React built by Facebook Open Source. As such, it shares many of the principles of React. It is a very simple but powerful system, where state is stored in atoms, and then derived via selectors. This allows us to, for example, store only the user input of a form in atoms, and a resulting payload in a selector, which derives its state from the atoms.

You can check out Recoil here: `https://recoiljs.org/`.

Jotai

Jotai takes a similar approach to Recoil but simplifies the system by getting rid of selectors and only dealing with atoms. Atoms can then derive state from other atoms. If you want a state management solution that is still simple, but more powerful than `useState`, Jotai is a great solution.

You can check out Jotai here: `https://jotai.org`.

Redux

Redux takes a different approach, offering a central store where all your state is contained, and then only allowing you to change it through actions. This ensures your application behaves consistently, and that the same user actions always result in the same state changes. Redux can be great for applications where actions are essential and when undo/redo functionality is needed (such as certain editors).

You can check out Redux here: `https://redux.js.org`.

MobX

MobX is a signal-based state management library that uses observables to track state changes. When a value is made observable, it can be mutated directly, just like a regular JavaScript variable, but all changes to it trigger observers of the state to execute and re-render components.

You can check out MobX here: `https://mobx.js.org/`.

xstate

xstate is a state machine library, which can be very useful when you have complex user interfaces with various states that need to be kept track of.

You can check out xstate here: `https://stately.ai/docs/xstate`.

Zustand

Zustand is a small state management library with a hook-based API that combines values and functions that change the values in stores. Each store then exposes a hook where its values and functions can be used.

You can check out Zustand here: `https://docs.pmnd.rs/zustand/getting-started/introduction`.

Now, let's wrap up by learning about some pointers on maintaining large-scale projects.

Pointers on maintaining large-scale projects

To keep this book as short and to the point as possible, as well as available to a wide audience, I intentionally left out some topics and technologies. However, these are still very important to get to know when maintaining large-scale projects, so I want to cover them briefly here.

Using TypeScript

TypeScript is JavaScript extended with syntax for types. A type system can be very useful in catching bugs early and give confidence when refactoring a large code base. While it can take some time to get used to typing everything, it becomes a blessing when you realize all problems appear as type errors in your code editor instead of runtime errors for your users.

I would recommend using TypeScript for all new projects. It is easy to learn when you already know JavaScript and integrates well with frameworks such as Next.js.

You can learn more about TypeScript here: `https://www.typescriptlang.org`.

Setting up a Monorepo

In this book, we were always dealing with a single app at a time. However, large-scale projects often consist of multiple apps, with potentially multiple internal libraries shared between them. For example, you might have two apps, which share UI components in a common UI library. Having all those libraries and apps in separate git repositories can often lead to organizational overhead.

To keep things simple, development teams often decide to set up a Monorepo, which contains all apps and libraries in a single repository. This also makes it easier to keep the code base consistent and keep track of large-scale refactorings.

You can learn more about Monorepos here: `https://monorepo.tools`.

To set up a Monorepo, use a package manager that supports workspaces, such as pnpm (`https://pnpm.io`) or yarn (`https://yarnpkg.com`). Certain tools make creating and maintaining Monorepos easier, such as Turborepo. Check out the guides on `https://turbo.build` to learn how to set up a Monorepo with Turborepo.

Optimizing the bundle size

As your project grows, the JavaScript bundle that's sent to the browser also grows. This can be problematic for devices on slower connections or with slower processors. Sometimes, certain dependencies add a lot to the bundle size, so it is a good idea to regularly check how changes in your project affect the bundle size.

For Vite, you can use `vite-bundle-visualizer` to find out which dependencies are increasing your bundle size: `https://github.com/KusStar/vite-bundle-visualizer`.

For Next.js, you can use the official `@next/bundle-analyzer` plugin: `https://nextjs.org/docs/app/building-your-application/optimizing/bundle-analyzer`.

Summary

In this book, we started with the motivation to become a full-stack developer. Then, we set up our development environment and learned about tools that make our lives easier. Next, we got to know Node.js and MongoDB, taking our first steps as backend developers. Then, we implemented a backend for a blog application using Express and Mongoose, and we wrote unit tests for it using Jest. Afterward, we integrated a frontend with our backend using React and TanStack Query, and as such, created our first full-stack web application. Next, we learned how to deploy our application with Docker, and we learned how to set up CI/CD. Then, we added authentication to our application using JWT. We learned how to improve the load time of our app using SSR and developed our own (simple) SSR solution in the process. We then learned how search engines work, and how to make sure customers can find our web application by facilitating SEO and providing metadata for social media embeds. Next, we implemented end-to-end tests using Playwright, making sure that our app always works as expected. Then, we learned how to aggregate and visualize statistics using MongoDB and Victory.

Afterward, we took a detour from REST APIs and developed a backend with a GraphQL API, learning what GraphQL is and what its benefits are. We then developed a frontend that consumes this GraphQL API. Next, we took a break from our blog application and built an event-based chat app using Socket. IO. While doing so, we learned how to create a backend and a frontend, and how to add persistence, in the event-based paradigm. In the last few chapters of this book, we learned about Next.js, a full-stack web development framework. We introduced the app router, a new way to structure your apps, and RSCs, which allowed us to merge the backend and frontend even more, reducing the need for boilerplate code to create APIs, and instead allowing us to directly access code from a data layer inside RSCs. We also learned about advanced concepts and optimizations in Next.js, such as caching, SEO, and optimized font and image loading. Finally, we learned how to deploy a Next.js app using Vercel, a cloud platform provided by the makers of Next.js, and we created a custom deployment setup using Docker so that we can deploy our app on any other cloud provider (or our own servers).

It has been a long journey. But, as we have seen in this chapter, there are still many more topics to dive deeper into, and the web development ecosystem is changing fast. New technologies keep coming out all the time, especially in terms of RSCs and Server Actions, which, at the time of writing, are still new and upcoming. I expect many more features to be released in this space, so keep an eye out for ground-breaking announcements in the React world!

"Stay hungry. Stay foolish. Never let go of your appetite to go after new ideas, new experiences, and new adventures." – Steve Jobs

Index

Y

yarn
URL 461

Z

Zustand 460
URL 460

`packtpub.com`

Subscribe to our online digital library for full access to over 7,000 books and videos, as well as industry leading tools to help you plan your personal development and advance your career. For more information, please visit our website.

Why subscribe?

- Spend less time learning and more time coding with practical eBooks and Videos from over 4,000 industry professionals

- Improve your learning with Skill Plans built especially for you

- Get a free eBook or video every month

- Fully searchable for easy access to vital information

- Copy and paste, print, and bookmark content

Did you know that Packt offers eBook versions of every book published, with PDF and ePub files available? You can upgrade to the eBook version at `packtpub.com` and as a print book customer, you are entitled to a discount on the eBook copy. Get in touch with us at `customercare@packtpub.com` for more details.

At `www.packtpub.com`, you can also read a collection of free technical articles, sign up for a range of free newsletters, and receive exclusive discounts and offers on Packt books and eBooks.

Other Books You May Enjoy

If you enjoyed this book, you may be interested in these other books by Packt:

Learn React Hooks

Daniel Bugl

ISBN: 978-1-83864-144-3

- Understand the fundamentals of React Hooks and how they modernize state management in React apps
- Build your own custom Hooks and learn how to test them
- Use community Hooks for implementing responsive design and more
- Learn the limitations of Hooks and what you should and shouldn't use them for
- Get to grips with implementing React context using Hooks
- Refactor your React-based web application, replacing existing React class components with Hooks
- Use state management solutions such as Redux and MobX with React Hooks

Micro State Management with React Hooks

Daishi Kato

ISBN: 978-1-80181-237-5

- Understand micro state management and how you can deal with global state
- Build libraries using micro state management along with React Hooks
- Discover how micro approaches are easy using React Hooks
- Understand the difference between component state and module state
- Explore several approaches for implementing a global state
- Become well-versed with concrete examples and libraries such as Zustand, Jotai, and Valtio

Packt is searching for authors like you

If you're interested in becoming an author for Packt, please visit `authors.packtpub.com` and apply today. We have worked with thousands of developers and tech professionals, just like you, to help them share their insight with the global tech community. You can make a general application, apply for a specific hot topic that we are recruiting an author for, or submit your own idea.

Hi!

I am Daniel Bugl, author of *Modern Full-Stack React Projects*. I really hope you enjoyed reading this book and found it useful for increasing your productivity and efficiency using React.

It would really help me (and other potential readers!) if you could leave a review on Amazon sharing your thoughts on this book.

Go to the link below or scan the QR code to leave your review:

`https://packt.link/r/1837637954`

Your review will help me to understand what's worked well in this book, and what could be improved upon for future editions, so it really is appreciated.

Best Wishes,

Daniel Bugl

Download a free PDF copy of this book

Thanks for purchasing this book!

Do you like to read on the go but are unable to carry your print books everywhere?

Is your eBook purchase not compatible with the device of your choice?

Don't worry, now with every Packt book you get a DRM-free PDF version of that book at no cost.

Read anywhere, any place, on any device. Search, copy, and paste code from your favorite technical books directly into your application.

The perks don't stop there, you can get exclusive access to discounts, newsletters, and great free content in your inbox daily

Follow these simple steps to get the benefits:

1. Scan the QR code or visit the link below

https://packt.link/free-ebook/978-1-83763-795-9

2. Submit your proof of purchase
3. That's it! We'll send your free PDF and other benefits to your email directly

Made in the USA
Las Vegas, NV
20 November 2024

12172994R10280